TOWNS *of* NEW ENGLAND

AND

Old England

IRELAND *and* SCOTLAND

Part I and II in One Volume

A VIEW OF PLYMOUTH

Photograph of an engraving in the Marine Museum, Boston   *Taken for the State Street Trust Company*

PLYMOUTH, MASSACHUSETTS

The Pilgrims landed at a place on the right of the three church spires near the center of the picture.   Burial Hill is on the right of the spires.

TOWNS
OF
NEW ENGLAND
AND
Old England,
IRELAND *and* SCOTLAND
❧ *PART I* ❧

Connecting Links between *Cities and Towns*
of NEW ENGLAND and *Those of the Same
Name* in ENGLAND, IRELAND *and* SCOTLAND
Containing Narratives, Descriptions,
and Many Views, some done
from *Old Prints*

Also much Matter pertaining to
The Founders and Settlers of New England
and to their Memorials on both sides of the Atlantic
By ALLAN FORBES

Written to Commemorate THE TERCENTENARY *of*
THE LANDING of the PILGRIMS
AND NOW ISSUED BY THE
Tudor Publishing Company
NEW YORK
MCMXXXVI

"WHILE you behold flourishing towns and villages abounding
in industry, prosperity, and happiness, where once all was
dreary, inhospitable, and desolate; think of the self-sacrificing forefathers, learn to emulate their virtues, and firmly resolve to transmit unimpaired, to the latest posterity, the glorious lessons of their
noble examples." —*From Pilgrim Almanac.*

*Edited and designed by direction of
Walton Advertising & Printing Co.
Boston, Mass.*

TABLE OF CONTENTS

LIST OF ILLUSTRATIONS

LIST OF ILLUSTRATIONS

LIST OF ILLUSTRATIONS

LIST OF ILLUSTRATIONS

ENGLAND,

showing, by capital letters and dots within the circles, locations of the English towns mentioned in this book and in Part II.

FOREWORD

THE Tercentenary of the Landing of the Pilgrims at Provincetown on November 11, 1620, and of the first Landing at Plymouth on December 21st of the same year, will be celebrated this autumn not only by the people of New England but by most of the other States, and also by England, Holland and doubtless other countries. We therefore believe this to be an appropriate year to issue this book treating of the connecting links between New England and Old England, including most of the cities and towns named after the places in England, Ireland and Scotland, from the beginning of the first settlement at Plymouth, Massachusetts.

It is our belief that there are many people who do not know who were the early settlers of the cities or towns, or of other places in the New England States. We think, too, there may be many who do not know how or why these New England communities have been given their present names, and we also believe few people realize the close relationship and the many links between many of our New England cities and towns and the mother cities and towns of the Old Country.

This idea was suggested to the author by Walter R. Whiting, Esq., who showed us several interesting pamphlets written by Rev. Louis C. Cornish describing the interesting exchanges of friendship that have taken place between New Hingham and Old Hingham.

We have attempted in this book to describe many of the messages, gifts and official or unofficial visits between the places of the same name in the New England States and the British Isles, and we believe most of this material has never before been collected; in fact, much of this information has never appeared in print, except perhaps occasionally in accounts of city or town celebrations, or in city or town records. Much assistance has been furnished by Mayors of cities, Town Clerks, Selectmen, officers of Libraries and Historical Societies, and by people in the different cities and towns in New England, who have very kindly forwarded to the Trust Company in many cases original documents, histories, letters, records, city and town reports, and photographs for our examination and reproduction, and it is to these persons the author and those who read this volume are particularly indebted.

We have endeavored to outline very briefly the early history of these cities and towns in New England which were named for cities and towns in Great Britain, and we also have included a short history of these places in the Old Country, which on account of their great age and long history we can only deal with very briefly. We have felt that New Englanders would like to know more of these English, Scotch and Irish places from which most of our settlers came. We furthermore believe that this history will result in further interchanges of friendship, gifts and correspondence, either official or unofficial, between cities and towns in America and places of the same name, and perhaps even other places, in Great Britain. We have not been able to include all the cities and towns in New England in this book, and have therefore reserved half of our material for a second number. These two volumes will describe most of the places in Massachusetts, and the most important ones in the other New England States, that have been named for places in Great Britain; it has been necessary to leave out all the towns and cities in New England that have been named for distinguished persons in the British Isles.

It has also been our endeavor to reproduce and describe the many tablets, memorials and statues on both sides of the Atlantic which connect the places of the same name in New England and Great Britain, and we think the reader will be surprised to find that England has erected almost as many memorials to the early explorers, settlers and Pilgrims of New England as we have done ourselves. We have also added pictures, or photographs of old prints, of particular places of interest to Americans in the English cities and towns, and have likewise included pictures and photographs of some rare prints of some of our largest New England cities and towns, which we think will be of particular interest both to New Englanders and to the people of Great Britain.

The author desires especially to thank Ian Forbes-Robertson, Esq., of Farnham, England, for having personally collected much valuable data and pictures of most of the cities and towns in Great Britain, of which mention is made, for without his valuable and efficient co-operation this book would have been impossible. The author also wishes to thank the many English Mayors, city and town officials, Secretaries of Museums and other societies, and photographers, for information and photographs forwarded through Mr. Forbes-Robertson.

The author is grateful for permission to use valuable material gathered by the late Oscar Fay Adams, a distinguished author of Boston, in checking up his material with that presented herewith. During his lifetime Mr. Adams published in various periodicals, such as the *New England Magazine*, Dedham *Historical Register*, Essex *Antiquarian*, Boston *Transcript*, and the *Christian Register*, a number of articles about "Our English Parent Towns." Among his posthumous papers is the manuscript of a complete and as yet unpublished volume upon the subject, the result of his wide research, historical, architectural and antiquarian, in England, which he dearly loved. Mr. Adams died at Truro, Massachusetts, in 1919. It is fitting that his work and his name should have their share in preparing a volume along this line in which he was especially interested. We wish to thank Miss Abbie Farwell Brown and Miss M. B. Lazenby for procuring for our use Mr. Adams' manuscript.

As much time has been spent in preparing this book, it seems proper to mention that the writer and compiler of this information has had able assistance in the research work from many. Among them being officers of the company of which he is president. The author especially desires to recognize the efficient services of Miss Florence H. Cabot who has given her time exclusively many months towards arranging this material and also to Miss Edith E. Olson and to Ralph M. Eastman, Vice President of the Trust Company.

The author also wishes to thank Perry Walton, Esq., and the staff connected with his company, the Walton Advertising and Printing Company, for much time and care given in the preparation of this volume.

A list of the persons who have helped us is appended, and we thank them for their great assistance and at the same time hope that they will approve of the results of our labours.

We thank His Excellency, Governor Calvin Coolidge, and his Secretary, Henry F. Long, Esq., who helped us in regard to Northampton; Hon. Andrew J. Peters, Mayor of Boston, and his Secretary, E. V. B. Parke, Esq., who helped us in regard to Boston, which we have had to postpone until next year. We also wish to thank Rt. Rev. Bishop Lawrence for valuable assistance in regard to interchanges, which we have treated in the second volume, between churches in the two countries; also Otto Fleischner, Esq., and other officials of the Boston Public Library, who have shown great courtesy and kindness in the selection of many books treating of these places in both countries; also Mrs. Mary Fifield King, for much valuable English material given to us.

PLYMOUTH AND SOUTHAMPTON, MASSACHUSETTS: Capt. Arthur H. Clark, Frederick W. Kitts (Plymouth, England), Wilfred H. Schoff, Secretary Commercial Museum, Philadelphia, Pa., Walter K. Watkins, Arthur Lord, Rev. Arthur Bryant Whitney, F. C. Holmes, Louis A. Law, Rev. Dr. J. Irving Brown of the Scots Church in Rotterdam, Capt. John A. Cook, Howard F. Hopkins, Josephine Young.

ANDOVER, MASSACHUSETTS: Bartlett H. Hayes, Claude Moore Fuess, Charlotte H. Abbott, Alfred L. Ripley, John N. Cole.

BARNSTABLE, MASSACHUSETTS: Thomas C. Thacher, Henry M. Hutchings, Miss Mary G. Hinckley, Miss Abbie L. Hinckley, Alfred Crocker, Richard Cobb, Sturgis Library. BATH, MAINE: Harold M. Sewall, Rev. Henry S. Burrage, Evelyn L. Gilmore, John Hatton (Bath, England), Fred D. Wardle (Bath, England). BELFAST, MAINE: David H. Smith, Henry E. Dunnack. BEVERLY, MASSACHUSETTS: Rev. E. J. V. Huiginn, H. Franklin Murray, Charles E. Ober. BRISTOL, MAINE, RHODE ISLAND, NEW HAMPSHIRE: Rev. Henry S. Burrage, Evelyn L. Gilmore, Rev. Albert C. Larned, Albert C. Bates, Thomas B. Steele, Wilfred H. Munro, Wallis E. Howe, Kate I. Stewart, Maria D. Norris.

CAMBRIDGE, MASSACHUSETTS: William C. Lane, Walter B. Briggs, Charles Belden, Librarian of the Boston Public Library, Elizabeth G. Norton, Edgar H. Wells. CHATHAM, MASSACHUSETTS: Augustus M. Bearse, Ernest E. Budder (Chatham, England), C. H. Smallhoff, William C. Smith. CHELMSFORD, MASSACHUSETTS: Rev. Wilson Waters.

DARTMOUTH, NEW BEDFORD AND BEDFORD, MASSACHUSETTS: George H. Tripp, Charles W. Jenks. DEDHAM, MASSACHUSETTS: Julius H. Tuttle, Miss Elizabeth Humphreys, Rev. William F. Cheney, Clifton P. Baker, Charles Stearns, Secretary of the Dedham Historical Society. DORCHESTER, MASSACHUSETTS: Mrs. Mary Fifield King, Rev. Simon B. Blunt, S. J. Willis, William B. Thurber, Frederick S. Brown, James E. Thomas, E. A. Huebener, Miss Lottie M. Allen, Edwin J. Lewis, Jr., H. Pouncy (Dorchester, England), John Acland (Dorchester, England), Rev. H. F. Burns. DUBLIN, NEW HAMPSHIRE: Henry D. Allison, Joseph Lindon Smith, Mrs. Jasper Whiting, Mrs. Florence C. Howes, Dr. Henry H. Piper, Herbert Maynard.

FALMOUTH, MASSACHUSETTS: Edward N. Fenno, Edward N. Fenno, Jr., Rev. Henry Herbert Smythe, Harry V. Lawrence.

GLOUCESTER, MASSACHUSETTS: Allen F. Grant, Henry D. Sleeper, Rev. Francis V. DeBem, Mrs. Joseph P. Mesquita, William J. Day, W. A. Reed. GROTON, MASSACHUSETTS: Rev. Sherrard Billings, Georgianna A. Boutwell, Mrs. Robert C. Winthrop, Frederic Winthrop.

HARTFORD, CONNECTICUT: Hon. Louis R. Cheney, Williston Walker, J. P. Morgan, William B. Bassett. HARWICH, MASSACHUSETTS: Thomas H. Nickerson, John H. Paine. HINGHAM, MASSACHUSETTS: Rev. Louis C. Cornish, Rev. Houghton Page, Walter R. Whiting, George S. Marsh, Gustavus O. Henderson, James Dean, Hugh Bancroft, Rev. H. K. Bartow, Rev. Milo H. Gates, D.D.

MELROSE, MASSACHUSETTS: Rev. Hugh Wallace Smith, John Larrabee, Franklin P. Shumway, W. De Haven Jones, Ashton L. Carr.

NORTHAMPTON, MASSACHUSETTS: J. L. Harrison, Malcolm B. Stone. NORWICH, CONNECTICUT: William C. Gilman, Mrs. E. E. Rogers, Albert C. Bates, Imogene A. Cash.

PORTSMOUTH AND RYE, NEW HAMPSHIRE: Wallace Hackett, William E. Marvin, William D. Turner.

SANDWICH, MASSACHUSETTS: Thomas C. Thacher, William L. Nye, Henry M. Hutchings, Capt. John S. Carpenter, James L. Wesson, John W. Dalton, Elsie M. Wing, J. A. Jacobs (Sandwich, England), Miss Annie A. Rogers.

WAREHAM, MASSACHUSETTS: Miss Hannah S. B. Dykes, Mr. and Mrs. Rudolph Weld. WOODSTOCK, VERMONT: W. Rodman Fay, George C. Lee, Edward H. Williams, Jr. WORCESTER, MASSACHUSETTS: Raymond Wyer, A. L. Stratton, Benjamin Thomas Hill, Clarence S. Brigham, Dwight S. Pierce, John B. Dyer.

YARMOUTH, MASSACHUSETTS: Thomas C. Thacher, Louis B. Thacher, Henry M. Hutchings, the late Willard T. Sears, Charles W. Swift, Richard Simpkins, Mrs. Lydia C. Matthews.

Those who have helped us in connection with towns which we have had to omit until next year, and those who have helped us in general matters connected with the New England cities and towns and to whom we are also greatly indebted, are:—

Miss Susan Ilsley Adams, W. F. Adams, John Albree, Charles F. Allen, Thomas H. Armstrong, Marion S. Arnold, M. M. Baker, G. C. Baldwin, Thomas Tileston Baldwin, Solon Bancroft, Francis Bardwell, Albert C. Bates, James Phinney Baxter, Mrs. Caroline A. Bill, Mrs. Charles S. Bird, Lillian E. Bishop, Hon. Chas. M. Blodgett, C. K. Bolton, Mrs. John P. Bowditch, John P. Bowditch, Nathaniel I. Bowditch, Charles H. Butler, A. M. Bragdon, Abbie Farwell Brown, Rev. Howard N. Brown, Peter N. Cameron, Everett Carleton, Imogene Cash, Librarian, Otis Library, Norwich, Connecticut, Howard M. Chapin, Mabel W. Chapin, Robert P. Clapp, A. L. Clarke, George K. Clarke, Rev. J. J. Cogan, Hon. George W. Coleman, Judge Louis A. Cook, Mary C. Copeland, Major Coxon, Hon. Walter H. Creamer, Mrs. H. A. Crosby, H. Ashton Crosby, Frederic H. Curtiss, R. M. De Cormis, Rev. Wm. H. Dewart, Harold T. Dougherty, John B. Dyer, Miss Emma Florence Eaton, Henry H. Edes, Erwin Edwards, George H. Eustis, Peter N. Everett, Fred T. Field, Redington Fiske, P. K. Foley, C. F. French, Mrs. Clara A. Fuller, J. Pennington Gardiner, C. H. Garland, E. Howard George, Agnes J. Goodwin, Miss Elizabeth Gorton, Francis Gray, Daniel M. Gurteen, N. Penrose Hallowell, Samuel King Hamilton, Mrs. G. G. Hammond, Edward M. Hartwell, City Statistician, E. R. Hastings, Jane A. Hewett, William L. Higgins, Edith M. Hodgman, Joshua B. Holden, Joseph I. Horton, Amos E. Jewett, Alfred S. Jewett, B. N. Johnson, C. S. Johnson, Harriette E. Jones, George E. Keith, Sinclair Kennedy, George S. Keyes, Virginia M. Keyes, Librarian, Lancaster Town Library, Rev. W. Appleton Lawrence, Miss H. G. Lee, Rev. Herbert Edwin Lombard, Henry G. Lord, Charles A. Loring, Edward Lovering, C. D. Lyons & Company, Mercy E. MacDermott, Rev. Alexander Mann, Moses W. Mann, Kenneth D. Marlatt, Herbert W. Mason, Miss Ida Mason, Lloyd Minton Mayer, Corwin McDowell, Herbert A. McElwain, William B. McSkimmon, Spencer P. Mead, John M. Merriam, Dr. Robt. T. Moffatt, Alfred A. Montgomery, Rev. Glenn Tilley Morse, Mrs. F. S. Moseley, John G. Moulton, E. I. Nye, Frank H. Page, Robert Treat Paine, Rev. Charles E. Park, Augustin H. Parker, Charles H. Pearson, A. W. Phinney, Fred S. Piper, Mrs. A. N. Rantoul, Josephine E. Rayne, Charles F. Read, J. A. Remick, Jr., E. H. R. Revere, Rev. Austin Rice, Dr. Austen F. Riggs, Ernest E. Rogers, Lawrence A. Ryder, Richard M. Saltonstall, E. L. Sanderson, Henry B. Sawyer, J. B. Shearer, T. Sheppard, Clarence E. Sherman, Librarian, Lynn Public Library, Frank Smith, Leonard W. Smith, Robert B. Smith, Jane Stevens, Ralph A. Stewart, Charles Stone, John H. Storer, Moorfield Storey, Thomas Sutton, Charles H. Taylor, Jr., Edward H. Temple, Edwin A. Tetlow, Bowen Tufts, Miss Sophia Turner, William D. Turner, Julius H. Tuttle, Rev. Wm. Harman van Allen, Henry G. Vaughan, Horace G. Wadlin, J. W. Walker, the late Rev. T. Franklin Waters, Walter K. Watkins, Rev. Francis E. Webster, Frank H. Whitmore, Moses Williams, Miss F. Mabel Winchell, Mrs. Marcia M. Winslow, Maj. Evelyn Wrench, Rev. Arthur H. Wright, Mrs. William E. Norman.

There may be other persons who have helped us, whose names through oversight have been omitted, and in such cases we wish to offer our thanks and apologies.

We trust that our efforts to bring before the people of New England historical material, much of which has never before been published, will be enjoyed and appreciated. Many celebrations will take place in New England during the next fifteen years, and while holding these anniversaries, let us not forget all we owe to the early settlers who endured such hardships when they left their homes and friends in England, Ireland and Scotland, to help found this Republic. To use again the Latin inscription on Governor Bradford's Monument on Burial Hill, which we have quoted under Plymouth: "Do not basely relinquish what the Fathers with difficulty attained."

BOSTON, 1920.   ALLAN FORBES

From a photograph by S. A. Chandler & Co., Southampton and Exeter, England   *Kindness Ian Forbes-Robertson, Esq.*

PILGRIM FATHERS MEMORIAL, SOUTHAMPTON, ENGLAND,

unveiled on Pilgrim Day, August 15, 1913, by the American Ambassador, Hon. Walter Hines Page. The Pilgrims sailed first from this port, but were obliged to return to Dartmouth to make repairs on the "Speedwell."

TOWNS of NEW ENGLAND
and
Old England, Ireland and Scotland

PLYMOUTH AND SOUTHAMPTON

"I hear the tread of pioneers,
Of nations yet to be,
The first low wash of waves where soon
Shall roll a human sea."

—Whittier.

FIVE kernels of parched corn per person comprised the Pilgrims' meal one day in the year 1623, when food became particularly scarce, and at the two hundred and fiftieth anniversary of their landing in Plymouth the guests at the banquet were surprised to find for the first course this same scant allowance of provisions on each plate as a reminder of the hardships endured by their forefathers in order that this great nation might live. To Provincetown and to Plymouth many Americans, and also a goodly number of Englishmen and people of other nationalities, will journey this autumn and next summer to do honour to that courageous little band of pioneers who laid, in the new world, "the corner stone of a nation," to use the words of Longfellow. There have been many pilgrimages to the historic "Old World Shrines" in England and Holland, and there will be many more this year and in the years to come; and each year both America and England will hold in greater reverence the little village of Scrooby, where the Separatist movement had its inception, and where is situated the old Manor House in which was born William Brewster, later called "Elder Brewster," the foremost planter of New Plymouth. On this old Brewster house is affixed a brass plate recording that this tablet was erected by the Pilgrim Society of Plymouth, Massachusetts, United States of America, "to mark the site of the ancient Manor House where lived William Brewster from 1588 to 1608, and where he organized the Pilgrim Church, of which he became a ruling Elder, and with which in 1608 he removed to Amsterdam, in 1609 to Leyden, and in 1620 to Plymouth, where he died April 10, 1644."

From Scrooby the usual pilgrimage takes the visitor to the nearby village of Austerfield, where is to be found the cottage in which was born William Bradford, the second Governor of our Plymouth, and the Historian of the Colony. At the early age of seventeen he used to walk across the fields to Scrooby to join his brethren in their meetings. A tablet in the Norman Church of Austerfield records that the aisle in which it was placed was built by the Society of Mayflower Descendants and other citizens of the United States, "in memory of William Bradford, who was born at Austerfield and baptised in this Church," on March 19, 1589. The quaint village of Gainsborough, the home of the Pilgrim Church, is another shrine, for here was the home for some time of John Robinson, the pastor of this Separatist Church, and the leader of this little flock that fled from Nottinghamshire into Holland. In the old Hall of this town the Church was founded in 1602, a more recent object of interest being the Robinson Memorial Church, the corner stone of which was laid by our Minister Hon. T. F. Bayard in 1896, the inscription reading:—

> To the
> Glory of God
> This stone, in memory of
> John Robinson, Pastor & Exile
> was laid on June 29, 1896
> by the Hon. T. F. Bayard, etc. etc.

Another tablet was placed in the vestibule of this Church in 1902 to commemorate the three hundredth anniversary, and the wording on this is as follows:—

> This tablet unveiled June 11th, 1902
> In the 300th year after the formation
> Of the Church in Gainsborough, with which
> The name of JOHN ROBINSON is associated,
> Stands as a record of the co-operation of
> AMERICAN with ENGLISH CONGREGATIONALISTS
> In erecting a building to commemorate him
> The thought of whom stirs equal reverence
> In ENGLISH and AMERICAN hearts.

At this dedication the Lord Lieutenant of the County of Lincoln quoted the prophetic words of our Minister James Russell Lowell, spoken at Wimbledon during a shooting competition between American and English marksmen, "If ever riflemen of both nations should be fated to meet in battle, may God grant that the rifles of both nations may be turned in the same direction."

The scene of the Pilgrim wanderings now moves to old Boston, where seven of the principal "offenders" were imprisoned in the old Guildhall, another Mecca for tourists, especially from New England. Bradford fortunately was so young that he was allowed to depart. After a number of weeks all the prisoners were liberated, and sailed, as every one knows, to Amsterdam, some of the voyagers taking fourteen days on the journey; from Amsterdam they went to Leyden, where they lived and worshipped for eleven years, and where John Robinson a short time afterwards succumbed, being buried in the Cathedral of St. Peter. A tablet was placed there to his memory in 1891, by the National Council of the Congregational Churches of the United States, and commemorates the fact that from there "at his prompting went forth the Pilgrim Fathers to settle in New England in 1620." A marble slab has also been placed on the building in which he lived, the inscription reading:—

On this spot lived, taught and died, John Robinson 1611–1625.

The committee appointed in Holland to celebrate the coming Pilgrim Anniversary will erect in his honour three memorial windows in this church; also other memorials will be erected in honour of the Pilgrims during the coming year at Amsterdam, Rotterdam and Delfshaven. The departure of the band from the latter port in the "Speedwell" and their arrival in Southampton was their next move, Robinson bidding them adieu as they sailed off "to a salute of small shot and three pieces of ordnance." Was it not quite fitting that the Dutch, in whose country they had lived so many years, should be the first nation to have its representative, from New Netherlands in New York, make an official visit to this little Pilgrim colony in the year 1627, which has gone down in history as its first diplomatic experience.

At Southampton they found the "Mayflower" at the West Quay waiting for them and near this spot in 1913 was unveiled by our Ambassador Page on Pilgrim Day, August 15 (N.S.) August 5 (O.S), the memorial shown in the cut on page 16.

IN GRATEFUL MEMORY OF
THOSE PILGRIMS OF THE "MAYFLOWER"
who crossed the Atlantic in the year 1620,
and became the founders
of the first of those settlements
which afterwards developed into the colonies
of New England
This tablet is placed here by the
Massachusetts Society of the Colonial Dames
of America.

Another tablet on the monument reads:—

On the 15th of August 1620
From the West Quay near this spot
The famous MAYFLOWER began her voyage
Carrying the little company of
PILGRIM FATHERS
Who were destined to be the founders
of the New England States of America.

Here the Pilgrims waited for a week while the "Speedwell" was being made ready for sea, and while in port they were joined by John Alden. The story of their return first to Dartmouth and then to Plymouth, where the "Speedwell" was finally

From "Home and Haunts of the Pilgrim Fathers," by Alexander Mackennal, D.D.

BARBICAN, PLYMOUTH, ENGLAND,

where the "Mayflower" lay before sailing for the New World. On the wall on the left is placed the tablet shown in the cut on page 22. The two men in the center of the above picture are looking at the plate shown below.

From a photograph taken for the State Street Trust Company by Heath & Stoneman   *Kindness Ian Forbes-Robertson, Esq.*

abandoned, is too well known to mention.   Of all the towns in the Old World Plymouth in County Devon, England, will of course always remain the one for which
New Englanders will have the warmest affection, and the particular place of interest.
there is the Barbican in Sutton Pool, now encumbered by the fishing nets, where
the "Mayflower" lay while her consort was undergoing repairs.   It was near here
on the "Hoe," on the cliff's top overlooking the Barbican, that Drake said to Admiral Howard, after it had been reported to him while playing bowls that the Armada
was entering the harbour, "There is plenty of time to win the game and beat the
Spaniards too."   The place where the "Mayflower" lay is recorded for all time by
a huge stone firmly embedded in the paved causeway, into which is cut the one
word "Mayflower" and the date "1620."   On the quay's wall a few feet away is
another memorial—a bronze tablet inscribed as follows:—

> On the 6th of September 1620, in the Mayoralty of Thomas Fownes,
> after being "kindly entertained and courteously used by divers
> Friends there dwelling," the Pilgrim Fathers sailed from
> Plymouth in the MAYFLOWER, in the Providence of God to
> settle in NEW PLYMOUTH, and to lay the Foundation
> of the NEW ENGLAND STATES—The ancient
> Cawsey whence they embarked was destroyed not many Years
> afterwards, but the Site of their Embarkation is marked by
> the Stone bearing the name of the MAYFLOWER in
> the pavement of the adjacent Pier.   This Tablet was erected
> in the Mayoralty of J. T. Bond, 1891, to commemorate
> their Departure, and the visit to Plymouth in July
> of that Year of a number of their Descendants and
>   Representatives.

These memorials were unveiled in 1891 in the presence of many Englishmen, and
also many Americans, who journeyed to England to witness the ceremony.   The
embarkation of the Pilgrims is shown in a painting in the House of Lords, London,
an engraving of which hangs in Pilgrim Hall, Plymouth, Massachusetts.

The little vessel of 180 tons after a tempestuous voyage of sixty-seven days,
best described by these lines of Dawes, cast anchor in Cape Cod Harbour, Provincetown, on November 11th (O.S.):—

> "Nobly the Mayflower bows
>   While the dark wave she plows
>   On to the West;
>   Till from the tempest's shock
>   Proudly she lands her flock
>   Where on old Plymouth Rock
>   Freedom found rest."

Often the little ship could carry no sail whatever, and the constant strain bowed
and cracked one of the main beams, and threatened to compel them to return to
England, but fortunately the crew was able to repair the break.   One hundred

From a photograph   *By Heath, Plymouth*

TABLET AND INSCRIPTION ON THE WALL OF THE BARBICAN, PLYMOUTH, ENGLAND,
recording the departure of the "Mayflower."

and two (sometimes stated as one hundred and one) souls left Plymouth, England, and the same number reached our shores, though one of the original members died on the way over, for one new life came into being in Cape Cod Harbour, Peregrine White, the first Englishman born in New England; in Pilgrim Hall are many articles used and worn by him. One of the passengers, John Howland, was washed overboard, but fortunately grabbed the topsail halyards and was hauled back on board the ship. Among the crew was a mariner described as being "proud and profane," who was always making fun of the misery of the passengers, and assailing them for being seasick, declaring that he hoped half of the passengers would die and that he might cast them overboard and "make mery" with their property. Of this incident a chronicler said, "It plased God before they came halfe seas over, to smite this yong man with a greeveous disease, of which he dyed in a desperate maner, and so was himselfe ye first that was throwne overbord." We think of the "Mayflower" as having made this one voyage to New England, but she was the ocean packet of her day, plying continuously between this country and England; she was one of the four vessels that brought Higginson and his company to Salem in

LANDING PLACE,
under Plymouth Hoe.

From an old coloured print　　　　　　　　　　　　　　　*Kindness Ian Forbes-Robertson, Esq.*

PLYMOUTH HOE, PLYMOUTH, ENGLAND,
as it must have looked at the time of the sailing of the "Mayflower."

1629, and was also one of Winthrop's fleet the following year. Her record after that cannot be traced, but she hailed, at different times in her career, from London, Yarmouth and Southampton. Dr. Harris of Manchester, England, claims he has proof that she was used as a whale ship in the Greenland whale fishery up to the year 1654.

It is a curious coincidence that the compact signed by the forty-one male members of the company was executed on November 11th, now known as "Armistice Day." This compact and the names of the signers have been inscribed on a memorial tablet in the Town Hall yard at Provincetown, and on the front of the tablet appear these words:—

> This Memorial stone is erected by the
> Commonwealth of Massachusetts
> to commemorate the compact, or
> Constitution of Government, signed
> by the Pilgrims on board the
> Mayflower in Provincetown Harbor
> November 11th, 1620, old style.

It is interesting to know that the seal of Provincetown has a picture of the scroll, upon which the compact was recorded, and on it are these words: "Compact

Photographed for the State Street Trust Company   *By W. G. Stiff*

TABLET PLACED NEAR THE SUPPOSED LANDING PLACE OF THE PILGRIMS, AT
PROVINCETOWN, MASSACHUSETTS

Nov. 11, 1620. Birthplace of American Liberty." Another tablet, shown above,
marks the supposed first landing place of the Pilgrims and is inscribed as follows:—

THE FIRST LANDING PLACE
of the
PILGRIMS, NOV. 11, 1620. O.S.
The map in Mourts' relation
Shows that near this spot
THE PILGRIMS
First touched foot on American soil

———

Erected by the Research Club of Provincetown
1917

This same organization is also planning to place a memorial on a boulder in the
oldest cemetery, in memory of the four Pilgrims who died while the "Mayflower"
was anchored in the harbour. There is still another inscription on a wooden marker
at the foot of Town Hill, indicating the place where the first washing was done.

The gigantic Pilgrim Memorial Monument in Provincetown was dedicated in 1910 by President Taft, the corner stone having been laid by President Roosevelt three years before. Miss Barbara Hoyt, a descendant of Elder Brewster, unveiled the tablet over the door facing the harbour, the inscription on it being as follows:—

On November 21st, 1620 (N.S.), The Mayflower, carrying 102 passengers, men, women, and children, cast anchor in this harbor 67 days from Plymouth, England.

On the same day the 41 adult males in the Company had solemnly covenanted and combined themselves together "into a civil body politick."

This body politic established and maintained on the bleak and barren edge of a vast wilderness a state without a king or a noble, a church without a bishop or a priest, a democratic commonwealth the members of which were "straightly tied to all care of each other's good and of the whole by every one."

With long-suffering devotion and sober resolution they illustrated for the first time in history the principles of civil and religious liberty and the practices of a genuine democracy.

Therefore, the remembrance of them shall be perpetual in the vast republic that has inherited their ideals.

The British Ambassador was present at the laying of the corner stone in 1907.

Congress has recently passed an appropriation to be used in improving the approach to this Provincetown monument, to make other suitable improvements, and to provide for a worthy celebration this autumn and next summer in

Photographed for the State Street Trust Company   *By W. G. Stiff*

PILGRIM MEMORIAL TOWER, TOWN HILL, PROVINCETOWN, MASSACHUSETTS,

which is a landmark for many miles around, was erected to commemorate the landing of the Pilgrims at Cape Cod on the eleventh day of November, 1620; their anchoring in this harbour; the adoption in the cabin of the "Mayflower," on the day of the arrival, of the Compact of Government, the first charter of a democratic government in the world's history; the birth here of Peregrine White, the first white child born in New England; the death of Dorothy Bradford, the wife of William Bradford, afterward Governor of Plymouth; the explorations in search of a place for permanent colonizations; and the entire train of events which preceded the settlement at Plymouth. In this monument are set stones from many Massachusetts towns which were founded, directly or indirectly, by these early Pilgrims who landed in Provincetown.

PLYMOUTH ROCK, PLYMOUTH, MASSACHUSETTS,

showing Cole's Hill, the Pilgrims' first burial ground, in the background. The bones of some of the
Pilgrims are in the canopy over the rock.

honour of the first landing place of the Pilgrims on New England shores, so well described by William Cullen Bryant in a poem sung at the celebration of the two hundred and fiftieth anniversary at Plymouth in 1870:—

> "Wild was the day; the wintry sea
> Moaned sadly on New England's strand,
> When first the thoughtful and the free,
> Our Fathers, trod the desert land."

While at Provincetown some of the more adventurous of the Pilgrims explored along the inner shores towards Truro, which town is named after the English place of the same name, and encountered Indians several times. The account of their stay at Provincetown and their rough sail to Plymouth has been told many times, but it is not generally realized that this first voyage of investigation was made in a small shallop, and that later the explorers returned to Provincetown and advised their companions to bring the "Mayflower" to Plymouth, as being more suitable to their needs. It was on the 9th of December (O.S.) 19th (N.S.) that the Pilgrims in their shallop reached their new destination, but it was two days later, the 11th of December (O.S.) 21st (N.S.), that historians agree the first landing party, called by Robert C. Winthrop "*The* Landing," stepped on Plymouth Rock, there being at the time a foot of snow on the ground. It is not always understood that there were many other landing parties on different days and also that many of the Pilgrims spent the whole winter on board the "Mayflower," there not being enough buildings for them,—buildings so well described by these lines:—

> "His home was a freezing cabin
> Too bare for the hungry rat;
> Its roof was thatched with ragged grass,
> And bald enough of that.
> The hole that served for a casement
> Was glazed with an ancient hat;
> And the ice was gently thawing,
> From the log whereon he sat."

Hundreds of people from all over the world have visited this historic rock, which has been proved to be the real one, and which is regarded with more veneration than any other in the world. In 1775 it was decided to move it to Town Square as a defiance to the Tory element, as it was thought it would encourage the slackers during the war, but while trying to do so the stone split in two and only half was ever placed there. In 1834 this half was again moved in front of Pilgrim Hall, the names of the forty-one signers of the compact of November 11th being recorded on it; both pieces of the rock in 1880 were placed together under the canopy. It is proposed by the Tercentenary Committee to lower the rock to its original position at the time of the landing, by removing the wharf and restoring the shore line to its original shape. An interesting incident to mention was the transfer of the bones of four of the Pilgrims who died during the early days of the colony and who

PLYMOUTH ROCK
This rock will be lowered to the position it was in at the time of the Landing.

were buried in the first burial ground on Cole's Hill, which is directly opposite the rock and the landing place. These remains were dug up accidentally not long ago in making a road, and placed on Burial Hill, whence they were removed and are now in the chamber on top of the canopy over the rock. Some years later, in 1883, while grading Cole's Hill, other remains were discovered and reinterred at the place of their original burial, over which is a stone slab, suitably inscribed. In this first burial ground fifty Pilgrims were interred during the first year of the colony, reminding the visitor of the frightful hardships that resulted in the death of forty-four persons in the first months of December, January, February and March. At the top of the steps on Cole's Hill the visitor can see a tablet which was placed there in 1917 by the descendants of James Cole, in his memory. He was born in London in 1600, was the first settler on this hill, in 1633, and died in Plymouth in 1692. It is hoped that funds will be provided to make a more suitable memorial of this hill, which will always be a hallowed spot for both Americans and Englishmen. It has been decided to place the statue of the Indian "King" Massasoit on

From "The Pilgrim Fathers," by Arthur Hall, Virtue & Co., London, 1853

BURIAL HILL, PLYMOUTH, MASSACHUSETTS

The second burial ground of the Pilgrims. Governor Bradford's monument is shown at the left of the center of the picture.

its summit. This hill was sown and continually levelled to conceal the awful loss of life both from the colonists and from the Indians.

The most inspiring place in Plymouth is the second cemetery used by the Pilgrims, on Burial Hill, the First Cemetery in New England, so well described by Rev. John Pierpont in a poem read at the celebration at Plymouth on December 22, 1824, part of which was as follows:—

> "The Pilgrim Fathers are at rest:
> When Summer's throned on high,
> And the world's warm breast is in verdure dressed,
> Go, stand on the hill where they lie;
> The earliest ray of the golden day
> On that hallowed spot is cast;
> And the evening sun as he leaves the world,
> Looks kindly on that spot last."

Here are marked by oval stone slabs the old fort and also the watch house, which were placed on the hill for protection, the sites of which are marked but will probably be made more discernible during this year. In this old cemetery are the Gov. William Bradford monument, and for his sons two tombstones, no doubt brought from England like many of the others; here is the oldest grave stone, dated 1681, in memory of Edward Gray; here also is probably the oldest grave, that of John Howland, the last man of the "Mayflower" to die in Plymouth; the Cushman monument; and also many other graves of great interest, too numerous to mention. The First Church, which is situated at the foot of Burial Hill, records on a tablet at the entrance:—

PILGRIM MONUMENT AT PLYMOUTH, MASSACHUSETTS

From a print in Pilgrim Hall, Plymouth, Massachusetts   *By George B. Brayton*

REMAINS OF THE WRECK OF THE ENGLISH VESSEL "SPARROWHAWK,"
wrecked off Orleans, Cape Cod, in 1626 and discovered in 1863. The frame of the hull as seen above is now in Pilgrim Hall, Plymouth, Massachusetts. This interesting relic was exhibited on Boston Common in 1865.

> The Church of Scrooby, Leyden, and the Mayflower gathered on this hillside in 1620, has ever since preserved unbroken records and maintained a continuous ministry, its first covenant being still the basis of its fellowship. In reverent memory of its Pilgrim founders this fifth meeting-house was erected A.D. MDCCCXCVII.

Numerous windows in the church commemorate events connected with the history of the Pilgrims.

The large Pilgrim monument at Plymouth to which eleven thousand persons contributed, was begun in 1859, but was not dedicated until 1889; on its sides are graphically portrayed the Departure of the Pilgrims from Delfshaven, the Signing of the Compact, the Landing, and the Treaty with Massasoit. The statue of Faith was contributed by the late Oliver Ames of Boston. The names of the passengers are on the monument, and also an inscription stating that it is a "National Monument to the Forefathers erected by a grateful people in remembrance of their labors, sacrifices, and sufferings for the cause of civil and religious liberty."

Pilgrim Hall, erected in memory of the Pilgrims, will be one of the great points of attraction during the approaching celebration; the corner stone was laid in 1824, the hall itself being later rebuilt by J. H. Stickney, formerly of Baltimore, Maryland. In this building are a number of pictures of Plymouth, England, and

From "The Pilgrim Fathers," by Arthur Hall, Virtue & Co., London, 1853

LEYDEN STREET, PLYMOUTH, MASSACHUSETTS,
as it looked about the middle of the nineteenth century.

also many treasures in the way of curiosities that form interesting connecting links between the Old and New Worlds. In this hall is the frame of the "Sparrowhawk," one of the most interesting and wonderful relics in this country, which was exhibited in 1865 on Boston Common; this little English vessel, of about a quarter less tonnage than the "Mayflower" was wrecked off Orleans, on Cape Cod, six years after the "Mayflower" first came to this country, her company finding refuge in Plymouth, Massachusetts. The "Sparrowhawk" is the first English vessel known to have been stranded on Cape Cod. Two hundred and thirty-seven years later a violent storm revealed the frame, consisting of old ribs, which was dug up and presented to Pilgrim Hall by Charles W. Livermore of Providence, Rhode Island. The rudder was presented by John Doane. Other relics in the hall that are of particular interest are bricks from the wharf in Delfshaven, from which the "Speedwell" sailed; the departure of the "Mayflower" from Southampton, photographed from the picture in Town Hall, Southampton, England; portrait of Edward Winslow, probably painted by Robert Walker in London in 1651, on one of Winslow's visits to England; Governor Bradford's Bible; the ancient sword of Miles Standish; the chair of Governor Winslow made in Cheapside, London, in 1614; also the chairs of Elder Brewster and Governor Carver; a model of the "Mayflower," the construction of which was passed upon by Capt. R. B. Forbes of Boston. One of the many beautiful paintings is Charles Lucy's "Departure from Delfshaven," which won the first prize of one thousand guineas at an exhibition in London. Other interesting relics are too numerous even to mention.

Leyden Street, which runs from the shore near the rock to the foot of Burial Hill, was originally called First Street, and then known by the names of Great and Broad Streets; it was not called by its present name until 1823.

> "There first was heard the welcome strain
> Of axe and hammer, saw and plane."

About one third of the way up the street on the left is the first, or common, house erected on the street, which bears an interesting inscription:—

> This tablet is erected by the Commonwealth of Massachusetts
> to mark the site of the first house built
> by the Pilgrims. In that house on 27 Feb.
> 1621 N.S. the right of popular suffrage was
> exercised and Miles Standish was chosen Captain by a
> majority vote. On or near this spot April 1 1621
> the memorable treaty with Massasoit was made.

Another fact of interest to both Americans and Britons was the return in 1897 by Rt. Rev. Mandell Creighton, Bishop of London, of the original history of the Plymouth Plantation, written by William Bradford, which is now in the Massachusetts State Library, the gift having been made through Minister Bayard.

One would suppose there would have been many more connecting links between

PRESENT VIEW OF LEYDEN STREET,

showing site of the first house in Plymouth, Massachusetts, where Miles Standish was chosen Captain February 27, 1621. This street was originally called First Street and later by the names of Great and Broad Streets. It was named Leyden Street in 1823. A copy of the inscription on this house is shown on page 33.

the two Plymouths, but the fact that the Pilgrims sailed from the English town of this name seems to have been sufficient to keep alive the friendship between the two places. There have been a number of visits of prominent persons to our Plymouth, chief of which perhaps was that of The Lord Bishop of Winchester, Rt. Rev. Ethelbert Talbot, who laid the corner stone of the new Christ Church in our Plymouth in 1912. At another celebration held in 1853 an invitation was sent to the Pastor of the Pilgrim Church at Southwark, London, but his extreme age prevented his acceptance; an interesting letter, however, was received from the Burgomaster, Aldermen and Councillors of Delfshaven, Netherlands. During the festivities, English and Dutch flags were flown beside that of our country.

Few people, we believe, know that Plymouth was not named by the Pilgrims, but was so called by Prince Charles (afterwards Charles the Second) and placed by Capt. John Smith on his map six years before, while he was in command of an

From "Pilgrim Fathers; or The Founders of New England in the Reign of James the First," by W. H. Bartlett

DELFSHAVEN, HOLLAND,

the port from which the Pilgrims sailed for Southampton, England, just previous to their voyage to New England.

expedition fitted out under the patronage of Sir Ferdinando Gorges, who was the governor of the castle in old Plymouth. Another curious fact is that the word "Pilgrim" was not used in connection with these early Plymouth settlers until about one hundred and seventy years after the landing.

The relation of the Indians to the pioneers at Plymouth will always be of great interest, and from these well-known lines it would appear as if the settlers were in constant fear of attacks:—

"So once, for fear of Indian beating,
Our grandsires bore their guns to meeting;
Each man equipped on Sunday morn
With psalm book, shot, and powder horn,
And looked in form as all must grant,
Like th' ancient true church militant,
Or fierce like modern deep divines,
Who fight with quills like porcupines."

(From Coffin's History.)

The most remarkable event in this connection occurred in the following March, when some of the colony met the Indian Samoset, who saluted them in good English and bade them welcome. This chief was one of the five Indians taken to London by Captain Waymouth a few years before, and while there he had picked up some of the language. On this occasion at Plymouth the Pilgrims entertained Samoset a day and gave him presents, and a few days later he returned with his friend Squanto, who had lived in Cornhill, London, and who always remained on friendly terms with the colonists. The great Sagamore Massasoit also came at the same time and made friends with the Englishmen, and on the first Thanksgiving in the New World he and some of his redskins were guests of the Pilgrims, a scene which has been depicted in a painting in Pilgrim Hall. This friendship between Massasoit and the colonists was further strengthened by Edward Winslow, when at Bristol, Rhode Island, he visited the Indian "King," who was desperately ill, though able to grasp the Englishman's hand and to say, "O Winslow, I shall never see thee again." Medicine was administered and he recovered, remaining always a firm friend of the Englishmen. Winslow in addition to his other good qualities is described as being a splendid horseman, for a story is told of him that while attending a "Saquish" in Plymouth Harbour with two friends he fell asleep, and when he woke up, to his surprise he found that his friends had ridden away, and that the tide had risen. He is said to have swum his horse across the channel, whereupon he took a short cut, and had a bowl of punch ready to greet his fellow countrymen when they arrived somewhat later.

Visitors to the Tercentenary will also visit the nearby attractive town of Duxbury, the home of Miles Standish, so called for Duxbury Hall in Lancashire, England, the home of his ancestors, and they will also visit the Standish Monument, his grave, and his spring.

As the pilgrims of 1920 stand on Cole's Hill or Burial Hill and gaze at Plymouth Harbour, let them remember that three hundred years before, when the "Mayflower," on April 5, 1621, after one hundred and ten days' stay, returned to England, not one passenger went back in her, not one soul that would not refuse to exchange the hardships in the New World for the luxuries and comforts in the Old World; and let the "modern pilgrims" make a vow to preserve the honour and integrity of this country, given to us by our English ancestors through such untiring determination. In the words of the Latin inscription on Governor Bradford's monument on Burial Hill: "Do not basely relinquish what the Fathers with difficulty attained."

We shall always esteem the people of old Plymouth, who, we are told, showed every kindness to these strangers within their gates, for curiously enough not one of those on the "Mayflower" hailed from there. Since the Pilgrims sailed there have been many changes in this attractive English port, often called "the deep-sea Venice," but there still exists the old church of St. Andrew, the massive

Photograph copyrighted International Film Service   *From the "Landmark," the Magazine of the English-Speaking Union*

THE ARRIVAL OF THE N. C. 4 AT PLYMOUTH, ENGLAND

The reception of the airmen of the N. C. 4 at the Barbican, where they were greeted by the Mayor standing on the "Mayflower Stone" from which the Pilgrim Fathers sailed in 1620. Commander Read is on the left of the line of airmen, nearest the Mayor. The N. C. 4 made the first air flight across the Atlantic, stopping at the Azores, and at Lisbon, Portugal, finally landing in Plymouth Harbour, England.

tower of which was built in 1460; and there is also standing part of the old castle, a dead remnant of the past, which gave hospitality to the Pilgrims; the advanced part of this fortress is called the Barbican, from which the "Mayflower" sailed. The old Hoe Gate, through which the voyagers to the New World must have passed, was unfortunately demolished in 1863. The Guildhall has many stained glass windows depicting scenes in Plymouth's history, one of which represents "The Departure of the Pilgrims."

From this same port sailed several of the Raleigh expeditions to colonize Virginia, which was at that time called Raleana; from there also in 1603 set sail the Gilbert explorers to Chesapeake Bay; and into this harbour returned Gosnold, Waymouth, and the Popham colony; from there, too, in 1572 Drake set out on his famous voyage; and also many fishermen sailed from this port to the New England coast in the early days. The most recent event of universal importance was the transatlantic flight of Commander Read of the American Navy, in his biplane N. C. 4, from Halifax to Plymouth, England, with stops on the way. With him was James L. Breese of New York.   Off the breakwater of the English port, Read and his crew were escorted into the harbour by British seaplanes flying the Stars and Stripes and the Union Jack.   It was a dramatic coincidence that Plymouth should have been chosen for the landing, and it was still more dramatic that the Mayor of Plymouth should have received the American airmen on the Barbican on the exact spot from which the "Mayflower" sailed two hundred and ninety-nine years before on a voyage of quite a different character.   It is no wonder that sailors are especially fond of this port, which has meant so much in the history of the two worlds, and they have many songs that tell of "their dear Plymouth town" and their "dear Plymouth sound."   These few lines written by Drayton also call to mind the importance of this seaport:—

> "Upon the British coast, what ship yet ever came
> That not of Plymouth heares? where those brave
> Navies lie,
> From Canon's thund'ring throats that all the world
> defie?"

This seaport on the river Plym, from which it gets its name, is well described in these words of Carrington:—

> "How oft by Fancy led,
> Sweet Plym, at morn or eve, I stray with thee:
> But chief at shadowy eve, I linger where
> The ocean weds thee, and delighted view,
> Proud rising o'er the vast Atlantic surge,
> Thine own,—thy Plymouth,—nurse of heroes—her
> Who bears thy noble name."

Plymouth was called by the Saxons, Tameorworth, and later on it became known as Sutton, or South Town.   In the time of Queen Elizabeth it became the chief port of England, and Devonshire became the most important county.

The latest exchange of greetings between Plymouth, England, and Plymouth, Massachusetts, took place June 24, 1920, when A. N. Hollely, official representative of Plymouth, England, after being conducted to Plymouth Rock where he was formally welcomed, and then proceeding to the Town Square, presented to the Board of Selectmen of the Massachusetts town the following set of resolutions commemorating the Tercentenary:—

"DUNSTAN, MAYOR

At a meeting of the Council of the Borough of Plymouth held on Monday, the 12th day of April, 1920.

WE, THE MAYOR, ALDERMEN AND BURGESSES OF THE BOROUGH OF PLYMOUTH in Council assembled send sincere and hearty greetings to the SELECTMEN, PLYMOUTH, MASSACHUSETTS, UNITED STATES OF AMERICA, on the occasion of the Tercentenary of the Sailing of the Mayflower from the Barbican, Plymouth, England.

From a print owned by a Boston collector   *Formerly in the collection of J. H. Seers, Essex, England*

THE WALLS OF SOUTHAMPTON, ENGLAND

Our records show that 'on this 6th day of September, 1620,' during the Mayority of Thomas Townes, after being kindly entertained and courteously used by divers friends there dwelling the Pilgrim Fathers sailed from Plymouth in the Mayflower in the providence of God to settle in New Plymouth and to lay the foundation of the New England States.

Even before the sailing of the Mayflower many expeditions sailed from this ancient Borough on voyages of discovery, notably in 1562–4–6–7 Sir John Hawkins to the West Indies; in 1570 Sir Humphrey Gilbert to North America; in 1575 John Oxenham to Mexico; in 1577 Sir Francis Drake in the Pelican on his tour of circumnavigation; in 1583 Sir Humphrey Gilbert to Newfoundland, and Sir Richard Grenville to Virginia; in 1587 Sir Walter Raleigh's expedition to Virginia under John White, and in 1607 the first settlers in New England who landed at the mouth of the Kennebec.

Coming to recent times, your late ambassador, Dr. W. Hines Page, an Honorary Freeman of Plymouth, made his great pronouncement in the Plymouth Guildhall, on the third anniversary of the declaration of war, with reference to the glorious entry of the United States into the war for the freedom of the world.

With great satisfaction we recall that during the war Plymouth was an American naval base of considerable importance.

Last year we had the honour of welcoming at the historic Barbican your Seaplane the NC 4, on the completion of the first Transatlantic Flight.

We rejoice to have this opportunity of giving expression to the feelings of friendship and goodwill which have for so long bound together our two countries, and to express the confident hope that our historical associations will ever be cherished to the great advantage of both nations.

In conclusion we hail our sister town of New Plymouth, and hope that her future may be one of unbroken peace and prosperity.

GIVEN under our Corporate

Common Seal—LOVELL R. DUNSTAN, *Mayor.*

E. J. LITTALS, *Town Clerk.*"

This greeting, in a handsome gilt frame, is now in the historic old town house of Plymouth, Massachusetts.

There are two other Plymouths in New England—one in Maine and one in Vermont—the latter being the birthplace of Hon. Calvin Coolidge, Governor of Massachusetts.

Southampton is an ancient walled town on the Test and Itchen Rivers, the latter the river of Izaak Walton. On every side the "modern pilgrim" sees relics of the past, for part of the old wall built in 1338 that once enclosed the town is still intact, and the West Gate leading down to the quay from which the "Mayflower" sailed looks much the same as it did in 1620 when the Pilgrims passed through it, which they must have done many times during their sojourn there. Bar Gate, a marvelous relic of olden times, has been restored and now bears a statue of King George III arrayed, oddly enough, as a Roman emperor. The "Mayflower" and the "Speedwell" sailed past the platform with its battery of guns, past Netley Castle, where the Earl of Hertford entertained Queen Elizabeth, and then into the Solent, past Hurst Castle and the Needles into the Channel. The old castle of Southampton, where long ago King Stephen reigned, has long since gone, but the ruins are carefully preserved.

WEST GATE SOUTHAMPTON

From an old print   Kindness Ian Forbes-Robertson, Esq.

WEST GATE, SOUTHAMPTON, ENGLAND

The Pilgrims must have passed through this gate in order to board the "Mayflower."

Southampton has always been a great seaport, but its most romantic trade occurred during the thirteenth, fourteenth, fifteenth and part of the sixteenth centuries, when the Venetians brought spices, Indian cotton, silks and other commodities to this port. These expeditions were organized by the Venetian Senate, and the voyages were made in galleys procured in Flanders, with which

WATER GATE, SOUTHAMPTON, ENGLAND

country they also traded. Indeed in the Middle Ages Southampton presented a cosmopolitan appearance, for there were seen many Normans, Gascons and Flemings, as well as Venetians. At the time of the survey, many French settled there, and French Street still recalls these days to the passerby. The history of this city, which will always be of the greatest interest to Americans, goes back to the third century, when it was called Clausentum; in 837 the Danes were repulsed, and in 840 Ethelwulf dated a charter from the "Royal town called Hamtun," his successors referring to it as the "celebrated place called Heamtun," which shows how important it was in the ninth century. The first authentic records in Saxon times call the place "Old Hamptun," the word meaning 'home town." In 962 it was named "Suthamtun," or "Suth-hamtun," to distinguish it from Northampton, as in our State of Massachusetts we have a Southampton, settled in 1732, which formerly was part of Northampton. Some historians refer to the English port as " Storied Southampton," as the place is so rich in history, legends and traditions.

Here King Alfred carried on his shipbuilding operations; here Canute was chosen king; here was the port of communication between the Norman and English courts; here Earl Godwin and his son, Harold, owned manors; from here also John of Gaunt sailed on his expedition to Brittany, returning also to the same port; here too Henry V assembled his fleet for an expedition to France; and here used to come many of the people of Charlemagne's court. Here Artemus Ward died and here also lies buried Edward A. Sothern, the actor, father of the well-known Edward H. Sothern of the present day. It is interesting to know that many of our New England soldiers composing the 26th (Yankee) Division stopped here on the way to France in 1917. In the eighteenth century the place became a fashionable seaside resort, and assembly rooms similar to those at Bath were built. At the present time the city has a big population and large suburbs, and is in a flourishing condition.

There is a town of Hampton in New Hampshire, said to be named for the English place at the request of Rev. Stephen Bachiler, whose last English living was the vicarage of St. Mary's in South Stoneham, near Southampton. The town of Southampton on Long Island, undoubtedly named after the English one, was formerly included in the State of Connecticut, this island being once owned by this New England State.

> "I heard, or seemed to hear, the chiding sea
> Say: 'Pilgrim, why so late and slow to come?
> Am I not always here, thy summer home?'"

> —*Emerson.*

ANDOVER, MASSACHUSETTS

"For our own Andover so old, and yet so young today,
Who ever to the Mother will loving homage pay,
To an old Borough on the Ande is namesake, mental heir,
Which Saxon men called Andover in English Hampshire Fair."

(Part of Poem "Historic Andover," by Annie Sawyer Downs, read at the 250th Anniversary of our Andover in 1896.)

DURING the Great War a well-known Major in the American Army, who hailed from Andover, Massachusetts, after being taken up in the air on a pleasure spin in England, was landed some distance from his camp, whereupon he set out to walk back. He read the nearest sign board and almost believed he was near his own home, when, to his surprise, he saw on it "Andover," and also the name of another town nearly as well known to him in this country. This officer was still more surprised to receive on Christmas Day presents of tobacco and other useful articles sent by Andover, England, and by Brechin, Scotland, to him and to all our Andover boys who could be found either in or behind the trenches in France. In welcoming our men in this way, the town of Brechin, not far from Aberdeen in Scotland, especially shared, for between our Andover and this Scotch town there have always existed very strong ties, owing to the fact that many of the settlers in our Andover during the nineteenth century came direct from Brechin. From there came the original John Smith in 1816, and, after some

other ventures, started in 1836, with his brother Peter and John Dove, a flax mill in our Andover. All three of these men were natives of Brechin, and they induced many other people of that town to come to Andover, Massachusetts, as operatives in their mill. The business is now conducted under the name of the Smith and Dove Company, carried on principally by Mr. George F. Smith, grandson of the pioneer, John Smith. They also gave to Andover Theological Seminary in 1865, a library, which was named Brechin Hall, after their birthplace. This building is now the administration center of Phillips Academy and is probably the most conspicuous structure on Andover Hill. Brechin Terrace, a short street in another section of the town, is a center for Scotch mill operatives, and is also named after the Scotch town.

From a photograph of picture in "An Old N. E. School,"
by Claude M. Fuess, Esq.

Kindness Claude M. Fuess, Esq.

BRECHIN HALL,

ANDOVER THEOLOGICAL SEMINARY,
ANDOVER, MASSACHUSETTS,

presented in 1865 by residents of Andover, Massachusetts, whose ancestors had come to this town from Brechin, Scotland.

Photograph taken by F. Frith & Co., England   *Kindness Ian Forbes-Robertson, Esq.*

UPPER CLATFORD VILLAGE, NEAR ANDOVER, ENGLAND

A picturesque bit of old English village life.

Photograph taken by F. Frith & Co., England   *Kindness Ian Forbes-Robertson, Esq.*

CHANCERY STREET, ANDOVER, ENGLAND

Our town and Brechin have for years been in constant communication, and during the World War many gifts were sent from Andover, Massachusetts, to Brechin, Scotland, including cigarettes, candy and clothing to be distributed among the Scotch soldiers. The relationship between the two towns is still very close, owing mainly to the fact that our Andover people have many near relatives in Brechin.

In May of 1917, Mayor F. W. Bingham of Andover, England, sent the fraternal greetings of his ancient borough upon the entry of America into the war of Liberty; this letter was addressed to "The Chief Citizen" and was handed to Harry M. Eames, Esq., Chairman of the Board of Selectmen of our Andover. This note was followed by further correspondence, most of which was published in the "Andover Townsman," together with extracts from the minutes of the quarterly meeting of the Town Council of old Andover, where the reply of Mr. Eames was read, describing the patriotism of our town in endeavoring to prosecute the war to a successful ending. The "Andover Townsman" in October, 1917, printed a letter written by a citizen of our town to the English town and we reproduce part of it, as it gives us an excellent idea of the early history of our Andover:—

"As most of our older citizens are descendants of British emigrants of two centuries or more ago, I need not say that under the conditions of the present war, our town, like all other towns of our New England, is enthusiastically on the side of our mother country in its war against the Prussian monarchy. . . . I notice (in the ancient Andover, Eng., pamphlet) the name of John Abbot. That name is of interest here as one of our early settlers, the town having been full of Abbots and Abbotts ever since, some of them very prominent in literary and other lines. It is understood that the name Andover was given to the town because some of the old settlers had hailed from your Andover, but I do not think it has ever been authentically understood as to the identity of these Andover emigrants. Chandler, Holt, Stevens, Russell are also old names of our Andover. . . ."

Gratification was expressed in the Council of the English town that of the eight American Andovers to whom the Mayor had written, the Massachusetts town was the first to respond. One member remarked that it was "extremely interesting to know that the name of their small community should be the source and origin of so many other towns in the American Republic." Another said that the greetings from our Andover would be of great interest to them and their children in years to come.

In 1634 some inhabitants of Newtowne (Cambridge) complained of lack of land, and desired leave to investigate other territory. They looked with favor upon the property along the Merrimack and Agawam Rivers and their wish was granted the following year, the Court ordering "that the land about Cochichewick shall be reserved for a plantation." This property was soon purchased from the Indians for six pounds and a coat, by John Woodbridge of Newbury, the first minister of Andover, who was probably assisted by Edmund Faulkner. The purchase was confirmed by the Court in 1646, and the town was incorporated as Andover, so named for some of the planters, who came from Andover in Hampshire County,

England, the names of Holt, Abbot, Stevens, Poor and Chandler being known in both Andovers. The names of other early settlers were found on the town records in our old style of handwriting, and were Simon Bradstreet, the most influential person in the plantation, and usually referred to as "the worshipful Mr. Simon Bradstreet," John Osgood, Joseph Parker, Richard Barker, John Stevens, Benjamin Woodbridge, John Frye, Edmund Faulkner, Robert Barnard, Nathan Parker, Henry Jaques, Richard Blake, John Lovejoy and others.

There is an English proverb relating to four English towns in Hampshire County, reading as follows:—

> Romsey in the mud,
> Southampton on the stones,
> Winchester eats the meat,
> Andover picks the bones.

The ancient borough and market town of Andover is situated in Hants County on the river Anton, the word Andover being derived from the Celtic "An," meaning spring, and "dour" or "dever" of similar significance. The discoveries there, including a number of tools and weapons, testify to the size of the population which lived there a thousand years before the advent of the Romans.

The romantic history of King Edgar's marriage with Elfrida occurred in Andover; he had heard of Elfrida's beauty, and sent Ethelwold to woo the lady for him, but she fell in love with the King's emissary, and concealing the facts from the King, they married; Ethelwold meanwhile reported to the King that Elfrida was a very ordinary person, but the King evidently discovered the treachery and, one day while hunting, Edgar slew Ethelwold by piercing him through the back, and Elfrida then became the wife of her husband's murderer. At Dead Man's Plack, a lonely place close to Andover, is a monument which marks the spot of this tragedy.

There are also Andovers in Maine, New Hampshire, Connecticut and Vermont.

BARNSTABLE, MASSACHUSETTS

THE Barnstable Church was organized in London in 1616, then went to Holland, came over the seas to Scituate, Massachusetts, in 1634, and then moved to Barnstable on Cape Cod five years later. The three hundredth anniversary of the founding of this First Congregational Church in London was celebrated in our town in 1916, on which occasion there was unveiled a memorial tablet that was placed on the side of a stone monument made of fragments of the former Sacrament Rock, which had been scattered in years gone by. This memorial is about a mile and a half west of the Court House on the main road to West Barnstable, and the inscription reads as follows:—

From a photograph   *Kindness Ian Forbes-Robertson, Esq.*

THE PARISH CHURCH OF ST. PETER AND ST. PAUL, BARNSTAPLE, ENGLAND

showing St. Anne's Chapel on the right.   The spire of the church leans over to one side and the bells hang on the outside of the steeple.

1 6 3 9

AT THIS ROCK

NOW IN FRAGMENTS

TRADITION REPORTS THAT

THE SETTLERS OF BARNSTABLE

RECEIVED THE SACRAMENT

FOR THE FIRST TIME

IN THEIR NEW ABODE

AND HELD

THEIR FIRST TOWN MEETING

THIS TABLET TO THEIR MEMORY

WAS SET UP

1 9 1 6

It is believed that the first sacrament was administered on the spot where this rock is situated, and that the first town meeting was also held there.

The site of the first meeting house adjoins the old burying ground on what is now known as Lothrop's Hill about one mile west of the court house, and it has been suggested that a tablet be placed there to record this fact.   The land of

From "Photographic Views of Barnstaple and North Devon," published by Sydney Harper & Sons, Barnstaple, England   *Kindness Walter K. Watkins, Esq.*

BARNSTAPLE, ENGLAND, SHOWING THE BRIDGE

From a print   *Kindness Henry M. Hutchings, Esq.*

SACRAMENT ROCK, BARNSTABLE, MASSACHUSETTS

At this rock in 1639 the first settlers of Barnstable received the sacrament and held the first town meeting. It is on the main road to West Barnstable.

which this site is a part was for many years owned by Captain Matthias Hinckley, a well-known packet master of Barnstable. The property now belongs to his grandson Henry M. Hutchings, Esq. The weathercock on the steeple of the present Unitarian Church building, it is believed, was made in England and was placed upon the steeple of the church building that was standing in 1723. At the time of the fire in 1905 which destroyed the building prior to the present edifice, this weathercock fell to the ground but was not destroyed, and was later placed upon the present meeting house. In this church there was erected in 1907 a tablet to the first minister of the Barnstable Church, the Rev. John Lothrop, the inscription written by Rev. Edward Everett Hale reading as follows:—

1 6 3 9
REV. JOHN LOTHROP
WAS THE
FIRST MINISTER OF THE BARNSTABLE CHURCH
HE HAD BEEN THE MINISTER OF THE
FIRST INDEPENDENT CONGREGATION IN
ENGLAND
HE WAS IMPRISONED FOR THIS SERVICE
BY ARCHBISHOP LAUD IN LONDON
FOR TWO YEARS
HE WAS RELEASED BY THE KING IN 1634
THAT HE MIGHT GO INTO EXILE
HE WAS BORN IN 1584
HE DIED AND WAS BURIED IN BARNSTABLE
NOVEMBER 8, 1653
A FAITHFUL WITNESS AND MINISTER
1 9 0 7

Among other families that went to Barnstable with the Rev. John Lothrop, or soon after, were the Annables, Bacons, Bournes, Cobbs, Hinckleys and Crockers. Lothrop was released on condition that he should leave the country, and he therefore sailed for Boston in 1634 whence he proceeded to Scituate and thence to Barnstable. He died in the house which is now incorporated in the building called the "Sturgis Library," in which house was born Captain William Sturgis, the well-known Boston merchant, who presented this building for use as a library and established a trust fund for its maintenance. The papers necessary to carry out this gift were executed by him only a few days before his sudden death.

It will be noticed that the English spell the name of the town "Barnstaple" whereas our way of spelling it is "Barnstable," yet, despite this difference there is no doubt that the New England town was named after the one in the romantic county of Devon on the river Taw. A curious thing about the older town is that many of the natives speak of it as "Barum," for what reason we have not been able to learn. The English Barnstaple, which is one of England's seaports, dates back to the year 925, when Athelstan came there in an attempt to drive the British out of what was then called "Damnonia." The ancient Britons called the place Tunge Abertawe, and the Saxons called it Berdenstaple.

The parish church of Barnstaple is in the heart of the town and is supposed to be the oldest building there, having been dedicated in 1318 to St. Peter and St. Paul. Its spire is considered one of the finest examples of such architecture in England. There are two unusual things connected with this church,—in the first place the spire leans over to one side, and in the second place its bells hang on the outside of the spire.

Many burgesses throve in this town on account of the newly discovered tobacco trade with Maryland and Virginia, and thereby became rich enough to build many large, handsome houses. For more than a thousand years Barnstaple has been famous for its pottery, called "Royal Barum Ware." Shakespeare is said to have visited the town during one of his theatrical tours. The annual fairs are events of great importance in both the American and English towns. A traveler to the mother town notices the singular similarity of the two harbours, especially at low tide.

BATH, MAINE

THE "Maine Gazetteer" states that Bath was named in 1781 by Col. Dummer Sewall, then a member of the General Court of Massachusetts, after Bath on the English Avon. His great-great-grandson, Harold M. Sewall, Esq., suggests that this name may have been chosen because of the hymn called Bath, a favorite in the hymn book of the early settlers. Certain it is that this frontier settlement presented not the slightest resemblance to the most fashionable spa of Europe. None of the settlers came from there, and the ships of our Bath had not yet begun to visit the older city's port of Bristol. Bath, England, has taken a great deal of interest in her namesake. About fifteen years ago Mr. Sewall attended a literary celebration in Bath, England, taking with him a letter from the Mayor, and was received with great consideration by the authorities in the old city. Later the Mayor of the English city requested that a committee be named from all the American Baths, of which there are about twenty-five, and Mr. Sewall was appointed a delegate and is still a member of this committee. In July, 1909, a great historical pageant was held in the English Bath, and each of the American Baths was requested to send a girl representative, many of the towns of this name responding. During the pageant a scene was arranged showing the introduction of the different towns in the New World to their English mother, and we quote a few lines of this interesting ceremony:—

"The Ladye Bath," who personifies the City, now makes her way to the Throne, which is set in the centre, to receive the

HOMAGE FROM THE WESTERN WORLD

By her side is the Swordbearer and a soldier with the British flag. Two maidens representing the Canadian Baths in Ontario and New Brunswick approach Mother Bath, while the Canadian Anthem, "O Canada," is sung.

LADYE BATH.

> Welcome! dear Daughters of brave Canada;
> All honour to that loyal-hearted land.

A procession approaches of silver-clad maidens, special envoys from the United States, in the dress of the Statue of Liberty, led by heralds and pages carrying banners with the arms of the States of Maine, New York, Illinois, New Hampshire, North Carolina, South Carolina, South Dakota, Ohio, Kentucky, Missouri, Pennsylvania, Michigan.   The band plays "The Star Spangled Banner."

LADYE BATH.

> Hark! 'Tis the coming of the white-robed Maids,
> Your neighbours in that wondrous Western World.
> Daughters of England, stand at our right hand
> The while we give them greeting to our shores.

Ladye Bath comes forward with outstretched arms.   The Maidens from the United States of America raise their banners simultaneously and advance towards Ladye Bath: as they approach they lower their banners and courtesy to Ladye Bath.

LADYE BATH.

> Illustrious Maidens of America,
> We welcome you to England and to Bath.
> The lintels of our doors are wreathed for you,
> The bread is broken, and your place prepared.

ONE OF THE MAIDENS.

> Ladye, we thank thee for thy courtesy.
> O'er the wide way of the unfathomed sea
> We come to bring thee homage from our land,
> And share thy tryst with mighty memories.
> Strangers we come—to find within thy gates
> An open-hearted hospitality.

LADYE BATH.

> God is the Father of all folk on earth.
> These words of the great Alfred, England's king,
> Counsel his sons and daughters to forget
> Man's sharp dividing in God's unity;
> Wherefore you are not strangers; we are kin.

Immediately after the foregoing words of Ladye Bath, the chorus sings the National Air common to Great Britain and the United States.

An interchange between the two cities occurred at the three hundredth anniversary of American shipbuilding, which was held in our Bath in 1907, and on this occasion the Mayor of the English city cabled his greeting. An ode to the sailing ship of the old days, written by W. Clark Russell, Esq., the novelist of Bath, England, was read on this occasion, accompanied by a letter to Mr. Sewall in which were these words:—

"I was cradled in wood when I came from New York to Liverpool at the age of six months. I also served in wood for eight years in frigate-like ships built at Sunderland. I shall be launched with most others on the sea of eternity in that odd little dug-out called a coffin.

From "The Beginnings of Colonial Maine," by Henry S. Burrage, D.D., Historian of Maine

SIR JOHN AND LADY POP-
HAM MONUMENT IN THE
PARISH CHURCH, WELL-
INGTON, ENGLAND

Sir John Popham was Chief Justice of England and helped to encourage many of the early voyages of exploration to Maine. He was an uncle of George Popham, who established on the peninsula of Sabino, at the mouth of the Kennebec, the first English colony on the shores of New England.

"Wood has played a large part in my life and this forthcoming Trans-Atlantic retrospective festival naturally put some little life of pensiveness into the gaze I fastened upon that nursling of American commercial shipping, Bath, beyond the sea."

Services were held at Bath and at Popham, nearby, which is the exact spot of the original settlement.

It is not generally realized that the early settlements of Maine antedated those in Massachusetts and that our industry of shipbuilding, so important to the early pioneers, was started in this little settlement at Popham, in 1607, when the early colonists built a little "Pynnace of thirty tonnes" which they called the "Virginia of Sagadahock," the first ship built by European hands on the American continent. There is no record of her career except that she took some of the early colonists back to England soon after the start of the settlement, and the following year sailed to Jamestown, Virginia.

Sir Ferdinando Gorges, friend of Raleigh and Governor of Plymouth under James I, the projector and patron of this little colony of George Popham,—the brother of the Chief Justice of England,—held out to his sovereign the vast territory which he sought to colonize, "as promising the increase of the King's Navy, the breeding of mariners and the employment of his people." Not to the glory of his sovereign, but of the sovereign people of America was this prophecy to be fulfilled, and in its fulfillment Bath and the banks of the Kennebec have had an illustrious part.

We have no record of the intermittent building of vessels which went on here for a century and a half following the Popham settlement. Sir William Phips, the first American to be knighted, and first Governor of Massachusetts Bay, was born

Kindness Miss Evelyn L. Gilmore

THE POPHAM MEMORIAL

at Fort St. George, on the promontory of Sabino. The memorial was placed there in 1907 to commemorate the landing of the first English colony on the shores of New England, in 1607, under George Popham. A copy of the inscription appears on page 55.

just across the river and learned the shipwright's trade there, and in 1762 the building of full rigged ships became an established industry, carrying the name and fame of Bath to the remotest ports of the world. The first ship was the "Earl of Bute" built in 1762 by Captain William Swanton. Over one hundred and forty years later the last wooden sailing ship was built in the District of Bath; her name was the "Aryan," and she was built by Minott.

From a print   Kindness Miss Evelyn L. Gilmore

FORT POPHAM AND SITE OF THE POPHAM MEMORIAL AT THE MOUTH OF THE KENNEBEC RIVER

Fort Popham is the old discarded fort in the center of the picture; the memorial is indicated by the arrow and the site of Fort St. George is just to the right of the arrow. This promontory is called Sabino.

Other famous ships of Bath were the first "Rappahannock," 1841; the second "Rappahannock," 1890; the "Roanoke" and the "Shenandoah," at the time of their launching the largest wooden ships afloat; the "Dirigo," 1894, the first steel sailing ship built in America; and the "William P. Frye" sunk by the German cruiser "Prinz Eitel Friedrich," January 28, 1915, the first American ship sunk by Germany; all of the above vessels were built and owned by the Sewalls. In the long roll of builders of Bath square riggers may be mentioned as types—space not allowing justice to all—the names of William King, Maine's first Governor, Crooker, Drummond, Houghton, Reed, Rideout, Patten and Rogers, and no history of Bath shipbuilding is complete without adding the name of Hyde, father and son, who gave to the Bath Iron Works its acknowledged pre-eminence in speed design and naval building. Four other plants connected with shipbuilding at present in Bath are the Texas Steamship Company, the Hyde Windlass Company, the G. C. Dearing Company and Percy & Small; the two last named concerns building wooden ships.

The original settlement by George Popham and his colony was on the peninsula of Sabino, at the mouth of the Kennebec, and here also was celebrated the two hundred and fiftieth anniversary of the inauguration of the first civil government on these shores, and likewise the building of this little ship "Virginia of Sagadahock" was again honoured. It must be remembered that the Kennebec River, known in the old days as Sagadahock, meaning "here it ends," has the honour of

Photograph by F. Frith & Co., England   *Kindness Ian Forbes-Robertson, Esq.*

"DOUGHBOYS" AT ROMAN BATHS, BATH, ENGLAND

Some of the three hundred "doughboys" who visited the old Roman baths in Bath, England, on Independence Day, July 4, 1918, as guests of the Mayor of the city. The soldiers of Rome bathed in these baths over one thousand nine hundred years ago.

having witnessed the first successful attempt of English colonization on the New England coast; it may also be of interest to mention that between the years 1607 and 1622 over one hundred and nine English vessels entered the nearby harbours.

At the time of this two hundred and fiftieth anniversary of the settlement, the United States Government began the construction of a fort near the supposed site of the old one erected by the Popham colonists. At the suggestion of the Maine Historical Society, a stone, with a suitable inscription, was gotten ready, but the building of the fort was postponed owing to the fact that the Government decided it would not be an adequate defence for the mouth of the Kennebec River.

In the meantime it was discovered that the Popham Colonists did not occupy the exact site of the old fort and, therefore, a new stone was placed at the proper site of Fort St. George on the promontory nearby, the dedication ceremonies being performed by Bishop Robert Codman, following the exact ritual read by Richard Seymour, the Chaplain of the Popham Colonists. The inscription on the memorial reads as follows:—

The First English colony
On the shores of New England
was founded here
August 29 N. S. 1607
under George Popham.

A salute was also fired on this occasion, in honour of Popham, the first Governor of the Colony, who died there and who was buried within the enclosure of the fort. This memorial is placed on a rocky point on Sabino Hill overlooking the fort and adjoining the Government reservation.   Several years before Popham landed at the mouth of the Kennebec, Captain George Waymouth made a voyage to this coast, landing at Monhegan Island, then called St. George's Island, whence he proceeded probably up the St. George's River.   He returned to Dartmouth, England.   To commemorate his discovery and exploration, the Maine Historical Society in 1905, on the three hundredth anniversary of his voyage, erected a cross on Allen's Island in St. George's Harbour, similar to the cross Waymouth himself set up at this place, thus making the earliest known claim of right of possession by an Englishman on New England soil.   These services were attended by J. B. Keating, Esq., British Vice-Consul at Portland, Maine, who made a speech on this occasion.   A tablet has also been placed in Thomaston in memory of Waymouth.

We have obtained a picture of some doughboys, three hundred of whom were guests of the Mayor of the English Bath on Independence Day, 1918, and who must have shown great interest in viewing the old Roman relics over nineteen hundred years old.   The Baths were turned over to the allied armies during the War, and many soldiers have regained their health at this famous spring, as generations past have done, according to these two well-known lines:—

"A seething bath which men yet prove
Against strange maladies a sovereign cure."

The discovery of the baths is somewhat uncertain; some historians claim that the father of Shakespeare's King Lear discovered these waters over eight hundred years before the Christian Era; while others are inclined to believe in the legend that Prince Bladud, son of Lud Hudibras, King of Britain, being banished from the kingdom on account of leprosy, hired himself out as a swineherd and, in the course of his wanderings, happened to cross the waters of the Avon where he discovered one of his sows, affected with the same malady, wallowing in the mud about some bubbling hot springs.   When the animal came out, he was amazed to find that it was entirely cured.   The young prince was also cured, returned to his father's palace, and later when he became king he is said to have founded a city at these springs.   Up to this day it has been one of the earth's secrets, unsolved by scientists.

The life at Bath, England, in the eighteenth century, presents a striking contrast to that of the little American city.   While the settlement upon the Kennebec was recovering from the hostile invasions of the Indians and was firmly establish-

BATH, ENGLAND,
from North Parade Bridge, showing the Abbey.

THE ROYAL CRESCENT, BATH, ENGLAND

ing itself upon the shores of the New World, the English city, under the rule of "Beau Nash," as "Master of Ceremonies," was the domain of fashion and gaiety, the center for the *beau monde* of England. Morning, noon and evening had their allotted pleasures, from the early revels at Spring Gardens to the fashionable balls at night. Varied indeed has been the history of this "Queen City of the West," as the English often call it, ever since its foundation, and not only has it been a health resort, but also a center of fashionable society and a Mecca for artists and men of letters. During the days of civil strife, Round Heads and Cavaliers fought in its streets.

At the time of Charles the Second, Bath was the favorite resort of royalty and celebrities, and among the latter have been Rochester, Addison, Walpole, Sheridan, Steele, Fielding and Pope, and that splendid circle of buildings known as "The Circus" has had many noted residents including Gainsborough the artist, and William Pitt, first Earl of Chatham; Jane Austen was also a frequent visitor at Bath, and her novels are said to be founded on Bath society; in fact Mrs. Siddons called herself a "Child of Bath." Pepys, too, visited the city, and recorded in his diary his experiences at one of the baths, concerning which he writes:—

"Methinks it cannot be clean to go so many bodies together in the same water."

Many kings and seven queens have gone there in search of health, and it has been said that the winter season at Bath was regarded as little less important than the spring season in London.

Edmund Burke, who in 1797 lived in the fine central house of the stately North Parade, tenanted in 1771 by Oliver Goldsmith, proved a true friend to the American colonists during their struggle for freedom, and an eloquent tribute to his political virtues was delivered by the late Hon. Whitelaw Reid, when he went to Bath on October 22, 1908, to inaugurate the memorial tablet commemorating Burke's last sojourn on the banks of the Avon. "There are few English cities," said Mr. Reid, "which more strongly appeal to my countrymen than Bath, once the abiding place of Burke and the elder Pitt." General Wolfe and Major André also lived there.

In King's Bath is an effigy of Bladud, with an inscription nearby, recalling the legend that he was "the founder of these baths 863 years before Christ."

The Abbey is the architectural feature of the city and in it is a monument to the memory of Hon. W. Bingham, President of the United States Senate in 1797.

Readers of Dickens will also remember that Pickwick visited Bath, and on the coach in which he travelled was painted the owner's name, which strangely enough was Moses Pickwick, as referred to by Sam Weller. Few readers of Dickens, however, realize that this name on the coach was actually an historical fact. Bath has often been called England's "Florence," "Waters of the Sun," "City of Fashion," and "Bath the Magnificent;" by the Romans it was called Aquæ Sulis.

Fittingly, we may conclude with an allusion to another link between the American and the English Bath: Thomas Pownall, Governor of Massachusetts, 1751–60, was a firm friend of the Colonists, and understood America as no other Englishman. He was born in Lincoln, England, and for this reason the ancient county of Lincoln in the Province of Maine, often styled the Mother of Maine Counties, received its name. This is the county in which Bath was situated, until set off into the County of Sagadahock. Pownalborough across the river was the shire town, and Thomas Pownall from whom it was named died in the English Bath.

BELFAST, MAINE

THE toss of a coin about the year 1770 decided the question as to whether Belfast, Maine, should be so called or whether it should be named Londonderry, from the town of the same name in New Hampshire whence most of the settlers in the Maine town had come a short time previously. A dispute had arisen as to the name of this new settlement, but James Miller, who with his wife and children was the first person to set foot on shore when their vessel reached these new lands, was determined that it should be named for Belfast, County Antrim, Ireland, the place of his birth. Some authorities claim that Miller's son, Robert, named Belfast, but this cannot be so because at that time the son was only twelve years of age. Miller finally, however, agreed to have this question decided in the manner already described. The town, now a city, was incorporated in 1773. The two Belfasts have often been thought to resemble one another in certain ways, for both places are divided by rivers which empty in each case into Belfast Bay; moreover both harbours afford very safe anchorage and are particularly attractive, the word "Belfast" signifying "Beautiful Harbour," an appellation most appropriate to both places.

The daring adventurers consisting of about thirty persons, first journeyed from Londonderry to Haverhill in May, 1770, and from there they went down the river and along the coast to Newburyport. From there they sailed north and after a hard week arrived at Northport, which they mistook for Belfast, and the name given to the harbour there was Saturday Cove, which name it still bears. These pioneers, who were of the same Scotch-Irish descent as the settlers of Londonderry, New Hampshire, then sailed along the coast from Northport a short distance until they reached Belfast. It is no surprise that they made such a success of this Maine enterprise, for we find them described by Hon. Charles H. Bell in these words: "There has been almost no place of eminence, political, literary, or professional, to which men of this descent have not attained. The number of them whose names have been written in history is endless." Among these settlers was John Mitchell who came from Ireland to New England with his young son and, on a visit to Passamaquoddy, Maine, in 1668, learned that this large tract of fifteen thousand

Photograph taken by F. Frith & Co., England   *Kindness Ian Forbes-Robertson, Esq.*

BELFAST, IRELAND,
showing the Albert Memorial Clock Tower.

From "Belfast and the Province of Ulster in the 20th Century," by Robert M. Young, B.A., J.P., published by W. T. Pike & Co., Brighton, England

From a water color in possession of Gt. Clark, M.P.

HIGH STREET, BELFAST, IRELAND, IN 1786

acres of land was for sale at the price of twenty cents per acre; he inspected it and was so impressed by its natural beauty and advantages that on his return to Londonderry, New Hampshire, he persuaded his friends to purchase it. A meeting was held at the house of David Craig, and a "Community" or "Proprietary" was formed to purchase these lands, then known merely as a "tract on the southerly side of a township granted to Co. Goldthwait at Penobscot Fort." There was a very interesting and unusual condition imposed in the purchase agreement that "we bind ourselves that no one shall own a right amongst us that is unable to produce a certificate of good moral character to the satisfaction of the community and to the gentlemen of which the purchase is made." Mitchell was the largest purchaser of land and is usually referred to as the founder of the town.

The lives of these settlers were full of hardship, and there is a record of one person who wrote home, "No cleared land in sight and no house except our cabin, composed of logs, through which holes were cut for doors and windows, with hemlock bark for roof."

From "Belfast and the Province of Ulster in the 20th Century," by Robert M. Young, B.A., J.P., published by W. T. Pike & Co., Brighton, England

CASTLE PLACE, BELFAST, IRELAND, IN 1843

The mother town in Ireland is situated on the river Lagan, just before it enters Belfast Bay, which was often the resort of roving Danes in the early centuries. Belfast has been spelled in many ways: Belfirst, Belfeirste, Ballfaste, Bealfast and Belferside being the usual way of spelling it in histories. The oldest name of the ground on which Belfast is situated was Ballyrecoolegalgie and this part of Ulster was originally named Uladh. The Irish name for Belfast was Beal-na-farsad or Bela Fearsad, meaning in the Irish language "mouth of the ford."

The authentic history of Belfast really begins with the Norman knight John de Courci who owned the counties of Antrim and Down and who built the first castle at Belfast in 1177. Belfast cannot claim the antiquity of Dublin as its history does not go back beyond the twelfth century, but during the latter part of the seventeenth century it is described by some writers as being the second town of Ireland. It is not known definitely when the Castle was built, but its career has been replete with history; it was held by De Maundeville, an Anglo-Norman, about 1300, later it came into the possession of Hugh O'Neill, and in 1560 it belonged to Queen Elizabeth. Still later the Castle again reverted to another member of the O'Neill family, one of the most important names in Belfast history, and finally it was granted at the beginning of the seventeenth century to Sir Arthur Chichester, who was the first Earl of Donegal, and who improved the city to such an extent that it reached its era of greatest prosperity at this time; in fact he was the real founder of modern Belfast in the year 1601.   The possession of the Castle in the early days was almost equivalent to the ownership of Belfast itself.   Sir John Chichester, younger brother of Arthur Chichester, once captured the Castle. He was killed and beheaded by MacDonnell.   The story is told that some time later MacDonnell went to see the Chichester family tomb in St. Nicholas' Church at Carrickfergus near Belfast, and upon seeing Sir John's effigy, the warrior inquired, "How the de'il came he to get his head again, for I was sure I had once ta'en it frae him?"

The old church near the town was called in the fourteenth century the "White Church," this name being later changed to "Church of St. Patrick of the Old Ford;" this was the mother church of the district, a branch chapel called "Chapel of the Ford" being the forerunner of the future church of Belfast.   Near the site of this church, on High Street, now stands St. George's.   The first Roman Catholic priest of Belfast was Rev. Phelomy O'Hamill, and the date of his coming was about the year 1704.

The first stage to Dublin was started in 1752 and three days were required in making the difficult journey; some years later another stage line was inaugurated to Newry and the coach traveled with such speed that it was called the "Newry Flying Coach."   In earlier days it is said that the female shopkeepers of Belfast, when they found it necessary to make a journey to Dublin, usually went by pillion.

In the eighteenth century Belfast was the scene of many sports, chief of which were cock-fights and the Ballymacash horse races.   Sugar refining was one of the leading industries of Belfast as early as 1683, George Macartney, one of the leading citizens of the town, owning a large plant.   The first Linen Hall, which was used as a trading market, was erected in the year 1739.   The town also had its salt works, its woolen mill, a ship building plant, glass works, a brewery and a rope walk.   Among the most prominent families of the city are the Warings, Pottingers, Knoxes and Legges.

BEVERLY, MASSACHUSETTS

BEVERLEY, England, which is always spelled with an "e" before the "y," is an attractive town closely associated with romance, traditions and struggles.   The town was in olden times called "Beverlega" and later "Beverlac" or "Beverlaco" from the great numbers of beavers that abounded in this locality, the name later being changed to "Beverley."   The beaver has always been accepted as the symbol of the town, and on a cloth shield which Constitutional Lodge No. 294 in Beverley, England, some years ago, sent over to Liberty Lodge in our Beverly, the figure of a beaver appears twice conspicuously among the other attractive decorations.   This beautiful present, which is shown in the cut on page 63,

From photographs taken for the State Street Trust Company

Kindness Worshipful Master H. Franklin Murray, and Rev. E. J. V. Huiginn

CLOTH SHIELD

in the rooms of Liberty Lodge, Beverly, Massachusetts, presented by Constitutional Lodge No. 294, Beverley, England. The beaver is the symbol of the English town, which received its name on account of the number of these animals which abounded in that locality in olden times.

REPLY OF THANKS

sent by Constitutional Lodge No. 294, of Beverley, England, to Liberty Lodge, Beverly, Massachusetts, for presents of a loving cup, moosehead, and beaver, sent to the English lodge by the Massachusetts lodge. For the wording of this letter see page 64.

hangs in the rooms of the Lodge. Interchange of friendly relations between the two Lodges was originated by the Earl of Londesborough of Beverley, England, and Charles Woodberry of Beverly, Mass., now deceased, who was a brother of George E. Woodberry, the author and poet; and pictures of these two men, who have done so much to promote these exchanges, now hang on the walls of the American Lodge. Liberty Lodge is also closely connected with the Alexandria-Washington Lodge in Virginia, of which George Washington was once Master, and on the walls of the Beverly Lodge is a very fine painting of the "Father of his Country" in his Masonic robes. Both these Lodges hold their great banquets each year on Washington's Birthday, and presents on these occasions are exchanged. The English Lodge always remembers the event and sends presents to Liberty Lodge. When the late Earl of Londesborough was alive he always sent large hampers of game from his own preserves, also ivy, mistletoe and laurel, to make the occasion an enjoyable one;

Photograph by F. Frith & Co., England   *Kindness Ian Forbes-Robertson, Esq.*

BEVERLEY MINSTER, BEVERLEY, ENGLAND,

one of the finest Gothic churches in England. On the walls of Liberty Lodge, Beverly, Massachusetts,
hang a number of pictures of this cathedral and of this English town.

and Thomas Foley, the present Secretary of the English Lodge, still continues the
custom of sending presents to the American Lodge. Some years ago, Liberty
Lodge, Beverly, sent over among other gifts a large moosehead, a loving cup and a
magnificent beaver which was captured by one of our backwoodsmen. The beaver
and loving cup are in the rooms of the English Lodge, while the moosehead is in the
residence of the late Earl of Londesborough, Blanckney Lodge. Their reply of
thanks elaborately illuminated is hung on the walls of Beverly Lodge, and reads
as follows:—

"To the W. M. and Brethren of Liberty Lodge, Beverly, Mass. U. S. A.
Fraternal Greeting. We the W. M. officers and Brethren of the Constitutional Lodge of Free and Accepted Masons, Beverley No. 294, on
the Register of the Grand Lodge of England, *Record* in open lodge assembled our sincere thanks and hearty good wishes to the Brethren of
Liberty Lodge for their handsome Present of a Silver Loving Cup given
in commemoration of the Constitutional Lodge attaining its Centenary.
17 June 1893"

From a photograph *Courtesy W. K. Watkins, Esq.*

NORTH BAR, BEVERLEY, ENGLAND

It is interesting to notice that this letter was dated June 17, Constitutional Lodge having thoughtfully picked out the date of the Battle of Bunker Hill in order to show that no ill feeling between the countries any longer existed. Return presents were sent to Liberty Lodge, including engravings, paintings, photographs, a Union Jack, two dozen old-fashioned "fireing" glasses, as they are called, and an attractive set of drinking glasses, each one of which has the picture of a beaver on it. On the walls of the American Lodge are a dozen or so photographs of Beverley and the Minster, and there is also a large photograph of the same church in the main room of the Lodge. It may be interesting also to record that the American Lodge raised a sum of money to help repair the statues on the outside of the English Cathedral, and in addition to this, during the war, the American Lodge sent money to Constitutional Lodge to take care of its wounded soldiers. Still another interchange of presents is interesting to note; while St. John's Church at Beverly Farms, Mass., was being built, the Beverley Minister sent to the Rev. E. J. V. Huiginn two splendid photographs to decorate the vestry room of the Church.

In 1906 Roland W. Boyden, Esq., of Liberty Lodge was the official representative to the English Lodge and was treated with great hospitality by the members

From a print owned by a Boston collector   *Formerly in the collection of J. H. Seers, Essex, England*

THE MARKET PLACE, BEVERLEY, ENGLAND

of the Beverley fraternity, among whom were John Elwell, Esq., the Master, Brother Hobson, Brother Gates, Brother Thomson Foley, the Secretary, and Brother Tom Turner. On his return Mr. Boyden gave an account of his visit at a meeting of Liberty Lodge held on October 31, 1906, and in this address he said: "The English, too, feel strongly the race tie which exists between the two countries, and they feel pride in the progress and success of the English blood on this side of the water."

Near the spot where the Beverley Minster now stands there used to be a monastery which was built in 721 A.D. by St. John of Beverley, who was at the time Archbishop of York; and to him the town, therefore, owes much of its prosperity. The Danes destroyed the town, together with the monastery, which was rebuilt, St. John of Beverley being then canonized and his bones enshrined in the new church. There is much interesting history attached to this place. Edward II visited Beverley previous to the battle of Bannockburn. His light horsemen in the battle were named "hobelers" on account of the small horses they rode, but they showed such bravery that they are supposed to have originated the well-known proverb, "Don't ride your hobby to death." In 1759 the Fifteenth York East Riding Regiment of Foot, which sailed against Quebec under General Wolfe and was captured, had its headquarters in the town, and they were jokingly called by some "The East Chalkshire Volunteers." In the old days the townspeople were much interested in bull-baiting and cock-fighting, which sports were indulged in by the

Athenians and the Romans. Beverley also held many horse races and had a famous hunt called the "Holderness Hunt," of which Tom Hodgson was the Master for many years beginning from the year 1824. He had his kennels at Beverley and lived only for hunting, and often after the runs the members dined together in the Beverley Arms Hotel. It is also mentioned that the cherry brandy used on these occasions was "no bad jumping powder in this country of drains," but that it went down a bit more easily if one looked at the attractive inscription on the bottle. The Master lived in such an humble room that it is said he could sit on his bed, stir the fire, and see his hounds through a hole in the wall, all at once. This well-known huntsman covered such distances on his runs that the people of the town said his men were made of cast iron, his horses of steel, and his hounds of india-rubber. In the very old days there was much horse-stealing in the country, which suggested the untrue saying, "If you shake a bridle over the grave of a York-shireman, he will arise and steal a horse."

Beverly, Massachusetts, was so named in the year 1668, the settlement having previously been called Mackerel Cove or Bass River. The place was originally part of Naumkeag, which included Salem, Marblehead, Manchester, Wenham, Danvers and some adjacent territory. It belonged to John, Sagamore of Agawam, who welcomed the new comers and made them a free grant of this entire territory. The first permanent settlement here was made by Roger Conant, John and William Woodberry, John Balch and Peter Palfrey in 1630. These five men all belonged to the Church of England. In 1668 Bass River was incorporated into a township by the name of Beverly, and the first selectmen included Thomas Lothrop, William Dixey, William Dodge, Sr., John West and Paul Thorndike. Three years later Roger Conant drew up a petition for a change of name which starts as follows:—

> "The humble petition of Roger Conant, of Bass River alias Beverly, who hath bin a planter in New England fortie yeers and upwards, being one of the first, if not the very first, that resolved and made good my settlement under God in matter of plantation with my family in this collony of the Massachusets Bay, and have bin instrumental, both for the founding and carrying on of the same;"

adding that

> "Now my umble suite and request is unto this honorable Court, onlie that the name of our towne or plantation may be altered or changed from Beverly to be called Budleigh. I have two reasons that have moved me unto this request. The first is the great dislike and dis-content of many of our people for this name of Beverly, because (we being but a small place) it hath caused on us a constant nickname of Beggarly, being in the mouths of many, and no order was given, or consent by the people to their agent for any name until we were shure of being a town granted in the first place.
> Secondly. I being the first that had house in Salem (and neither had any hand in naming either that or any other town) and myself with those that were then with me, being all from the western part of Eng-

land, desire this western name of Budleigh, a market towne in Devon-shire, and neere unto the sea, as wee are heere in this place, and where myself was borne.   Now in regard of our firstnesse and antiquity in this soe famous a collony, we should umblie request this small preveledg with your favors and consent, to give this name above said, unto our town.   I never yet made sute or request unto the Generall Court for the last matter, tho' I think I might as well have done, as many others have, who have obtained much without hazard of life, or preferring the public good before their own interest, which, I praise God, I have done."

The Court replied that it could "see no cause to alter the name of the place as desired," much to the disgust of the petitioner.   Conant was born in Budleigh, England, in 1591; in 1623 he came over here to Plymouth, then moved to Nan-tasket, later to Cape Ann, and finally to Salem, living to the ripe age of eighty-nine.   John Balch came from Bridgewater, Somersetshire, England.

BRISTOL, MAINE

(Also New Hampshire, Vermont, Rhode Island and Connecticut)

THERE is a Bristol in each of the New England States with the exception of Massachusetts, and most of them have derived their name from Bristol, England, which port almost takes rank with Plymouth, England, as having been the home or starting point of many of the early voyages of exploration to the New England coast, and particularly to Maine.   The merchants of the English Bristol, in the early days, took a great deal of interest in all the suggested ventures to the American shores, and their interest was encouraged in many cases by the city authorities.   The earliest explorers whose names are connected with the Eng-lish city were John Cabot, who resided there, and his son Sebastian, who claimed he was born at "Bristowe," meaning Bristol.   In 1497 Henry VII granted letters patent to John Cabot, who with his son Sebastian set sail in the "Matthew," and succeeded in discovering the continent of North America, landing first at Cape Breton.   Cabot also made a second voyage along the Atlantic coast, and it has often been asserted that he opened the way towards the English colonization of our shores.   A large tower was erected to the memory of John Cabot on Brandon Hill, Bristol, England, in 1897, commemorating the four hundredth anniversary of his great discovery.   There are three bronze tablets on the tower, one recording the laying of the corner stone by the Marquess of Dufferin and Ava, in June, 1897, and the dedication of the tower by him in the following year.   The second tablet reads as follows:—

> This tablet is placed here by the Bristol Branch of the Peace Society in the earnest hope that Peace and Friendship may ever continue between the kindred Peoples of this Country and America.
> Glory to God in the Highest, and on Earth Peace, Goodwill toward men.   LUKE II. 14.

THE CABOT TOWER, ON BRANDON HILL, BRISTOL, ENGLAND,

erected in 1897 to the memory of John Cabot, to commemorate the four hundredth anniversary of his discovery of the continent of North America.

The third tablet is worded as follows:—

> This Tower
> was erected by public subscription
> in the 61st year of the Reign of Queen Victoria,
> to commemorate the fourth centenary of
> the Discovery of the Continent of
> North America
> on the 24th of June, 1497 by
> John Cabot
> who sailed from this port in the
> Bristol Ship 'Matthew' with a Bristol crew
> under Letters Patent granted by King Henry VII
> to that Navigator and his Sons
> Lewis, Sebastian, and Sanctus.

Another memorial has been raised to John and Sebastian Cabot in the form of a bronze tablet placed on St. Augustine's Bridge in Bristol, bearing the following inscription:—

From "The Beginnings of Colonial Maine," by Henry S. Burrage, D.D., Historian of Maine

PRING MEMORIAL

in St. Stephen's Church, Bristol, England, placed there to commemorate the well-known voyages of Capt. Martin Pring to the Maine Coast and to the East Indies. The first part of the inscription is given in our text on page 72.

From this port John Cabot and his son Sebastian (who was born in Bristol) sailed in the ship Matthew A. D. 1497 and discovered the continent of North America.

In the Church of St. Mary Redcliffe is still to be seen the "Dun Cow" bone, the rib of a cow whale, which is the only remaining trophy of Cabot's expedition, and which for some time was considered part of the body of George Warwick. This great seaport is also closely associated with the adventures of Martin Frobisher, and it may also be interesting to mention that here lie the remains of Admiral William Penn, the father of the famous Lord Proprietor and governor of Pennsylvania. It may interest the reader also to mention that the steamships "Great Britain" and "Great Western," the latter being the pioneer of transatlantic steam traffic, were launched at this English seaport. Shipping is still carried on quite extensively, although not by large vessels, and a particularly picturesque feature is that ships can sail into the very heart of the town, as shown in one of our cuts. A few feet from these docks is the fashionable shipping street, and nearby is the cathedral.

Photograph taken especially for the State Street Trust Company by F. Frith & Co., England   Kindness Ian Forbes-Robertson, Esq.

BRISTOL, ENGLAND,
showing the center of the city and the docks, the latter being a picturesque feature of this seaport.

An object of interest to Americans is the Portland Street Wesleyan Methodist Chapel, which was founded by Captain Webb who is said to be the founder of Methodism in America. A window in this chapel represents him preaching in his scarlet uniform with his sword beside him. Another interesting fact connected with Bristol is the splendid collection of pastel portraits exhibited in the Bristol Art Gallery by James Sharples who lived in America for several years and who died in New York in 1811. He made portraits of all the famous persons of his time including George Washington, Mrs. Washington, Alexander Hamilton, John Adams, Thomas Jefferson, James Madison, Mrs. Madison, Aaron Burr and many others. Bristol, England, is situated on both banks of the Avon, and was regarded at one time as the second capital of the kingdom. When the Queen of James II made a visit to the town in 1613 she enjoyed it so much that she said "she never knew she was Queen until she came to Bristol."

There is an interesting memorial in St. Stephen's Church, Bristol, England, to Captain Martin Pring, who sailed twice, probably from Bristol, on his well-known voyages to the Maine coast. His first achievement in 1603 was celebrated in Portland, Maine, on its three hundredth anniversary. We give a cut of this monument in Bristol, England, on page 70. Part of the inscription reads as follows:—

To the Pious Memorie of Martin Pringe, Merchaunt, etc., etc.

> His painefull, skillfull, travayles reacht as farre
> As from the Artick to the Antartick starre;
> He made himself A Shippe.   Religion
> His onely Compass, and the truth alone
> His guiding Cynosure: Faith was his Sailes,
> His Anchour Hope.

There are also tablets erected in St. Peter's Church in Bristol to Robert Aldworth and Giles Elbridge, two prominent Bristol merchants who in 1626 bought Monhegan Island, off the Maine coast, from Abraham Jennings, and who also obtained a grant of twelve thousand acres of land at Pemaquid in 1631, from which territory has sprung Bristol, Maine. This island of Monhegan, formerly called St. George's Island, was one of the fishing ports used in the early days by the fishermen of the British Isles.

Bristol, Maine, was incorporated as a town in 1765 and was so called because of the connection of its early history with so many citizens of England, although it is not known by whom the name was suggested. The first title to these lands was acquired by John Brown who bought the present territory and Damariscotta in 1625. The early conveyancer of these lands was Abraham Shurt, and Nathaniel I. Bowditch, the well-known Boston conveyancer, dedicated his book "to the memory of Abraham Shurt, the father of American conveyancing, whose name is associated alike with my daily toilet and my daily occupation." There is a tablet erected to commemorate the execution of this first deed in America which conveyed a large part of Pemaquid, including Bristol, from the well-known Sagamore Samoset to John Brown. Sewall wrote that "Pemaquid under titles from the President of the Council of New England became a noted place and the busiest on the coast." Pemaquid at this time included the land east of Falmouth, now Portland, and west of the Penobscot River.

It may be interesting to mention that some of the Popham people are supposed to have landed at Pemaquid in 1607, and there is a tablet placed in the tower built over the Fort at Pemaquid Harbour to commemorate the landing of these Englishmen on the New England shores.

Bristol, Rhode Island, received its name in 1681 and was probably named for the English town of this name, although we have been unable to trace any connecting links; however, its broad street was laid out by an Englishman. At one time this Rhode Island town was the fourth largest seaport in the country, and a large commerce with the world was carried on from there.

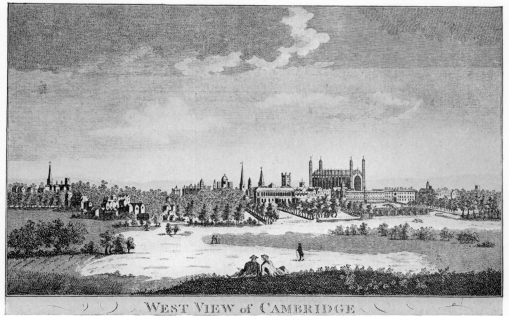

From an old print   *Kindness Ian Forbes-Robertson, Esq.*

From a photograph by F. Frith & Co., England   *Kindness Ian Forbes-Robertson, Esq.*

CAMBRIDGE, ENGLAND
View on the Cam.

Bristol, Vermont, was originally granted to Samuel Averill and sixty-two of his associates and was first called "Pocock" for the distinguished English Admiral of this name; the name Bristol was given in the year 1789.

CAMBRIDGE, MASSACHUSETTS

AFTER GOD HAD CARRIED US SAFE TO NEW ENGLAND
AND WEE HAD BUILDED OUR HOUSES
PROVIDED NECESSARIES FOR OUR LIVELI HOOD
REARD CONVENIENT PLACES FOR GOD'S WORSHIP
AND SETLED THE CIVILL GOVERNMENT
ONE OF THE NEXT THINGS WE LONGED FOR
AND LOOKED AFTER WAS TO ADVANCE LEARNING
AND PERPETUATE IT TO POSTERITY
DREADING TO LEAVE AN ILLITERATE MINISTERY
TO THE CHURCHES WHEN OUR PRESENT MINISTERS
SHALL LIE IN THE DUST

THESE memorable words on a tablet at the right of the Johnson Gate, on the west side of Harvard College Yard, are taken from "New England's First Fruits," a pamphlet published in London in 1643; these lines show us that the struggling colony, which could raise only sixty pounds to defend itself from the Indians, appropriated four hundred pounds to guard itself against ignorance. Opposite this tablet near the Johnson Gate is another one which records that the "colledge is ordered to bee at Newetowne;" that "Newetowne henceforward be called Cambrige;" and that the "colledge shallbee called Harvard." There is another tablet on the corner of Boylston Hall facing Massachusetts Avenue, which probably has been read by very few of the thousands of students who have been at Harvard, and who, therefore, may not be aware of the fact that Cambridge was once called Newtown, sometimes also spelled Newtowne. The words on this tablet are as follows:—

Here was the homestead
of Thomas Hooker
1633–36
First pastor at Newtown.

It will be remembered that this is the same Hooker who journeyed to, and founded, Hartford, Connecticut. There are other tablets in the yard which must be especially interesting to the many English visitors who have been at Harvard, as they show that three of the oldest and finest buildings of Harvard College were named for English benefactors. Hollis Hall, built by the Province in 1763, was named in honour of Thomas Hollis of London, merchant, and members of his family who were benefactors of the College; Holworthy was built by a state lottery in 1812 and was named for an English merchant, Sir Matthew Holworthy, who in 1681 gave one thousand pounds, the largest gift received by Harvard College up to that

From a photograph

Kindness Mrs. Mary Fifield King

EMMANUEL COLLEGE, CAMBRIDGE, ENGLAND,
the college John Harvard attended.

time; Holden Chapel was built by the wife and daughter of Samuel Holden, M.P., who was a liberal benefactor of the College. Massachusetts Hall is the oldest building in the University, having been erected by the Province in 1720. It was occupied by the American Army during the Revolutionary War and was used for students' rooms until 1870, when it was remodelled within and lectures and examinations began to be held there.

The College, founded in 1636, was the only one in the country up to the year 1693, when William and Mary in Virginia was started. Two years after the founding of the College, the name of Newtown was changed to Cambridge, owing to the fact that the town had been selected as the site of the new seat of learning, and also for the reason that most of the ministers and leading men of our colony had been educated at old Cambridge in England. That the erection of the new college was not delayed for many years through lack of adequate funds, was due in no small measure to the generous gift of "that gentle and godly youth" John Harvard, a young minister of Charlestown, who at his death in 1638 left to the College his entire library and one half of his estate, which, it has been estimated, was worth about sixteen hundred pounds. Out of gratitude for this splendid gift, as every

From pictures in Harvard College Library, Harvard University   *Kindness William C. Lane, Esq.*

HARVARD MEMORIAL CHAPEL AND WINDOW IN ST. SAVIOUR'S CHURCH, SOUTHWARK, LONDON

The window was the gift of Hon. Joseph H. Choate. The arms of Harvard University can be seen on the left and those of Emmanuel College on the right. The chapel, restored by Harvard men, was dedicated in 1907, to commemorate the three hundredth anniversary of the baptism of John Harvard in this church. The altar and its ornaments were also presented by Harvard graduates.

HARVARD MEMORIAL WINDOW IN THE CHAPEL OF EMMANUEL COLLEGE, CAMBRIDGE, ENGLAND,

given by Harvard graduates on the occasion of the tercentenary celebration of Emmanuel College, Cambridge, England. Prof. Charles Eliot Norton represented Harvard University, and Hon. James Russell Lowell, Minister to the Court of St. James, represented America.

HARVARD HOUSE, THE EARLY HOME OF JOHN HARVARD'S MOTHER, IN STRATFORD – ON – AVON, ENGLAND,

now owned by Harvard University. The house is supposed to have been built in 1596 by Thomas Rogers, and here in the year 1605, Robert Harveye, as the name was then spelled, was married to K a t h e r i n e, daughter of Thomas Rogers. They were the parents of John Harvard.

one knows, the new college was named after him. John Harvard was one of those "Great-hearts of his generation, whom England begot, Cambridge bred, and Emmanuel in special nurtured." He was the son of Robert Harvard and his second wife, formerly Katherine Rogers of Stratford-on-Avon, who was born in a small house there which now belongs to Harvard College, and is known as Harvard House, shown in the cut above. His childhood was spent in Southwark, London, where in the baptismal records of St. Saviour's Church is found the following entry:—

"1607 November 29 JOHN HARVYE S. of Robt. a Butcher."

In 1627, young Harvard entered Emmanuel College, Cambridge, that institution of which its founder, Sir Walter Mildmay, said, in reply to Queen Elizabeth when she accused him of having erected a Puritan foundation, "No, Madam, far be it from me to countenance anything contrary to your established laws, but I have set an acorn, which when it becomes an oak, God alone knows what will be the fruit thereof." Although

> "In vain the delving antiquary tries
> To find the tomb where generous Harvard lies,"

nevertheless in 1828, at the suggestion of Hon. Edward Everett, the alumni of our University erected a granite shaft in the Phipps Street Burial Ground, Charlestown, at the dedication of which Mr. Everett paid him a splendid tribute in his dedicatory address. A tablet in the Harvard Church of Charlestown, formerly called the First Church, is placed there to the memory of Harvard and other early ministers of the church. Some years later, in 1836, at the banquet held at Harvard to celebrate the two hundredth anniversary of its

Photograph taken for the State Street Trust Company by George B. Brayton

GRANITE SHAFT TO THE MEMORY OF JOHN HARVARD,

in the Phipps Street Burial Ground, Charlestown, Massachusetts, where he was buried. This memorial was placed there in 1828 at the suggestion of Hon. Edward Everett. On the monument are these words: "On the 26th day of September, A.D. 1828, this stone was erected by the Graduates of the University at Cambridge, in honor of its Founder, who died at Charlestown, on the 26th day of September, A.D. 1638."

founding, the entire company rose to do honour to the following toast:—

> "The sacred memory of John Harvard, who set the first example, on the American continent, of a union between private munificence and public education, which has bound successive generations, as with links of steel, together, and has given to an unknown stranger a deathless name."

Another event of interest connecting Harvard College with her founder occurred in 1884 at the tercentenary celebration of Emmanuel College, Cambridge, at which time a window to his memory was placed in the college chapel, the gift of Harvard men. There were present at this anniversary Prof. Charles Eliot Norton of Har-

From a picture in Harvard College Library, Harvard University
Kindness William C. Lane, Esq.

CUP GIVEN TO EMMANUEL COLLEGE, CAMBRIDGE, ENGLAND,

by Harvard men in England as a testimonial of their loyalty to the College of their founder.

From an old print in Harvard College Library, Harvard University   *Kindness William C. Lane, Esq., and Walter B. Briggs, Esq.*

CHURCH AND PRIORY OF STE. MARIE OVERIE (NOW ST. SAVIOUR'S),
SOUTHWARK, LONDON,

showing London Bridge. In this church John Harvard was baptized in 1607, and here his father was buried in 1625. Harvard Chapel, given by Harvard graduates, is in this church. Here is also a monument to William Emerson, an ancestor of Ralph Waldo Emerson.

vard University, sent over by Harvard especially for this occasion, and Hon. James Russell Lowell, who was at that time American Minister at the Court of St. James.   That same year there was erected on the Delta in the grounds of Harvard University the well-known memorial statue of John Harvard presented by Samuel J. Bridge, an alumnus of the University.   Two years later, in 1886, at the celebration of the two hundred and fiftieth anniversary of the founding of the College, the college which John Harvard attended was represented by Bishop Mandell Creighton, who gave a splendid tribute to the founder of America's great seat of learning, a man who was, he said, "at once a scholar, a statesman, a philanthropist, a man whom Emmanuel may be proud to have trained, and Harvard may be proud to recognize as her founder."   Another gift that especially links the old university town with the new, is a memorial brass inscription which was placed under the Harvard window in Emmanuel College on August 25, 1904, the gift of Harvard alumni, and made to perpetuate their gratitude "to their founder in the college which fostered his beneficent spirit." The most important memorial, however, is the Harvard Chapel in St. Saviour's Church, Southwark, London, dedicated July 17, 1907, where John Harvard was baptized in 1607 and where his father was buried in 1625, the idea having been carried out by Harvard men while Hon. Joseph H. Choate was our Ambassador to England. In this chapel is also a beautiful stained-glass window, the gift of Mr. Choate. This chapel received in 1909 the gift of an altar from Ralph W. Hickox, '72, which was dedicated by the Bishop of Southwark, and also altar ornaments presented by Amory A. Lawrence, '70, of Boston, and Francis Appleton, '75, of New York.

An event of great interest to Cantabrigians on both sides of the ocean was the gift of a cup during the winter of 1918 to Emmanuel College by Harvard men in England as a testimonial of their loyalty to the college of their founder. There is yet another connecting link between our Cambridge and John Harvard's early days in the form of a stone set in the wall of Appleton Chapel, in Harvard College Yard, which came in 1908 from the archway of this same old church in London, which Harvard attended. Underneath the stone are the words

A stone from St. Saviour's Church, Southwark, in which John Harvard was baptised, Nov. 29, 1607.

Mrs. F. P. Kinnicutt of New York was instrumental in procuring this stone.

It may be well also to mention the recently founded Choate fellowship, which enables graduates of the English university to study at Harvard. It would be fitting if some one should found a similar fellowship in honour of John Harvard's descendant, Lionel de Jersey Harvard, who graduated here in 1915, and then straightway entered the English Army and gave his life fighting for the freedom of the world. There are several pieces of a communion service in Christ Church in our Cambridge bearing the arms of King William and Queen Mary which were part of a set given to King's Chapel, Boston, in 1694, by these sovereigns. It was used there up to the year 1772, when it was divided, Christ Church receiving three pieces.

Our town of Cambridge, now a city, was founded in 1630 by Governor Winthrop and a party of men from Boston, who rowed up the Charles River in search of a suitable place to build a fortified town where the government officials might live in safety. They landed near the present Harvard Square, and decided that this situation was admirably suited for their purposes. The land was then purchased from the Mystic Indians for the sum of about fifty dollars and the promise of an annual present of a coat to the squaw sachem as long as she lived. The colony called "Newetowne" was soon established. Although only three miles inland, at that time it was a frontier settlement, and evidence of this fact still exists in the clumps of willows standing on college land and adjacent parts of Cambridge, which have sprouted from the old stockade used for defence against the Indians. New

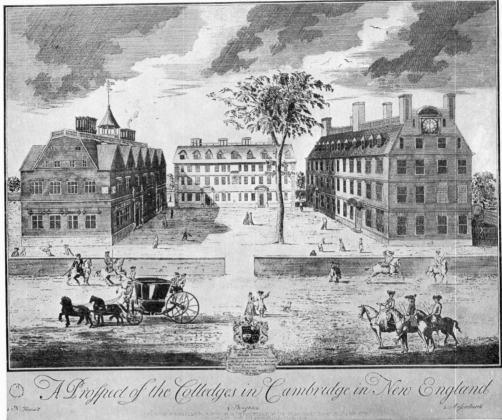

A Prospect of the Colledges in Cambridge in New England

From Burgis's engraving of 1726 in Harvard College Library, Harvard University, published by   *Kindness William C. Lane, Esq. and*
Charles E. Goodspeed, from original in Massachusetts Historical Society   *Walter B. Briggs, Esq.*

HARVARD COLLEGE, 1726,

showing on the right Massachusetts Hall, the latest to be added (1720) to the group of three buildings
then composing the College and the only one which remains to the present date.

lands were added to the settlement about the year 1648, which included our present
Brighton, Newton, Arlington, Lexington, Bedford, Carlisle, Chelmsford, Billerica
and part of Tewksbury, the last five towns being withdrawn soon after from the
Cambridge territory.   In 1688, Newton, known originally as "Cambridge Village,"
was formed into a separate township; Lexington, which had been known previously
as "Cambridge Farms," was separated in 1713, and in 1807 Arlington and Brighton
were made separate townships.

In the Cambridge market place in 1636, Rev. Thomas Hooker with a hundred
men and women of his congregation assembled, with their possessions, including a
hundred and sixty head of cattle, and after a prayer by the minister, they adjusted
their burdens on their shoulders, and to the beating of the drum which used to

summon them to church, they slowly made their way along the Watertown road on their march to Hartford, Connecticut, driving their cattle before them. This exodus, so history tells us, was occasioned by the fact that this Puritan minister did not approve of the religious test for voting. A picture of these wanderers is shown on page 152. Before leaving our Cambridge for Cambridge across the water it seems fitting to repeat the amusing lines written by Oliver Wendell Holmes describing the New England city:—

> "Know old Cambridge? Hope you do.
> Born there? Don't say so! I was, too.
> Nicest place that ever was seen,—
> Colleges red, and common green,
> Sidewalks brownish with trees between,—
> Sweetest spot beneath the skies
> When the canker-worms don't rise,
> When the dust, that sometimes flies
> Into your mouth and ears and eyes,
> In a quiet slumber lies,
> Not in the shape of unbaked pies,
> Such as barefoot children prize."

It may be well to mention that the press of Harvard College was the first printing press in this country and for forty years was the only one in the British Colonies. It was originally owned by Rev. J. Glover, an Englishman, who embarked for this country in 1638, and who died on the way over; but Stephen Daye, who accompanied him as printer, brought the press safely to Cambridge, where it was superintended by President Dunster of Harvard College and later was set up in the President's house. The present University Press, which traces its origin to the old College press, is under the management of Herbert H. White, Esq.

Old Cambridge on the river Cam, from which it is called, has endured a multiplicity of names: in 875 A.D. it was called Grantanbrycge; in 1142 Cantebruggescir; in the fourteenth century Cantbrigge; in 1436 Canbrigge, later on being changed to Cawnbrege, Cambrigge and Caumbrege, until we come to the present name of Cambridge. The old university must have had a modest beginning, for we are told that it may ascribe its origin to a traveling teacher who once lectured there at the fair and, having attracted a large audience, returned the following year; or it may have originated from the monasteries of the Fenland which by degrees developed until a corps of masters was secured. We are certain, however, that it was a place for student monks at such an early period that there is no precise date known. It has also been ascertained beyond doubt that the University dates back at least to 1229, the time of Henry III. The college that is of greatest interest to New Englanders is, of course, Emmanuel, to which also went Samuel Whiting, Nathaniel Ward, Thomas Hooker, Nathaniel Rogers, Thomas Shepard, John Cotton and Samuel Stone. It also may be interesting to New Englanders to remember that

John Eliot attended Jesus College, also that John Winthrop went to Trinity, also Charles Chauncey, the second president of the College, and Hugh Peters, as well as Bacon, Dryden, Newton, Byron, Macaulay and Tennyson. About seventy of the early settlers of New England may, in fact, be traced to Cambridge University, England.

In 1896, Mayor William A. Bancroft of Cambridge, Massachusetts, sent a letter of greeting and a history of his city to the Mayor of Cambridge, England, Mr. William C. Hall. The letter and history were presented by Alderman Charles P. Keith of Cambridge, Massachusetts, and a very cordial letter of thanks was later received by Mayor Bancroft from the Mayor of the mother town.

In closing this article on Cambridge, we can do no better than to quote the last two lines of verses written by Rev. John Wilson, which first appeared in Mather's "Magnalia" in 1702:—

"And as old Cambridge well deserved the name,
May the new Cambridge win as pure a fame."

CHATHAM, MASSACHUSETTS

IT is the common belief that the early settlers of Chatham in New England named the town for Chatham in England in the belief that the Massachusetts town, on account of its commanding position at the heel of Cape Cod, would sometime become a government naval station similar to its English counterpart on the Medway with its wonderful dock yard. It is a curious fact that this prediction should in a way have been realized in 1917 when the United States Government established a flying school in the town, which is still continued. It may be interesting also to recall the fact that it was off these waters of our Chatham that several of our flyers had a battle with a German submarine. Another possible reason for the name was that many of the Cape Cod towns were named for English ones.

The person who was chiefly responsible for the changing of the name from the Indian Monomoit to its present one was Rev. Hugh Adams, who went there as a minister in 1711 from our Boston, and who was able in the following year to incorporate the settlement. Mr. Adams remained there some years, finally getting into a long and bitter fight with a tavern keeper named Ebenezer Hawes, because he claimed the latter placed his tavern too near the parsonage. This old settlement of Monomoit was originally owned by William Nickerson, of Norwich, England, who, unauthorized by the Plymouth Colony, bought it from the Indians and settled there as early as 1656. The Plymouth Court allowed him to keep part of his territory and he then established his dwelling near Ryder's Cove. Nickerson had followed the trade of a weaver before coming to New England in 1637 on a vessel

THE ROYAL DOCK YARD AT CHATHAM.

THE ROYAL DOCK YARD AT CHATHAM, ENGLAND

This view was taken from the banks of the river Medway near Upnor Castle.

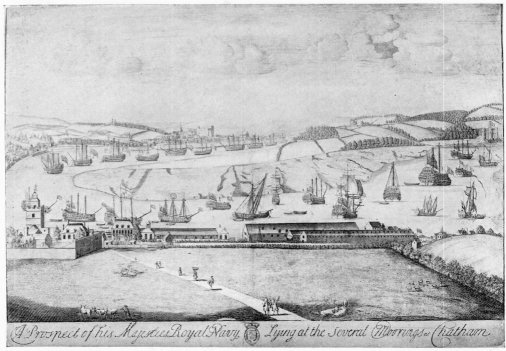

A Prospect of his Majesties Royal Navy. Lying at the several Moorings at Chatham.

From an old print in the possession of Perry Walton, Esq.   *Kindness Max Williams, Esq.*

A PROSPECT OF HIS MAJESTY'S ROYAL NAVY,
lying at the several moorings at Chatham.

on which Samuel Lincoln, an ancestor of President Lincoln, was also a passenger. It is said today that about nine-tenths of the families in Chatham trace their ancestry back to this William Nickerson, and most of the other one-tenth can follow their lineage back to either the Eldredge or Taylor families, so frequently found in the town's history.   Nickerson was in continual difficulties with the Plymouth Court as to his possessions, and in 1665 it was ordered that the plantation should come within the limits of the township of Yarmouth, a few years later being transferred to Eastham.   The growth of the new settlement at first was slow, but after 1674 Nickerson sold part of his lands to some of his friends, the records showing that those who came soon after him were John Downing, Thomas Crow (or Crowell as he was sometimes called) and Edward Cottle of Salisbury, England, who had first lived in Salisbury and then in Amesbury, Mass.   Another early purchaser of lands here was Captain James Forster of London, who purchased Morris Island, then known as Quitnesset, and who in his will, dated 1686, gave it to his sister "Elizabeth Torlton Lately Living in Jacobs Street in Southworke near London."   This property later came into the possession of Morris Farris for whom it was then named.

A person of the greatest importance in the early history of Chatham was the Indian Tisquantum, sometimes called "Squanto," who had traded along the shores of Cape Cod near Chatham. He was so fond of Englishmen that on his deathbed he beseeched Governor Bradford to pray that he might go to the "Englishman's God in Heaven" and at the same time he bequeathed much of his property to his English friends as a token of his love for them. Charles Francis Adams claims that for a certain time he was "the most essential factor in the prolonged existence of the Plymouth Colony," as he helped them to grow maize or Indian corn, assisted them to fish, and acted also as interpreter and pilot for them. It was through Tisquantum that trading relations were established between the Pilgrims and the Indians at Monomoit, and over his grave was cemented between the Colonists and their Indian neighbors a bond of friendship which was never broken. He died while accompanying the Governor on one of his expeditions and was buried probably within the present boundary of Chatham. His loyalty to the English is especially remarkable in view of the early treatment he had received, for he was one of the group of redskins who had been captured by Capt. Thomas Hunt in 1614 and sold

Photographed by C. H. Smallhoff

"MAYFLOWER" INSCRIPTION IN FRONT OF THE OLD TWIN LIGHTS, CHATHAM, MASSACHUSETTS,

marking the point on the coast at which she turned back to Provincetown.

Photographed by C. H. Smallhoff

BOULDER AND TABLET MARKING THE PROBABLE GRAVE OF WILLIAM NICKERSON IN
CHATHAM, MASSACHUSETTS

He was the owner of, and the earliest settler in, Chatham, then called Monomoit.   He was born in Norwich,
Norfolk County, England.   The tablet reads in part as follows:—

IN MEMORY OF
WILLIAM NICKERSON
ENGLAND 1604—MASSACHUSETTS 1689-90
BOSTON 1637—FREEMAN 1638—YARMOUTH 1640.
DEPUTY TO GENERAL COURT 1655. FOUNDER OF CHATHAM.
RELIGIOUS TEACHER—USEFUL CITIZEN—FIRST OF THE NAME IN AMERICA.
PROGENITOR OF FIFTY THOUSAND DESCENDANTS.

HIS WIFE
ANNE (BUSBY) NICKERSON
ENGLAND 1609—MASSACHUSETTS 1686

THIS TABLET SET UP ON THIS THE PROBABLE BURIAL PLACE OF
WILLIAM NICKERSON I WITH THE PERMISSION OF THE TOWN OF CHATHAM A.D. 1915.
BY WILLIAM EMERY NICKERSON OF CAMBRIDGE 9 AMOS 8 JONATHAN 7 JONATHAN 6
SETH 5 JONATHAN 4 THOMAS 3 WILLIAM 2 WILLIAM I
(The figures after these names represent genealogical numbers.)

into slavery. The Indian, however, won the friendship of his captors, learned
their language, and rendered them very valuable service, finally succeeding in
reaching England and later Newfoundland, where he was found by Capt. Thomas
Dermer, an Englishman employed by Sir Ferdinando Gorges, who took him on
many of his voyages to the Cape.

It is interesting to recall that the treacherous sand bars which extend for miles off the Chatham shore forced the "Mayflower" to abandon her southern course around Cape Cod to the Hudson River or the Jersey shore, where the Pilgrims had a grant of land, and caused her navigator to turn back to Provincetown. A tablet on the shore records this event. Governor Bradford in describing their experiences said: "While attempting to finde some place aboute Hudson's River for their habitation, but after they had sailed yt course about halfe ye day, they fell amongst deangerous shoulds and roring breakers, and they were so farr intangled therwith, as they conceived themselves in great danger; and ye wind shrinking upon them withall, they resolved to bear up againe for the Cape, and thought themselves hapy to gett out of those dangers before night overtooke them, as by God's providence they did. And ye next day they gott into ye Cape-harbor." Thus it was that New England, instead of New York or New Jersey, became the home of the Pilgrims. It is believed that fourteen years before the arrival of the "Mayflower" a French colony set foot on the Cape, led by Jean de Poutrincourt and Samuel de Champlain.

The Cape Cod town has continually been called upon to assist shipwrecked mariners, and as early as 1711 it was stated that the village "has often heretofore been a place of relief to many shipwrecked vessels and Englishmen cast ashore in storms."

The English Chatham, now united with Rochester, is known to us on account of its important dockyard with its battleships and its armies of workmen; there Peter the Great gained part of his education as a workman, and there also within the dockyard is a figurehead of Lord Nelson, taken from one of the old wooden ships. Charles Dickens lived in the town for many years. Chatham is situated in County Kent on the south side of the Medway and about twenty-seven miles east of London.

There is also a Chatham in New Hampshire and in Connecticut.

CHELMSFORD, MASSACHUSETTS

ON the walls of the Adams Library in Chelmsford, Massachusetts, there are several framed photographs of Chelmsford, England, for which town ours was named, and also a portrait of Lord Chelmsford, once Lord High Chancellor of Great Britain. In the year 1905, on the two hundred and fiftieth anniversary of the incorporation of the town, an invitation was sent to the Mayor of the English town, to which the following reply was received:—

"MAYNETREES, CHELMSFORD,
26 April, 1905.

Dear Sir:—

I have been hoping that I should be able to accept your very kind invitation to the celebration of the Quarter Millennial Anniversary of the Incorporation of your Town.

CHELMSFORD, ENGLAND,

showing the procession of Judges, attended also by the High Sheriff and his officers.

An old view from a print photographed by Fred Spalding & Sons, Chelmsford, England   Kindness Ian Forbes-Robertson, Esq.

Alas! the distance and time form an impassable barrier. . . . Allow me to wish the celebration every success. We shall think of you, and offer heartiest greetings in the four appointed days. I will send over to you, as you request, one or more specimens of our native trees. With repeated thanks and assurance of the peculiar interest which we take in your prosperity,

Very truly yours,

WALTER PAYNE GEPP, *Mayor.*

Walter Perham, Esq., Chairman of Selectmen,
Chelmsford, Massachusetts."

Another letter was sent from the English Rector to the American Rector, which reads as follows:—

"CHELMSFORD, May 15.

Dear Mr. Waters:—

May I write to thank you for your very kind letter. I, indeed, wish that it were possible for some one from the old home to be with you at your commemoration; but I fear that it is not possible. Perhaps the old blood is not so enterprising as the new, but it is very difficult to leave the work here for so long a time as a visit to Massachusetts implies. May I, as Rector of Chelmsford in the old Country, offer all who are taking part in your Commemoration, the very best wishes. We shall think of you and trust that, as such a Commemoration must be a link between all, so it may be a help on to further progress, social, moral, religious. I shall like very much to see a paper of your arrangements as it will enable me to put a short account in our Magazine, which will help to bring it to the notice of our people generally. I am sending one or two specimen photos in this envelope. This will, I hope, give a slight idea of the old town.

Yours sincerely,

H. A. LAKE, *Rector of Chelmsford, England,
Honorary Canon of St. Albans."*

Cables were also received on the day of the celebration. During the four days of the festivities there were shown several copies of old engravings of scenes from Chelmsford, England, which were sent by Mr. Fred Spalding to Mr. Walter Perham, the Chairman of Selectmen of the New England town, who, by the way, visited the mother town in Essex in 1902. While there he made an examination of the records of St. Mary's Parish and discovered that there were in the old English town, between the years 1538 and the time of the settlement of our town, a number of people of the same name as in our town, or its offshoots, the most prominent names being Adams, Butterfield, Spaldyng, Chamberlyne, Fletcher, Parker, Warren and Purkis. Edwin H. Warren, Esq., formerly Town Treasurer of our Chelmsford, also visited the town of the same name in England some time in the 70's, and likewise Mr. Shurtleff, the Unitarian minister, made a similar visit only a few years ago. The Rev. Wilson Waters of our Chelmsford, who gave us this information, also mentions that E. Percy Boulter, a resident of the town, and gunner in the Canadian Heavy Artillery, made several visits there during the Great War, and met the officials of the town. Mr. Waters also speaks of having sent to Canon Lake several books relating to our town, receiving from him in return a number of

ALL SAINTS CHURCH, CHELMSFORD, MASSACHUSETTS
In this church are pictures of St. Mary's Parish Church in Chelmsford, England, and other relics from English towns.

photographs and other objects of interest that are now in the Sacristy of All Saints Church.

During the two hundred and fiftieth anniversary one of the speakers claimed that he had a right to be present, as he had an ancestor named Chamberlain who was born in Chelmsford but who moved to Billerica, which was also named after the English town of Billericay. "He is sorry for it now," said the speaker, "but he partly made up for it by going to Concord."

A few families settled in our Chelmsford as early as 1650, but the first recorded movement occurred two years later, when a number of people went there from Woburn and Concord. The town was actually settled in 1653. The original grant included what is now the large city of Lowell. Our Chelmsford was named for Chelmsford, England, as the latter town had been the home of some of these early settlers. The President of the United States, John Adams, while in England in the year 1786, further confirms this by mentioning in his diary that "Chelmsford was probably named in compliment to Mr. Hooker, who was once minister of that town in Essex." It will be remembered that Rev. Thomas Hooker had been curate of St. Mary's Church in Chelmsford, England.

The Rev. John Eliot, apostle to the Indians, who did much for the Indians living on the Chelmsford grant, at one time taught school near the English Chelmsford.

The first family that came to settle on the new tract, according to tradition, was that of Abraham Parker, a prominent name in the history of our Chelmsford even up to the present time.

The town was not incorporated, however, until 1655, at which time Groton and Billerica were also recognized as distinct towns. During the early years of the colony Rev. John Fiske, who was once a school teacher in Chelmsford, England, was induced to leave Wenham with several families and to take up his residence at Chelmsford, thereby greatly assisting the progress of the settlement. Cotton Mather, in his "Magnalia," says of him, "Twenty years did he shine in the golden candlestick of Chelmsford." The Chelmsford meeting house was erected in 1659 or 1660 upon or near the site of the present Unitarian Church. Chelmsford furnished the granite for the first stone block ever erected in the city of Boston and for a number of its finest buildings.

Chelmsford was an important frontier town during the Indian wars, and many of her soldiers fought at Concord and Bunker Hill. Five hundred and forty-four of her men out of a population of thirteen hundred and forty-one served in the War of the Revolution.

A merchant of Boston in "The Present State of New England," printed in London in 1675, relates an amusing incident which took place near Chelmsford:—

"About the 15th of August, Captain Mosely with sixty men met a company, judged about three hundred Indians, in a plain place where few Trees were, and on both sides preparations were making for a Battle; all being ready on both sides to fight, Captain Mosely plucked off his Periwig, and put it into his Breeches, because it should not hinder him in fighting. As soon as the Indians saw that, they fell a Howling and Yelling most hideously, and said, '*Umh, Umh, me no staw merre* [*stay here?*] *fight Engis mon, Engis mon got two hed, Engis mon got two hed; if me cut off un hed, he got noder, a put on beder as dis*'; with such like words in broken English and away they all fled and could not be overtaken, nor seen any more afterwards."

The English Chelmsford is the shire town of Essex, is twenty-nine miles from London, and is celebrated for its corn and cattle markets. Before bridges were built, there was a ford across the river Chelmer at this place, and hence the name Chelmer's Ford. The name appears in ancient records as "Chelmersforde," "Chelmereford," and "Chelmesford." Its church, which dates from the year 1427, is one of the chief objects of interest in the town, and has been made the cathedral of the diocese of Chelmsford. A Roman villa was unearthed there in the middle of the nineteenth century.

From original in Adams Library, Chelmsford, Massachusetts   *Kindness Rev. Wilson Waters*

CHELMSFORD, ENGLAND, AND THE RIVER CHELMER

From picture in All Saints Church, Chelmsford, Massachusetts   *Kindness Rev. Wilson Waters*

ST. MARY'S CHURCH, CHELMSFORD, ENGLAND

The records in this church show that there were at the time of the settlement of our Chelmsford, many names the same as those in the early days of the Massachusetts town. Rev. Thomas Hooker, in whose honour Chelmsford, Massachusetts, was probably named, was once curate of this English church.

All Saints Church, Chelmsford, Massachusetts, contains a number of objects of interest to us. Within its walls are some curious panels and other ancient carvings from the church in South Hadleigh, England, which are kept in the Rector's study; there are also some carvings on either side of the central arch of the roodscreen, which came from Chester Cathedral; also in the sacristy hang some framed photographs of St. Mary's Parish Church, Chelmsford, England, which were presented by the Rector and Wardens of the English church.

DARTMOUTH, NEW BEDFORD AND BEDFORD, MASSACHUSETTS

"Not any lovelier spot, I ween,
Had England's noble captain seen,
Since, by the Virgin Queen's command,
From Dartmouth's old historic strand,
The widespread ocean field to plough,
He guided forth the 'Concord's' prow,
Upon his venturous quest!"

(Part of a verse written by James B. Congdon on the two hundred and fiftieth anniversary of the founding of Dartmouth. The lines refer to Bartholomew Gosnold's expedition.)

THE part of Dartmouth, Massachusetts, now occupied by the city of New Bedford was owned by the Russells, which was the family name of the Duke of Bedford, whose English home, called Woburn Abbey, is in Bedfordshire. The first mention of the name Bedford in any of the Dartmouth records was in 1773 when the following entry occurs:—

"It was voted to raise by way of tax the sum of Eighty-seven pounds eight shillings and four pence Lawful money to defray the charges accrued to said town by Building the New Workhouse in Bedford in Dartmouth."

The story of the naming of New Bedford is a most interesting one. Ralph Russell, who came from England, was one of the earliest settlers in the town, being engaged in the iron business. He was a progenitor of the Russell families of New Bedford and was the ancestor of Joseph Russell from whom New Bedford really received its name. In 1765 Joseph Rotch, father of William Rotch, moved from Nantucket to Dartmouth to pursue the whale fishery and here he met this Joseph Russell. These two men met again on some public occasion in 1787, and in talking about a possible name for the town, Rotch suggested that the place should be called Bedford in honour of a distinguished member of the Russell family, the Duke of Bedford. This suggestion was promptly adopted by the rest of the inhabitants and from that time on Russell was always referred to as "the Duke." It was discovered, however, that there was another Bedford in the state, so that

"NEW BEDFORD FIFTY YEARS AGO" (in 1808)

The last building shown on the left of the picture was the mansion of William Rotch, Sr., who is represented in the chaise, the only private carriage then in the village. He was the son of Joseph Rotch who was one of the founders of the whaling industry which has made the city known throughout the world. The large man in the center of the street, called Water Street, is William Rotch, Jr., the leading merchant of the place, and the man in conversation with him is supposed to be Abraham Russell, grandson of the Joseph Russell, who, with Joseph Rotch, gave the town its name. The two men shaking hands are Captain R. R. Crocker and Samuel Rodman, Sr. One of the boys harnessed to the small cart is George Howland, Jr.

EAST VIEW OF BEDFORD BRIDGE TAKEN IN THE YEAR 1790

It crosses the river Ouse, which runs through the center of the town. Tradition says that it was erected with part of the materials of the Castle demolished by King Henry III in the year 1224. Bedford Castle stood on the right of the bridge.

the prefix "New" was added, and the town was, therefore, called New Bedford. Joseph Russell, who was born in the old township of Dartmouth, was, therefore, the real founder of New Bedford, and he was also the originator of the whale fishery there. Francis Rotch has the honour of having launched the first vessel in the town, which he named the "Dartmouth." Joseph Rotch, the first of the Rotch family who went to Nantucket, later moving to New Bedford, was born in Salisbury, England, in 1704. The Indian name of New Bedford was Acushnet, the settlement having been bought from the Indians in 1652.

In the early days there was a minister in the town who was very absentminded, and once after the services in the church had started, he remembered that he had forgotten his sermon. Therefore, he gave out a long hymn to be sung by the congregation, and in the meantime he ran home and got his sermon, appearing in the pulpit at the right time.

There have been individual visits of interested citizens to the town of old Bedford, England, but the official interchanges of congratulations occurred between Dartmouth, Massachusetts, and Dartmouth, England, on the occasion of the two hundredth anniversary of the incorporation of our Dartmouth. A very elaborate programme was carried out, and was participated in by the various towns which were formerly parts of our Dartmouth, namely, New Bedford, Dartmouth, Acushnet, Fairhaven and Westport. George Howland, Jr., was Mayor of New Bedford at the time of this celebration, which took place on September 14, 1864, and the notice sent out by him was in part as follows:—

"CENTENNIAL CELEBRATION.

To the Sons & Daughters of Old Dartmouth abroad, the undersigned on behalf of the children at home, send Greeting.

Two Hundred Years Ago

'The tracte of land called and known by the name of Acushnet, Ponagansett & Coaksett was allowed by the Court to bee a townshippe:—to bee henceforth called and knowne by the name of Dartmouth.' The villages which then formed the town of Dartmouth now constitute the towns of Dartmouth, Westport, Fairhaven and Acushnet and the City of New Bedford."

The committee appointed to handle the celebration was composed of the following: H. J. Taylor, A. G. Pierce, Lemuel M. Kollock, Cornelius Davenport, John W. Macomber, Wm. C. Taber, Jr., and Charles H. Gifford. It was voted that an address be sent to the Mayor, Recorder, and Aldermen of the city of Dartmouth, county of Devon, England, and a very beautiful engrossed return message was received by the city of New Bedford, the original of which hangs in the Free Public Library.

Many of the original thirty-six proprietors settled in New Bedford two hundred years before, and among them were the families of Howland, Morton, Kempton.

REPLY FROM DARTMOUTH, ENGLAND,

to New Bedford, Dartmouth, Westport, Fairhaven and Acushnet, Massachusetts, on the occasion of the two hundredth anniversary of the incorporation of Dartmouth, Massachusetts.

Dunham, Shaw, Cooke, Soule, Faunce, Sampson, Delano, Bartlett, Palmer, Doty, Hicks, Brown and Bumpass. Among other early settlers are found the names of Howland, Hathaway and Slocomb, and in Fairhaven were the families of Pope, Taber, Delano, Jenny, Spooner, Tripp, Sherman and Aaron Davis.

The town was called Dartmouth probably on account of the fact that the "Mayflower" and the "Speedwell" both put back to Dartmouth, and also because some of the earliest settlers of our Dartmouth probably came from the English town of the same name. It is also a fact that Gosnold procured his vessel the "Concord" in Dartmouth, England.

A few years later, on July 4, 1876, a centennial was held in New Bedford to celebrate the anniversary of the naming of the town, which, as the old deed says, was bought from the Indians for "thirty yards of cloth, 8 moose-skins, 15 axes, 15 hoes, 15 pair breeches, 8 blankets, 2 kettles, 1 clock, 2 pounds in wampum, 8 pair of stockings, 8 pair shoes, 1 tin pot and 10 shillings in other comoditie." It may be interesting to record that St. Martin's Church, New Bedford, has on the wall of its chancel, with a proper inscription, an old Roman stone that was seen by Miss Julia Rodman of New Bedford in the church of the same name in Canterbury, England, and which was sent over to New Bedford by the authorities of the English church. The font is a reproduction of the one in the English church.

As Bartholomew Gosnold was about to sail from Falmouth, England, in March, 1602, his parting words to Raleigh were:—

"My lord, I will hoiste saile, and all the wind my bark can beare shall hasten me to find a great New World."

Although he did not settle in New Bedford his name is thoroughly linked with the town owing to the fact that he sailed into Buzzards Bay and made a settlement on Gosnold's Island, which is part of the Elizabeth Islands. He named Buzzards Bay "Gosnold's Hope," which name was changed later to "Buzzards Bay" by the early settlers at Dartmouth on account of the abundance of fish hawks, which in olden times were called "buzzards." The whole group of islands today is called "Elizabeth Islands," but at the time of his discovery the island of "Cuttyhunk" was called by him "Elizabeth" for the Queen. He also named Gay Head "Dover Cliff." He remained here only a short time, returning to Exmouth, Devonshire, England, but his short stay entitled him to the honour of being called the first Englishman to set foot on New England soil and also the first Englishman to establish a settlement in the New England states. In 1902 there was held a tercentenary of his landing at Gosnold on the island of Cuttyhunk, and the corner stone of a monument was laid which was dedicated in September of the next year, which is not only a memorial to him, but to all the other explorers who were inspired by him. The shaft of this memorial stands on the exact spot where Gosnold's

From a photograph   *Kindness George H. Tripp, Esq.*

GOSNOLD MEMORIAL,

placed at Gosnold, on an island in a pond on the larger island of Cuttyhunk, near New Bedford, to commemorate the first English settlement in New England.

From a painting by William A. Wall in the Old Dartmouth Historical Society   *Kindness George H. Tripp, Esq., and Frank Wood, Esq.*

LANDING OF BARTHOLOMEW GOSNOLD,

the first Englishman to establish a settlement in New England. He landed at Gosnold, on the island of Cuttyhunk, off the coast near New Bedford.

storehouse and fort stood and the corner stone was taken from the original wall of the fort laid out by the explorers three hundred years ago. The memorial reads:—

Tercentenary Memorial
to
Bartholomew Gosnold
and his companions who landed here
June 4 (O. S. May 25) 1602
and built on this Islet the First
English habitation on the Coast of
N. E. Corner stone laid June 4,
1902. Dedicated Sept. 1, 1903 on
the anniversary of Gosnold's death at
Jamestown, Virginia.

The whole island on which this memorial is situated was given to the Dartmouth Historical Society by Messrs. Perry, Nye and Swift, who purchased it on account of their interest in the event. People of Cuttyhunk jokingly used to say that so few people died there that they had to kill a man in order to start a cemetery. At

From a photograph by Balley & Flower　　　　　　　　　　　　*Kindness Ian Forbes-Robertson, Esq.*

DARTMOUTH, ENGLAND, AND THE HARBOUR,

taken from one of the precipitous hills upon which the town proper is built.　The tower is that of the Parish Church of St. Saviour.

From an old print by R. Ackermann, 1821　　　　　　　　　　　*Kindness Ian Forbes-Robertson, Esq.*

DARTMOUTH, ENGLAND, SHOWING DARTMOUTH CASTLE,

and the Church of St. Petroc as it looked when the Pilgrims sailed by on their voyage to the New World. The church is considerably changed today.

one time pilots were taken on at Cuttyhunk for New Bedford, and there was such rivalry among them that they would watch the incoming vessels from the tops of the houses with spyglasses.

It may be interesting to go across the water and say a few words about Dartmouth and Bedford in England. To the New Englander, Dartmouth in the beautiful county of Devonshire is second only in interest to Plymouth. To this haven the "Mayflower" and "Speedwell," as every one knows, put in to overhaul the reported defects of the latter vessel, after the two ships had been at sea only about eight days. As it took a week to make the necessary repairs, the Pilgrims had an opportunity to familiarize themselves with the town, and we can imagine them roaming about the quaint streets of Dartmouth and climbing some of the steep hills of the city. The picture on page 100 is taken from one of the most precipitous of these hills and shows the parish church of St. Saviour in the distance, which dates from 1372. The other picture shows Dartmouth Castle and the church of St. Petroc as they looked when the adventurers sailed down the river Dart. In this picture is also seen the quaint steeple of the church tower which no longer exists. The castle in its present condition dates from Henry VII, but other castles both Saxon and Norman have previously stood on its site. The church was built in the fourteenth century. Dartmouth has had a prominent place in the naval history of England, and several colonial expeditions to the Western Hemisphere have set out from there, chief of which was that headed by Sir Humphrey Gilbert.

Bedford is the county seat of Bedfordshire and is situated in an agricultural district fifty miles north of London. The country is watered by the river Ouse which some one said "winds more meandrous than Meander." Another writer said that the river ran eighty miles to reach a distance of eighteen and then adds, "Blame it not, if sensible of its sad condition, and presaging its fall into the foggy fens of the next county, it be loath to leave this pleasant place; as who would not prolong their own happiness?" The name "Bedford" can be traced back to the ninth century or earlier, when there was a military station on the river at this point called Bedicanford, which was shortened into Bed-an-ford, meaning fortress on the ford. Offa, King of Mercia, was buried on the river bank, and this incident has suggested to some antiquarians the possibility of another derivation. Bede is the Saxon for prayer, or place for praying—hence Bedford may mean the prayer-ford or the chapel at the ford. "Bede-houses" were not uncommon at that time and when built near a ford or bridge they would suggest a prayer for a safe passage. A castle was built after the Norman Conquest by the third baron of Bedford who was involved in many of the internal struggles of England. One of the most memorable occasions was the siege conducted by Henry III, and some of the stones thrown during the siege were used to build parts of the churches of Bedford. The barony of Bedford was given to John Plantagenet, third son of Henry IV, who was created Duke of Bedford and became Regent of France for the English. The chief part of

From a painting by William A. Wall in the Free Public Library, New Bedford, Massachusetts   *Kindness George H. Tripp, Esq.*

BIRTH OF THE WHALING INDUSTRY, NEW BEDFORD, MASSACHUSETTS

This city is known the world over as having been the leading whaling port of America. This painting represents the first whaling carried on from here in sloops, and the scene is laid in the lower river where the blubber was brought ashore to be tried out. Indians are bartering for the oil.

the monastic property was bestowed upon the Russell family with the Earldom of Bedford. In 1694 the dukedom was restored by William III in consideration of the services of the family for civil and religious liberty, and the title continues to this day.

The name best known in connection with Bedford is that of John Bunyan who was born in 1628 in the nearby village of Elstow in the house which is still standing and which is shown on page 103. The church nearby has two memorial windows to Bunyan illustrating his "Pilgrim's Progress." There is a tower in the church which contains a chime of bells upon which Bunyan practiced the art of bell ringing which was indulged in so much by the English at that time. Bunyan was possessed of the Puritan spirit and became deacon of a non-conformist body in Bedford. He was put in jail for twelve years "because he strove to mend souls as well as kettles." In his church is a door with scenes from "Pilgrim's Progress" given by the Duke of Bedford. After his death which occurred in London in 1688,

From a photograph   *Kindness Mrs. Mary Fifield King*

JOHN BUNYAN'S COTTAGE, ELSTOW, NEAR BEDFORD, ENGLAND

He was born in this house in 1628.   There is a statue to him in Bedford and memorials in the church near his house.

many Puritans for years afterwards begged for the privilege of being buried as near his grave as possible.   There is a bronze statue of Bunyan in Bedford and on the pedestal is the following inscription:—

Presented to the
Borough of Bedford
by
Hastings IX Duke of Bedford
June 10, 1874

The town of Bedford, Massachusetts, in 1892 or 1893 sent a copy of its history to Bedford, England, which was acknowledged by F. A. Blaydes, Mayor, February 2, 1893, who said in his letter,—"I shall be very pleased to send to your public Library a copy of my work 'Genelogia Bedfordiensis.'"   This was duly received and is now in the Bedford Library.

DEDHAM, MASSACHUSETTS

"Across the winding Charles,
From this sturdy Rock of renown,
You discern the sloping roofs
Of yon quaint old Dedham town."

AS Edward Alleyn, Richard Everard (the old name for Everett), John Gay, John Ellis and Samuel Morse were paddling up the Charles River in the year 1635, they complained that there were so many turns in the river that it seemed to get them nowhere. They were, however, much impressed with this part of the country and succeeded in obtaining from the General Court at Newtowne (later called Cambridge) a grant of a tract of land south of the Charles River to twelve men, including themselves, and this grant was later increased so that it included the present Dedham, Norwood, Westwood, Dover, Natick, Needham, Wellesley, Walpole, Medfield, Medway, Millis and parts of Hyde Park, Readville, West Roxbury, Sherborn, Bellingham and Franklin. It was agreed among these first settlers, whose numbers soon increased, that every married man should have a house lot of twelve acres of land, and as early as 1654 there were as many as ninety-five small houses along the river near the location of the present Court House. These early settlers wanted to call the plantation "Contentment" and this name was actually written in the town records of the first two meetings and still appears on the seal of the town, but the name was soon changed to "Dedham" in honour of the three Johns—John Dwight, John Page and John Rogers—who were among the early comers. The best known of these three was Rogers, who with some of his friends had come over from Dedham, England, having been forbidden to preach in the town of his birth, and it was this fact undoubtedly that induced the General Court to name the settlement Dedham. John Dwight was a forbear of the late President Dwight of Yale University. There are a number of other Johns in the early town records, including John Kingsbury, John Coolidge, John Gay and John Ellis. Others who came from England were John Allin, who was a pastor in the new town; Major Eleazer Lusher, leader of the train band and one of the founders of the Ancient and Honorable Artillery Company; Captain Daniel Fisher, a selectman; Michael Metcalf, school teacher; Joshua Fisher, tavern keeper; Deacon Francis Chickering and Samuel Guild. Many of these families still live in the town. Those who settled in West Dedham, now called Westwood, were Avery, Baker, Colburn, Fales, Farrington, Kingsbury, Wright and Wilson. Major Lusher was one of the most prominent of these pilgrims, and his duty was to keep the town records, which he did so well that it was later said of him,

"When Lusher was in office, all things went well,
But how they go since, it shames us to tell."

From "Barber's Historical Collections"

SOUTHERN VIEW OF THE COURT–HOUSE IN DEDHAM, MASSACHUSETTS

From an old print   *Courtesy of The Dedham Club, formerly the Dedham Polo Club, Dedham, Massachusetts*

NORFOLK AGRICULTURAL SOCIETY'S EXHIBITION,

held in Dedham, Massachusetts, sixty or more years ago. The grounds were near Dedham Common, on what is usually called the Nickerson property. Mrs. Nickerson, who lived here, married the late Admiral Hood of the Royal Navy.

The records of the town are complete from the first entry made by him in 1635 to the present time, a fact which can be said of few towns of Massachusetts.

The old Fairbanks house was erected by Jonathan Fairbanks soon after the settlement of the town and has been in the family ever since, a place of interest to thousands of tourists annually.

Curiously enough, another minister of the same name lived in the English Dedham at almost the same time that John Rogers came to Dedham, Massachusetts; their relationship has never been definitely determined, but the latter may have been a brother or cousin of Nathaniel Rogers, son of the Rev. John Rogers, who never came to this country, and whose name appears on old Dedham records up to the year 1651. The former had been preaching to large congregations in Dedham church, near the beginning of the seventeenth century, but had been continually persecuted. He did much to encourage emigration to New England and so did his son Nathaniel, who was instrumental in naming our Ipswich, Haverhill and Chelmsford for the towns near his home in England. The church in Ipswich, America, for one hundred and fifty years was presided over by descendants of John Rogers. When he died in England he was widely mourned. In the churchyard of the Dedham Parish Church of old Dedham is a tombstone to mark his burial place and around the margin the following words in Latin were deciphered some years ago:

I, John Rogers, a preacher of the Word of God, 42, in this place 31 years . . . my work being finished, I have resigned my soul . . . my body . . . I wait for the day . . . Aged 65, October 18, 1636.

In the center the following words are still left although the rest of the inscription has been obliterated:—

True-hearted worshipper of God,
No Boanerges more courageously
Gave forth his thunder, and no Barnabas
Spake with more dulcet tone than he. . . .

Photograph by F. Frith & Co., England
Kindness Ian Forbes-Robertson, Esq.

BUST OF REV. JOHN ROGERS, in the parish church of Dedham, England. He may have been a relative of the John Rogers who was one of the three men in whose honour Dedham, Massachusetts, was named. His son, Nathaniel, was instrumental in naming Ipswich, Haverhill and Chelmsford, Massachusetts.

There is also a bust of him in the Parish Church on the south chancel wall. There is another tablet to the memory of Daniel Sargent Curtis, who was born in Boston in 1825 and who lies buried beneath the tablet on the outside of the south wall.

Old Dedham existed before it was called Dedham, before Essex had become the land of the East Saxons, and before the country was known

THE "VALE OF DEDHAM," ENGLAND

This print is from a painting by John Constable, who was closely associated with old Dedham and the neighboring towns.

From "Picturesque Dedham; Essex"
Published by The Clacton-on-Sea Graphic Printing & Publishing Co., Ltd., Clacton-on-Sea   *Kindness Mrs. Mary Fifield King*

DEDHAM STREET, DEDHAM, ENGLAND

as England, or by the older name of Britain. The river Stour on which the town is situated was nameless for many centuries. When Cæsar invaded Britain in 55 B.C. the region near Dedham was thickly inhabited by a tribe called Trinobantes, this country later being known as Middlesex and Essex. The Trinobantes submitted to Cæsar, who restored their native prince to the throne. The old Romans made no permanent conquest until ninety years later, when they established a Roman station in Dedham called "ad Ansam" or "Roman Dedham." The Saxons settled near Dedham and called it "Home in the Valley." The first information of old Dedham, as of most English places, is derived from a survey made in the time of William the Conqueror contained in the Domesday Book, and here we find an account of the Manor of "Delham" (as it was then called) as it was at the death of Edward the Confessor in 1066. In these early days it belonged to "Aluricus Camp," meaning Ælfric the Champion, and later it fell into the hands of the Normans under Roger de Ramis. Here many Flemings were encouraged by Edward III to come and teach the English the art of making cloth. Dedham played an important rôle in Henry VIII's matrimonial adventures; he gave the town to Catharine of Aragon on their marriage, but immediately transferred the property to his later wife Anne

From "Picturesque Dedham; Essex"   *Kindness Mrs. Mary Fifield King*
Published by The Clacton-on-Sea Graphic Printing & Publishing Co., Ltd., Clacton-on-Sea

DEDHAM CHURCH, ENGLAND

Boleyn, and still later gave it to Jane Seymour, another of his wives. On the execution of the latter, the King gave Dedham to his brother-in-law, Charles Brandon, Duke of Suffolk, later transferring it to his minister, Thomas Cromwell, and when the latter fell, another wife of King Henry, Anne of Cleves, became possessor of these lands.

The picture of the "Vale of Dedham" on another page is from a print taken from one of the paintings by John Constable, who has always been closely associated with Dedham and the neighboring towns. In his boyhood he worked for his father, who was a miller, and the young lad could be seen every day in his white suit and hat on his father's cart going to and from the mill. He went to the Grammar School at Dedham where he showed especial skill in penmanship. His master noticed his pupil's talent, and on several occasions during his lessons there would be a long pause which was broken by the master, who would say: "Go on; I am not asleep. Oh, now I see you are in your painting room!" Constable spent most of his early days working for a glazier and painter. He died in London. He made his reputation by his English landscapes, and his "Cornfield" and "Flatford Mills" are recognized by all Dedhamites as nearby scenes. When asked once what style he intended to imitate, he said, "None but God Almighty's style." He

From a drawing of a print

In the Historical Register of the Dedham Historical Society

DEDHAM, ENGLAND

Copies of this print are hung in the Dedham National Bank and in The Dedham Club, Dedham, Massachusetts.

thought he came into the world to convince mankind that nature was beautiful, and he often used to say, "I love every stile and stump and lane in the village; as long as I am able to hold a brush I shall never cease to paint them." His painting of "Dedham Hill," showing the conspicuous and attractive Dedham church tower, is in the Sheepshanks collection in the South Kensington Museum.

Edmund Sherman and his wife are buried in old Dedham churchyard. Rev. W. F. Cheney of the Church of the Good Shepherd of Dedham, Mass., who preached in the parish church of Dedham, England, on July 17, 1892, corroborates the fact that this Edmund Sherman was an ancestor of Gen. William T. Sherman, some members of the family having come to our Boston as early as 1634. The family tomb is in bad condition and at one time there was a movement on foot to renovate it.

There is also a Dedham in Maine, and one in Tennessee.

DORCHESTER, MASSACHUSETTS

"It was Thanksgiving Day, and the sea-meadows lay
In long russet curves round old Dorchester Bay;
The sturdy oak mansions had opened their halls,
The chimneys had smoked on the Mystic and Charles,
And Grandfather Minot looked out on the Sea—
The last of the Dorchester Pilgrims was he—
And he leaned on his cane, and he said, 'They are gone,
The Pilgrims who sailed on the "Mary and John,"
That old Thanksgiving Day,
Into Dorchester Bay.

I love the strange tales of the Pilgrims of yore,
And of those who first landed on Dorchester's shore.
How they sang on the sea! They are gone, all are gone,
The Pilgrims who sailed on the "Mary and John;"
On that Old Summer Day,
Into Dorchester Bay.

Give thanks for such men on the Thanksgiving Morn,
Such heroes as sailed on the "Mary and John,"
Let the bells ring today
Around Dorchester Bay.'"

(Part of poem written by Hezekiah Butterworth on the two hundred and fiftieth anniversary of the First Parish Church in the Town of Dorchester.)

TWO attractive tablets, the gift of Deacon Henry Humphreys, one on each side of the doorway of the First Parish Church of Dorchester, Mass., honour the Rev. John White and his friends, whom he persuaded to come over to this country in 1630 to found a colony in our wilderness. Rev. John White, who was known to his contemporaries as the "Patriarch of Dorchester" and to later

DORCHESTER
NAMED
FROM THE TOWN OF DORCHESTER,
IN DORSET, ENGLAND.

The first settlers
sailed from Plymouth, England,
in the Mary and John,
(one of the Winthrop fleet.)
March 20, 1630.

Arrived at Nantasket, (now Hull) May 30.
And landed in Dorchester,
June 6, 1630.

THE FIRST CHURCH OF THIS PARISH
WAS BUILT NEAR THE CORNER OF
COTTAGE AND PLEASANT STREETS, IN 1631

SECOND CHURCH BUILT,   1646
REMOVED TO MEETING HOUSE HILL, 1670
THIRD CHURCH BUILT,   1677
FOURTH CHURCH BUILT,   1743
FIFTH CHURCH BUILT,   1816
SIXTH CHURCH BUILT,   1896

Presented by Deacon Henry Humphreys.

FIRST PARISH
DORCHESTER
1630

Church formed in Plymouth England
under the guidance of
REV. JOHN WHITE
of Dorchester England

MINISTERS

REV.		
JOHN WARHAM	1630	1635
JOHN MAVERICK		
RICHARD MATHER	1636	1669
JOSIAH FLINT	1671	1680
JOHN DANFORTH	1682	1730
JONATHAN BOWMAN	1729	1773
MOSES EVERETT	1774	1793
THADDEUS M. HARRIS	1793	1836
NATHANIEL HALL	1835	1875
SAMUEL J. BARROWS	1876	1880
CHRISTOPHER R. ELIOT	1882	1893
EUGENE R. SHIPPEN	1894	1907
ROGER S. FORBES	1908	1917
HARRY FOSTER BURNS	1918	

Presented by Deacon Henry Humphreys

From a photograph

TABLET
IN THE FIRST PARISH CHURCH,
DORCHESTER, MASSACHUSETTS,
in memory of the early settlers of the town.

By F. A. Frizell

TABLET
IN THE FIRST PARISH CHURCH,
DORCHESTER, MASSACHUSETTS,
in memory of Rev. John White, with the names
of all the ministers of the church from his time.

writers as the "Father of the Massachusetts Colony," had previously interested himself in encouraging the settlement at Plymouth and had furnished money to the settlers here, also urging at the same time many of the old Dorchester fishermen to make voyages into American waters.   His failure at Cape Ann in 1624 only stimulated him to new undertakings, and we soon find him, with about one hundred and forty of his friends, in the New Hospital at Plymouth (shown on page 113) where they spent the night previous to sailing for America.   White himself did not come over on the "Mary and John," but preached to them just before sailing.   Among the notable passengers were Captain Roger Clap, Henry Wolcott, an ancestor of the late Governor Wolcott, Thomas Ford, George Dyer, William

From an old print
Photographed by F. A. Frizell

Kindness Mrs. Mary Fifield King
and Rev. H. F. Burns

"THE NEW HOSPITAL," PLYMOUTH, ENGLAND,
the building (taken down in 1869) in which the members of the First Church in Dorchester gathered before sailing in the "Mary and John," March 20, 1629-30, for Dorchester, Massachusetts. This picture hangs in the Minister's Room in the First Parish Church of Dorchester, Massachusetts.

Gaylord, William Rockwell, William Phelps, Israel Stoughton, George Minot, George Hall, Richard Collicot, Nathaniel Duncan, Captains John Mason and Richard Southcote. Much to their disgust Captain Squeb landed them in Hull on May 30, 1630, instead of near the Charles River where they hoped to disembark. Some of their number, therefore, rowed up the Charles and settled at Charlestown, but the larger part of the colony landed at Savin Hill, Dorchester, then called Mattapan. This was the second parish in the colony and the third in New England. The settlement was called after the old town in England, for the reason that among the early settlers "were some from Dorset Shire and some of ye town of Dorchester" and they furthermore wished to do special honour to the Rev. Mr. White, who was the Rector of St. Peter's Church and who held this position for forty years. In appreciation of this great man, Richard C. Humphreys, a member of the First Parish Church in our Dorchester, and some of his friends, placed in the parish church of

MEETING HOUSE HILL, DORCHESTER, MASSACHUSETTS, IN 1847,
showing the First Parish Church.

St. Peter, old Dorchester, where his body lies, a memorial tablet shown in the cut on page 119, the inscription on which reads as follows:—

> In this Porch lies the Body of the Rev^d. John White, M.A., of New College, Oxford. He was born at Christmas, 1575. For about forty years he was Rector of this Parish, and also of Holy Trinity, Dorchester. He died here 21 July, 1648. A Man of great Godliness, good Scholarship, and wonderful Ability and Kindness. He had a very strong sway in this Town. He greatly set forward the Emigration to the Massachusetts Bay Colony, where his name lives in unfading remembrance.

The first winter in America was exceedingly cold and Judge Sewall wrote that the communion bread was frozen pretty hard and rattled sadly in the plates during church service. In these early days Dorchester included Milton, Dedham, Hyde Park, Canton, Sharon, Foxboro and part of Stoughton, all this land being known to the English as the "land beyond the Blue Hills." Other settlers came over from Weymouth, England, to Dorchester, in 1633, and at this time, three years after the establishment of the plantation, it was the richest in the colony.

The old church in our Dorchester is most attractive, and contains a number of relics of interest both to Englishmen and Americans. The clock in the vestry, of Chinese design, dated 1770, came from England; the pulpit also came from England, and was used in the old West Church in our Boston until it was given up, when the pulpit was presented to the Dorchester meeting house. There is also a Bible of the time of King George III, which is still in use. There is also an attractive memorial room to Mrs. Emily A. Fifield, whose family came from the town of Fyfield, England. This room contains the old key of Fyfield Church and a copy of the Rev. John White's book "The Tree of Life," which was written in 1647 and given to the church by William Taylor of London. This book contains advice to the colonies and is very rare. The church, too, owns most of the original records which were started in the earliest times and which have been continued up to the present time. The old Pierce house in Dorchester contained some furniture which came over with the early settlers, but these rare articles were sold about a year ago. The Pierces also owned a piece of bread which was brought over in the "Mary and John" and which is now preserved by one of the descendants.

Since 1855 there have been two anniversaries in Dorchester to commemorate the settlement of the plantation. The first one was held on Easter Sunday, March 28, 1880, to commemorate the gathering of the Church in England and its departure for America, and the second was held on June 17th of the same year to commemorate the anniversary of the planting of the church in Dorchester, and the settlement of the town, which took place June 6, 1630. This second celebration was attended by Governor John D. Long of Massachusetts, who in his speech referred to the fact that there was also a John Long who had been a resident of Dorchester, Eng-

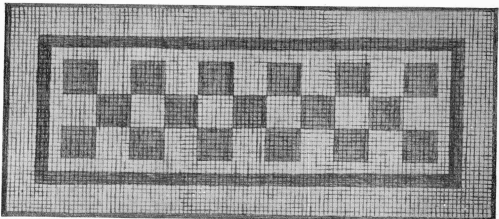

From a photograph   *Kindness Edward A. Huebener, Esq.*

ANCIENT ROMAN PAVEMENT AT THE ENTRANCE OF THE DORCHESTER HIGH SCHOOL,
DORCHESTER, MASSACHUSETTS

It was originally a section of the "Fosse" or Roman Way laid by the Romans in Dorchester, England, after they had subjugated the Britons in 55 B.C. It was secured by the Dorchester High School in 1905 through the enterprise of Charles J. Lincoln, Esq., then principal of the school, and the late Richard C. Humphreys, Esq., president of the Dorchester Historical Society. It was discovered when the crypt of All Saints Church, Dorchester, England, was being repaired and was presented to Dorchester through the kindness of the Rev. S. E. V. Filleul, rector of the church. It is composed of red and white cubes of various sizes enclosed within a brass border and is almost ten feet long and six feet wide, containing about nine thousand blocks.

land. In the church on this occasion were some roses from roots brought over from England in the early days, and also other flowers that had come from Plymouth and other towns in England. The vestry was hung with pictures of Dorchester, England, which were loaned by Rev. E. G. Porter of Lexington, Massachusetts. The following telegram from the Mayor of Dorchester, England, was read during this celebration and was followed by great applause:—

"Old Dorchester sends cordial congratulations to New Dorchester upon its two hundred and fiftieth anniversary and warmly reciprocates its affectionate attachment."

The town of Windsor, Connecticut, which was founded by settlers from our Dorchester, was also represented at this meeting. In the minister's room in our Parish Church are many interesting pictures of Dorchester, England, and on pages 113, 118 and 119 we give illustrations taken from these prints.

In 1904 and 1905, after considerable correspondence, our Dorchester received part of an old Roman pavement which was discovered while the crypt of All Saints Church was undergoing repairs, and it seemed appropriate that young Dorchester should have some legacy from the early home of so many of her pioneers. The Dorchester High School finally became the possessor of this historic relic and it was placed in the floor within the entrance of the school, and the following tablet nearby describes it:—

From a photograph by Bernard Griffin *Kindness Ian Forbes-Robertson, Esq.*

HANGMAN'S COTTAGE, DORCHESTER, ENGLAND

In the early days Dorchester kept its own hangman.

Photograph by Bernard Griffin *Kindness Ian Forbes-Robertson, Esq.*

THE BIRTHPLACE OF SIR THOMAS HARDY, O.M., THE NOVELIST, BOCKHAMPTON,
DORCHESTER, ENGLAND

John Lothrop Motley also lived and died near Dorchester. He was a relative of the Motleys of Boston,
Massachusetts.

Photographed by F. A. Frizell from a print in the Minister's Room of the First Parish Church, Dorchester, Massachusetts
Kindness Mrs. Mary Fifield King and Rev. H. F. Burns

ST. PETER'S CHURCH, DORCHESTER, ENGLAND

Rev. John White, who organized the colony that came to Dorchester, Massachusetts, in 1630, is buried in this English church, of which he was rector for many years.   The tablet which was erected to his memory by residents of Dorchester, Massachusetts, and which is shown in another cut, is in this church.

The
Tessellated
Pavement
below
was originally laid in Dorchester, England, during
the Roman occupation of that country
55 B.C.–410 A.D.
It was discovered while
repairs were being made in
the crypt of All Saints Church
and through the kindness of
Rev. S. E. V. Filleul
The Rector of that Parish
was received by the friends of
the Dorchester High School
and was placed in its present
location March
1906

There are also some colored pictures of old Dorchester below this tablet. This pavement is composed of red and white cubes of various sizes, and contains about nine thousand small blocks. It is to the efforts of Mr. Charles J. Lincoln, then principal of the Dorchester High School, and the late Richard C. Humphreys, for many years president of the Dorchester Historical Society, who cheerfully bore the expense of the removal of this pavement, that we are indebted for this old relic.

Interchanges also took place between the two towns in 1855, and in anticipation of the celebration the committee in charge of the event sent a very friendly letter to the Mayor of Dorchester, England, parts of which are as follows:—

"Your place being the residence of many of our progenitors, and from which this town derived its name, we address you with an affectionate interest. It is comparatively but a few years since our ancestors left their quiet home and launched forth upon the ocean, to make a new home for themselves and posterity, and to take up their abode in this then inhospitable wilderness of savages and wild beasts. . . . We believe that this is almost the only country ever settled that had not the lower motive of gold, plunder, or conquest, for its paramount object. . . . It is supposed that this town was called Dorchester, on account of the great respect of its early settlers for Rev. John White, a clergyman of your place at that time, and an active instrument in promoting the settlement and procuring its charter. They sailed from Plymouth, England, March 20, and arriving May 30, 1630, they came in the ship Mary and John, Capt. Squeb, and were finally settled down here as a body politic about June 17, 1630. They were reinforced from time to time, and many remained here only for a short period, and then went to other places and made new homes. It is estimated that there are now living, in this country, two hundred thousand persons who are descendants of the early settlers of this town. . . . The inhabitants of this town propose to celebrate the 79th anniversary of our birthday as a nation, on the coming July 4th. Hon. Edward Everett, a native of this place, and late Minister Plenipotentiary to Great Britain, will address the assembly. The sons and daughters of the town, wherever scattered, are invited to come to their ancestral home and unite with us on this occasion. It is too much for us to ask that a delegation might be sent from your Borough to add

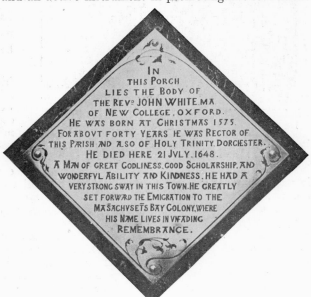

From a picture in the Minister's Room in the First Parish Church, Dorchester, Massachusetts
Kindness Mrs. Mary Fifield King and Rev. H. F. Burns

TABLET IN THE PARISH CHURCH OF ST. PETER'S, DORCHESTER, ENGLAND,

placed there in memory of Rev. John White, by residents of Dorchester, Massachusetts. He is called the "Patriarch of Dorchester," as he was instrumental in sending a colony to our Dorchester in 1630.

Photograph by Bernard Griffin   *Kindness Ian Forbes-Robertson, Esq.*

REMAINS OF THE HOUSE IN DORCHESTER, ENG-
LAND, IN WHICH REV. JOHN WHITE LIVED

It stands behind the parish church and is now used as
an ironmonger's workshop.

to the interest of this festival; but should one or more of your citizens whom you would approve be in this country, it would give us great pleasure to have them attend as our guests. . . . distance is computed by time and not space, so that you seem neighbors as well as friends, and by this epistle we reach forth across the ocean and offer you the right hand of fellowship.

signed by EDMUND P. TILESTON
EDMUND J. BAKER
EBENEZER CLAPP, JR.
WM. D. SWAN
WM. B. TRASK
WM. H. RICHARDSON
JAMES SWAN
SAMUEL BLAKE
EDWARD HOLDEN"

In answer a return message was received, part of which is given below:—

"Your letter, which as Mayor it fell to my lot to receive, has created a feeling of interest amongst us, and we welcome with great cordiality the communication from those whom we may style kinsfolks. I have caused your letter to be printed, and have circulated it amongst such persons especially as are likely to assist us in our inquiries on the subject of it. . . . We feel that we cannot furnish you with an account of our town and neighborhood in such a manner as we would wish, in time for your anniversary but we hope by the 80th anniversary to be able to collect a portfolio for you, which, if you wish, we shall gladly forward to you. I have already a nucleus of the collection. . . . Mr. White's name is still known in the Borough and there are still names amongst us enumerated by you. . . . Our design is to furnish you, if acceptable, with full description of the town and neighborhood, accompanied by such views as we may be able to procure or furnish to illustrate our account. We do not think we can do this with justice to the subject before next summer, but if you will then accept it as a pledge of good feeling and good fellowship, it is humbly at your service.

Signed THOMAS COOMBS, *Mayor*."

During the recent war an invitation was sent to American soldiers from Dorchester who should pass through England, to accept the hospitality of the English borough, a courtesy much appreciated.

Minot and Humphreys were two of the early settlers in new Dorchester and it

From a photograph   *Kindness Ian Forbes-Robertson, Esq.*

HIGH STREET WEST, DORCHESTER, ENGLAND,
showing St. Peter's Church in background.

is said that these lines appeared on the former's tomb in the old Upham's Corner
burial ground:—

> Here lie the bodies of Unite Humphreys and Shining Minot,
> Such names as those, they never die not.

In the cemetery at Upham's Corner, Dorchester, there is a tablet in memory of
the early settlers who are buried there, also some old English tombstones similar
to those in Plymouth, Massachusetts.

The old seal of the town is an interesting one; on it appears the old thatch-roofed
meeting house, also the Blue Hills which served to pilot these early settlers to our
harbour, and the triple towered Castle placed there in memory of the Castle in
Dorchester, England, which was copied from the seal of the old town of Dorchester,
England. The most recent interchange between the two Dorchesters is the stone
sent towards the latter part of 1919 by Rev. Grosvenor Bartelot, M.A., Vicar of
St. George's, Fordington, Dorchester, England, to Rev. Simon B. Blunt, Rector

of All Saints Church, Dorchester, Massachusetts. This stone is to be set in the top of the altar. The English Rector writes that this stone formed a part of the ancient stone altar of his Church which dates back to the year 1200 or earlier.

An altar was found in Dorchester, England, which records that Dorchester was a flourishing Roman settlement before the invasion by the Saxons. The Romans called it Durnovaria which meant "water way" or "channel."

Photograph by F. A. Frizell   *Kindness Mrs. G. F. Pierce*

PIECES OF BREAD AND CORN-COB,

brought to Dorchester, Massachusetts, by Robert and Ann Pierce in the "Mary and John," in 1630. These relics of the early settlers have been in the Pierce family of Dorchester, Massachusetts, ever since.

The old town has some interesting places, which include the Roman walls and the amphitheatre called "Maumbury Rings," which is one of the finest in England and goes back to the time of Agricola. There are also the large earthworks of Maiden Castle. The cut on page 117 shows Hangman's Cottage, which is one of the sights pointed out to visitors. At one time it would seem that the mother town was not over virtuous, as the records show that the hangman was kept very busy. The house of Judge Jeffreys, who was called the "Bloody Judge," is also pointed out to the sightseer. John Endicott was born in Dorchester, England, and Sir Thomas Hardy, the novelist, and Barnes, the poet, both lived there. Another interesting fact is that John Lothrop Motley, the historian, who was born and lived in our Dorchester lived and died in the English Dorchester. The town is supposed to be a place of health-giving qualities, if we judge by the remark made by one of the physicians of the town who said that a "doctor could neither live nor die in Dorchester."

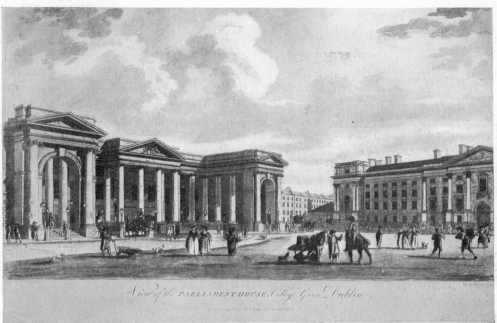

From an old print by J. Malton, 1790   *In the possession of a Boston collector*

VIEW OF THE PARLIAMENT HOUSE AND COLLEGE GREEN, DUBLIN, IRELAND

From a print published by T. S. Roberts, 1796   *In the possession of a Boston collector*

BLARNEY CASTLE,
near Dublin, Ireland.

DUBLIN, NEW HAMPSHIRE

HENRY STRONGMAN forms the connecting link between Dublin, New Hampshire and Dublin, Ireland. He was born in the Irish capital and was the only one of the original Scotch-Irish settlers to remain permanently in this New England town. These facts furnish us with sufficient proof that the name Dublin was given in his honour, the previous name having been "Monadnock No. 3." The late Thaddeus Morse has corroborated this reason for the naming of the town, for he describes hearing a discussion concerning this subject when he was a boy, and he remembered that "the name Dublin was chosen because the earliest settlers were Scotch-Irish and the capital of their native country was Dublin." Strongman was a weaver by trade, came to this country about 1736, lived in Boston for a short time, and then moved to the vicinity of Deerfield, Massachusetts. Soon after, his family became the fifth to take up a residence in Dublin, New Hampshire. In the year 1800, the several branches of the family changed their name to Strong. The first meeting of the incorporated town was held in 1771, although the name Dublin may have been used previously. The first board of selectmen chosen at this meeting in addition to Strongman, comprised Thomas Morse and Benjamin Mason, Joseph Greenwood being elected town clerk. Strongman is described as being well educated and most helpful to the town in its early days. Morse was supposed to have been the first permanent English settler in this attractive New Hampshire town.

This territory was settled many years before 1771, a deed dated November 3, 1749, having been given by Colonel Joseph Blanchard, Jr., of Dunstable, by power vested in him by the proprietors, by vote of a meeting held in Portsmouth, New Hampshire; this grant ran to Matthew Thornton, Samuel Stoddard and thirty-eight others. The allotment of land and drawing of shares took place on the first Tuesday of June, 1750, at Dunstable. The first settler was William Thornton, a brother of Matthew, and one of the signers of the Declaration of Independence, who stayed, however, only a short time, and who had a daughter born there named Mollie, the first white child born in the town. A tablet was erected in the town about twenty-five years ago to his memory. About ten years later some Scotch-Irish families came from Londonderry, New Hampshire, to Peterborough, New Hampshire, and several of them moved over to Dublin, among them being John Alexander, William McNee, Alexander Scott, with his son William, and James Taggart. A number of people also moved to Dublin from Sherborn, Massachusetts, and also from Natick, Medfield, Holliston, Framingham, Temple and Amherst, until in the year 1775 there were three hundred and five settlers in Dublin as compared to twenty-three voters five years before. Most of these settlers, however, came from Sherborn, and the greatest friendship has always existed between

CASTLE OF DUBLIN.

From an old print   *In the possession of a Boston collector*

Dedicated by permission to his Exe^y the Right Honble CHARLES EARL WHITWORTH, G.C.B. Lord Lieu^t of Ireland, and Grand Master of the Order of S^t. Patrick by his respectful & Obedient Servant (Signed) James Del Veechio

CASTLE OF DUBLIN

In the center is seen the New Castle Chapel, on the right the Treasury, on the left the entrance to the Ordnance Office and avenue leading to Great Ship Street.

the two towns, resulting in 1771 in the gift of a communion set to the church in Dublin by a Mrs. Whitney of Sherborn. The one hundredth anniversary of the settlement of Dublin was held on June 17, 1852.

Of the ancient capital of Ireland on the river Liffey, Thackeray said, as he looked at the view from Carlisle Bridge:—

"beautiful the Four Courts and dome to the left, the Custom House and dome to the right, vessels on the river, the scene animated and lively."

Carlyle also visited Dublin and described the terrible week that it took him to sail there from England. Another description of the city was given by the well-known Irishman, George Moore, who said there were four objects of interest, the Castle, Shelbourne Hotel, the Kildore Street Club and Mrs. Rusville, the fashionable dressmaker of that time. It was there also, in Hoey's Court, in Castle Street, where Jonathan Swift, Dean of St. Patrick's, was born in the year 1667, though no trace of the building can be seen today; and in this cathedral so closely associated with Dean Swift, lie side by side his body and that of Stella, whose real name was Esther Johnson; she was married to Swift, but this fact was kept a secret to the day of his death. Sir Walter Scott in speaking of St. Patrick's Cathedral, declared that the church was Swift's tomb and that his face could be seen in every corner.

The history of Dublin Castle is said to be practically the history of Ireland after the twelfth century. It has been claimed that Dean Swift almost burned it up by trying to read there in bed one evening. King Henry II presented Dublin to five hundred citizens of Bristol, who came over to view the newly acquired possessions, but their reception was not very cordial, for they were attacked by the hill people, who killed all of them. At the beginning of the thirteenth century, Fitz Henry determined to erect a strong fortress on Cork Hill, and began therefore to build the ancient castle of Dublin, of which so much has been written. In its chapel the Viceroy and his court held sway and received the fashionables of the City. The great balls, the acme of a debutante's desire, were held in Beefeaters Hall in the Castle and there we are told that the ladies who wanted to dance were placed in rows or tiers reaching all the way from the floor to the ceiling, an arrangement described as "being in paradise." On these occasions great etiquette was enforced and only persons of sufficient social prominence were allowed to meet the King's representative. The more recent balls were given in St. Patrick's Hall, and here the annual festival in honour of this Saint was held on every March seventeenth at which the Lord Lieutenant was always obliged to go through with the formality of "drowning the shamrock," and on this day of carnival all made merry. In the evening St. Patrick's Ball took place. Here also levees were held once a year, and all the "belles and beaux" of Dublin drove to Cork Hill, one of the greatest "belles" of her day being the daughter of Sir David and Lady Roche. In the nineteenth century Dublin was the second capital in the British dominions and was such a center of fashion and gaiety that the Viceroy's Court exceeded the brilliancy of that of George III. We are told that of all the viceroys the Duke of Abercorn, who gave most wonderful dinners during the season, was the most magnificent, and second to his entertainments were the fancy dress balls given by Mrs. Guinness, which are described as being most attractive.

To the little theatre in Smoke Alley came many of the leading actors and actresses of the day, including Garrick, Peg Woffington, Fannie Kemble and Mrs. Siddons. The scene after the theatre let out has been described as one of great commotion, for the lane was very narrow, and the sleepers nearby were much disturbed at the noise, and could be seen with their heads out of the windows, swearing at the audience as it filed out, the torch bearers, the coachmen and the footmen.

Some writers have claimed that Dublin, called both Dublana and Eblana in the olden days, resembled London, and certainly College Green with its attractive buildings as shown in the cut reminds one of the English capital; this Green once formed part of a village called Hogges or Le Hogges, from the word Hoge, meaning small sepulchral mounds, found there during the time of Charles I. The word Dublin is derived from Dhu-b-linn, meaning "the black or dark pool," its name in ancient days having been Baile Atha Cliath.

There is an interesting legend in connection with St. Patrick and the ford over the river Liffey; as the Saint was going home to Armagh he stayed in the city over night and while there his hosts complained of the bad water, whereupon it is claimed he caused a fountain to spring up at a place near the present site of St. Patrick's Cathedral which was entirely restored at one time by Benjamin Lee Guinness.

The Danes continually landed and sacked the town and in 840 the people of Dublin erected a fortress on the same place, probably, where the Norman castle was later built. In the next century the same troublesome tribe was beaten by Malachi II, who as Moore wrote "wore the collar of gold, that he won from the proud invader."

Trinity College Library, the Royal Irish Academy and the Royal Dublin Society are some of the most important organizations of the city, the Dublin Horse Show being an annual event known the world over. A memorial was erected in Sackville Street to Nelson in 1803. *And was blown up on the morning of Tuesday 8th March 1966.*

FALMOUTH, MASSACHUSETTS

"ARE you a man of Kent?" was usually the first question asked by the people of County Kent, England, when they met a stranger, and if one could answer in the affirmative, he was considered of very superior quality. In the early history of our colony a company of persons arrived in Scituate, Massachusetts, from this county in England and, in describing their landing, the Massachusetts Historical Society Collections say that "Scituate, indebted to the substantial character of some of its founders, many of whom it is evident came from Kent, England, soon became a respectable town, which superiority it maintained to the latest annals of the colony." There is a street in Scituate called "Kent Street" that still recalls to us these early settlers from that county. Part of this Scituate company removed to West Barnstable and began the settlement of that town in 1639. Some years later, in 1660, some of this colony again moved from Barnstable to Falmouth. They arrived in boats and landed between Fresh and Salt Ponds, where they lived, until their homes were constructed, near "Consider Hatch's Pond," called "Sider's Pond" for short. Most of the names of these Falmouth settlers were Scituate and Barnstable names and include the families of Hatch, Robinson, Chapman, Jenkins, Hamlin, Lothrop, Nelson, Cobb, Hinckley and Bacon. When these first settlers arrived in Falmouth the wife of Jonathan Hatch unexpectedly gave birth to a son and when asked what she would call it, she replied,

From an old coloured print

Kindness Ian Forbes-Robertson, Esq.

FALMOUTH, ENGLAND,
showing Pendennis Castle on the left.

"He was born among the flags and his name shall be Moses," and from that time until now this name has been a familiar one in the town.

Falmouth across the seas is on the river Fal, as its name implies, and is an attractive seaport in Cornwall built on very steep hills. There has been much rivalry between this town and Plymouth which caused a Falmouth writer to say: "Likewise as Plymouth vaunteth richer and fairer towne and greater plenty of fish than Falmouth, so Falmouth braggeth that a hundred sayle (sail) may anker within its circuit and no one of them see the other's top, which Plymouth cannot equal." Falmouth is an important port and many noted persons have frequented it. Lord Exmouth, who was a Pellew and whose family were at one time well known in Maryland, sailed on the waters of the harbour, as did also Nelson and other famous admirals; the news of the great victory of the Nile was brought to this seaport first. It is interesting besides to remember that Napoleon on his way to St. Helena put in there. Falmouth was noted chiefly as having been the leading port of the packet service, and the following lines give an excellent idea of the town during these flourishing days which lasted for about one hundred and sixty years.

"We past in sight of St. Maurs, a little fishing town on the east of the bay, and anchored about noon at Falmouth. There is a man always on the look-out for the packets; he makes a signal as soon as one is seen, and every woman who has a husband on board gives him a shilling for the intelligence. . . . The perpetual stir and bustle of this inn is as surprising as it is wearisome. Doors opening and shutting, bells ringing, voices calling to the waiter from every quarter, while he cries 'coming' to one room, and hurries away to another. Everybody is in a hurry here; either they are going off in the packets, and are hastening their preparations to embark, or they have just arrived, and are impatient to be on the route homeward. Every now and then a carriage rattles up to the door with rapidity which makes the very house shake. The man who cleans the boots is running in one direction, the barber with his powder-bag in another; here goes the barber's boy with his hot water and razors; there comes the clean linen from the washer-woman; and the hall is full of porters and sailors, bringing in luggage or bearing it away;—now you hear a horn blown because the post is coming in, and in the middle of the night you are awakened by another because it is going out."

This packet service started in the year 1688 and really made the town of Falmouth. A few brigs also were sent to Spain, Portugal, New York, the West Indies and other ports, the "Mercury," which sailed to New York, being particularly well known. The ships were small and have often been referred to as "bathing machines" and "coffin ships." One of the well-known captains was John Goodridge who took a great interest in America and at one time owned land in Albany, New York. There was a packet memorial erected in Falmouth in 1899, and a few of the old packet-men were on hand to witness the celebration. The inscription reads:—

> To the memory of the gallant officers and men of H. M. Post Office
> Packet Service sailing from Falmouth 1688–1852.

Also in the library is a list of the packets and their commanders and the places to which they sailed. There are also tablets in the Falmouth and Mylor churches.

Our chief interest, however, in connection with this English town is that Bartholomew Gosnold, the first Englishman to found a colony in New England, sailed from this port to America.

One of the objects of interest in Old Falmouth is Pendennis Castle which was built by Henry VIII, and which has always been closely associated with the Killigrews, who were styled "the Lords of both fort and town" and who were believed to be invincible. A member of this family has been governor or owner of this Castle for generations. When coaches first came in, one of the Killigrews made the remark that it was "more like flying than rideing." In this Castle the Prince of Wales, afterwards King Charles II, took refuge in the "King's room" and after a long siege the stronghold was obliged to surrender.

Sir Walter Raleigh, who figured so prominently in the history of England during this great epoch, was the first to draw attention to the possibilities of the harbour. In his time only two houses stood in the town, which was then known as "Smithick." In later years, it was called "Pennycomequick," a word derived from the Celtic Pen-y-cum, meaning "Head of the Vale," and "wick," signifying the Saxon for village. It was not, however, until the time of King Charles II that the town was called Falmouth by Royal proclamation. The Russell and Rogers families were two of the most important in the town,—Captain Rogers of the Royal Navy being distinguished for gallantry in the year 1807.

In the old days there was a doctor in old Falmouth in whose diary has been found the following amusing entry: "Did this day administer to old Mrs. Jones for her ague." The next day: "called on Mrs. Jones and found she had died in the night in much agony. N.B. Not use . . . again!"

There is also a Falmouth in Maine, from which the territory of the present Portland was taken.

GLOUCESTER, MASSACHUSETTS

"Gloucester is fair, yes wondrous fair
For artist's brush, or poet's pen,
Yet still its wealth beyond compare
Is in its race of sturdy men."

THE English names of city, town, stream and street in New England will be lasting memorials to the love borne by the early settlers on these shores, for the beautiful English towns which they had left behind them. Gloucester is another example, for between the quaint old cathedral city of Gloucester, England, and the picturesque seaport of Gloucester, Massachusetts, there still exists this strong bond of kinship and friendliness. One of the first invitations issued by the officials of our Gloucester on the occasion of the two hundred and fiftieth anniversary of its incorporation, in 1892, was to the Lord Mayor and

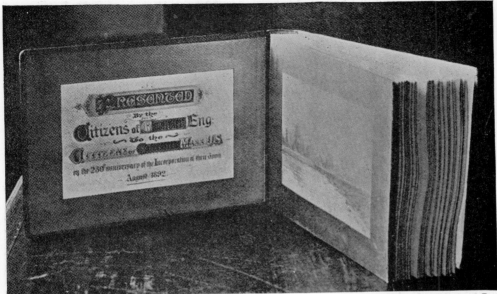

From Report of the 250th Anniversary of the Town of Gloucester, Massachusetts *Kindness Allen F. Grant, Esq.*

THE ALBUM PRESENTED IN 1892 BY THE MAYOR AND TOWN COUNCIL OF GLOUCES–
TER, ENGLAND, TO GLOUCESTER, MASSACHUSETTS, AND NOW IN
THE CITY HALL OF THE LATTER PLACE

It contains views of the English city and was sent on the occasion of the two hundred and fiftieth anniversary
of the incorporation of Gloucester, Massachusetts.

Town Council of Gloucester, England. A beautifully embossed parchment reply was received, expressing their appreciation of the invitation and regret at being unable to accept it, the message being addressed to Mayor Asa G. Andrews of Gloucester, Massachusetts, by Hon. James Platt, Mayor of the English city:—

"Dear Mr. Mayor,—

In common with all the members of our City Council, I appreciate very much the kind invitation of your citizens to be present at the celebration of the two hundred and fiftieth anniversary of Gloucester, Massachusetts. It would have given me great pleasure to have been able to accept the honour and to participate in the celebration, but the time is not convenient for me, as our musical festival commences on September 6th, and I must be present on the occasion. We have also just entered into the occupation of our new Guild Hall which takes up a good deal of my time for the present. It would have been all the more pleasant to me, as I have some little knowledge of your city and experienced the hospitality of one of your predecessors, Mayor Williams, in the summer of 1882. Our City Council have resolved to send you an address of congratulation which they will sign, and also an album illustrating various objects of interest in our city, present and past. Wishing you a very successful celebration and continued prosperity, I remain," etc.

From Report of the 250th Anniversary of the Town of Gloucester, Massachusetts   *Kindness Allen F. Grant, Esq.*

EXTERIOR VIEW OF THE ALBUM PRESENTED BY GLOUCESTER, ENGLAND,
TO GLOUCESTER, MASSACHUSETTS

The album referred to in this letter was presented to Mayor Asa G. Andrews at the Mayor's luncheon on August 25th, by John Platt, Esq., son of this Mayor Platt of Gloucester, England; the younger Platt was present at the anniversary celebration and took a prominent part in its observance.   This beautifully illustrated album, now in City Hall, is bound in Russia leather, and on the outside is a silver plate on which are engraved the words:—

"Views of Gloucester, England, 1892."

On the inside of the cover is the following inscription:—

"Presented by the Citizens of Gloucester, England, to the Citizens of Gloucester, Massachusetts, on the 250th anniversary of the incorporation of the town, August 1892."

TABLET AT STAGE FORT PARK, GLOUCESTER, MASSACHUSETTS,
placed to commemorate the first English settlement there.

LARGER VIEW OF TABLET ON ROCK AT STAGE FORT PARK, GLOUCESTER,
MASSACHUSETTS

During this anniversary week cablegrams were exchanged by the mayors of the two cities, thereby further cementing the friendship that existed between the Bay State city and its English counterpart. Mayor Platt has several times visited our Gloucester. Further correspondence ensued between the two towns, as shown below:—

"At a quarterly meeting of the Council of the City of Gloucester, England, held at the Guildhall, on Wednesday, the 28th day of July, 1909, James Bruton, Esq., Mayor, in the chair, the following letter from Gloucester, Massachusetts, was read:—

GLOUCESTER, MASS.
July 6, 1909.

THE HONORABLE THE TOWN COUNCIL,
      Gloucester, England.

Gentlemen:

The preliminary announcement for Gloucester Day, Wednesday, August 4th, has been forwarded to you. In behalf of the Committee I am pleased to extend you a cordial invitation to visit Gloucester on that day as the guest of our people. As you will see, the principal event will be the evening pageant and play. 'The Canterbury Pilgrims' is based upon the Canterbury Tales of Geoffrey Chaucer, and must especially appeal to you. The Pageant as it will be presented in our city will be the most ambitious so far attempted in this country. We wish that it may be possible for you to honor us on this occasion, and we can assure you that your welcome will be one that you will remember with pleasure.

Might we ask also for a word of greeting to be given at the Pageant in case you could not accept our invitation.

With sincere regards,

Yours truly,

FRED W. TIBBETS, *Secretary.*"

to which the following reply was sent:—

"GUILDHALL, GLOUCESTER, ENGLAND
23rd July, 1909.

Dear Sir,

I beg to acknowledge receipt of your letter of the 6th instant inviting the Council of this city to visit Gloucester, Mass. as the guests of the Citizens on 'Gloucester Day,' August 4th, 1909, on the occasion of a Festival in honour of William Howard Taft, President of the United States; and I also thank you for the separate invitation sent to me personally. . . . I am quite sure the Members of the Council would very much like to attend the Festival and that they would be specially interested in the Pageant and Play 'The Canterbury Pilgrims,' though they would need no such inducement to visit Gloucester, Mass., if able to do so, as they are mindful of the friendship which has so long existed between the two Cities and the very cordial welcome which has been extended to some old Gloucestrians who have visited your City.

On behalf of the Members of the Council and my fellow citizens, I heartily thank you for your very kind invitation, and I sincerely hope that the visit of the President of the United States and the success of your Pageant and Play may cause 'Gloucester Day,' 1909, to be long remembered as a red-letter day in your City.

PORTUGUESE CHURCH, GLOUCESTER, MASSACHUSETTS,

called "Our Lady of Good Voyage." The Virgin Mary is holding in her arm a Gloucester fishing vessel. Over the door is shown another model of a vessel. Once a year a service is held here known as "The Crowning," which is described in the text.

Trusting that some Members of the Council may be able to visit your City on some future occasion, and with the assurance that any of your Citizens will ever receive a cordial welcome in this City, I am

Yours very faithfully,

FRED W. TIBBETTS, Esq.,　　　　　　　　　　　　　　JAMES BRUTON, *Mayor.*
Secretary 'Gloucester Day' Committee,
Gloucester, Mass."

In 1915, John J. Somes, Esq., the present City Clerk of our Gloucester, gladly accepted the offer of Hon. W. J. Johnston-Vaughan, an ex-Mayor of Gloucester, England, to send to our city a bell made in the old Gloucester Bell Foundry, one of the most important foundries in the Kingdom in mediæval times. This bell, marked "1779" and "T. R." for the founder's name, now hangs in the corridor of City Hall in our Gloucester with a suitable card below indicating how it came into the possession of our city.

In 1899, Captain Howard Blackburn of our Gloucester, who had lost most of his fingers on the fishing grounds, sailed alone a small boat about thirty feet long from Gloucester, Massachusetts, to Gloucester, England, where he was received by the officials and others of the town, among whom were the members of the firm of Fielding and Platt, the latter a relative of the Platt who is described above as having come over to our Gloucester to attend one of the celebrations here. Captain Blackburn carried with him a letter from the Mayor of our Gloucester and while in the English Mayor's office his attention was called to a framed address hanging in that office which had been sent by Mayor William W. French of Gloucester, Massachusetts, acknowledging receipt of the album sent to our city. The captain was entertained at the Gloucester Theatre and over his box floated the Stars and Stripes, and in the evening Yankee Doodle was played.

The first Englishman to plant his foot on the soil of Gloucester was Captain John Smith who landed here in the year 1614, and called the point "Tragabigzanda" which was soon changed to Cape Ann by Prince Charles in honour of his mother, Anne of Denmark. Captain Smith was much interested in the fishing industry, and wrote home to England, "Is it not pretty sport to pull up two pence, six pence, or twelve pence as fast as you can hale and veare a line?" Gloucester was originally settled three years after the Plymouth Colony by a group of colonists from Dorchester, England, who came there in the year 1623 to establish a fishing industry. The Cape Ann town, however, was not incorporated until 1642, when it was given the name of Gloucester either in honour of its first minister Richard Blynman or in memory of the English city on the Severn from which many of the pioneers had come that year; it is an interesting fact that many of the leading citizens of the city at the present time are descendants of the original settlers, among them being the families of Parsons, Sargent, Conant, Wonson, Babson and Tarr. This small fishing settlement grew steadily until it is today the largest fishing port in this country and it was quite fitting that a memorial should have been erected in honour of these sturdy men who founded this industry in Gloucester. The memorial, which consists of a bronze tablet set in a huge boulder, was placed near Half Moon Beach on Fishermen's Field, now called Stage Fort Park, near the place where the early settlers landed, where the fishing stages were placed, where the first house, that of Roger Conant, and the First Church were situated. The inscription on this beautiful tablet is as follows:—

On this site in
1623
A Company of Fishermen and Farmers from Dorchester, Eng.
under the direction of Rev. John White founded
THE MASSACHUSETTS BAY COLONY

From that time, the Fisheries, the oldest industry in the Commonwealth,
have been uninterruptedly pursued from this Port

HERE IN 1625 GOV. ROGER CONANT BY WISE DIPLOMACY
AVERTED BLOODSHED BETWEEN CONTENDING FACTIONS
ONE LED BY MYLES STANDISH OF PLYMOUTH
THE OTHER BY CAPT. HEWES
A NOTABLE EXEMPLIFICATION OF ARBITRATION
IN THE BEGINNINGS OF NEW ENGLAND

Placed by the citizens of Gloucester, 1907.

Two hundred and sixteen vessels were enrolled in the town in the year 1916, carrying a total crew of about 3,000 men, and the value of the catch from the early days to now totals over $500,000,000. Great, however, has been the sacrifice of human life, as those know who have watched in vain for the return of their loved ones, for between the years 1830 and 1916, four thousand five hundred and thirty-four men were lost at sea from this port.

"On a sea in a night that with horror is crazed
With the torture and passion and fury of storms,
On an old fishing-craft that is beaten and dazed."

There are two very interesting and impressive ceremonies which take place in Gloucester each year connected with the fishing industry which, we believe, are unique in this country. One of these, known as "The Crowning," was inaugurated two decades ago by Captain Joseph P. Mesquita, one of the foremost fishing captains of this noted fishing port. After having been delivered from extreme peril at sea, he vowed that each year at the Feast of the Pentecost he would consecrate himself to the Lord in gratitude for this deliverance by carrying out a ceremony similar to that held for years in Portugal, from which country came many of the ancestors of Gloucester's fishermen. He and the members of his crew donated funds to purchase in Lisbon, Portugal, a silver crown surmounted by a dove to be used in carrying out his vow. The ceremony usually begins with a procession from his house to the Portuguese Catholic Church of Our Lady of Good Voyage headed by Captain Mesquita bearing the crown. When the church is reached,

From Report of the 250th Anniversary of the Town of Gloucester, Massachusetts   *Kindness Allen F. Grant, Esq.*

STAGE FORT, THE FIRST SETTLEMENT AT GLOUCESTER, MASSACHUSETTS, 1623
A tablet on the boulder at the right records this fact.

the crown is received by the priest, and the Captain and other persons who have prepared themselves for this ceremony by special prayers for the week preceding, follow him to a place before the altar where, after High Mass is celebrated, the crown is lowered on the heads of those participating in the ceremony, solemn thanks being offered to the Holy Ghost for past blessings with prayers for a continuation of His favor.   The dove surmounting the crown is a symbol of the Holy Ghost, and the crown is a reminder of Queen Elizabeth of Portugal, who at a time of great famine in her country was so charitable to the poor and ministered to their wants with such a holy spirit that she was later canonized.   In further remembrance of the good works of this Queen, many loaves of sweet bread are prepared, and these, after being blessed by the priest, are distributed among the people present at the ceremony, each man, woman and child in the audience receiving a loaf.   One selected loaf of immense size is especially decorated for the celebrant.

The other ceremony, which is held under the auspices of the Gloucester Fishermen's Institute, consists of a memorial service for the men of the city who have gone down to the sea in ships never to return. The schoolchildren with arms laden with flowers proceed to the bridge over the Squam River, just outside the city, and after an appropriate service the flowers are cast on the waters and are carried out to sea, the beautiful thought behind this ceremony being that the flowers shall seek the unknown graves of the victims of Neptune's wrath.

From Report of the 250th Anniversary of the Town of Gloucester, Massachusetts
Kindness Allen F. Grant, Esq.

ROGER CONANT HOUSE, FIRST HOUSE ERECTED
IN GLOUCESTER, AT STAGE FORT, IN 1623

From an old print in the Islesboro Inn, Dark Harbour, Maine   *Kindness David H. Smith*

GLOUCESTER, MASSACHUSETTS

Many are the quaint superstitions which have arisen from Gloucester's famous industry, for instance: fishermen believe that if they accidentally drop a cake of ice overboard when preparing for a fishing trip, they will have good luck and a full fare, but if they turn a hatch bottom up or drop it into the hold, they will meet the direst misfortune throughout the voyage, and may consider themselves indeed fortunate if they ever see land again.   They will also tell you that

> "Sunday sail, never fail;
> Friday sail, ill luck and gale."

And so, in spite of the other flourishing industries that have sprung up in Gloucester, it will always be as the quaint, picturesque old fishing port that we shall think of her, and her name will bring to our mind, not the picture of her granite quarries or her cement works, but a vision of the old docks lined with smartly rigged fishing-craft and tramp steamers, and as we listen there comes to us the sound of

> "The chimes a-striking, sweet and low,
> While softly, sweetly, gently steals
> The lullaby of drifting keels."

Our Gloucester is also known as the town where the name "schooner" was first given to a vessel, the word being suggested by a bystander who exclaimed, "See how she scoons!"

From "The City of Gloucester," England, by John Jennings, Brunswick Road, Gloucester, England   Photographed by George B. Brayton

ANCIENT WEST GATE HOUSE AND BRIDGE, GLOUCESTER, ENGLAND,
as in the time of George III.

Back of the town is an abandoned settlement named Dogtown, so called because of the fact that towards the end of the seventeenth century the women settlers
near the seacoast, for better protection, were sent several miles back into the country
with their dogs.   Dogtown today, with its huge primeval boulders, its sunken cellars,
and its grass-grown streets, is a weird, romantic, and pathetic place, a world be-
witched, as one of the few visitors there expressed it.   In this unique settlement
there were supposed to be many witches, the names of Judy Rhines and "Tammy"
Younger, the "Queen of the Witches," being the more often quoted in the Dogtown legends.   The latter was supposed to be able to bewitch a load of wood so
that it wouldn't stay on the ox team until part of it had been unloaded at her door,
and it was also claimed that she exacted a certain amount of fish when a vessel
came in or, otherwise, she would bewitch the next catch.   This settlement, one
of the few ruined towns of America, so little known to either the visitor or the native,
and now completely deserted, was once the home of the ancestors of some of the
best citizens of Gloucester and Rockport.

Some of the settlers of our Gloucester as early as 1650 moved to and founded

Photograph by A. B. Fitcher   *Kindness Ian Forbes-Robertson, Esq.*

COLLEGE COURT, GLOUCESTER, ENGLAND,
showing the First Sunday-school.

New London, Connecticut, and in 1727 were responsible for the settlement of Falmouth, Maine, and a few years later of New Gloucester also in Maine.

Gloucester, England, is a city of great antiquity. It was first called "Caer Gloui" before the Romans came to Britain, being the site of an important fort they called "Glevum," which was changed by the Saxons to "Glow-ceastre," "Glewancester," and "Glew-ceastre" from which the present name "Gloucester" is apparently derived. The name was supposed to suggest "Fair City." Many relics of the Roman days have been discovered, including coins of the Emperor Claudius, who came to Britain and pushed his conquest toward the interior of the island. A monastery was founded in 679 and in 1022 Bishop Wolstan of Worcester established the Benedictine rule there. In 1541 the diocese of Gloucester was constituted, with the Abbey Church for its Cathedral. From the early days, Gloucester seemed to be marked for distinction. In 577 the Saxon King of Wessex captured the town, and in 836 the Danes possessed the place, they in their turn being badly beaten in 918. In 1051, Edward the Confessor took up his residence there and some years later William the Conqueror held Court at Gloucester, where he usually spent his Christmas. In 1264, the King lost possession of the castle by

Photograph by F. Frith & Co., England

Kindness Ian Forbes-Robertson, Esq.

THE CITY OF GLOUCESTER, ENGLAND, AND GLOUCESTER CATHEDRAL FROM THE RIVER SEVERN

Photograph by F. Frith & Co., England   *Kindness Ian Forbes-Robertson, Esq.*

THE DOCKS OF GLOUCESTER, ENGLAND

fraud, some knights dressed as "woolmongers" being let in through the gates by treachery. The town also figured in the wars of 1642 and 1643.

In 1734, there was only one stage coach between Gloucester and London, which left on Monday morning and arrived in the latter city on Wednesday evening, and in these early days this was considered such an achievement that the words "Gloucester Flying Machine" were painted on the coach doors in large letters. It may be interesting to mention that several wills in the Registry begin, "Whereas I am about to take a journey to London, and whereas it is uncertain whether or not I may live to return, I do therefore think it necessary to make my last will and testament."

The Gloucester Cathedral, which is one of the finest in England, was dedicated by the Bishops of Worcester, Rochester and Bangor. Gloucester also has an old castle which dates back to the early days when such a fortress was necessary there on account of the town being the key to South Wales. The city is situated on the river Severn which is well described by these words:—

> "Queen of the Western Rivers, Severn, hail!
> The boast of Gloucester, glory of her vale,
> Long may thy broad expanse of waters sweep
> In rolling volumes to the kindred deep!"

GROTON, MASSACHUSETTS

GROTON, County Suffolk, England, is the ancestral home of our first Governor, John Winthrop, and on the south side of the church in the old town is a stone tomb placed there as a memorial to Adam Winthrop, the first of the name, who was Lord of the Manor of Groton. Here are buried Governor Winthrop's father, grandfather and possibly great-grandfather. The Winthrop coat of arms is on one end of the tomb and the Latin inscription on the side now partially obliterated translated into English reads as follows:—

> Heaven the country Christ the way. Here lies the body of Adam Winthrop, Esq., son of Adam Winthrop, Esq., who were Patrons of this Church and Lords of the Manor of Groton. The above named Adam, the son, married Anna the daughter of Henry Browne of Edwardston by whom he had one son and four daughters. He departed this life in the year of our Lord 1623, and of his own age 75. But Anna his wife, died 1628. She also is buried here with him.

> Blessed are the peacemakers; for they shall be called the sons of God.

Inside the church stands the old baptismal font and at the back of the church are two tablets, one that was taken from the old tomb outside, probably to make place for the long inscription quoted above. The inscription below came into the possession of Hon. Robert C. Winthrop of Boston, Massachusetts, who returned it to the English church. It is worded as follows:—

> Here Lyeth Mr. Adam Wynthrop Lorde and Patron of Groton, whiche departed owt of this worlde the IXth day of November, in the yere of oure Lorde God MCCCCCLXII.

The other tablet explains itself:—

> The above plate removed at some remote period from the grave in this chancel of Adam Winthrop, Esq., First Lord of this Manor and Patron of this church after the Reformation, and long in the possession of his family in America, was restored in 1878 by the Hon. Robert C. Winthrop of Boston in New England, his descendant in the eighth generation.

On the east end of the church is a large colored glass window placed there in memory of Governor John Winthrop and presented to the church by some of the Winthrop family in America, chiefly through the instrumentality of Hon. Robert C. Winthrop. There is a double window on the south side of the church just above the tomb which was placed there as a memorial to John Winthrop's first and second wives, Mary Forth and Thomasine Clopton.

The house in which the Governor of Massachusetts and his son, the Governor of Connecticut, lived is not standing today but its situation is well known. The place was sold soon after John Winthrop left there to lead the great Puritan emigration in 1630 to New England.

The town of Groton, Massachusetts, is directly indebted for its name to Deane Winthrop, a son of Governor Winthrop, who was born in the parish of Groton, County Suffolk, England, in 1622. Our plantation of Groton, therefore, was closely associated with the old home of Governor Winthrop and the birthplace of his son, Deane, who was one of the original petitioners for the incorporation of our town. Deane Winthrop lived in Groton, Massachusetts, for a number of years, dying at Pullen's Point, now part of Winthrop. He was a brother of the first Governor of Connecticut. Several of the Winthrop family living in Massachusetts today have called their residences after the old town in England.

Our Groton is closely associated with the stage coach days and once contained a number of typical New England taverns. Two of the best known stage coach drivers, whose names have come down to us, are Aaron Corey and Horace George, the latter being so obliging that he delivered messages, newspapers and packages along the road; he was particularly popular with the boys of the town because he would slow down in sleighing time to allow them to grab the straps on the back of the coach and so enable them to "ketch on behind," as it was then called. "Phin" Harrington was also another well-known driver and he was particularly noted for his great speed; he was very small and the story is told of him that on cold nights he was able to crawl into one of the large lamps on the side of the coach and warm his feet. He held the reins of the Groton stages for forty years. In 1800, or thereabouts, a stage left Boston every Wednesday, arriving in Groton in the afternoon, and it was advertised to leave Groton each Monday morning, which gives some idea of the lack of regular transportation in these early days. The charge for a single trip was two dollars.

The Massachusetts town has not placed any memorials, as far as we can learn, to any of the Winthrop family, but in 1879 the town erected a monument to commemorate the site of the first meeting house which was burned by the Indians, from whom the town suffered much. Another memorial was also set up in the town to the memory of the Longley family, ten of whom were either killed or taken into captivity by the redskins. The earliest minister of this first parish was Rev. John Miller of Cambridge College, England, who first served as assistant to Rev. Ezekiel Rogers of Rowley, and who later was one of the first ministers at Yarmouth. The original grant of the Massachusetts township was made in 1655 and this is the date of the incorporation of the town. Groton Academy, now called Lawrence Academy of Groton, was founded in 1792 and has been helped many times by Amos Lawrence and William Lawrence, this family being one of the most important in the history of the town. Other well-known names connected with Groton are Morse, Blaisdell, Blood, Ware, Woolson, Gove, Prescott, Bancroft, Waters, Mansfield, Green, Eldredge, Williams, Nelson, Stearns, Farnsworth, Bullard and Hall. Colonel

WINTHROP FAMILY TOMB, GROTON CHURCH,
GROTON, ENGLAND, SHOWING THE WINTHROP
COAT OF ARMS ON THE FRONT END

Here are buried the father, grandfather and possibly the great-
grandfather of Governor Winthrop, the first Governor of
Massachusetts. The inscription on the side of the tomb is
given in the text.

William Prescott of Bunker Hill
fame was born and lived in
the town. Groton School, also
in this town, is one of the best
known boarding schools in this
country.

There have been a few ex-
changes of presents between
the English town and its American namesake, the chief remembrance from the old town in
England being a photograph of
the church in old Groton, which
is framed together with small
pieces of stained glass from one
of the old windows in the
church, which was brought
over by the late Dr. Samuel
A. Green, a well-known resident of Groton and historian
of the town; it now hangs in
the Groton Public Library.

Groton, England, is also indirectly responsible for the
naming of Groton, Connecticut, in the year 1705, during
the Governorship of Fitz-John
Winthrop, out of respect for
the Suffolk home of his family.
There was also at one time a
Groton, New Hampshire, and
there is still in existence a Groton, Vermont, both of which were named by some
of the early settlers who came from our Groton; New York also claims a Groton,
which was likewise named after Groton, Massachusetts, and Groton, Connecticut,
there being also a Groton, Ohio, named for the Connecticut town, and one, too, in
South Dakota.

We quote a few lines of verse written by Mrs. James Gordon Carter of Groton,
although they give a rather exaggerated idea of the excitement at Groton Junction
station (now called Ayer). These verses would be better suited to this place at
the time of Camp Devens, the large New England training camp for troops during
the Great War:—

From a photograph now in the Groton Public Library, Groton, Massachusetts   *Kindness Miss Georgianna A. Boutwell and Rev. Sherrard Billings*

GROTON CHURCH, GROTON, ENGLAND,

showing the Winthrop family tomb in the outside corner of the church. Above this tomb is the double window placed there as a memorial to Governor John Winthrop's first and second wives. The large window on the right end of the church is the memorial window to John Winthrop, Governor of Massachusetts, given by members of the Winthrop family in America, at the suggestion of Hon. Robert C. Winthrop of Boston, Massachusetts. In the same frame with this picture are pieces of stained glass from Groton Church, England, shown in the cut below.

PIECES OF STAINED GLASS FROM GROTON CHURCH, GROTON, ENGLAND,

brought to Groton, Massachusetts, by the late Samuel A. Green, and presented by R. F. Swan, Esq., Postmaster of Boxford, England.

"Who, pray, in any age or nation
E'er saw a place like Groton Station?

. . . . . .

The bell is ringing, steam is hissing!
Bipeds pour out—your trunk is missing!
'What train is this? tell me, pray!'
'Why, Ma'am, these go to Nashua.'

. . . . . .

Squeezed as in nightmare or a witch hug,
In comes the upper train from Fitchburg!

.   .   .   .

All while this host of ills you're summing,
'Look out! the Boston train is coming!'
And now, alas! the plot so thickens,
The heart of the lone maiden sickens.

.   .   .   .

'This way, Miss,' some one cried,—'don't hurry;
No use in making such a flurry!'

.   .   .   .

'Take care, there!' 'Here, that's my trunk, porter!'
'Look out! I'll make you one head shorter!'
'Where do you go,—to Fitchburg? Worcester?'
'What's in this basket, John?' 'A rooster!'
'Here, take this box!' The cars are starting,
And through the air John's legs are darting.
A woman calls, 'Hannah, where's Peter?'
'Munching an apple.' 'What an eater!'
'There, now, the baby's set to crying;
For mercy's sake! what's father buying?'
'That's the wrong car,—get out, Susanna!'
'Don't cry—where did you hurt you, Hannah?'
'Where's Mr. Stiles? such work, I never!
I wish he'd come, he looks so clever.
Children, get in! the bell is ringing!
Why, do hear Mr. Fairbanks singing!'
My Muse, alas! see her wings flutter;
Panting, one warning word she'll utter:
'Beware,' she says without compunction,
'Beware, at night, of Groton Junction!'"

There was an odd character in Groton who had lost her husband whereupon a number of changes had to be made around the place, including the removal of the pigsty; the old lady was particularly downcast when this was demolished as she declared it was the only memorial of her husband she had left.

Groton, England, is an ancient town and owing to its geographical position played an important part in early English history. In the days of Norman rule this part of the country was studded with castles and fortresses, the greater part of which were in the vicinity of Groton, which in Domesday Book is called Grotena.

Samuel A. Green, Esq., in an address delivered at Groton, Massachusetts, in 1905, on the two hundred and fiftieth anniversary of the American town, speaks thus of Groton, England:—

"During my boyhood I always had a strong desire to visit Groton in England, which gave its name to this town and indirectly to six other towns in the United States. Strictly speaking, it is not a town but a parish; and there are technical distinctions between the two. . . . All my previous knowledge in regard to the

From prints in the collection of Mrs. R. C. Winthrop   *Kindness Mrs. R. C. Winthrop*

EAST WINDOW, GROTON CHURCH, GROTON, ENGLAND, 1875,

placed there in memory of John Winthrop, leader of the great Puritan emigration to New England in 1630, first Governor of Massachusetts, and founder of Boston, Massachusetts, by his descendants in America, at the suggestion of Hon. R. C. Winthrop of Boston, Massachusetts.

SOUTH WINDOW IN GROTON CHURCH, GROTON, ENGLAND, 1880,

placed over the Winthrop tomb, to the memory of the two wives of Governor John Winthrop, both of whom are buried in the chancel of the church. This window is the gift of Hon. R. C. Winthrop.

place was limited to the fact that it lay in the county of Suffolk, near its southern border. After a somewhat close study of the Railway Guide, I left London in the month of October, 1854, for Sudbury, which is the only town of considerable size in the immediate neighborhood of Groton. . . . From Sudbury I drove in a dog-cart to Boxford, where I tarried over night at White Horse Inn, and in the morning walked over to Groton, less than a mile distant. This place, the object of my pilgrimage, I found to be a typical English village of the olden time, very small both in territory and population, and utterly unlike any of its American namesakes. . . . On reaching the end of my trip I called at once on the Rector, who received me very kindly and offered to go with me to the church, which invitation I readily accepted. He expressed much interest in the New England towns bearing the name of Groton, and spoke of a visit made to the English town a few years previously, by the Honorable Robert C. Winthrop, of Boston, which gave him much pleasure. We walked over the grounds of the old manor, once belonging to John Winthrop, first Governor of Massachusetts; and Groton Place, the residence of the lord of the manor at that time, was pointed out, as well as a solitary mulberry tree, which stood in Winthrop's garden, and is now the last vestige of the spot. . . . I remember with special pleasure the attentions of Mr. R. F. Swan, post-master of Boxford, who took me to a small school of little children in that parish, where the teacher told the scholars that I had come from another Groton across the broad ocean. He also kindly made for me a rough tracing of the part of the parish in which I was particularly interested; and as I had left the inn at Boxford when he called he sent it by private hands to me at the Sudbury railway station. All these little courtesies and many more I recollect with great distinctness, and they add much to the pleasant memories of my visit to the ancestral town, which has such a numerous progeny of municipal descendants in the United States."

The English home of the Winthrop family lies midway between Hadleigh and Sudbury in the County of Suffolk. It was formerly the lordship of the Abbot of Bury and was granted in 1544, soon after the dissolution of the Monasteries, to Adam Winthrop, Esq., and this grant may be seen in the Patent Rolls of the Public Record office in London.

HARTFORD, CONNECTICUT

MAYOR and Mrs. Louis R. Cheney of Hartford, Connecticut, and several friends accepted the invitation of Hertford, England, to attend the one thousandth anniversary of the rebuilding of the old Borough, and we believe that his own words best describe his visit, the celebration, and the wonderful reception given to him and the other Hartfordites who accompanied him:—

"When I went to England in 1914, to attend the Hertford Millenary Celebration, I little imagined what was before us. It was during my term as Mayor, in response to several most urgent invitations, that I accepted, and our party sailed for Southampton about the 20th of June.

We were met at the Waterloo Station, in London, by the Mayor, Town Clerk, and a councillor of Hertford, who escorted us to our hotel and told us of the honors in store for us. The first one was that we were to be invited to dine and sleep at the Marquess of Salisbury's as he was their Lord High Steward. The invitation duly arrived from Lady Salisbury, and we accepted without any unnecessary delay.

We arrived at Hatfield House, a party of six, in time for tea and were most cordially greeted by Lady Salisbury, who had visiting her, Miss Balfour (sister of the Hon. Arthur James Balfour), Lord and Lady Eustace Cecil (brother of the late Marquess, the great statesman and diplomat and father of the present Lord Salisbury), Lady Mary Cecil and Lady Arran.

The exercises, on the following day, were conducted on the Castle Grounds, before an audience of about three thousand people. After the presentation ceremonies, I was given the freedom of the platform (unexpectedly to me at that time) and presented the congratulations and best wishes of our Hartford to the Mother City. The credit of naming our Hartford after their Hertford was attributed to John Haynes, the first elected Gov. of Connecticut. I was very proud to claim him as an ancestor on that occasion. He came from Essex, near Hertfordshire, with Rev. John Hooker, and Samuel Stone, and was very prominent, owning quite an estate of his own over there.

After the exercises in the open, we sat down to a bountiful luncheon (about one hundred of us) at which the nobility was largely represented. We drank to the king's health standing, and when Lord Salisbury toasted Mr. Balfour, the latter broke down, and it was very touching to see a great statesman so moved. I was then toasted and got out of the dilemma as best I could. We next went to the castle grounds to see a wonderful pageant, setting forth the history of Hertford, up to Queen Elizabeth's time. As a delicate attention to our party they sang the words of 'America' to the tune of 'God Save the King'—a custom of our own.

The pageant was given every day for a week. I was greatly honored by being made President of the Pageant on one of the following days. On this occasion the deputy mayoress was presented with a bouquet of flowers by the school children. All of the townspeople were most cordial and showed their appreciation of our coming so far to participate in their celebration by seeing that many doors were opened to us, which are generally closed to the usual visitor."

It is particularly interesting to note that Mr. Cheney was descended from John Haynes who had come from Essex, near Hertfordshire, and who named the Connecticut town "Hartford" in honour of his friend Samuel Stone of Hertford, England, who accompanied Hooker on the pilgrimage from Massachusetts, as shown in the cut on page 152. These three men organized the First Church of Hartford and founded the colony on the banks of the Connecticut River, first calling it "Newtowne" after the town they had left in Massachusetts (now called "Cambridge"). Haynes later became the first Governor of this little Connecticut colony.

Among the interesting things brought back from England by Mayor Cheney was the photograph of the baptismal record on parchment in All Saints Church, which gives an account of the baptism of Samuel Stone in these words:—

"July 1602. Samuell, soone of Jhon Stones was baptyzed 30th."

In parentheses under the photograph appears this note:—

"One of the founders of Hartford, Conn. U.S.A. 1636."

Another interesting relic in the old church is the baptismal font which was used to baptize Stone.

The Mayor of the Connecticut town made several speeches, which he has been too modest to give us but we feel sure that he did justice to the occasion. His visit was of particular interest both to England and America for the reason that within the last nine years, our Hartford has had a Mayor who was a lineal descendant of one of the principal personages connected with the founding of the town, and

From "History of Antiquities of New England, New York and New Jersey"

REV. THOMAS HOOKER AND HIS CONGREGATION ON THEIR LONG JOURNEY FROM
NEWTOWNE (NOW CAMBRIDGE) TO FOUND HARTFORD, CONNECTICUT

another Mayor who could trace his ancestry back to Hooker. Americans will also
be interested in the number of Hadhams in the vicinity of the borough of Hertford
which reminds them of the variations of the same name in New England.

Hartford, Connecticut, received the following message, sent over after Colonel
Cheney's return home:—

"Borough of Hertford
    in the
County of Hertford
    England.

At a Quarterly Meeting of the Council of
the Borough of Hertford, duly convened and
holden at the Town Hall, Hertford, on
Wednesday, the 29th day of July, 1914, at
6 o'clock in the evening, precisely,

It was Unanimously Resolved:—

That the Members of this Council have received with the utmost
pleasure an Address from the MAYOR, ALDERMEN and COUNCILMEN of
the CITY of HARTFORD, in the STATE of CONNECTICUT and UNITED
STATES of AMERICA, on the OCCASION of the CELEBRATION of the
MILLENARY of the REBUILDING of this TOWN by KING EDWARD THE
ELDER, and desire to return their sincere thanks for the kindly greetings
and good wishes therein expressed.

THEY most earnestly reciprocate the hope that the cordial and
friendly relations that exist between this Borough and its Offspring
beyond the seas may long continue.

THEY further desire to express their intense gratification that the
Deputy Mayor and Mayoress (Colonel and Mrs. Cheney) and a number

Photograph by Arthur V. Elsden   *Kindness Ian Forbes-Robertson, Esq.*

ALL SAINTS CHURCH, HERTFORD, ENGLAND

In this church is the baptismal register of Samuel Stone, the founder of Hartford, Connecticut.   He was baptized in 1602.

From a photograph   *Kindness Hon. Louis R. Cheney*

MAYOR, ALDERMEN AND COUNCILMEN OF HERTFORD, ENGLAND

This picture, taken in front of Hertford Castle, is part of a collection of framed pictures of the English town in City Hall, Hartford, Connecticut.

of the Citizens of Hartford, Connecticut, were able to attend the Millenary Celebration, and sincerely trust that their guests will carry home with them the happiest recollections of their visit, and of the welcome they received.

THE CORPORATE SEAL of the Mayor, Aldermen and Burgesses of the Borough of Hertford, England, was hereunto affixed by WILLIAM FRAMPTON ANDREWS, Mayor, in the presence of Alfred Baker,
      Town Clerk."

                 W. F. ANDREWS
                      Mayor.

In the offices of the Town Clerk in Hertford Castle hang the photographs of the Common Council of our Connecticut city, which were presented about 1904 by Mayor William F. Henney. We also understand that in 1891 Americans subscribed a considerable sum of money to build St. Nicholas Hall in the Parish of St. Andrew's which adjoins All Saints Church, the church of Samuel Stone. At this time a fête was held in Hertford, which was attended by the American Ambassador, who referred to the fact that when his native city, Chicago, was destroyed by fire it was from England that the first help came. Some of the prominent manufacturers of the Connecticut city sent over articles to help make the occasion a success. Many views of Hartford were presented to the Marchioness of Salisbury, when she opened the fête.

There has been much speculation and curiosity as to why the English town is spelled with an "e" and the Connecticut town with an "a." Colonel Cheney tells us that our town was not misspelled, and claims that it is the English town that really has made the error. In proof of this assertion he explains that the seal of the English town, upon which appears the figure of a hart, or deer, has on the margin the word "HArtforde," the additional "e" being the old English form of spelling. Another proof perhaps is the fact that the English town is always pronounced as if it were spelled "Harford." It is also interesting to note that in an account of Hertford Castle published in 1589, the name is spelled with an "a" instead of an "e," which should prove to us pretty conclusively that it is the mother town that has strayed from the correct method of spelling, while her child, our town, adhered to the original and proper spelling.

Hertford was four hundred years older than the thousand years for which this celebration was held, being inhabited by a sturdy race of Britons before the Saxons conquered the country. It was a flourishing town when the great Saxon king, Alfred, allowed the cakes of the peasant's wife to burn, thereby enduring a scolding by the angry woman, who, of course, did not know she was tongue-lashing her sovereign.

Hertford is situated at the meeting point of three rivers, the Maran, the Beane, and the Lea, and as far back as the time of the Cæsars there was a British

From "Picturesque Hertford"   Published by Rose & Sons

PORT HILL, HERTFORD, ENGLAND

From "History of the First Church in Hartford"   By Rev. George Leon Walker, D.D.

MONUMENTS IN THE CENTER CHURCH BURYING GROUND IN HARTFORD,
CONNECTICUT, TO THE MEMORY OF ITS EARLY SETTLERS

The Haynes, Hooker and Stone memorials are on the right.

settlement on this site, which was at that time called "Durocobriva," meaning "conflux of waters." The situation was one to attract the East Saxons, who renamed the town "Hertsforda," and it became the residence of the Saxon kings. Others claim that Hertford, which gives its name to the county as well as to the borough and market town, is named for "Ford of the Harts," while other historians assert that its name is derived from the Saxon word "Herudford," meaning "Red Ford." The river Lea connected Hertford with London before the days of the rail-road, and this may be the reason that the National Synod was held there in 673 by King Ecfried, sometimes spelled Egfrid, which is claimed to have been the precursor of the English Parliament. The Saxons in their turn were subjected to the attacks of the Danes and in the reign of Alfred the town was raided and burned to the ground; but the great Saxon king built a dyke to keep out the tides, thereby preventing the Danes from using the Lea, as they previously had done, and by this act he saved the town.

Edward the Elder built Hertford Castle in the year 906, and after the conquest the Normans rebuilt it, surrounding it with a moat and walls of steel and flint, some of which remain to this day. It is especially interesting to find that the first Governor of the Castle appointed by William the Conqueror was an ancestor of Governor Haynes and Mayor Cheney of our Hartford. This post was afterwards

Photographed by Arthur V. Elsden   *Kindness Ian Forbes-Robertson, Esq.*

HERTFORD CASTLE, HERTFORD, ENGLAND

On these grounds the Hertford Millenary celebration took place in 1914, at which Mayor Louis R. Cheney of Hartford was present as the official representative of the Connecticut city.

given to one of the Norman barons who had distinguished himself against the English, and as a reward the castle was bestowed upon him, remaining the property of his family for years. It may also be of interest to mention that in this old castle were married Isabel of Castile and Prince Edward Plantagenet, the fourth surviving son of King Edward III. When Henry VIII ascended the throne the castle was in a dilapidated condition, but as he desired it for a future residence, he gave orders to have it restored. Both Queen Mary and Queen Elizabeth spent much of their girlhood there, their presence being still recalled by a path called the "Queen's Bench Walk." Another fact of historical interest is that during the plague in London both in 1563 and 1589 Parliament sat in Hertford Castle. In 1628 it was granted by King Charles to William Cecil, the second Earl of Salisbury, and has been in the family ever since. Charles Lamb has been closely associated with Hertfordshire, and sometimes we hear it mentioned as "Lamb's County." An old proverb asserts that

> "He who buys a house in Hertfordshire,
> Pays three-quarters for the air."

The name of Morgan seems to have been distinguished in Hertford, as well as in Hartford, for we read that there was a Robert Morgan in the English city who was granted by the King special permission "that henceforth during his life in the presence of us, or our heirs, or in the presence of any other, or others, whomsoever, at any times hereafter be covered with his hat on his head, and not take off or lay aside his hat from his head, for any reason or cause, against his will or pleasure." He undoubtedly bestowed great favors upon the town, as his namesake, J. P. Morgan, has bestowed upon our city.

If we turn again to the American city we find that Hooker, with Stone (who it will be remembered was born in Hertford), first came to Newtowne from England on the invitation of certain Newtowne settlers who had in England attended worship with the Rev. Mr. Hooker. They sailed for this country in 1633 and when they arrived their friends said that their "three great necessities were now supplied, for they had *Cotton* for their clothing, *Hooker* for their fishing, and *Stone* for their building." Monuments have been

Photographed for the State Street Trust Company by Arthur V. Elsden
Kindness Ian Forbes-Robertson, Esq.

THIS TABLET IS PLACED IN ST. NICHOLAS HALL IN HERTFORD, ENGLAND,

to record the assistance of citizens of Hartford, Connecticut, who subscribed funds to help rebuild this hall, which is in the Parish of St. Andrew, adjoining that of All Saints, in the church of which parish can still be seen the baptismal register of Samuel Stone, who was one of the founders of Hartford, Connecticut.

placed in Hartford over the graves of Hooker, Stone and Haynes and we give a picture of them on page 155.

It may be interesting to Harvard men to record that as early as 1644 a small colony in Connecticut "took measures conserneing the mayntenaunce of scollers of Cambridge."

HARWICH, MASSACHUSETTS

A PICTURESQUE Cape Cod village, with here and there a velvety, green lawn bordered with whitewashed stones; trim gravel paths leading up to scrupulously neat white cottages, where a few gray-haired sea captains still pace up and down the porches, as they once trod the decks of the old ships in the days that are past,—such is the little town of Harwich, Massachusetts. Far across the ocean where the rivers Stour and Orwell meet in old England is the ancient borough of Harwich, called in olden times Har-wic, from which the New England town receives its name. By whom or under what circumstances the name was given will always be a matter of conjecture, but it was probably suggested by Patrick Butler, one of the residents of the Massachusetts village, who is said to have walked all the way to Boston to obtain the act of incorporation, which was granted on September 14, 1694. Certain it is that there must have been some of those early settlers for whom the old maritime town in Essex County, England, held tender memories, and this link which bound the old England town to the one in New England was strong and continued so through all these many years.

In 1907, Charles M. Robbins, Esq., a native of our Harwich, made a trip to Europe, and while in England he visited the ancient borough for which his native town was named, and purchased numerous prints and pictures of old Harwich, which he presented, on his return, to the Massachusetts town; some of these are now hanging on the walls of the town clerk's office, while others are in the Chase Library at West Harwich.

From a photograph   *Kindness John H. Paine, Esq.*

FLAGSTONE FROM A STREET IN HARWICH,
ENGLAND,

now placed in the pavement at the entrance to the Exchange
Building, Harwich, Massachusetts.

HARWICH.

LONDON PUBLISHED BY McKINSTONE, 106 LEADENHALL STREET 1840.

HARWICH, ENGLAND

From a rare old print by W. J. Huggins, in the possession of a Boston collector

Formerly in the collection of Brooks Reed, Esq.

Mr. Robbins also visited the borough officials of Harwich, England, including the Mayor, the Clerk, and the Superintendent of Public Works, and intimated to them that he would appreciate some suitable souvenir which he might present to Harwich, Massachusetts, in memory of its worthy namesake across the sea. He persuaded the Superintendent of Public Works to ship to Harwich, Massachusetts, a flagstone that had been in the sidewalk in front of the City Hall for over two hundred years, but which, owing to its position in a jog, or corner, was only slightly worn. Upon its arrival at the Cape Cod town, this stone was properly inscribed by Mr. Henry T. Crosby, the marble worker of Harwich, and was placed in the sidewalk in front of the Exchange Building, owned by the town, which prominent position it now occupies.

Like the English Harwich, the Cape Cod town is a popular seaside resort; and for those who appreciate history as well as fresh air, there are also to be found in each town numerous historical associations. Off the coast of Harwich, England, Alfred's fleet encountered the Danes in the year 885, and many years afterwards, in 1666, there, too, occurred a memorable engagement between the Dutch and the English.

Less stirring, but no less interesting to lovers of history, are the associations which cluster about the Bay State town. The territory comprised in the township, with the exception of a large tract on the southwest, is a part of the original section selected by the "Purchasers or Old Comers" of the Plymouth colony, and granted to them upon the surrender of the patent in 1640. Across the mouth of the inlet of Muddy Cove, or Long Cove, as it is sometimes called, where the Wading Place bridge connects the towns of Harwich and Chatham, the Indians used to ford the river on their way from one town to the other, and near the boundary stone where the tide gate has been built stood their weir. A short distance northwest of the mouth of the cove is the site of the farm where lived Micah Ralph, the last full-blooded Indian in Harwich. The first settler in the town of Harwich, as far as is known, was Gershom Hall, who was born in our Barnstable in 1648 and who came from the territory now called North Dennis; as a farmer, millwright and lay preacher he was a prominent person in the colony.

The Massachusetts town was not destined to compete as an industrial center with her English prototype, where shipbuilding and fishing are carried on quite extensively and where large cement works are also located. During the early part of the nineteenth century the manufacture of marine salt was an important industry at Harwich, Massachusetts, but in time the decline in the price of salt and the increase in the cost of the works unfortunately led to the abandonment of the business. At one period, however, in her history, the Cape Cod town had quite a reputation as a fishing center, and her sturdy sons became expert in the use of the harpoon on their whaling expeditions. At first a large number of whales were to be found in the vicinity of the Cape, and small boats were employed in the pursuit of them, but later, as they withdrew to more peaceful feeding grounds, the whalemen went after them in sloops, and finally schooners were used. Cod and

From an old print   *Kindness Perry Walton, Esq.*

HARWICH, ENGLAND

mackerel fishing each enjoyed a period of prosperity, but now they, too, have declined. The cultivation of cranberries is now the principal industry of the town. The goddess of industry has tarried at this picturesque town, and passed on, leaving to Harwich only the memory of those glorious days when her ships sailed the many seas.

The harbour of Harwich, Essex, England, is large enough to hold a hundred ships of war, and is almost the only feature of this town. It is now the permanent headquarters of the Admiral of Patrols and of the Torpedo Destroyer Flotillas operating in the North Sea, with a range of action extending from Dover to the Firth of Forth. The town itself is of little interest, though to the stranger some of its narrow streets and wooden houses would appeal strongly. The Old Cups Hotel is interesting, its oak-panelled rooms reminding one of its age. There is still shown the room in which the great Lord Nelson slept during his visits there, but it is, alas! fast passing into decay.

Just south of the town is Beacon Hill, upon which is situated one of the most powerful forts along the coast, but so artfully concealed that the visitor might easily pass by without knowing it. Strangely enough, there is a Bunker's Hill a mile out from the town, but it is only a nickname taken from the name of a man who kept a public house at its foot.

The Saxon Chronicles mention a battle fought near Harwich in 885 between King Alfred the Great's fleet and sixteen Danish ships. Orwell was the name of the town in bygone times, but the sea washed it entirely away, and upon its ruins Harwich rose. Being the only harbour of refuge between the Thames and the Humber, it naturally became an important place for shipping. Edward II gave the first charter to Harwich in 1318. It was his successor, Edward III, who sailed from this port in 1340 with a fleet of 260 sail to attack the French fleet at Sluys near Flanders, where he gained the great victory.

The most notable event, however, in the history of the town was the German capitulation which began on November 20, 1918, with the surrender to Admiral Tyrwhitt of over two hundred German U-boats. These vessels that were to cause the destruction of England, found a safe anchorage in Harwich Harbour.

Queen Elizabeth immortalized the name of Harwich by calling it "Happy-go-lucky Harwich," lucky indeed, for although the Germans made many raids upon the town, only twice did a bomb fall there, and fortunately neither of them exploded.

Dovercourt, the "West End" of the Borough of Harwich, is fast becoming a summer resort. The famous diarist Pepys once represented Harwich in Parliament.

HINGHAM, MASSACHUSETTS

BETWEEN the years 1633 and 1639 a good many persons migrated to Hingham, which was then called Bare Cove. A few families came over here in 1633 and took up land on Planter's Hill, now part of the Brewer estate and known as "World's End Farm." This strip of land is situated across the water in front of the late Hon. John D. Long's residence. Several followed in 1634, but the largest number came over in 1635, most of them from old Hingham, Norfolk, arriving in Charlestown, after an extended voyage; they then came down the harbour in an open pinnace into the small stream which runs by the mill-dam and through the town, almost up to the present jail, and started their settlement near the foot of the present Ship Street. On this historic spot is a memorial which reads as follows:—

In grateful memory of
Reverend Peter Hobart and
that company of English men and women
who founded the town of
Hingham
landing near this spot in September
1635
Erected by Old Colony Chapter
Daughters of the American Revolution
1913

THE OLD MEETING HOUSE, OFTEN CALLED "THE OLD SHIP CHURCH," HINGHAM,
MASSACHUSETTS. ERECTED 1681

The Memorial Tower in honour of the early settlers stands on the right of the Old Meeting House.

HINGHAM, ENGLAND

ROOM ON SECOND FLOOR OF THE HINGHAM MEMORIAL TOWER,

placed there in memory of Rev. Peter Hobart, first minister of this settlement and a settler here in 1635. He was born in Hingham, England, in 1602. The inscription over the mantlepiece is given in the text. The desk and chair on the left were brought over from old Hingham by Rev. Louis C. Cornish and date from about 1650. The chair on the right was brought from old Hingham, probably in 1635, by a member of the Lincoln family, in which it continued in unbroken succession until recently presented to the Hingham Memorial. The Lincoln family of Hingham, Massachusetts, are descendants of the Lincolns of Hingham, England. Abraham Lincoln was of the Hingham family.

Mr. Cushing, the third town clerk, gives a record "of such persons as came out of the town of Hingham, and the towns adjacent, in the county of Norfolk, in the kingdom of England, into New England, and settled in Hingham." He also stated that "The whole number who came out of Norfolk, chiefly from Hingham and its vicinity, from 1633 to 1639, and settled in Hingham, was two hundred and six." There is no question but that this town was named after the town of the same name in England where most of these early settlers had lived. Among the earliest to move to the new town were Peter Hobart, the first minister, and Robert Peck, who were the most prominent men of their time in the plantation; also among other early comers were the Lincolns, Herseys, Cushings, Jacobs, Wilders, Burrs, Thaxters, Spragues, Chubbucks, Andrews, Bates, Stoddards, Stowells, Gardners,

Beals, Towers, Leavitts, Ripleys, Joys, Marshes, Lanes and Whitons. On a hill across the creek opposite this early settlement were established earthworks and a fort and the remains can be seen today in the center of the old cemetery. On top of this hill is the First Meeting House, whose congregation was gathered in 1635 in an earlier meeting house, and later moved to the present building which was erected in 1681. This meeting house is the oldest place of public worship now in use in the United States and is well worthy of a visit. On entering one notices particularly the bell rope which hangs down in the center of the church, just as it did in the early days of the plantation, one of its functions being to give warn-

ing of any Indian attacks. In a corner of the church are still preserved the old pews, numbered 6, 37, 46, 47, and 51, which were occupied by the early church-goers, and many of the families of the original settlers still own pews in the church. There is a bronze tablet near the pulpit which gives the ministers' names from the time of Rev. Peter Hobart in 1635 to the present, there having been only eleven preachers in all these many years. Nearby is a carving of St. Peter's keys on a block of wood taken from the church in Hingham, England, and sent to our Hingham; it dates back to the Reformation. The church also uses the baptismal bowl which, according to the best authorities, dates prior to the year 1590, and which was brought over by the early comers. One should be sure to climb to the top of the church and see the curious curved rafters which support the roof and which are shaped like the ribs of a ship; it is on account of these unusual old beams, that the meeting house has been called the Old Ship Church. This form of building was commonly known in England as a ship church and, from being one of many, it is now the only survivor of the type in this country.

From a photograph   Kindness Rev. Louis C. Cornish,
                           Rev. Houghton Page and
                           Gustavus O. Henderson, Esq.

REAR VIEW OF THE TOWER IN HINGHAM, MASSACHUSETTS,

showing part of the ancient cemetery used by the early settlers. This tower was erected by the people of our Hingham and descendants of the settlers on the occasion of the two hundred and seventy-fifth anniversary of the founding of the town, and dedicated to the memory of the early settlers. Rev. Louis C. Cornish was chiefly responsible for the building of this campanile. The mounting-block, sent from Hingham, England, is on the ground floor. In the belfry are bells, copies of those in Hingham, England, and other nearby towns in Norfolk County, England. On the second story of the tower is the Hobart room shown in another cut.

The Massachusetts Hingham has had closer relations with its English mother than have most of the other American towns which have been named for English ones. On the two hundred and seventy-fifth anniversary of the founding of the new Hingham, a memorial tower was erected in memory of the first settlers by public subscription and through the efforts of Rev. Louis C. Cornish. It is situated at the entrance of the old burying ground where many of the forefathers are buried and adjacent to the Old Ship Church. In the belfry of this tower are eleven bells made in London, which are copies of the bells in churches at Hingham, Norwich, and several other adjacent towns in the county of Norfolk, England. In the lower part of the tower is the following inscription:—

This Memorial
erected by public subscription on the 275th anniversary of the settlement
commemorates the men and women
who for the sake of liberty and at great sacrifice
came out from Hingham, England, and towns adjacent
between the years 1633 and 1638
and on the edge of the wilderness
established this free plantation of New Hingham

1633 Ralph Smith, Nicholas Jacob, Thomas Lincoln,
Edmund Hobart, Theophilus Cushing, Edmund Hobart, Sr.,
Joshua Hobart, Henry Gibbs
etc., etc.

Also in this tower is one of the most interesting relics in new Hingham, the Hingham Stone, which was sent by old Hingham to its namesake here as an anniversary gift, and which is supposed to be the only stone that could be found in Hingham, England. The following inscription in the tower describes this stone:—

The Hingham Stone
long used as a mounting block
is believed to have stood
for centuries on the Village Green
and to have been known
to the Forefathers before the migration.
It was given by Hingham, Norfolk
to Hingham, Massachusetts
for this Memorial
and was presented to the Town
on October 9, 1911 by the
Right Hon. James Bryce, D.C.L.
Ambassador for Great Britain
to the United States.

On the second story of the tower is a room dedicated to the memory of Peter Hobart, and over the fireplace in the corner are inscribed on a panel the following words:—

To the Memory of the Revd. Peter Hobart, M.A. Born in Old Hingham 1602 Died in New Hingham 1678 Educated in Cambridge University, Lecturer and Preacher in English Parishes, he emigrated to America in 1635, and became one of the Founders, and the First Minister of this free Plantation. Leader in religious and civil affairs, courageous champion of the rights of man, for forty three years Preacher of the Word of God on this far Edge of the Wilderness, he walked by faith, and left upon this community & upon New England the impress of his high ideal of reverent freedom, which endures & shall endure "Here shall the light of memory be kindled."

This room is panelled with wide pine boards given by someone in Michigan who showed a particular interest in Hobart. The room contains a desk and chair which were brought to this country from old Hingham by Rev. Mr. Cornish, who in 1913 visited the English Hingham as one of a committee appointed by the town to present a substitute stone as a recognition of the action of the English town already described. Besides Mr. Cornish and his wife, this committee included Mr. and Mrs. Isaac Sprague and their son. This is the only official visit made from our Hingham, though many citizens of our town have visited the English town of the same name. The official presentation of this stone, which took place before the townspeople, is shown in the cut on page 170. Between the poles on each side were the words "Old—Hingham—New" and on the other side appeared "1637—Welcome—1913." Upon the platform stood the block of granite which now has been placed on the edge of the village green, where it replaces the old mounting block which stood outside the blacksmith shop and which now is in this country. The inscription above the stone is given under the cut on page 168.

After appropriate remarks a luncheon was served in the White Hart Inn, which was followed by a reception at the residence of Rev. Canon Upcher, the Rector of the Hingham Parish. Rev. Mr. Cornish in his pamphlet says:—

"The gift also expressed a great hope. May not these stones exchanged between the Hinghams be stepping stones to closer friendship between Anglo-Saxon people? . . . When all the towns in both countries feel the same hearty good will no ill will can exist between the nations. . . . The two Hinghams, when all is said, are strands in the bonds of confidence that bind English speaking people together."

The following day as the Committee left the village many of the inhabitants were in their doorways waving the visitors a farewell. Near the old English town are to be found Norwich, Yarmouth, Ipswich, Weston, Wrentham, Boxford, Stoneham, Lynn, Sudbury, Attleboro, Cambridge and Boston, all of which names can be found in both countries.

Just before America entered the Great War our Hingham took up a public subscription for the benefit of the war sufferers in English Hingham, and collected fifteen hundred dollars for this purpose. In return, a copy of the roll of honour of the English town during the war was sent over here and is now in the town building.

From a photograph sent by Hingham, England, to Rev. Louis C. Cornish, formerly of Hingham, Massachusetts
Kindness Rev. Louis C. Cornish

MOUNTING BLOCK NEAR THE VILLAGE GREEN, HINGHAM, ENGLAND

The inscription above the stone reads: "This stone was given in 1913 by the people of Hingham, Massachusetts, to replace the Ancient Mounting Block which stood upon this spot, presented to them in 1911 by Hingham, Norfolk." (England)

Very recently Mr. Cornish made another visit to old Hingham and made a speech on the village green listened to by a large number of the inhabitants of the old town.

Rev. Ebenezer Gay, known as the father of American Unitarianism, seems to have been one of the wits of our Hingham in the early days. Once he was riding to Boston with a friend and as they were crossing Boston Neck he was asked jocosely by his companion, "Where would you be, my friend, if those gallows had their due?" "Riding alone to Boston" was the prompt reply.

The second parish of Hingham was formed at Cohasset, where an interesting interchange of presents with the old Hingham took place only a few years ago. The Rector of St. Stephen's Church in Cohasset obtained from St. Andrew's Episcopal Church in Hingham, England, part of the old baptismal font which now forms part of the font in the Cohasset church. This font dates from the fourteenth century and in it five generations of Lincolns in England were baptized. In return a former Cohasset Rector, Rev. Milo H. Gates, D.D., obtained subscriptions from a number of persons in this country for a bust of Abraham Lincoln which was sent to the Church in old Hingham, the home of Lincoln's ancestors, and which was unveiled in 1919 by Hon. J. W. Davis, American Ambassador to the Court of St. James. Samuel Lincoln, a Norfolk weaver, was the first of the family to migrate to America and the name of Lincoln has ever since been closely

identified with the old and new Hinghams. The inscription on this tablet reads as follows:—

From the "Landmark," the Magazine of the English-Speaking Union

BUST OF ABRAHAM LINCOLN IN THE PARISH CHURCH OF HINGHAM, ENGLAND,

presented by some of his descendants, and others living in America, through the instrumentality of Rev. Milo H. Gates, D.D., former rector of St. Stephen's Church, Cohasset. Cohasset was originally a part of Hingham, Massachusetts.

> In this Parish for many generations
> Lived the Lincolns,
> Ancestors of the American,
> ABRAHAM LINCOLN
> To him, greatest of that lineage,
> Many citizens of the United States
> Have erected this memorial,
> In the hope that for all ages,
> Between that land and
> This land and all lands,
> There shall be
> "Malice toward none,
> With charity for all."

The American Ambassador said in the course of his speech:—

"It was from this village that Lincoln's progenitors set out almost three hundred years ago to taste the great adventure of the new world, and to join with those bold and hardy pioneers who were carving a new home out of the Transatlantic wilderness. Samuel Lincoln, the Norfolk weaver, left Hingham, according to tradition, in the year 1637, Abraham Lincoln, his remote descendant, returns today in this memorial."

There is also a Lincoln statue in Manchester, England, and in Edinboro, Scotland.

Mr. Cornish, at the request of the Trust Company, describes Hingham, England, in these words:—

"Hingham, Norfolk, lies sixteen miles distant from the city of Norwich, and about seven miles from the nearest railway station. A rich farming country naturally centers in this ancient village. A beautiful and large Gothic church with a lofty tower stands adjacent to the village square, which is surrounded by low brick houses. From this village between the years 1633 and 1638 about two hundred families removed for conscience

From a photograph   *Kindness Rev. Louis C. Cornish and Rev. Houghton Page*

SCENE ON THE VILLAGE COMMON OF HINGHAM, ENGLAND,

at the time of the presentation, on August 11, 1913, of the stone sent by residents of Hingham, Massachusetts, to replace the mounting block now in the memorial tower in our Hingham. The committee from
the Massachusetts town on this occasion was composed of Rev. Louis C. Cornish and Mrs. Cornish, Mr.
and Mrs. Isaac Sprague and their son.

sake and established the Free Plantation of New Hingham, now the town of Hingham,
Massachusetts. An ancient record preserved in the Library of Cambridge University,
England, begins with these words, 'The humble petition of the poor ruinated town of
Hingham, Norfolk,' and tells of the empty houses and forlorn condition after half the
people had come overseas. The exodus is still held in remembrance in Old Hingham."

MELROSE, MASSACHUSETTS

WE believe that there are a good many residents of our Melrose who do
not realize that in Trinity Church is a carved stone taken from the
ruins of Melrose Abbey, Scotland. It was brought to this country
largely through the efforts of Mr. William L. Williams of our Melrose, and at the
present time it is under the support of one of the trusses on the south side of the
Church, the tablet nearby marking its history in these words:—

The above carved stone once formed a part of the Abbey Church of St.
Mary, Melrose, Scotland, built about A.D. 1400. It was obtained

through the kind offices of Alexander T. Simson, Esq., Gildon Grove, Melrose, and the Rev. James C. Herdman, Melrose and presented to William L. Williams of this town, and by him to Trinity Parish, A.D. 1886.

Except for occasional visits to the old town by citizens of our Melrose, we know of no other connecting links, excepting a stained glass window in the Melrose Highlands Club, the gift of Frank A. Messenger, Esq., which shows portions of the Abbey. The latest inhabitant of our Melrose to receive a present from the old country was Lieut. Carl E. Shumway, who while in Boston, England, in 1918, was presented by the Mayor with a stone from the old church there.

Our Melrose was formerly called "Malden North End" and "North Malden" and still before that "Pond Feilde." Originally it belonged to Charlestown, which then included what is now Somerville, Malden, Everett, Woburn, Melrose, Stoneham, Cambridge, West Cambridge and Reading, and a large part of Medford.

Many townships were later formed from these original lands, which reduced this territory to its present limits. Melrose was settled in the early days, although the town was not incorporated until 1850. It is certain that it was called after its Scotch namesake, but there has seemed to be a controversy as to whether the name was given by William Bogle of Glasgow, Scotland, who moved to our Melrose, or by Rev. John McLeish, pastor of the Methodist Protestant Church at that time. It is apparent that there was a meeting at Mr. Bogle's house at which the question of the name was discussed, one of those present making the remark:—

Photograph taken for the State Street Trust Company   *By George B. Brayton*

TRINITY CHURCH, MELROSE, MASSACHUSETTS

In this church is a stone from Melrose Abbey, Scotland.

MELROSE, SCOTLAND
Market Square from East.

CHANCEL AND EAST WINDOW, MELROSE ABBEY, SCOTLAND

From a photograph   *Kindness Ian Forbes-Robertson, Esq.*

MELROSE ABBEY, FOUNDED BY DAVID I, KING OF SCOTLAND

A stone from this Abbey was sent as a present to Trinity Church, Melrose, Massachusetts.

"I know a beautiful little town in Scotland which resembles this section so much that I should like to have our new town named after it. It is Melrose."

The prominent names connected with the present city have been Sprague, Green, Barrett, Lynde, Upham, Vinton, Howard and Guild.

The name of the Scotch town, often spoken of as "Fair Melrose," is derived from the British "Moal Ross," meaning a projection of meadow. At one time it was also known by the name of "Malerose." Poets have sung of Melrose and its Abbey, and of the river Tweed, which runs by the town, and therefore, we will not attempt to write of the place, or the wonders of this Abbey, of which Chambers made the remark, "To say that it is beautiful is to say nothing." The Abbey was founded by David I, and was dedicated in 1146 to the Virgin Mary. David I entrusted the Abbey to a body of Cistercian monks from Yorkshire. The abbots of Melrose were noted for their sanctity and knowledge. The Abbey was restored by Robert Bruce in 1326 and Sir Walter Raleigh also did much to preserve its ruins. The winding river, gardens and village, and hamlets nearby make the scenery most attractive. The town suffered much during the wars between England and Scotland.

Photograph by Henry Cooper & Son   *Kindness Ian Forbes-Robertson, Esq.*

THE ELEANOR CROSS, NORTHAMPTON, ENGLAND

One of the three crosses that remain standing today, out of a total of ten or twelve which King Edward I erected for his beloved Queen, one on each of the successive spots where the body rested on its "funeral way" to Westminster Abbey, November, 1290.

NORTHAMPTON, MASSACHUSETTS

NORTHAMPTON is known to New Englanders and to many persons throughout the whole United States as being the home of Hon. Calvin Coolidge, the esteemed Governor of Massachusetts and Republican nominee for Vice President in 1920, whose name during the important election of 1919 "for law and order" traveled across the seas to the mother town and other places in England and even in France.

The English Northampton has always shown great interest in her daughter and at the time of the two hundred and fiftieth anniversary of the Massachusetts town, held in 1904, Hon. Samuel S. Campion, Alderman of Northampton, England, happened to be visiting the St. Louis Exhibition and was invited to be present. He was able to accept and began the ceremony with an address to the children of the Sunday-schools, saying among other things:—

"Boys and girls,—or shall I say brothers and sisters,—I am from Northampton, England, and am standing on the sacred soil of New England. I am sure that no person sang with more earnestness than I the hymn this morning,

'O God, beneath Thy guiding hand
Our exiled fathers crossed the sea.'

Those brave old Puritans and Pilgrims were your fathers and my fathers. I come from Northampton, England, to greet you, boys and girls, and you children of an older growth, on this auspicious anniversary, and it is with peculiar pleasure that I find myself addressing a Sunday-school gathering in the City of Northampton, Mass. First, let me say how warmly I appreciate the kind words which the Governor has said in regard to my coming here. . . . I come to bring the greetings of the Sunday-school children and workers of old Northampton to the Sunday-school children and workers of this old city in the new Continent. . . . And I know they feel the greatest interest in your Celebration, and wish you all the greatest happiness and the highest success in your school work."

After the address, the school-children voted to send a reply to the school-children of the old town. Mr. Campion in a later speech told the Northamptonites of the first Norman church and castle in his town, the history of which is connected with the life of that remarkable figure in history, Thomas à Becket, Archbishop of Canterbury. These buildings are still standing, as is also another monument known as Queen Eleanor's Cross. Mr. Campion continued his remarks by adding that the people of old Northampton in the seventeenth century "were men, men with strong convictions and unbendable backbone, and their womenfolk were of the same heroic mould as themselves. It was of such stuff that the early settlers were made, whom the old country sent over to form your settlements here—to create a new Northampton in Massachusetts." Later in the celebration, Mr. Campion told his hearers of the Norman Conquest, when William the Conqueror

From large hanger printed in commemoration of British-American Peace Centenary, Christmas Eve, A.D. 1814–1914

THE ANCESTRAL HOME OF THE FAMILY OF GEORGE WASHINGTON, IN SULGRAVE,
NORTHAMPTON, ENGLAND

took possession of Northampton, and then handed the city over to his niece, Judith. He also mentioned Simon de St. Liz, the first Earl of Northampton, the brave crusader, who when he returned from battle erected as a memorial the church which is still standing, establishing also a monastery which he dedicated to St. Andrew. Mr. Campion also mentioned that in 1546 the Mayor of old Northampton was named Lawrence Washington, a direct ancestor of George Washington, and that within six miles of the town, in Great Brington, the family remains lie buried. On the tomb is a coat of arms of the Washington family composed of the Stars and Bars, which according to tradition gave us our Stars and Stripes. He also mentioned the fact that the father and mother of Benjamin Franklin came from the little village of Ecton, only five miles from Northampton; also that Henry Wadsworth Longfellow's ancestry on his mother's side claimed as their residence a village within ten miles of the town. After his address the English Alderman then read the following cablegram from the Mayor of his town:—

From a photograph   *Kindness Walter K. Watkins, Esq.*

NORTHAMPTON, ENGLAND

"Convey to the Mayor, City Council and the inhabitants heartiest greetings from myself, the Council and Burgesses of Northampton, England, on the two hundred and fiftieth anniversary of settlement of our namesake American City.

LEWIS, *Mayor*."

It may be interesting to mention that an invitation to attend this two hundred and fiftieth anniversary was sent to his Honour the Mayor and City Council of Northampton, England, to which a very gracious reply was received reading as follows:—

"To his Honour the Mayor,

    and the City Council of Northampton, U.S.A.

Mr. Mayor and Gentlemen:—

On behalf of myself and the Corporation of the ancient Borough of Northampton, England, I beg to acknowledge and to thank you for the invitation with which you have honoured us, and for the cordial feeling which prompted the invitation, to join with you in your celebration of the 250th anniversary of the settlement of your prosperous city. . . . Mr. Mayor and Gentlemen, I feel certain that the Council will appreciate highly your kindness and will join with me in heartiest good wishes for the growth and progress of

Photographed from an old print by Henry Cooper & Son   *Kindness Ian Forbes-Robertson, Esq.*

VIEW OF MARKET SQUARE, NORTHAMPTON, ENGLAND

From a photograph   *Kindness Walter K. Watkins, Esq.*

MARKET SQUARE, NORTHAMPTON, ENGLAND
A more recent view.

your City and the best welfare of its inhabitants. I shall also ask the Council to order your invitation to be duly inscribed in the records of our Borough, which received its first charter from King Richard I on 18th November, anno Domini, 1189. I have the honour to be,

Mr. Mayor and Gentlemen,

Yours very faithfully,

EDWARD LEWIS, *Mayor."*

One of the interesting features of the celebration was an old stage coach sent by Southampton, which was marked "Northampton to Southampton Mail 1809."

Another speaker on this occasion mentioned the amusing words of Mr. Choate, who said:—

"The Pilgrim Mothers were more worthy of our admiration than the Pilgrim Fathers, for they not only endured all the hardships which the Pilgrim Fathers did, but they had to endure, in addition, the Pilgrim Fathers themselves."

When Mr. Campion returned to England he made a report to his Mayor of the Northampton celebration, and his account of the proceedings was published in the "Northampton Mercury," a few quotations from which may be of interest:—

"I was made, as your representative, the honoured guest of the city, and in every function connected with the Celebration, I was not only placed in positions of honour, but the kindliest allusions were made to my presence as the representative of the mother city in the old country. For it was made clear that Northampton, Old England, was the source from whence sprang Northampton, Mass. I was informed that the New England city received its name out of respect to some of the earliest settlers who had come from our ancient borough. . . . Nor did I forget to make suitable reference to the Washington tomb at Great Brington Church. . . . His Excellency, John L. Bates, the Governor of Massachusetts, was also present, and in his address gave me a most cordial welcome as the representative of the old mother city. In response to my greetings, the large assembly stood up in token of their approval of a proposition to reciprocate the good wishes of which I was the bearer to the whole of the Sunday-school workers and scholars of Northampton, Old England. And through you, Mr. Mayor, I hope I may be permitted to convey this reciprocal greeting from the Sunday-schools of Northampton, Mass., as an example of one of the important ties which bind together the Old and the New Worlds."

The English Mayor, in a few appreciative words, moved that the thanks of the Council be accorded to him and that his report be entered as public minutes of the borough.

The first church in our Northampton was gathered in 1661, the congregation then consisting of only eight persons, whose names were Eleazar Mather, David Wilton, William Clarke, John Strong, Henry Cunliffe, Hervey Woodward, Thomas Roote and Thomas Hanchett. In these days the worshippers were reminded of the service by trumpet or drum, as bells were not used in the very early days. The first minister was Eleazar Mather, son of Richard Mather of Dorchester, a brother of Increase Mather, the greatest of the name, and uncle of Cotton Mather. Eleazar was born in Dorchester in 1637. During the later years of the church

NORTHAMPTON, MASSACHUSETTS, SHOWING MAIN STREET IN 1838

NORTHAMPTON, MASSACHUSETTS, IN 1842
From Warner's Coffee House.

other ministers serving, after Mather, were Stoddard, Edwards, Hooker and Williams, Edwards perhaps being the most illustrious of all.

Our Northampton was first settled in 1654, was incorporated a city in 1884, and has often been spoken of as "The Meadow City," as it lies in one of the most fertile plains in this country. Most of the early settlers were natives of England, who were emigrants to this country in 1630, later journeying from Boston to Hartford, Windsor, or Springfield, and thence proceeding up the river to Northampton, which was in those days called Nonotuck. Springfield had a hand in the early settlement of this town, for we find that out of the twenty-four people who signed the petition in 1653, three of them, John Pynchon, Elizur Holyoke and Samuel Chapin, came from this flourishing city to help in the new settlement at Northampton. Joseph Hawley, Seth Pomeroy, Caleb Strong and Isaac C. Bates are important names in the later history of the town.

The second plantation created from Northampton lands was called Hadley, from a town of similar name in Suffolk, England; Hatfield was also set off, being likewise named from a town in Hertfordshire, England.

In the eighteenth century Northampton, England, was spoken of as "the proud beauty of the midlands," and today she still lays claim to this name. It is situated in the heart of England, easily accessible, and from every angle is rich in history and antiquity. The town is said to have been founded by Belinus, a British king, and for centuries it was alternately ravaged by Saxons, Danes and Normans. After the Norman invasion, and the marriage of Simon de St. Liz, the first Norman earl, to Maud, the daughter of Judith, the widow of the last Saxon Earl of Northampton, the town became the resort of royalty. Here came Henry I, Henry II and King John, and in 1564 Queen Elizabeth visited the town and was received in great state. Many years later, when Charles I and his queen passed through the town, they were presented with costly gifts of plate. Only fourteen miles away, at Naseby, on June 14, 1645, the army of Charles I met with defeat. The townsmen, since Queen Elizabeth's time, were ever strong Puritans and during the civil war favored the Parliamentary party. Charles II, when he "came into his own," marked his displeasure by ordering the demolition of the castle and walls of the town.

America's first woman poet, Anne Bradstreet, was born in this English town.

NORWICH, CONNECTICUT

THE people of Norwich, Connecticut, have always appreciated the fact that their city on the Thames, above New London, is named for the large city of the same name in Norfolk County, England, and it is for this reason that there have been many official and unofficial exchanges of friendship. Members of the Gilman family of Norwich, Connecticut, have made a number of visits to the ancient city in England and have also corresponded for many years with the

Lord Mayor and other officials. In 1859, Daniel C. Gilman, once president of Johns Hopkins University, and brother of William C. Gilman, a citizen of Norwich, who has carried on a good deal of correspondence with the English Norwich, delivered an historical address, which has been published in a volume called "The Norwich Jubilee," giving an account of the Connecticut city. William C. Gilman has given to us an interesting account of the two hundred and fiftieth anniversary of the founding of Norwich, and also mentions the interesting correspondence that took place between the two cities in 1905, of which we give copies:—

"GUILDHALL, NORWICH, 10th January, 1905.

Dear Mr. Mayor:—

I have the honour to transmit in a wooden case a Resolution which was unanimously passed by the Council of this City on the 22nd November last, with newspapers containing an account of such meeting; likewise the cushion cover referred to in the Resolution.

I trust that the case will arrive safely, and that the contents thereof will prove an object of interest to your Citizens, and remind them of the old City from which yours has taken its name.

I am, Mr. Mayor,

Yours faithfully,

ARNOLD H. MILLER, *Town Clerk.*

The Worshipful,
The Mayor of Norwich,
Connecticut, U.S.A.

NORWICH   At a meeting of the Council of the Mayor, Aldermen, and Citizens of the City of Norwich, held on the twenty-second day of November, one thousand nine hundred and four

Mr. Alderman Wild moved, Mr. Councillor Howlett seconded and it was unanimously

Resolved,   On the Report and recommendation of the City Committee that two of the cushions presented to the Corporation by Thomas Baret, Mayor of the City in 1651, for use at, but not now required at the Cathedral, be given one to the Castle Museum Committee and the other to the Mayor and Corporation of Norwich, Connecticut, U.S.A. for preservation and exhibition in the Museum of that City, and that the Town Clerk be authorized to affix the Corporate Seal to this Resolution.

ARNOLD H. MILLER,
Town Clerk,"

"City Clerk's Office, Norwich.

WHEREAS, The Council of the Mayor, Aldermen and Citizens of the City of Norwich, England, by resolution bearing date November the twenty-second, 1904, did, on behalf of that Corporation present to the Mayor and Corporation of this City, one of a set of cushions presented to the first named Corporation in 1651 by its then Mayor, Hon. Thomas Baret, and said gift has now come into the possession of this Council for preservation and exhibition,

Resolved, That said gift be and it is hereby accepted in the name and behalf of the Mayor and Corporation of the City of Norwich, Connecticut, and

Resolved, That the same be and hereby is perpetually loaned to the Norwich Free Academy to be by said Corporation placed in the Slater Museum for preservation and exhibition, together with the certified copy of the original resolution of gift accompanying the same, and

Resolved, That the thanks of the Court of Common Council and of the citizens here represented by its membership are due and are cordially extended to the Donors; and

Resolved, That a copy of these resolutions suitably engrossed be forwarded to the Mayor, Aldermen and Citizens of Norwich, England, in testimony of our appreciation of their distinguished consideration.

Attest, *City Clerk*, STEVEN D. MOORE."

The Thomas Baret mentioned above was a brother of Margaret Baret Huntington, who came from Saybrook, Connecticut, in 1633, and who is the ancestress of all the Huntingtons in New England. Another exchange of felicitations took place in 1909 at the two hundred and fiftieth anniversary of our city, at which time the following telegram was received:—

"NORWICH, ENGLAND, July 5, 1909.

GILBERT S. RAYMOND,
Secretary of Anniversary Celebration Committee,
Norwich, Conn. U.S.A.

City of Norwich sends hearty congratulations to American daughter on her attaining two hundred and fifty years.

Signed   Walter Rye, Mayor."

A suitable reply was sent by the Connecticut city. In many places in the city, the English flag was flown beside the Star Spangled Banner.

Invitations were also sent to the Mother City to attend the Quarter Millennium held in 1909. An interesting ceremony during this celebration was held in Old Norwich Town burying ground where the guests of the occasion assembled, among the moss-covered stones that marked the graves of many of the forefathers, the graves of four being marked by a tall tree, upon the trunk of which were the names of the pioneers who were buried there,—Thomas Adgate, Simon Huntington, John Post and Thomas Waterman,—and also the name of Christopher Huntington, Jr., the first male child born in Norwich. We give on page 184 a cut of the monument

SENT. THOS. LEFFINGWELL
RICHARD WALLIS
THOMAS ADGATE
JOHN OLMSTEAD
STEPHEN BACKUS
THOMAS BLISS
JOHN REYNOLDS
JOSIAH REED
RICHARD HENDYS
CHRISTOPHER HUNTINGTON

MAJOR JOHN MASON
BORN IN ENGLAND
DIED IN NORWICH
JAN. 30, 1672.
AGED 73.

From a photograph   *By W. R. Stevens*

THE FOUNDERS' MONUMENT,

erected to Major John Mason and thirty-seven others who
were settlers in Norwich, Connecticut, in 1659 and 1660.

erected in the first burial place in Norwich Town to Major John Mason, often spoken of as the "Myles Standish of Connecticut," who with Winthrop, Fenway, Gardner, Higginson and Fitch formed the first of the little colony at Saybrook on the coast. Interesting monuments have been placed on Sachem Street to Uncas, chief of the Mohegans, who captured Miantonomo, chief of the Narragansetts, names too well known in history to be described again. There is also a monument erected to Miantonomo on Sachem's Plain. There is still another memorial that has been erected to Thomas Leffingwell, who carried provisions to Uncas for the relief of the Mohegans when they were being besieged by their enemies. Our Norwich is called the "Rose of New England," which name perhaps would be disputed by many other towns and cities.

Norwich, England, the capital of Norfolk County, is often called the "City of Churches," and one writer describes it as "either a city in an orchard" or "an orchard in a city," as the houses and trees are so attractively blended together. Norwich is about twenty miles from Yarmouth and is noted for its great antiquity and interesting history, having been at one time the seat of the Anglo-Saxon princes; it has also been the scene of many happenings among the Iceni, Romans, Angles, Saxons, Jutes and Danes, its earliest name being, "North-wic," found on the early coins. The city has one of the finest market places in England, and in the old days it was said that at the Saturday markets the people showed more interest in the advance or fall in the price of butter than in any other event of the week. Americans are particularly interested in the "Maid's Head Hotel," which is very old, and which is situated in Tombland, the ancient name of the market place.

The story is told of a Norfolk laborer who decided to migrate to America, and who was seen one day driving along the road near Norwich in his farm cart. He was asked where he was going, and he replied that he didn't "fare rightly to know by what route they were going to the United States," but added, "We'm gwine ter sleep't Debenham [thirty miles from Norwich] the first night, so's to kinder break the journey." An interesting event that took place in East Anglia was the "camping" contest, which was a form of football game between Norfolk and Suffolk, and which took place on the common with three hundred or more on a side. These matches were often fatal and it is claimed that one contest resulted in the death of nine men during the fortnight of play. In one special event Suffolk won after fourteen hours of play, and just as the ball was being thrown in, the Norfolk men inquired of their opponents whether they had brought their coffins with them.

One of the coach routes was between London and Norwich, and at certain times of the year the country nearby supplied so many turkeys and geese that the would-be passengers complained, particularly near Christmas time, that they could not get seats on the coach, as it was piled high, inside and out, with birds on their way to the London markets. There are amusing pictures showing the Norwich coach loaded with fowl and not a passenger anywhere to be seen.

The history of the See at Norfolk dates back to the seventh century, when its seat was at Dummoc, a Roman station on the coast of Suffolk, now called "Dunwich;" in 1094 the See was transferred to Norwich, and in 1096 Bishop Lozinga founded the present cathedral, and also a Benedictine Abbey. The castle which is the next important building to the cathedral, and which once covered many acres of land, was plundered in 1216 and later made a prison; it goes back thirteen hundred years and perhaps has seen more fighting than any other castle in England.

The Gurney family, well known in America, has been associated especially with Norwich, England, and at one time owned Gurney's Bank. It may be interesting also to mention that Edith Cavell's body was brought back from Belgium with great ceremony and was buried in an enclosure at the east end of the Cathedral.

At one time the town of Castor nearby was larger than Norwich as shown by this rhyme:—

"Caistor was a city when Norwich was none,
And Norwich was built of Caistor stone."

PORTSMOUTH AND RYE, NEW HAMPSHIRE

THE histories of Portsmouth and Rye are so closely connected that we think it best to mention them together.

The first actual settlement in New Hampshire was made in 1623 at Odiorne's Point, opposite Newcastle and across Little Harbour at the mouth of the Piscataqua River. The first visitor to this part of New Hampshire was Martin Pring from Bristol, England, who has been further described under our article on "Bristol." This first colony at Odiorne's Point, Rye, has usually been referred to as the "Thompson Settlement," for the reason that David Thompson was the most prominent person connected with the undertaking, he having been authorized "To found a Plantacon on the river of Piscataqua, to cultivate the vine, discover mines, carry on the fisheries, and trade with the natives, to consecrate this soil to the service of God and liberty." He came over in the ship "Jonathan," and on this point of land erected a dwelling called "Mason Hall." Thompson was associated with Sir Ferdinando Gorges and Captain John Mason, who had been granted a charter from King James for "planting, ruling, ordering and governing New England in America;" the latter is usually regarded as the "founder of New Hampshire." Gorges and Mason we have also mentioned under "Bristol," for it is with that town in England that their names are so closely associated. We give on this page a picture of the tablet that has been erected to commemorate this first settlement in the State of New Hampshire. This settlement was called Sandy Beach for a number of years until the incorporation of Newcastle in 1693, when with parts of Portsmouth and Hampton it was formed into a parish under the name of Rye. The few early pioneers, however, became discouraged, as they soon had the misfortune to bury forty of their number in the cemetery nearby, and had it not been for the courage of Captain Walter Neale, the Governor of the Colony, the settlement which finally resulted in the

From a photograph   *Kindness Wallace Hackett, Esq.*

TABLET PLACED ON ODIORNE'S POINT, RYE, NEW HAMPSHIRE, OPPOSITE NEW-CASTLE,

to commemorate the first planting of an English colony on the soil of New Hampshire.

From a photograph   *Kindness Ian Forbes-Robertson, Esq.*

TABLET PLACED IN GARRISON CHURCH, PORTSMOUTH, ENGLAND,

by seven well-known residents of Portsmouth, New Hampshire, in honour of Captain John Mason, who was the original proprietor of Portsmouth, New Hampshire, and who held the title of Vice-Admiral of New England.

formation of the State of New Hampshire might have been abandoned. Some years later John Odiorne built a house here and established such a large farm that the point was finally named after him, and is so called to this day.

Among the early settlers in Newcastle was Francis Jennings, or Jenness as he has sometimes been called, who in 1665 came here with some of his friends from Rye, England. A few years later he moved across the river to Sandy Beach and it was probably due to him that the name Rye was given to the New Hampshire town. Here it is said he established a bakery and distributed his bread among towns along the coast in his small pinnace.

The city of Portsmouth was named in honour of Captain John Mason, who as we have said, was the original proprietor of the Province of New Hampshire, and who was at one time Governor of Portsmouth, England. He had for some time been interested in the trade with the New England colonies, and foresaw the possibilities of this country. To his memory seven prominent citizens of Portsmouth, New Hampshire, John Scribner Jenness, Charles Levi Woodbury, Charles Wesley Tuttle, Alexander Hamilton Ladd, Charles Henry Bell, Eliza Appleton Haven and Charlotte Maria Haven, placed gas standards and a brass tablet, in 1784, in Garrison Church, Portsmouth, England, the words on the tablet being as follows:—

> To the glory of GOD and in memory of CAPTN
> JOHN MASON—Captain in the Royal Navy—
> Treasurer of the Army—Captain of South
> Sea Castle—Governor of the Colony of
> Newfoundland—Patentee and Founder of
> New Hampshire in America—Vice Admiral
> of New England—Born 1586 Died 1635.
> This faithful churchman, devoted patriot
> and gallant officer of whom England and
> America will ever be proud was buried
> in Westminster Abbey.

It was not until 1653, though, that Brian Pendleton, Renald Fernald, John Shere-bourn, Richard Cutt and Samuel Gaines actually petitioned for the change of the name of this territory to its present one, the plantation having previously been called "Piscataqua Settlement" or "Strabery Banke" so named by reason of a bank near there where strawberries were found. The name Portsmouth was thought by many to be especially appropriate, as the land was situated near a good port and at the mouth of a river.

Several times our city and its namesake in England have corresponded and exchanged presents; one of these occasions was in 1874 when the Mayors interchanged views of their respective cities and on another occasion the Mayor of our city, Hon. Wallace Hackett, who has kindly placed at our disposal a history of the English Portsmouth, received views of the English seaport and also a letter from the Mayor which read as follows:—

> "MAYOR'S OFFICE.
> THE TOWN HALL,
> PORTSMOUTH, 28th October, 1908
>
> *Dear Mr. Hackett:*—
> Before retiring from Office, I should like to thank you very much for the Mementos of your City which you kindly sent me, and think it very appropriate indeed that the Mayor of Portsmouth in the new World should send such a friendly letter to the Mayor of this ancient Borough. I reciprocate the kindly sentiments which you express, and beg to extend to yourself or any Member of your Corporation a hearty welcome, should you at any time be visiting this part of the Country.
> With hearty good wishes for the success of yourself and Colleagues and the prosperity of your City,
>
> I am
>
> Yours very truly,
> F. G. FOSTER, *Mayor.*"

In speaking of the early settlements in New Hampshire we must not forget to mention the Isles of Shoals which are situated about eight miles from the mainland. It is difficult for us to realize that in the early days they were the rendezvous of hundreds of English and other ships, that fishing there was carried on very actively, and that their population at one time was larger than that of any other place in the Eastern provinces. It was also there that the English fishermen called in order to learn the latest news from their country. These early days at the Shoals are well described by John S. Jenness in these words:—

> "During the entire sixteenth century fishing vessels came hither from our eastern waters. Doggers and Pinckies of the English, clumsy Busses of Holland, light Fly-boats of Flanders, the Biskiner and Portingal and many other odd high-peaked vessels were attracted thither summer after summer."

At one time, about 1661, it was suggested that these islands be called "Apledoore" from the Devon fishing village of Appledore, and even to this day one of the group bears this name. The islands are closely associated with that great explorer, Captain John Smith, who at first called the group by his own name, "Smith's Isles" and it was, therefore, quite fitting that the Society of Colonial Wars in the State of New Hampshire should dedicate in 1914 a memorial to him on Star Island, the services being held three hundred years after Captain Smith's visit to the shores of New England. The words on the tablet are as follows:—

Photographed by St. Clair Studio

CAPTAIN JOHN SMITH
1579–1631
After proving his valor in
Europe and America became
Governor of Virginia
and
Admiral of New England
While exploring this coast in the
Spring of 1614 made the first recorded
visit to these islands, named by him
Smith's Isles.

Not only has this country honoured this early explorer, but England has also placed an epitaph to his memory in the church of St. Sepulchre, London, and the inscription thereon begins as follows:—

> "Here lies one conquer'd that hath conquer'd Kings,
> Subdu'd large Territories, and done things
> Which to the World impossible would seeme."

TABLET PLACED ON STAR ISLAND, ISLES OF SHOALS, OFF THE COAST OF NEW HAMPSHIRE,

in honour of the noted English explorer, Captain John Smith, who visited the islands in 1614, naming them "Smith's Isles."

Smith was the author of a book called "Generall Historie of Virginia, New England and the Summer Isles." Those who have read the story of his life remember that at one time he slew three Turks in the Transylvania Campaign and it was in memory

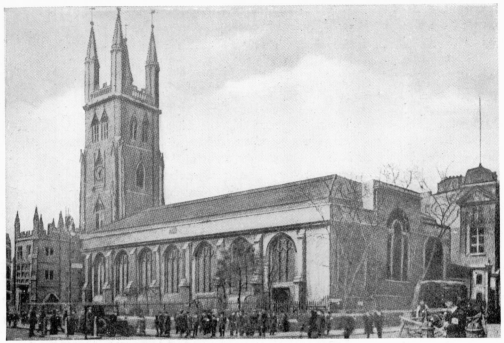

From "The Beginnings of Colonial Maine," by Henry S. Burrage, D.D., Historian of Maine

ST. SEPULCHRE CHURCH, LONDON,

in which Captain John Smith was buried.   He was one of the earliest explorers of the New England coast,
and first named the Isles of Shoals "Smith's Isles."

of this achievement that the three islands off Cape Ann were named by him "Three Turks' Heads" and there is still a Turk's Head Inn at Rockport near Gloucester. It is also interesting to mention that he was granted the right by the Heralds' College to use three Turks' heads on his coat of arms.   Professor Smith, Governor of the New Hampshire Society for Colonial Wars, at the dedication of the memorial, referred to him as "the navigator, the sailor, the traveller, the explorer, the colonizer, the ruler, the author and one of the finest types of the race to which he belonged."   On the same day as the dedication of the Smith memorial another tablet was erected on Star Island to the memory of Rev. John Tucke, whose remains were placed under the obelisk.   Tucke was born in Hampton, New Hampshire, to which town his great-grandfather had come from Suffolk, England.   The younger Tucke lived at the Isles of Shoals for forty years, and, as the place was primarily a fishing settlement, he was paid at one time in "winter fish," and was often referred to as the "fisher of men."   Another minister of the early days was Rev. John Brock; one day the fishermen all came to him begging him to postpone his meeting as they wished to go fishing.   The minister replied, "If you will go away I say unto you,

catch fish if you can, but as for you that will tarry and worship the Lord
this day I will pray unto Him for you that you may catch fish until you are
weary." The story reads that thirty of the number went fishing and caught
four fish, while the five who stayed went out in their boats later and hauled in
five hundred fish. It is also related that church meetings after this were always
well attended.

"God save Englonde and the town of Rye." (From Old Customal.)

Rye in England is in the County of Sussex, and to the millions of
people who have followed the British Army in Flanders, Ypres Castle in Rye will
always be of special interest. This castle, which is really only a tower, is of
great antiquity and was for centuries before the British soldiers fought over the
famous battlefield of France called "Wipers" Tower, and it was, of course,
natural that the battle of Ypres and the
town where it was fought should be
spelled and pronounced the same way
as was the old tower in their native
land. This structure which was built by
William of Ypres, Earl of Kent, in the
twelfth century, is in a good state of
preservation.

Old Rye is very quaint, with its red-
roofed dwellings clustered about the huge
rock, which rises sharply from the flat
green stretches of Romney marshes. It is
said that some of the streets of the town
have grass growing between the cobble-
stones, and there is a story that the Rye
Corporation used to top-dress this grass
every spring in order to make it grow so
well. It is no wonder that artists have
thronged this attractive place, which was
called "Rye Royal" by Queen Elizabeth
during her visit there. The earliest notice
in history was at the time the Danes
landed near there in A.D. 893. During the
reign of Edward the Confessor, he gave
Rye to the abbots and monks of Fécamp
in Normandy, France, because he liked
that country and wanted to help her
people. Henry III, however, at once ex-

Photograph by F. Frith   *Kindness Ian Forbes-*
& Co., England   *Robertson, Esq.*

HOUSE IN RYE, ENGLAND, IN WHICH
HENRY JAMES LIVED FROM
1898 TO 1916

It is on the right of the street and is known as
the "Lamb House." The house in the background is known as the banqueting-hall and
was used by Mr. James as his library, where
he did all his work.

Photograph by F. Frith & Co., England   *Kindness Ian Forbes-Robertson, Esq.*

MERMAID STREET, RYE, ENGLAND, SHOWING MERMAID INN (on right)
Rye is a most attractive town, with its quaint and narrow streets, many of which are cobblestoned.

changed Rye for other property in Gloucestershire and Lincolnshire, which he allowed the monks to hold.

Rye is said to have received its name from the Latin Ria, or from the British word Rhy, meaning a ford or bay, although the best authorities claim the name came from the French Rie, meaning a bank of the sea. To New Englanders the connection of Henry James with the English town is of special interest, for it was there that he lived for part of each of twenty years, in the old Lamb house, which we show on page 191 together with his library, in which he wrote many of his books. Mr. James was a familiar figure in the town and when he died he was much missed by the inhabitants. There is an interesting tragedy connected with this Lamb, who was the previous owner of the house in which James lived. Lamb once sentenced a certain butcher for false weights, whereupon the latter stabbed by mistake a man called Grebell, who had lived in the house before Lamb bought it and who was a relative of Lamb. This murder of an innocent man caused such a tremendous sensation that the skull of the butcher and the gibbet upon which he was hung are both preserved in the town hall. One of the attractive streets of the town is called Mermaid Street, upon which is situated Mermaid Inn.

From a copy of a picture by Turner, owned by a Boston collector   *Formerly in the collection of J. H. Seers, Essex, England.*

PORTSMOUTH, ENGLAND, 1825

Portsmouth Harbour, England, and the long sea road between the Isle of Wight and Hampshire is so safe for vessels that seamen often call it the "King's Bed-chamber." Portsmouth is one of the famous cities of England and, of course, received its name from the mouth of the port, which was believed in this case would become *the* port of England. The name was originally derived from the Roman word Portus. The earliest record of the island of Portsea, upon which the city is situated, was during the time of King Ethelred, who granted it to the new Minster at Winchester. Portsmouth Harbour was used by the Romans, who built the fortress of Porchester; the port was also used by Henry III as the place for assembling his expeditions to Gascony, between which place and Portsmouth much trade was carried on at one time. To Portsmouth also came Charles I. A bust of this king is set up high in the wall of the great tower at the foot of High Street and beneath the bust is the following inscription:

> After his travels through all France into Spain, and having passed very many dangers both by sea and land, he arrived here the 5th day of October, 1623.

Here also landed Catherine, consort of Charles II, from Lisbon just previous to their marriage; here too landed the present Prince of Wales on his return from his recent visit to Canada and the United States.

A curious custom of the place was for the rope-makers from the great rope-walks to escort the kings when they visited the city. There was also in the city an old gun wharf, as it was called, which was built in 1662 by a contractor, whose name, curiously enough, was William Shakespeare, and the place where his workmen were paid off is still called Shakespeare's Head. In the center of the town is the parish church, which was erected in the early part of the thirteenth century, and which was dedicated to Thomas à Becket; in the cupola of this church was a lantern in which was a bell that used to be rung whenever a ship appeared in the harbour. Portsmouth was also a great shipbuilding center as early as the days of King John, and from then until now many notable vessels of the English Navy have been launched there. The Free Mart Fair, which has been held in Portsmouth for many years and which we believe is held there to this day, is spoken of in these words:—

"Ye lovers of Fun to Portsmouth repair
And see the delights that abound at our fair."

It is impossible to mention all the important events that have taken place in this great English seaport, but it will be of special interest to Americans, as well as to Englishmen, to mention that Charles Dickens was born in the Borough of Portsmouth.

Portsmouth, on the island of Newport, Rhode Island, was also named after the English city. Some of its early settlers became dissatisfied and removed to the other end of the island, founding Newport, one of the foremost watering places of the world. Among these early settlers of Newport were William Coddington, William Brenton and Thomas Hazard. Brenton owned a large farm on Brenton's Point, so called to this day.

SANDWICH, MASSACHUSETTS

IN 1900 the late Col. Charles L. Norton of our Sandwich visited the town of the same name in England from which our Cape town got its name, and several years later he received three seals from the English Mayor, one of which he succeeded in having adopted by Sandwich, Massachusetts, as its official seal. In 1912, Henry B. Russell, Esq., of the neighboring town of Bourne, which was once part of Sandwich, visited the old town of Sandwich, England, and brought back a number of pictures, which now hang in the reference room of the Sandwich Public Library. Just before the Great War, William L. Nye, Esq., another resident of our town, had some correspondence with the Curator of the mother town, who sent a number of photographs which we have had reproduced on page 195. Mr. Nye has just been able to trace a piece of the wainscoting from the town hall of old Sandwich, which was sent in 1913 to a member of the Wing family of our town, by Mr. J. A. Jacobs, Curator of the Sandwich archives in England. This relic of old England,

SANDWICH, ENGLAND—SANDOWN ROAD

CATTLE MARKET AND TOWN HALL, SANDWICH, ENGLAND

From a photograph   *Kindness James L. Wesson, Esq.,*
and Henry M. Hutchings, Esq.

NYE FAMILY BOULDER, SANDWICH,
MASSACHUSETTS

Erected by the Nye family in America in
memory of their ancestors, the Nyes and the
Tuppers, early settlers in this Cape Cod town.
The inscription is given on page 197.

dating back to the year 1570, has just been returned by Colonel Wing from out West, at the suggestion of Mr. Nye, and will now be placed among the antiquities in the Sandwich Historical Society. Members of the Wing family for many years have been corresponding with Mr. Jacobs. The Mayor of the English town also sent over to the Wing family (on the occasion of one of their family reunions) some books and papers. Further than this we have been unable to trace any direct communications between the two towns.

This old Cape Cod town vies with its sister Yarmouth in attractions, and perhaps suggests something of the picturesque old English town of Sandwich on the river Stour, which was one of the Cinque-ports of the ancient days. Nothing but a forest wilderness, reaching down to the salt marshes which bordered the stretches of white beach, greeted the eyes of those first settlers who early in the year 1637 chose this spot on the Cape as a satisfactory place "to sit down." This territory had previously been used as a trading post, for it formed a most convenient halting place on the route between Plymouth and the Dutch colonies of New York. Its actual settlement, however, dates to that year, 1637, when, as stated in the old Plymouth records, "it is also agreed by the Court that these tenn men of Saugust, viz, Edmond Freeman, Henry Feake, Thomas Dexter, Edward Dillingham, William Wood, John Carman, Richard Chadwell, William Almy, Thomas Tupper, and George Knott shall have liberty to view a place to sitt down and have sufficient lands for three score famylies upon the conditions propounded to them by the Governor and Mr. Winslowe." The settlement was incorporated as a town on September 3, 1637, and named for Sandwich in Kent County, England, where several of the early settlers once lived. The boundary lines were established by the Puritan Captain, Miles Standish, and his friend John Alden, when Plymouth ordered the town to be laid out. Before the end of the year this little group of pioneers was joined by fifty others who came chiefly from Lynn, Saugus, Duxbury and Plymouth. The names that have appeared often in the history of the town are Freeman, Dillingham, Tuttle, Allen, Besse, Blackwell, Bodfish, Bourne, Briggs, Burgess, Ewer, Hallett, Harlow, Holway, Sanders, Nye and Wing; the few lines of poetry which we quote and which were written at the time of the two hundred and fiftieth anniversary make further mention of some of the names that have meant so much to the town:—

"The names of Freeman and of Bourne,
Nye, Dillingham, and their compeers;
We trace, from first to last, upon
The annals of this ancient town."

In 1908 there was erected in the village of Sandwich, in the village square near the present town house, a large boulder shown on page 196 to which was affixed a tablet in memory of the an-cestors of Benjamin Nye, the earliest an-cestor of the Nye family in this country, and the inscription thereon reads as follows:—

1637

ERECTED BY THE NYE FAMILY OF AMERICA
TO THE MEMORY OF THEIR ANCESTORS
BENJAMIN NYE AND
KATHARINE TUPPER HIS WIFE
WE BEST SERVE THE INTEREST OF POSTERITY
BY TREASURING THE MEMORY OF OUR ANCESTORS

1908

From a photograph

*Kindness Captain John S. Carpenter, U.S.N., and Henry
M. Hutchings, Esq.*

THE "SADDLE" ROCK, SANDWICH,
MASSACHUSETTS,

placed over the grave of Edmond Freeman, who was one of the earliest settlers in our Sandwich, and who was born in England in 1590.

On the farm still owned by the descen-dants of Edmond Freeman there are two large boulders called the Saddle and Pil-lion Rocks which mark the graves of him-self and his wife. The tradition is that after the death of his wife, Freeman, who was the first settler in Sandwich of that name, had these boulders drawn by oxen to their present location, placing the Pil-lion stone over the grave of his wife, giving at the same time instructions that the Saddle stone should be placed over his own grave, upon his death.

Within a few years descendants of Edmond Freeman and his wife have had a tablet set into each of these stones. The inscription on the Saddle stone reads as follows:—

EDMOND FREEMAN
BORN IN ENGLAND 1590
DIED IN SANDWICH 1682
A FOUNDER OF THE TOWN OF SANDWICH IN 1637
ASSISTANT TO GOVERNOR BRADFORD
1641–1647

From a photograph
Kindness Captain John S. Carpenter, U.S.N., and Henry M. Hutchings, Esq.

THE "PILLION" ROCK, SANDWICH, MASSACHUSETTS, marking the grave of Edmond Freeman's wife, Elizabeth. These two stones, known as the "Saddle" and "Pillion" Rocks, are on the farm still owned by Edmond Freeman's descendants. After the death of his wife, Edmond Freeman placed the "Pillion" over her grave and directed that upon his death the "Saddle" should be placed over his own grave.

The inscription on the tablet on the Pillion Rock reads as follows:—

ELIZABETH WIFE OF
EDMOND FREEMAN
BORN IN ENGLAND 1600
DIED IN SANDWICH 1675–6

During King Philip's War, which resulted in the devastation of so many frontier towns, Sandwich and several other Cape Cod towns invited the dwellers in the stricken settlements to take refuge with them, for none of the Cape tribes joined with Philip in this uprising, many even serving against him. The friendliness on the part of these Indians was due in no small measure to the work of the Cape Cod missionaries, among whom were Richard Bourne and Thomas Tupper of Sandwich. The former settled in the town in 1637, became an instructor to the Mashpee Indians in 1658, and was ordained as a preacher by Eliot and Cotton in 1670. So great was the affection of the Indians for this missionary and his family, that in 1723, forty-one years after his death, when a Bourne child was suffering from a disease which the physicians believed incurable, the Indians came with their medicine men, and, with the mother's permission, gave the child their simple remedies which resulted in a cure. Thomas Tupper was a missionary among the Herring River Indians, and in the diary of Judge Samuel Sewall are found extracts relating to a church which was built for the Indians at this place under Tupper's supervision, and at the expense of Judge Sewall. This was the first meeting house in this vicinity to be made of sound and lasting material, in the English fashion, the carpenter, Edward Milton of Sandwich, having been ordered to build a "convenient, comfortable meeting-house for the natives at Sandwich" and to finish it properly, "by making and well hanging the doors, clapboarding in the inside well and filling the walls with shavings or other suitable matter for warmth." From that time to the present, Sandwich has well maintained its churches. There are now five church buildings in the village, and the sight of the spires and towers across the meadows which meets the eye of the traveler on the railroad when approaching the town is an inspiring one. The spire of the Congregational Church, although

From a photograph   *Kindness Ian Forbes-Robertson, Esq., and J. A. Jacobs, Esq.*

BARBICAN, SANDWICH, ENGLAND,
a picturesque gate of the town.

somewhat reduced in dimensions, is on the same beautiful lines as that of the Park Street Church in Boston.

There was a curious law in our Sandwich in the early days forbidding a young man to marry until he had killed so many blackbirds, which was a condition that was imposed in order to keep a constant ratio between the number of spinsters and the number of poor marksmen. It was quite natural that Sandwich, situated as it was upon the seacoast, should have become a seafaring community. Here maritime pursuits were carried on sometimes in defiance of the King, as in the case of drift whales which from time immemorial had belonged to the crown. Another reference to this industry appears in the records of the year 1702, when the town voted to its pastor, Rev. Rowland Cotton, as part of his salary, "all such drift whales as shall, during the time of his ministry, be driven or cast ashore within the limits of the town, being such as shall not be killed with hands." It may be assumed that some of the funds thus diverted from the King's treasury went towards a new Sunday gown for Madam Cotton. The revenue that the settlers derived from a tax on mackerel was used for the support of the public school.

The Earl of Sandwich, who died in 1792, derived his title from Sandwich, England.   He was the First Lord of the Admiralty in 1778, when Captain Cook discovered the Sandwich Islands, which were named for him.   There is so much history surrounding the English town that we can mention only a few of the important events that are connected with the ancient seaport, which was at one time known as "Sondwic."   Most of the pioneers who came from Kent to this country doubtless often had visions of this sleepy, picturesque Old World town, with its ancient churches, its crooked streets, and its high gables—the port where once the galleys of imperial Rome lay at anchor.   The town is first mentioned in 664 during the life of St. Wilfrid, when it is related that the Bishop returning from France arrived "happily and pleasantly" in the haven of Sandwich, the town probably having been founded about that time.   The territory about Sandwich was reclaimed from the seas in historic times, but it can hardly be said to be a port now, as the sands have shifted to such a great extent.   Its decline began during the Tudor days and during the reign of Henry VII the river diminished so much that the harbour became very poor, while during the reign of Queen Elizabeth it was hardly used at all.   Few vessels now go up the river Stour, and the shipping that once existed there to a considerable degree has been abandoned.   At one time the Corporation of Sandwich complained that the people carried off too much sand that was left when the river fell; the Corporation claimed that these persons should be sentenced to capital punishment, but that the river had become so low it would be impossible to drown them if it got much lower.   Many more attempts were made to improve the harbour but without much success.   Soon after the time of Queen Elizabeth the town grew very prosperous, and many serge, baize and flannel workers came to the town, which fact has been commented upon in England in the following words:—

> "Hops, Reformation, baize and beer
> Came into England all in a year."

Fortunately, as the town lost the use of its harbour, a number of Huguenots were brought over by Queen Elizabeth from the Netherlands and they founded the industries of weaving and market-gardening, thereby causing great prosperity.   It is also said that celery was first grown in England by these new-comers to Sandwich.   We will mention only a few names connected with the town and not necessarily in chronological order.   In 851, Athelstan, King of Kent, fought a battle here against the Danes, which resulted in their defeat and the capture of nine of their ships.   A few months later, the enemy again appeared in the mouth of the Thames with three hundred and fifty vessels, landed on the Kentish shore, and pillaged Sandwich and Canterbury; there is a legend that King Arthur set out from here with his army and a great multitude of ships to give battle against Rome, returning also to this port; here Edward the Confessor lived for some time, while collecting his fleet; from here in 1164 Thomas à Becket, after his flight from Northampton, set sail on a fishing vessel, later returning to the same port, where he was received with great joy by the towns-people; here, too, in 1194 King Richard I landed after imprisonment by Leopold, Duke of Austria; here Edward III went to rendezvous his fleet before sailing for France. About this time a curious regu-lation was made that the dredgers were not allowed to sell their oysters to strangers until all the inhabitants of Sandwich had first been supplied. Another event that we might mention was the arrival at Sand-wich in 1357 of Edward the Black Prince, with his prisoner the luckless John, King of France, on their way from Bordeaux, after the battle of Poitiers. Queen Eliza-beth was so interested in the town that in 1572 she made a visit there and was re-ceived with much splendor. The house where she stayed is now used as a private residence. In 1670, Queen Catherine

From a photograph   *Kindness Ian Forbes-Robertson, Esq., and J. A. Jacobs, Esq.*

STRAND STREET, SANDWICH, ENGLAND

Most of the streets in Sandwich are narrow and winding.

visited the town with her great cavalcade, and her visit has been commemorated by a series of paintings which were formerly in a private house, but which have now been removed to the Guildhall. The old town was also the resort of many others of the royalty of England.

There is also a Sandwich in New Hampshire.

WAREHAM, MASSACHUSETTS

THE only official correspondence between the Warehams of old England and New England took place in 1879 at the time of the bi-centennial of Rochester, now part of our Wareham, when Hon. Thomas Lean Skewes of the English town wrote to our town. There is no question but that the Cape Cod town, like many others nearby, was named after the old town in Dorset County, England, which is a quaint, sleepy village of about two thousand inhabit-ants, dating back to the time when the Romans held possession of England. It is occasionally enlivened, however, at the time of the election for the local member of Parliament, when the respective candidates address their constituents from the "hustings," as they are called, where many a battle royal has been fought and many

From a photograph　　　　　　　　　　　　　　　　*Kindness Ian Forbes-Robertson, Esq.*

ST. MARTIN'S CHURCH, WAREHAM, ENGLAND

A rare example of a Saxon building, having remained practically intact for over twelve hundred years.

a head has been broken.   The town is very tranquil, as another picture on the following page shows, and all that remains of the ancient days are the huge earthworks of Roman construction which almost surround the town.   There is also evidence that the place was a British camp even before the Romans landed on English soil and fortified the place.

The eastern part of Wareham, on Cape Cod, was known to the Indians as "Agawam" and was sold to the Plymouth colony in 1655, which some years later resold it to Joseph Warren, William Clark, Joseph Bartlett, Josiah Morton, Isaac Little and Seth Pope.   The western part belonged to Rochester, and in the year 1739 both tracts of land were incorporated under the name of Wareham.   The earliest permanent settlers, however, came from Hingham, Massachusetts, chief of them being Israel Fearing, whose family played an important part in the history of the town.   The township was incorporated in July, 1739, the first minister chosen being Rev. Roland Thatcher, who was born in Barnstable, Massachusetts, and who was ordained December 26th, 1739.   He was succeeded by Rev. Josiah Cotton.   Other settlers of Wareham came from Sandwich, Rochester and Barnstable, Massachusetts.

Wareham, at the mouth of the Frome River in Dorsetshire, occupies the site of the old Roman station Morino, and takes its name from the Roman designation of the town.   Its fame is undoubtedly due to the fact that Horace Walpole was a native of the town, and that from there lime and cement are exported, as well as potter's clay, much of which is sent to America and various parts of the Continent.

An historian says: "In Saxon times it was already a place of note, and it is said that Beohrtric, King of Wessex, was buried here A.D. 800.   During the period of the Danish invasions those piratical marauders continually landed at Wareham, and made it their headquarters.   In 1015 Canute entered the Frome, and having ravaged Dorset, Somerset and Wilts, and plundered Cerne Abbey, returned hither, and sailed thence to Brownsea.   At the time of the Domesday Survey the unfortunate town was in very sunken fortunes, but it revived again under the rule of the Conqueror, who appointed two mint masters here, the same number it had in the time of Æthelstan.   The strength of its position brought much misery on the inhabitants during the struggle between Stephen and the Empress Maud.   It was seized for the latter by Robert of Gloucester in 1138.   The next year Baldwin de Redvers, one of the Empress' warmest adherents, landed here and seized Corfe Castle.   It was taken and burned by Stephen in 1142 during the temporary absence of the Earl of Gloucester, who on his return with young Prince Henry, then a boy of nine, retook the town and castle, the latter after an obstinate defence of three weeks. In 1146, when Prince Henry was forced to leave the kingdom, he took ship here for Anjou.   After this the poor town seems to have enjoyed a breathing time.   John landed here in 1205, and again eleven years later.   In 1213 Peter of Pomfret, the hermit, who had foretold the king's deposition, was brought out of his prison at

From a photograph   *Kindness Ian Forbes-Robertson, Esq.*
TOW PATH, SOUTH BRIDGE AND TRINITY CHURCH TOWER, WAREHAM, ENGLAND

From a photograph   *Kindness Ian Forbes-Robertson, Esq.*
NORTH STREET, WAREHAM, ENGLAND,
showing St. Martin's Church on the right in the background.

Corfe, and, after being dragged through the streets of the town, was hanged and quartered here.

"During the civil wars of the seventeenth century it again became the object of contention between the two parties, being repeatedly taken and retaken, after its first occupation for the Parliament in 1642.   The townspeople were chiefly loyal to the Crown.   Their 'dreadful malignancy' was used as an argument by Sir Anthony Ashley Cooper for the complete destruction of the town, as it would certainly be occupied by the royal forces on the first opportunity, unless it was 'plucked down and made no town.'   The ruin averted then was accomplished one hundred and twenty years later, July 25, 1762, when nearly the whole town was consumed by fire; but two years after, it rose from its ashes 'fairer than before.'"

WOODSTOCK, VERMONT, AND WOODSTOCK, CONNECTICUT

IN St. James Episcopal Church at Woodstock, Vermont, shown in the cut, are two carved wooden panels which came from St. Mary Magdalen's Church in Woodstock, England.   One of these panels is on each side of the chancel, and below one is the following inscription:—

> These panels were given by the Rector and Parishioners of St. Mary Magdalen's Church Woodstock (Oxfordshire) England and once formed a part of the eighteenth century organ loft of that ancient church.

This attractive Vermont town was named after the place of the same name in Connecticut, which in turn was so called from the town of Woodstock in England. The first person to settle in the Vermont town was James Sanderson, who came there about 1670 from Leicester, Massachusetts, having previously lived in Watertown, Massachusetts.   The records show that he was chosen one of the hog drivers of Woodstock in the year 1774.

Woodstock, Connecticut, is closely associated with Massachusetts, for we are told that Rev. John Eliot was wont to pray from his pulpit in Roxbury for his parishioners, the fathers of the Connecticut town, many of whom went there from Roxbury.

A town meeting was held in Roxbury in 1683 to arrange for the new settlement in Connecticut, and at this meeting a number of prominent citizens drew up a petition to the General Court of Massachusetts which was at once granted.   The following year, after the terms set forth were accepted by Roxbury, Samuel and John Ruggles, John Curtis and Edward Morris were sent out to "view the wilderness and find a convenient place."   At first the settlement was called New Roxbury after the Massachusetts town, but finally the citizens, desiring to have a name of

From a photograph   *Kindness Wm. Rodman Fay, Esq.*

ST. JAMES CHURCH, WOODSTOCK, VERMONT
In this church are two panels given by St. Mary Magdalen's Church, in Woodstock, England.

their own, adopted the suggestion of Judge Sewall, that it be called Woodstock, his notes on this subject appearing in his diary as follows:—

> "I gave New Roxbury the name of Woodstock, because of its nearness to Oxford, for the sake of Queen Elizabeth, and the notable meetings that have been held at the place bearing that name in England, some of which Dr. Gilbert informed me of when in England. It stands on a Hill. I saw it as I (went) to Coventry, but left it on the left hand. Some told Capt. Ruggles that I gave the name and put words in his mouth to desire of me a Bell for the Town."

The two New England Woodstocks remember with pride their historic mother town, which is about eight miles from the town of Oxford, and fifty odd miles from London. The appearance of the town has hardly changed an iota during the last three quarters of a century. Here have dwelt many of the kings of England; here King Alfred translated Boethius' Consolations of Philosophy; and here, to the displeasure of his French wife, Eleanor, Duchess of Aquitaine, Henry II brought the fair Rosamond, around whose name cluster so many stories which the light of modern research has proved untrue. Algernon Charles Swinburne has made use of one of the myths in his "Rosamond," the first scene of which is laid in "The Maze at Woodstock," while Tennyson refers to Rosamond's terror of Queen Eleanor in his "Dream of Fair Women." Here Becket came, and Chaucer too,

Kindness Ian Forbes-Robertson, Esq.

From a photograph by Henry W. Taunt

WOODSTOCK, ENGLAND, SHOWING PARK STREET AND THE MARKET PLACE

who laid one of his scenes in "The Dream" in the park of Woodstock; Princess Elizabeth was also imprisoned here by her sister Mary. Tennyson also has faithfully reproduced the scene and the inscription made by Elizabeth on her prison window:—

> "Much suspected, of me
> Nothing proved can be,
> Quoth Elizabeth, Prisoner."

From this town Sir Walter Scott, too, procured the material for his novel "Woodstock."

Saxon and Norman kings for centuries hunted and feasted in Woodstock. One of the last royal banquets was held here for James II in 1687. Some years later the palace was declared to be beyond repair, and in 1704 the royal manor of Woodstock was given to John Churchill, Duke of Marlborough, as a reward for his famous victory at Blenheim. Parliament bestowed £500,000 with which to build the present palace that bears the name of the little village where the Duke of Marlborough attained his victory, and in the park the trees are said to be arranged in the order of the battle of Blenheim. The acorns from one of the oaks in this park were collected a few years ago and sent either to Woodstock, Vermont, or to Woodstock, Connecticut. Much of the beauty of the modern park is due to the genius of "Capability" Brown, the landscape gardener, who by damming the river Glyme, formed a lovely lake on the grounds of the palace, boasting that

> "The Thames will never forgive me for what
> I have done at Blenheim!"

Doctor Johnson, however, who visited the park many years later, irascibly remarked, "The epigram has been drowned!" The present Duke of Marlborough, Charles John Spencer Churchill, K.G., married Consuelo, the daughter of W. K. Vanderbilt, Esq., of New York.

WORCESTER, MASSACHUSETTS

WORCESTER, Massachusetts, was undoubtedly named after the Battle of Worcester which was fought on Worcester Plains in 1651 between the armies of King Charles II and Cromwell. An ancient building in old Worcester called The Commandery, founded by St. Wulfstan in 1095, is pointed out as the house in which the King took refuge, and from which he escaped by the back door. Many relics of this battle have been dug up, and in 1908 the mother city sent to her namesake two suits of armour which had been worn by soldiers of King Charles in this conflict. On page 210 is a picture of one of these suits, both of which were placed in the Mayor's office in City Hall. The

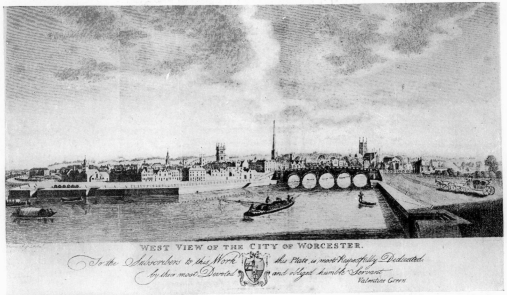

WEST VIEW OF THE CITY OF WORCESTER.

To the Subscribers to this Work this Plate is most Respectfully Dedicated by their most Devoted and obliged humble Servant
Valentine Green

Photographed from "The History and Antiquities of the City and Suburbs of Worcester," by Valentine Green, 1796

Photograph by F. Frith & Co., England   *Kindness Mrs. Mary Fifield King*

WORCESTER, ENGLAND

ONE OF TWO SUITS
OF ARMOUR USED
IN THE BATTLE OF
WORCESTER

brought over in 1908
by Col. Albert Webb of
Worcester, England, as a
present to Worcester,
Massachusetts. It is now
in the City Hall, Worcester,
Massachusetts.

presentation of these interesting gifts was made by Col. Albert Webb, who brought them over as a donation from the Corporation of Worcester, England, together with this letter from the Mayor of old Worcester, Hon. John Stallard:—

"The Mayor, Aldermen and citizens of the city of Worcester and county of the same name in England send a hearty greeting to the Mayor and Corporation of the city of Worcester in Massachusetts, and beg their acceptance, as a token of friendly remembrance, of the accompanying two suits of armour, forming part of nine suits, which, with a brass cannon, were presented to our city by a former member of the corporation as having been used by the soldiers of King Charles the Second at the battle of Worcester, September 3d, 1651, and we have intrusted Col. Albert Webb, V.D., J.P., a member of our corporation to make the presentation of the said suits of armour, with a hearty assurance of our good will toward the city of Worcester in America. Given under our common seal this 16th day of October, 1908."

A committee of well-known Worcester people which included Louis H. Buckley, Charles W. Stevens, Frederick Midgley, John A. Larkin, Frederick H. Luke, George H. Coates, Arthur B. Brunell, John P. Holmgren, Peter F. Sullivan, Samuel S. Green and Nathaniel Paine was appointed to receive Colonel Webb, who during his visit stayed at the house of Mr. Paine. The presentation took place in the Mayor's room in City Hall and the gifts were received by Hon. James Logan, who was Mayor of Worcester at the time. Colonel Webb in his speech made the following remarks:—

"Good-will and high esteem exist all over our country towards this great and powerful nation. We hope that this incident will create an always broadening movement of cordial good feeling in America towards the mother country that will be felt even to the farthest confines of this continent. We wish it to be a token and a proof that only the best of good feeling prevails in England towards America and we hope that the good-will which now exists, and is so essential to the peace of the whole world, will be welded into an unbreakable tie between us. I hope that you will always see in the significance of this gift the guarantee that the two great English-speaking nations of the earth are indissolubly bound together by ties of blood and friendship that nothing can sever."

Mayor Logan's reply included these words:—

"We will give these relics an honored place in our city as a memorial of the men who fought for both you and us in Worcester, England, so many years ago."

The first settlers of Massachusetts at an early date began to move from the coast towards the beautiful Lake Quinsigamond, which was the name of the set-

N.E. VIEW OF WORCESTER CATHEDRAL, 1789.

To the Honourable and Reverend the Dean, and the Reverend the Chapter of Worcester This Plate (Presented by Them to this Work) is most Respectfully Dedicated by their Most Devoted and Obliged humble Servant Valentine Green

From an old print in "The History and Antiquities of the City and Suburbs of Worcester," Valentine Green, 1796

NORTHEAST VIEW OF WORCESTER CATHEDRAL, ENGLAND, 1789

Some fragments from this cathedral were sent to All Saints Church in Worcester, Massachusetts.

tlement on the place where Worcester now is. It was called Quinsigamond, meaning "fishing place for pickerel," until 1684, when it was changed to Worcester. There had been a settlement at Springfield and the General Court thought it desirable to have a place midway between this town and Boston where travelers and horses could rest and spend the night. Daniel Gookin, Edward Johnson, Joshua Fisher and Thomas Noyes were therefore appointed a committee in 1665 to survey the land near the lake and to determine if there was a "meet place for a plantation." A few years later, the committee, though somewhat changed in personnel, reported that the place showed great prospects of being made into an attractive village, and recommended that the Court "reserve it for a town." From 1657 to 1664 the Court made grants of this land to the church at Malden, to Increase Norwell of Charlestown, and to Thomas Noyes of Sudbury. The latter sold his land to Ephraim Curtis of Sudbury, who has been considered the first white settler of Worcester. He was the only white man between Marlboro and Brookfield, and it is said that after a hard day's work he would sit down and, look-

From a photograph   *By E. B. Luce*
ALL SAINTS CHURCH, WORCESTER, MASSACHUSETTS
In this church are relics, shown in another cut, sent as a present by Worcester Cathedral, Worcester, England.

ing towards Sudbury, in his loneliness would shed tears.   He distinguished himself later during the attack of King Philip at Brookfield.   The village, destroyed by the Indians several years later, was rebuilt, but again was destroyed, remaining unoccupied until 1684, when Captain Henchman and his associates returned and built a citadel.   Curtis' son was one of the number and has gone down in history as the first of his family to become a permanent settler.   This settlement was again destroyed by the Indians, but was rebuilt in 1713 by Jonas Rice, who was really responsible for the establishment of the first permanent settlement in the town.   A tablet to his memory has been placed on a boulder on Heywood Street, the inscription reading as follows:—

On this site
In 1713
Major Jonas Rice
Made the first
Permanent Settlement
in Worcester
Placed by
The Worcester Society of Antiquity.

There have been some other interchanges of presents between the two cities, the chief one being some fragments of the Cathedral of Worcester, England, which have been placed as an attractive decoration in the wall of the porch of All Saints Church in our Worcester. At the time of the dispute over the Oregon boundary, when our relations with England were somewhat strained, letters were sent from Worcester, America, to Worcester, England, assuring them of our friendship, and a cordial answer was returned, both of which are preserved in the Worcester Public Library here. Other correspondence followed, including a letter written during the Mexican War by friends in Worcester, England, to the superintendents, teachers and friends of Sabbath-schools and religious education in Worcester, Massachusetts. Some years later, in the year 1874, John Davis Washburn, representing a committee, took over to the English town a collection of books as a present. It was at this time that the fragments from the Cathedral of Worcester were brought back to this country, and the tablet shown in the cut below carefully describes their history.

The English Mayor a few years later wrote to the American city as follows:—

"I truly am doubtful which is best; to have a comfortable past behind you all settled and arranged or a future before you, with all its possibilities."

At the formal opening of the Public Library and Hastings Museum at old Worcester, in 1881, our minister at the Court of St. James, Hon. James Russell Lowell, performed the ceremony, and the librarian of the Free Public Library at Worcester, Massachusetts, sent a cable of greeting to the Mayor of old Worcester which was received as the procession was entering the building. The English Mayor replied by cable.

At the time of the celebration of the two hundredth anniversary of the naming of Worcester, Massachusetts, held in 1884, the Mayor of old Worcester, Hon. W. M. Williamson, was invited to attend the ceremonies, but owing to pressing duties at home he was unable to accept. Several residents of old Worcester, however, have visited the Massachusetts city which bears its name.

From a photograph   By E. B. Luce

RELICS FROM WORCESTER CATHEDRAL,
WORCESTER, ENGLAND,

presented to All Saints Church, Worcester, Massachusetts. The tablet records the event.

From a photograph   *Kindness Mrs. Mary Fifield King*

FRIAR STREET, WORCESTER, ENGLAND

Another Englishman who visited our Worcester was Henry Willis, and shortly after our city sent over numerous other books and pamphlets. Samuel S. Green also visited the English town as a representative of our Worcester, and was received with great courtesy. It should also be mentioned that Mayor Williamson of old Worcester visited our city, and after his return home sent over two beautiful albums of photographs of members of the Corporation of Worcester, England, taken during the Jubilee year, 1887, and other presents.

English Worcester is a quaint and large cathedral city situated on both sides of the river Severn. It became important in early English history owing to the fact of its close proximity to Wales which made it the scene of much fighting in repelling invaders, and time after time the gallant little garrison of the town stemmed the attacks. In 1113 the Welsh burned the town; in 1140 it was taken by the Empress Maud; in 1150 Stephen burned the town, but failed in his attack on the Castle; again in 1189 and 1202 Worcester was burned. The city dates back to 585 A.D., having been built on the site of a Roman town. It was the Wigorna-ceastre of the Saxons, from which comes Worcester, meaning "War Castle," which is an appropriate name, as Briton, Roman, Saxon, Dane and Norman have all fought there. Bishops St. Dunstan and St. Oswald both lived there, the latter becoming the patron saint of the city. St. Oswald dedicated the Cathedral, which was destroyed and rebuilt in the eleventh century by Wulfstan II, who was an even greater saint. The present church in 1218 was again partially rebuilt and dedicated with great

From "Barber's Historical Collections"

WORCESTER, MASSACHUSETTS (MAIN STREET)
An old view.

pomp, St. Wulfstan's body being enshrined in the altar.   In this church there also
is a tomb of King John, which is the oldest regal tomb in England; in 1797 it was
opened to prove to archæologists that the body was really that of the king.

The Guildhall was built in 1721 and contains many suits of armour which were
worn during the Battle of Worcester and which are similar to the ones sent to
this country.

Queen Elizabeth on her visit to Worcester in 1574 granted a charter to some
clothiers, forming them into a corporation which still exists.   Another item of
interest is that Sir Henry Washington who was made Governor of Worcester in
the absence of the regular Governor, while the latter was a prisoner during the
siege of Worcester, was supposed to be connected with the ancestry of Gen.
George Washington.   Dean Swift was also a resident of the city.

The present Mayor of the English Worcester, Hon. Arthur Carlton, during the
war suggested that the citizens of his town "adopt" Worcester, Massachusetts,
and invite all officers and men of the American Army hailing from Worcester, and
who took part in the Great War, to visit the homes of the people of his city during
any leave of absence.   This idea of the English Mayor was enlarged upon and about
three hundred towns in England "adopted" other towns in America, in most cases
choosing those of the same name as their own.

The latest expression of interest towards England was shown very recently by
the Worcester Art Museum, which assumed responsibility for, and made possible,
the tour of the British Government Exhibition of War Pictures in this country.
The paintings were by Sir William Orpen, the well-known Irishman and other
artists of the British Empire.

YARMOUTH, MASSACHUSETTS

AT Yarmouth, England, also known as Great Yarmouth, Admiral Nelson was given the freedom of the city, and the Town Clerk, as he administered the oath, said, "Hold up your right hand, my Lord," to which came the reply, "That is at Teneriffe," whereupon the people renewed their shouting in their jubilation over the recent successes of the British Navy. It is said that Yarmouth watched the Admiral's career with unusual interest, and it is certain that on this visit the people showed special enthusiasm, for they took the horses from his carriage and themselves drew him through the crowded streets of the town. This incident took place in 1800 after the battle of the Nile, and to the present time the Nelson room in the "Old Star Hotel" on the Quay is pointed out with interest to the visitor, as Nelson is said to have lodged there on another occasion when he landed at that seaport. The panelling from the Nelson room was sold to an American some years ago and is believed now to be in Washington, D.C. This hotel was not used always as an inn, having been built in the last part of the sixteenth century by William Crowe as his private residence.

Many jokes have been made about Yarmouth and its herrings, it having often been said that the town was "built upon herring bones." Another person in describing it said it was known for its herrings and excursionists, while still another writer in speaking of its herring fishery says, "It is the worthiest herring fishery in Europe, which draweth great concourse of people, which maketh the town much richer all the year following, but very unsavory for the time." Once a year Yarmouth used to hold a herring fair. At one time this port registered six hundred and thirty-one sailing vessels, and claimed that its herring nets, added to those owned by the nearby town of Lowestoft, would stretch over two hundred miles. Certainly the Yarmouth bloater has made a world-wide reputation, although in the old days it was claimed that there was so much smuggling between Holland and the English coast that spirits were sometimes more profitable than fishing. On the town arms are three herrings with lions' heads, a symbol of the prosperity of the town and also a recognition of loyalty to the King.

It was the beachmen's colony in Yarmouth that especially attracted the attention of Dickens; these beachmen used to derive their living from salvaging boats that went ashore off the Yarmouth coast, and according to one of the historians of the town the customary prayer of the children of this little colony was, "Pray God send daddy a good ship ashore before morning." There are many people in Yarmouth who remember Dickens' "Mr. Peggotty's house," which was an old ship on the beach where he lived. Dickens must have been very fond of the town, because he is said to have made the remark that if one had a grudge against any particular insurance company the best way to gratify it would be to buy a large annuity and then retire to Yarmouth to live.

CUSTOM-HOUSE, TOWN-HOUSE, and SOUTH-QUAY, YARMOUTH

From an old print; photograph by Alfred Yallop   *Kindness Ian Forbes-Robertson, Esq.*

THE QUAY, YARMOUTH, ENGLAND,

as it looked in 1814, showing Custom-House and Town House.   The Quay is over a mile in length.

In the town there are many quaint houses, which have a very foreign appearance, resembling very much the old buildings of Amsterdam and Rotterdam; David Copperfield himself thought they looked very Dutch, also saying that "if land had been a little more separated from the sea and the town and the tide had not been quite so mixed up, like toast and water, it would have been much nicer," but after he had smelt the fish, pitch, oakum and tallow, and had seen the sailors walking about, he said he felt he had done the place an injustice. Characteristic of the town are the numerous "Rows," or narrow alleys, one of which, called "Kitty Witches," is at one point only twenty-nine inches wide.

An interesting visitor to Yarmouth was Charles II who was received there in 1671, and who was presented with four herrings made of gold with ruby eyes. These few words describe his visit:—

> " Yarmouth had first (O, more than happy port!)
> The honour to receive the King and Court,
> And entertain, season providing dishes,
> The King of England with the king of fishes!"

It may be interesting also to mention that Governor Winthrop in the "Arbella" sailed from this port, while still another occasion of interest was a dinner along the Quay which was held in 1814 to celebrate the restoration of King Louis XVIII of

From an old print owned by a Boston collector   *Formerly in the collection of J. H. Seers, Essex, England*

THE QUAY, YARMOUTH, ENGLAND

France.   There was a curious superstition in the town that when an old maid died the steeple nodded.

The old seaport contains one of the largest parish churches in England, Herbert de Lozenga, the first Norman Bishop of Norwich, being responsible for its erection in 1101.   It is dedicated to St. Nicholas, the patron saint of fishermen.   It is claimed that the people of Yarmouth have some Danish fighting blood in their veins, but however this may be, they have always proved great fishermen, sailors and fighters.   At one time the town also pursued both the cod and whale fisheries.

Yarmouth is situated on a peninsula at the mouth of the Yare River, from which, of course, it gets its name.   Much of the land was marsh land and was eaten away by the sea, which caused an old salt once to remark quite truthfully that "it would take a heap of money to make us quite safe."   Much of the land, however, has been reclaimed, and many cattle now graze on pastures where Roman galleys once sailed.

When the Dutch lived in the town the friendship between them and the other residents of Yarmouth was so strong that the Yarmouthites inaugurated what they called a "Dutch" Sunday, which was the Sunday before September 21st, when the herring fishing began.   This important event began with a ceremony called "Wetting the Nets," the nature of which is easily guessed. Of course, the Dutchmen arrived in time for this important occasion, and Nall, the Yarmouth historian, quotes the words of an eye-witness to their arrival: "With the afternoon's tide the Dutchmen began to enter the haven's mouth; and it was pleasing to see them proceed, one after the other, up the river to the town. . . . Of these vessels about fifty came up this year. All of them arrived in the course of Friday evening; and at night I took a walk to view them by moonlight. The odd line of masts, exactly uniform; the yards and furled sails disposed in a regular row, the crews sitting on deck with their pipes, calmly enjoying their repose, and conversing in a strange tongue, impressed the imagination in a forcible but pleasing manner; the quiet and order which reigned among so large a number was much to be admired. On Saturday the streets were sprinkled with parties of Dutchmen, easily distinguished by their round caps, short jackets and most capacious breeches. . . . On the ensuing Sunday, called 'Dutch Sunday' all the country round, as far as Norwich, flocked to see the show. The Dutch did honour to their visitors by decorating their schuyts with flags in the gayest manner they were able. The whole length of the quay was crowded by people of all ranks, in their best apparel. . . . It was a view equally striking and singular, and not to be matched in any part of the kingdom." "Dutch Sunday" is now an obsolete festival, and the Dutchmen no longer "wet their nets" at Yarmouth; but they still come here and to Lowestoft in considerable numbers at Christmas for pickled herring, and then look very like their forerunners of a century and a half ago. They are still distinguished by their "round caps, short jackets, and most capacious breeches." The Great Yarmouth Public Library possesses many books, pamphlets, prints and photographs relating to our Yarmouth and sent over by our town.

Yarmouth on Cape Cod is one of the most beautiful towns on the Cape, and at one time included not only the present Yarmouth but also Dennis, which was made a separate township in 1794. The First Church of Yarmouth was founded in 1639, the early ministers in their order being Rev. Marmaduke Matthews, Rev. John Miller, Rev. Thomas Thornton and Rev. John Cotton, a grandson of John Cotton. It is particularly interesting to learn that one hundred and ninety-one Indians attended this little church during the pastorates of Miller and Thornton. The names of those to whom the first grant was made were Antony Thacher (usually spelled Anthony), Thomas Howes and John Crow, who proceeded at once to organize the town, erecting a fort at Fort Hill near the old cemetery. Anthony Thacher was the oldest settler of the town and the most helpful man in the colony, his descendants being among the leading citizens of Yarmouth and Boston at the present day. The farm now owned by a member of the family, Hon. Thomas C. Thacher, belonged to his ancestor, and in his memory in 1905 he and others of his family placed a stone on the supposed site of the old house; the inscription reads as follows:—

Photograph by F. Frith & Co., England · · · · · · · · · · · · Kindness Ian Forbes-Robertson, Esq.

GREY FRIARS ROW, YARMOUTH, ENGLAND

These very narrow "Rows," or alleys, are characteristic of the town.

Near this Site Lived and Was Buried
ANTONY THACHER
He came to America in 1635
from Somersetshire England.
Shipwrecked on Thacher's Island 1635.
Settled in Yarmouth 1639.

Three years later the Thacher family gave to the town a road called the Thacher Shore Road, built over what is supposed to be the location of the old Colonial road laid out by the early settlers of Yarmouth. Much of it runs through the Anthony Thacher farm. There is an inscription on a tablet placed at its eastern end, worded as follows:—

THACHER SHORE ROAD
Given to the Town of Yarmouth
in memory of
HENRY C. THACHER
by his wife and children
1908

Thomas Howes later went to North Dennis, where a memorial shaft was set up in 1834 to his memory in the old Howes burial ground and, as it was one of the earliest monuments to the early settlers erected in this country, we give the inscription:—

Thus from the central part of Britton's isle they came
And on Columbia's soil did propigate a name
We their descendants the Patriarch own
And to the first Howes do dedicate this stone.
This monument was erected in 1834, etc.

Richard Sears, usually referred to as "The Pilgrim," was another important man in the history of the Cape and particularly at Yarmouth and Chatham, where in the cemeteries of these towns monuments have been set up to the memory of himself and his descendants. He married Dorothy Thacher, the daughter of Anthony, and is said to have attended the Yarmouth church for twenty-three years. This Richard Sears, the founder of the American line, sought refuge in Leyden and in 1630 sailed for the New World, landing at Plymouth in May of the year 1630. In 1643 he removed to Yarmouth. The monument at Yarmouth bears the following inscription:—

Sacred to the memory of
RICHARD SEARS,
Son of John Bourchier Sears and
Marie L. Van Egmont,
In lineal descent from
Richard Sears of Colchester
And Ann Bourchier Knyvet,
England.
He landed at Plymouth in 1630.
Married Dorothy Thacher,
And died in Yarmouth in
1676.

MARKET PLACE, YARMOUTH, ENGLAND

From an old print owned by a Boston collector   *Formerly in the collection of J. H. Seers, Essex, England*

RATHMINES PUBLIC LIBRARY

There are also tablets on this monument to the memory of his three sons, Knyvet, Paul and Sylas. The monument in the Chatham cemetery, which is similar in form to the one in Yarmouth, bears inscriptions to the memory of Daniel Sears, a grandson of Richard Sears, and other descendants of "The Pilgrim."

The original family name in England was Scearstan, the more modern spelling having been Sarre, Syer, Sayer, Saers, Sayers and Searston. There is a village on the Isle of Alney, in the county of Gloucester, named Scearstan. The family of Sayers or Sears is to be found in the vicinity of Colchester in the county of Essex, this branch being the direct descendants of Adam Sare, whose great-grandson served in Parliament for the town and port of Sandwich. Members of this family appear frequently on the early records of Colchester, one John Sayer having held the office of Alderman. There is a monument and many tablets to the Sears family in the parish church of St. Peter in Colchester, England. On the two hundred and fiftieth anniversary of the founding of the Massachusetts

From a photograph *Kindness of the late Willard T. Sears and Hans Eberhard, Esq.*

MONUMENT TO RICHARD SEARS IN YARMOUTH, MASSACHUSETTS

He was the founder of the American line of Sears, coming to Massachusetts in 1630. Some of his descendants settled at Chatham, among them being his grandson, Daniel Sears, over whose grave a monument similar to the one in Yarmouth has been erected. The name of Sears is closely associated with the early history of Cape Cod. Richard Sears married Dorothy, daughter of Antony Thacher of Yarmouth, Massachusetts, one of the first three grantees of land in that town.

town, which was held in 1889, one of the descendants of Richard Sears, Philip Howes Sears, was the orator of the day. One of the inscriptions over the lunch tent on this occasion was "Mattacheese 1639—Yarmouth 1889," the former word being the Indian name of the town. Another inscription on the tent was the motto, "We will our celebration keep," which were the words of King Henry IV. It is especially interesting to mention that our Yarmouth was as much interested in whaling as its forefathers in the old town in Britain, and has also furnished many shipmasters and sailors. It is also interesting to record that Yarmouth, Barnstable and Sandwich were all founded on the same day, as one orator at the Yarmouth celebration pointed out, and which fact, he said, may have prevented his making two more speeches. The following lines written by Mrs. Mary M.

Bray at the time of this celebration tell us of those names so well known in this quaint Cape Cod town:—

"We search the records once again and read
The names of those who pioneered the way,
Hallett and Matthews, Thacher, Howes and Crow,
Simpkins and Ryder, Taylor, Sears and Gray."

Other lines written for the occasion we also quote:—

"We lift the Pilgrims' war cry still
For freedom and for God,
And wear as proudest title yet
The sons of old Cape Cod."

NAMES

From Somerset and Devon,
From York and Worcestershire,
The younger sons came sailing
With hearts of steel and fire.

From leafy lane and valley,
Fair glebe and ancient wood,
The counties of old England
Poured forth their warmest blood.

Out of the grey-walled cities,
Away from the castled towns,
Corners of thatch and roses,
Heathery combes and downs,

With neither crown nor penny,
But an iron will they came;
Heirs of an old tradition
And a good old English name.

A stark great silence met them
On a nameless, savage shore;
But they called the wild,—"New England,"
For the sake of the blood they bore.

"Plymouth, Exeter, Bristol,
Boston, Windsor, Wells."
Beloved names of England
Rang in their hearts like bells.

They named their rocky farmlands,
  Their hamlets by the sea,
For the mother-towns that bred them,
  In racial loyalty.

"Cambridge, Hartford, Gloucester,
  Hampton, Norwich, Stowe."
The younger sons looked backward
  And sealed their sonship so.

The old blood thrills in answer,
  As centuries go by,
To names that meant a challenge,
  A signal, or a sigh.

Now over friendly oceans
  The old towns, each to each,
Call with the kinship in a name;
  One race, one truth, one speech.

This poem, "Names," is used by permission of Miss Abbie Farwell Brown, from her new volume of verses, "Heart of New England."

END OF PART I

TOWNS *of* NEW ENGLAND

AND

Old England

IRELAND *and* SCOTLAND

Part II

Photographed from a rare coloured engraving in the St. Botolph Club, Boston, Massachusetts   *Kindness of the Governors of the St. Botolph Club*

MAY SHEEP FAIR, BOSTON, LINCOLNSHIRE, ENGLAND,

showing St. Botolph's Church in the background. This rare engraving is taken from a painting by George Northouse, of Boston, England. There are several other similar prints owned and highly prized by collectors in Boston, Massachusetts. One of these prints is owned by the State Street Trust Company.

TOWNS
OF
NEW ENGLAND
AND
Old England,
IRELAND and SCOTLAND
❧ PART II ❧

Connecting Links between *Cities and Towns*
of NEW ENGLAND and *Those of the Same
Name* in ENGLAND, IRELAND *and* SCOTLAND
Containing Narratives, Descriptions,
and Many Views, some done
from *Old Prints*

Also much Matter pertaining to
The Founders and Settlers of New England
and to their Memorials on both sides of the Atlantic

By ALLAN FORBES

Written to Commemorate THE TERCENTENARY *of*
THE LANDING of the PILGRIMS
AND NOW ISSUED BY THE
Tudor Publishing Company
NEW YORK
MCMXXXVI

It was but natural that the Lion
and the Unicorn should have been used
on the Old State House for decorative purposes when the building was first erected before
the Declaration of Independence. At the time that
the name of King Street was changed to State Street,
the original figures were destroyed, being replaced, however,
when the building was restored in 1882. Still again there was
a change due to the fact that the old wooden figures began to decay,
necessitating the substitution, soon after 1900, of the present ones, which
are made of copper. The wooden Lion and Unicorn now beautify a lawn in
Chestnut Hill, on the outskirts of Boston. The Lion and the Unicorn are called
in heraldic terms "supporters," for the reason that they are the figures placed on either
side of a coat of arms shield, suggesting their support of it. They seem to have been originally introduced by the engravers of seals purely from an artistic point of view to fill up the
space between the shield of arms and the circle in which it is usually set, but they have nothing
to do with the coat of arms itself. The Unicorn is a favorite "supporter" in Scottish heraldry,
having first appeared about the year 1480. In 1505 it is recorded that the Scottish
Arms were supported by two Unicorns. As late as the year 1766 the Unicorn was
still placed on the right, but after the Union it became the left supporter, the
Lion being the right supporter. The Unicorn is, of course, a fabulous animal. The earliest heraldic lion known is the rampant lion of Flanders,
which appeared in the seal of Richard I. These two present supporters of the shield of the United Kingdom were introduced
by King James I of England and VI of Scotland on his
accession to the throne of England in 1603 and have
remained unchanged to this day. Before this date,
however, supporters were constantly being
changed. A picture of the Old State
House, upon which appear the Lion
and the Unicorn, is on page 39.

Edited and designed by direction of
Walton Advertising & Printing Co.
Boston, Mass.

TABLE OF CONTENTS

LIST OF ILLUSTRATIONS

———

PAGE

LIST OF ILLUSTRATIONS

LIST OF ILLUSTRATIONS

LIST OF ILLUSTRATIONS

ENGLAND,

showing by capital letters and dots within the circles, location of the English towns mentioned in Part I and in Part II.

FOREWORD

THIS book, as in the case of Part I, has been written by the author with the object in view of placing before the people of New England, in commemoration of the Tercentenary of the Landing of the Pilgrims, information concerning those cities and towns in New England which have been named for places in England, Ireland and Scotland. The work endeavors to relate the experiences of the early settlers, to make clear the origin of the names of the new communities and to record the connecting links between places in the old country and their New England namesakes. The sketches of the early history of these cities and towns in New England include pictures and inscriptions of many tablets and memorials on both sides of the Atlantic which connect places of the same name in New England and Great Britain, together with many photographs and prints of interest.

The author has endeavored to include in this volume the most important cities and towns in New England which were named after those in England, Ireland and Scotland and which were not included in Part I. The places described last year were Plymouth and Southampton, Andover, Barnstable, Bath, Belfast, Beverly, Bristol, Cambridge, Chatham, Chelmsford, Dartmouth, New Bedford and Bedford, Dedham, Dorchester, Dublin, Falmouth, Gloucester, Groton, Hartford, Harwich, Hingham, Melrose, Northampton, Norwich, Portsmouth and Rye, Sandwich, Wareham, Woodstock, Worcester and Yarmouth.

There are a few towns in the New England States which, for lack of space, it has been necessary to omit from both Part I and Part II, but we believe that we have described in the two volumes most of the important places in New England which have connections with the places in the British Isles whence they derived their names.

We have thought it fitting to begin Part II with Boston, the other towns following alphabetically.

We repeat here that the idea was suggested to us by Walter R. Whiting, Esq., who showed us several pamphlets written by Rev. Louis C. Cornish showing the connecting links between Hingham, Massachusetts, and Hingham, England.

The author is very grateful for the assistance given by the Mayors of the towns in the British Isles, heads of Museums and of Historical Societies who contributed much valuable material but all of whose names, unfortunately, we do not have.

The author wishes to give credit again to Ian Forbes-Robertson, Esq., of Farnham, Surrey, England, who gave such valuable assistance concerning the places in Great Britain and who obtained most of the pictures of points of interest in those towns, for without such help as his these two volumes could not have been compiled.

The author, too, is indebted to the late Oscar Fay Adams, who compiled a history of many towns in Great Britain but who unfortunately died before it could be published. This material was presented to us through the kindness of Miss Abbie Farwell Brown and Miss M. B. Lazenby. His manuscript was of great help in checking the information concerning these towns across the water and it is fitting that his work and his name should share in the preparation of these two publications.

Thanks are due to Mayors of our cities, Selectmen of towns, officials of Libraries and Historical Societies and other residents of places in New England who have forwarded to the author for examination letters, records (in many cases original documents) and photographs; to these persons the author and the readers of this book are especially indebted. It has been our endeavor to remember all who have assisted us, and we have included these in a list below. There may be others, however, who, through the great volume of correspondence, may have been overlooked, and to these persons the author offers both his apologies and his thanks.

Much credit is due likewise to Perry Walton, Esq., of the Walton Advertising and Printing Company, who has assisted in compiling and arranging all our publications for the past sixteen years, and to his efficient staff which includes Josephine Sullivan, Hans Eberhard, Mary N. Cornell, Cornelia Randall, Ruth P. Wedge and William Bond Wheelwright. Thanks are also due for the assistance given by Mrs. Louise Ames Norman.

At the suggestion of a number of readers of Part I of this commemorative series, the author of both books has reluctantly subscribed his name at the end of this Foreword and wishes at the same time to add that he was assisted in their preparation by Ashton L. Carr, Vice President of the Trust Company, by Ralph

M. Eastman, Assistant to the President, by Miss Edith E. Olson of the Trust Company staff and by Miss Florence H. Cabot, now Mrs. Herman H. Fardelman.

The author thanks the people of New England for the appreciation with which Part I was received and trusts this one, its successor, will prove equally interesting. Although these books were prepared to commemorate the Tercentenary of the landing of the Pilgrims, and are of special interest to Americans, they also appeal to the peoples of the British Empire. This has been shown by the demand for Part I from all parts of the English-speaking world, and it is hoped that these books will cement a closer friendship between the two nations.

In the preparation of this volume we are indebted especially to Hon. Andrew J. Peters, Mayor of Boston, and his Secretary, E. V. B. Parke, Esq., who helped us in regard to Boston. We also wish to thank Rt. Rev. Bishop Lawrence for valuable help given us in connection with interchanges between churches in the two countries; Rev. William S. Key, formerly of Boston, England; Charles F. Belden, Esq., Otto Fleischner, Esq., and other officials and clerks of the Boston Public Library, for untiring efforts in procuring information of value for this book; also Mrs. Mary Fifield King, Walter K. Watkins, Esq. and George Francis Dow, Esq., for a number of pictures of towns in Great Britain.

The list of those who helped us on different cities and towns is appended.

BOSTON: Thomas Tileston Baldwin, Abbie Farwell Brown, Rev. Howard N. Brown, George W. Coleman, Frederic H. Curtiss, Rev. William H. Dewart, Henry H. Edes, Rev. Prescott Evarts, P. K. Foley, J. Pennington Gardiner, Edward M. Hartwell, Rev. W. S. Key, Fred H. Kimball, Rt. Rev. William Lawrence, Rev. Alexander Mann, Robert Treat Paine, Rev. Charles E. Park, Charles F. Read, Henry B. Sawyer, Ralph A. Stewart, Charles H. Taylor, Jr., Julius H. Tuttle, Rev. William Harman van Allen.

ATHOL: Duke of Atholl (Blair Atholl, Scotland), William G. Lord, Pearl L. Mason, William B. McSkimmon, F. E. Wing. ATTLEBORO: Mrs. Walter M. Kendall, Walter O. Lochner, Rev. Charles H. Pennoyer, Mrs. Lucinda F. Spofford, Mrs. Joseph L. Sweet.

BIDDEFORD: Walter H. Bradley, Frank C. Deering, Rev. George A. Gordon, Emma Hatch, E. L. Morrill, Burton H. Winslow. BRAINTREE: Marion S. Arnold, Mrs. Caroline A. Bill, Charles H. Taylor, Jr. BRIDGEWATER: Lucia L. Christian, Joshua E. Crane.

COVENTRY: William L. Higgins, Mrs. W. R. Thurber.

DOVER: Clara P. Atkinson, Arthur G. Fuller, C. H. Garland, Corwin McDowell, Augustin H. Parker, Frank Smith.

EXETER: Edmund S. Boyer, Miss Carrie W. Byington, Minnie T. Knight, Harry V. Lawrence, Winifred L. MacKay, Dr. Edward O. Otis.

FRAMINGHAM: Nathaniel I. Bowditch, Peter N. Everett, John M. Merriam.

GREENWICH: H. Ashton Crosby, Erwin Edwards, Spencer P. Mead, Major Evelyn Wrench, Dr. James F. Muirhead.

HAVERHILL: Paul E. Gray, Daniel M. Gurteen (Haverhill, England), John G. Moulton, Leonard W. Smith, C. S. Whittier. HULL: John H. Grout (American Consul, Hull, England), Charles H. Pearson, T. Sheppard (Hull, England).

IPSWICH: Francis R. Appleton, Joseph I. Horton, Herbert W. Mason, Mrs. Augustus N. Rantoul, Augustus N. Rantoul, the late T. Franklin Waters.

LANCASTER: Virginia M. Keyes, Mrs. Nathaniel Thayer. LINCOLN: Mrs. John P. Bowditch, John P. Bowditch, Moorfield Storey, George G. Tarbell. LONDONDERRY: A. E. Cudworth, Norreys Jephson O'Conor. LYNN: John Albree, Luther Atwood, Major Coxon (Lynn Regis, England), Hon. Walter H. Creamer, R. M. De Cormis, Francis Gray, Mrs. G. G. Hammond, Joseph F. Hannan, B. N. Johnson, Rev. W. Appleton Lawrence, Walter R. Whiting.

MALDEN: Hon. Charles M. Blodgett, A. L. Clarke (Maldon, England), Dr. Godfrey Ryder, F. A. Shove, W. G. A. Turner. MANCHESTER, NEW HAMPSHIRE: E. Howard George, Alfred S. Jewett, H. A. McElwain, A. W. Phinney, C. W. Sutton (Manchester, England), Miss F. Mabel Winchell. MEDFORD: N. Penrose Hallowell, Moses W. Mann.

NEWBURY: Miss Susan Ilsley Adams, Harriette E. Jones, Rev. Herbert Edwin Lombard, Rev. Glenn Tilley Morse, Mrs. F. S. Moseley, J. B. Shearer, Rev. Arthur H. Wright. NEWCASTLE: Wallace Hackett, William D. Turner. NEW LONDON: M. M. Baker, Miss Elizabeth Gorton, P. Le Roy Harwood, Dr. J. F. Muirhead, Ernest E. Rogers, Major Evelyn Wrench.

OXFORD: Everett Carleton, William Arthur Dupee, Mrs. Clara A. Fuller, Dr. Elliott P. Joslin, Mrs. William B. Scofield, Harry Worcester Smith, Benjamin H. Stone, Stead W. Rodgers.

READING: The late Solon Bancroft, Rev. J. J. Cogan, Miss Emma Florence Eaton, Charles A. Loring, Rev. Austin Rice, Horace G. Wadlin. ROWLEY: Charles F. Allen, Amos E. Jewett.

SALISBURY: Edmund Chase Eastman. SHERBORN: Francis Bardwell, Henry G. Vaughan. SPRINGFIELD: W. F. Adams, G. C. Baldwin, Frank H. Page. STRATFORD: Edward Fox, Esq., J. P. (Mayor of Stratford-on-Avon, England), Miss Frances B. Russell. SUDBURY: Mrs. John P. Bowditch, John P. Bowditch, Rev. Paul Revere Frothingham, Frank F. Gerry, J. V. Lee, John M. Merriam.

TAUNTON: The late Edith M. Hodgman, Frank Walcott Hutt, Edward Lovering, Edward H. Temple, Edwin A. Tetlow. TOPSFIELD: George Francis Dow, T. W. Pierce.

WALTHAM: Thomas H. Armstrong, C. F. French, E. L. Sanderson, Charles Stone, John H. Storer, Rev. Francis E. Webster. WARWICK: Herbert O. Brigham, Howard M. Chapin, H. R. Curtis, Mrs. H. W. Marsh, H. W. Marsh (Warwick, England), Thomas S. Longridge, Herbert H. White. WATERTOWN: R. M. Saltonstall. WEYMOUTH: Judge Louis A. Cook, E. R. Hastings, *The Times*, London. WINCHESTER: George H. Eustis, Sinclair Kennedy, Librarian at Guildhall Library, London, Henry G. Lord, Bowen Tufts, Major Evelyn Wrench. WINDSOR: Julia M. Clapp, Gilbert F. Davis, G. G. Wilder. WOBURN: Judge Edward F. Johnson.

YORK: Mrs. J. P. Bowditch, A. M. Bragdon, Henry S. Burrage, D.D. (Historian of

Maine), Alfred Johnson, Edward C. Moody, James Brown Thornton, M.D., Sophia Turner.

GENERAL: Rodolphe L. Agassiz, Hon. Thomas W. Bicknell, Mrs. Charles S. Bird, Grace Blanchard, Mrs. Alice E. Boynton, F. B. Brightman, Thomas G. Brown, Howard M. Buck, Charles H. Butler, Mrs. George Leonard Chaney, Howard M. Chapin, George K. Clarke, Luther Conant, Rev. Louis C. Cornish, Mrs. George H. Davis, Mrs. Henry Dorrance, Richard H. Evans, Fred T. Field, Redington Fiske, George S. Godard, Mrs. Albert L. Hall, Henry M. Hutchings, Mrs. Minnie T. Knight, Miss Mabel E. Knowlton, Willard P. Lewis, C. D. Lyons & Company, E. A. Marsh, Louis L. Robinson, Samuel Russell, Robert B. Smith, Louis E. Stoddard, Thomas Sutton, J. B. Taylor, Lucien Thompson, Hon. John J. Treat, Walter K. Watkins, George E. Watters, Harold E. Watters, Miss Florence E. Wheeler, Elbert W. Whitney, Robert Whittaker, Miss Elizabeth Wilkinson.

In closing this Foreword we would like to express our belief that the spirit of our forefathers so well referred to in a poem by John Pierpont almost one hundred years ago in 1824, at the Plymouth celebration, will always endure in America.

> "The Pilgrim Fathers,—where are they?
>   The waves that brought them o'er
> Still roll in the bay, and throw their spray,
>   As they break along the shore;
> Still roll in the bay, as they rolled that day
>   When the Mayflower moored below,
> When the sea around was black with storms,
>   And white the shore with snow.
>
> The mists that wrapped the Pilgrim's sleep
>   Still brood upon the tide;
> And the rocks yet keep their watch by the deep,
>   To stay its waves of pride.
> But the snow-white sail that he gave to the gale,
>   When the heavens looked dark, is gone;
> As an angel's wing, through an opening cloud,
>   Is seen, and then withdrawn.
>
> The Pilgrim exile,—sainted name!
>   The hill whose icy brow
> Rejoiced, when he came, in the morning's flame,
>   In the morning's flame burns now;
> And the moon's cold light, as it lay that night
>   On the hill-side and the sea,
> Still lies where he laid his houseless head;
>   But the Pilgrim,—where is he?
>
> The Pilgrim Fathers are at rest:
>   When Summer is throned on high,
> And the world's warm breast is in verdure dressed,
>   Go, stand on the hill where they lie.

The earliest ray of the golden day
  On that hallowed spot is cast;
And the evening sun as he leaves the world,
  Looks kindly on that spot last.

The Pilgrim spirit has not fled:
  It walks in noon's broad light;
And it watches the bed of the glorious dead,
  With the holy stars, by night.
It watches the bed of the brave who have bled,
  And shall guard this ice-bound shore
Till the waves of the bay, where the Mayflower lay,
  Shall foam and freeze no more."

(The fourth verse of this ode was printed on page 29 of Part I.)

This poem was also on the program of the Tercentennial Celebration held at Plymouth, Massachusetts, on December 21, 1920. On this occasion Governor Calvin Coolidge of Massachusetts sat in the chair brought over by Governor Bradford, which is now owned by William R. Hedge, Henry R. Hedge and their sister, direct descendants of this early Governor.

ALLAN FORBES,

BOSTON, 1921.

———————

From an engraving in the St. Botolph Club, Boston, Massachusetts   *Kindness of the Governors of the St. Botolph Club*

ST. BOTOLPH'S CHURCH, BOSTON, ENGLAND

There is also an etching of this church in the St. Botolph Club, presented in 1903 by William Harwood of Boston, England.

TOWNS of NEW ENGLAND
and
Old England, Ireland and Scotland

BOSTON, MASSACHUSETTS

"St. Botolph's Town! Hither across the plains
And fens of Lincolnshire, in garb austere,
There came a Saxon monk, and founded here
A Priory, pillaged by marauding Danes,
So that thereof no vestige now remains;
Only a name, that, spoken loud and clear,
And echoed in another hemisphere,
Survives the sculptured walls and painted panes.

St. Botolph's Town! Far over leagues of land
And leagues of sea looks forth its noble tower,
And far around the chiming bells are heard;
So may that sacred name forever stand
A landmark, and a symbol of the power
That lies concentred in a single word."

S T. BOTOLPH'S TOWN, so well described by Longfellow in these well-known lines, and our Boston have had many interchanges, one of the most interesting being the collection of six seals of old Boston which now hangs in the Committee Room of the City Council in our City Hall, a present sent by Hon. Meaburn Staniland, Mayor of the old town, at the suggestion of John Lewis Clark, Esq., who made a visit to Boston, England, in 1849. Mr. Clark in a letter now on file in our City Hall gives an account of this gift in a communication addressed to Mayor John P. Bigelow of this city in 1851. The seals are all of the period of Henry VIII, when the borough was incorporated, and the wooden frame was made from one of the original timbers of St. Botolph's Church, of which Rev. John Cotton was vicar for twenty-one years. The frame bears the following inscription:—

Photographed by George B. Brayton   Kindness Hon. Andrew J. Peters, Mayor of Boston, Massachusetts, and E. V. B. Parke, Esq.

SMALL BOX SENT IN 1919 TO HON. ANDREW J. PETERS, MAYOR OF BOSTON, NEW ENG–
LAND, BY HIS WORSHIPFUL A. COOKE YARBOROUGH, MAYOR OF OLD BOSTON

It is made from the railings that formed part of the dock in the old Guildhall, where the Pilgrim Fathers
were tried in 1607. The message that came within the box appears in another illustration.

TO THE CITY OF BOSTON, UNITED STATES
FROM
MEABURN STANILAND, ESQUIRE, MAYOR
OF BOSTON, OLD ENGLAND, 1849.

Our Mayor gratefully acknowledged receipt of the seals and at the same time sent
some books and reports of our city to the English city. Another interesting present sent over here in 1919 to our City Hall is an oak box containing a scroll upon
which the Mayor, Aldermen and Burgesses of Boston, England, congratulate the
Mayor and Governing Body of our Boston on the victories of the American armies
in France and the valuable assistance given to the Allied cause by the American
Navy. The English officials also refer with pride to the connection between their
ancient borough and the capital of Massachusetts. The plate on the outside of
the box explains its history:—

To the Honourable Andrew J. Peters,
Mayor and to the Governing Body
of the City of Boston, Massachusetts:

This box (which is made from the rails which formed a part of the dock in
the old Guildhall, where the Pilgrim Fathers were tried in the year 1607)
with the enclosed address of good fellowship, is presented by the Worshipful the Mayor and Corporation of the Borough of Boston, England.

A. COOKE YARBOROUGH, *Mayor.*

Photographed by George B. Brayton

Kindness Hon. Andrew J. Peters, Mayor of Boston, Massachusetts,
E. V. B. Parke, Esq., and E. M. Hartwell, Esq.

OLD SEALS OF BOSTON, ENGLAND,

now in the Committee Room of the City Council in City Hall, Boston, Massachusetts. They are of the period of Henry VIII and were presented to our city in 1849 by Hon. Meaburn Staniland, Mayor of Boston, England. The frame was made from one of the original timbers of St. Botolph's Church, Boston, England.

Among other documents in City Hall is a communication sent in 1856 from old Boston to our City Government expressing appreciation of the visit of Hon. Joseph Story, President of the Boston Common Council, who made a visit to St. Botolph's Town the year before. Still another document was written in 1865 expressing the sorrow of the people of old Boston at the time of the death of Abraham Lincoln.

Another interchange of greetings occurred during the Mayoralty of the Hon. Frederick O. Prince of our Boston, who invited the Mayor of the English town to be present at the two hundred and fiftieth anniversary of the founding of our city. The Vicar of Boston at this time wrote:—

"I beg you to convey in such way as you deem most suitable my most grateful acknowledgments to those, who with yourself have been the cause of my late invitation, assuring them that both as a successor of John Cotton, one of your honoured founders, and as an inhabitant of the Town from which your city takes its name, I shall ever cherish the deepest interest in its welfare, both political and religious, and desire the blessing of Almighty God upon it.

MESSAGE FROM THE MAYOR OF BOSTON, ENGLAND, TO THE MAYOR OF BOSTON, MASSACHUSETTS

It was enclosed in the box shown in another illustration.

I need hardly say that the Mother regards not only with no envy but with honest pride of all right minded parents the far greater progress which the daughter across the Atlantic has made and is likely to make . . .

I have the honour to remain

Your faithful and obliged servant,
G. B. BLENKIN, *Vicar of Boston.*"

Soon after the sending of the box to City Hall our Public Library received a valuable present from St. Botolph's Town, which was presented by Alfred J. Ogston, Esq., acting British Consul in Boston, and which was received on behalf of this city, by Hon. Andrew J. Peters, our Mayor. Hon. George W. Coleman, President of the City Council in 1915, and a member of the Council in 1914 and 1916, made a visit to the old town in 1918 and while walking along the river he noticed part of an ancient oaken balustrade that once stood in the Court Room of the old Guildhall before which some of the Pilgrim Fathers, among whom was Elder William Brewster, had appeared as prisoners in 1607. The association of this relic with our city is even more closely brought home to us when it is realized that Richard Bellingham, Governor of the Massachusetts Bay Colony, held the position of Recorder of the city of old Boston, doubtless passing by the railing many times a day during his routine of business. Mr. Coleman suggested to Hon. A. Cooke Yarborough, Mayor of old Boston, that it would be a very fitting thing if his town could send the rail, which was then being used as a back-yard fence along the river bank, to the daughter across the Atlantic and it arrived in May of the following year and is now one of the most interesting relics owned by the Library, standing on the Huntington Avenue side of the delivery room of the central office at Copley Square, the inscription on it reading:—

Before this railing,
once part of the dock
in the Guildhall of Boston,
Lincolnshire,
stood on trial in 1607
some of the Pilgrim Fathers

The gift of the City of Boston, England, 1919.

Mr. Ogston in presenting it said in part:—

"I have the pleasure, your Honour, of requesting your acceptance of this ancient railing, as a token of the kindly and cordial feeling entertained by the City of Boston in England for the City of Boston in New England, and emblematic of the feeling of love and esteem which exists between the two nations."

Photographed by   *Kindness Charles F. Belden, Esq.,*
George B. Brayton   *and Otto Fleischner, Esq.*

**SECTION OF RAILING FROM THE GUILD-
HALL, BOSTON, ENGLAND,**

once part of the dock in the Guildhall, before which
some of the Pilgrim Fathers were tried, now an interesting relic in the Boston Public Library, Boston,
Massachusetts. This ancient railing was discovered by Hon. George W. Coleman, of our city,
on a visit to the mother town, and given to our
Library by Hon. A. Cooke Yarborough, Mayor of
old Boston. The presentation, which took place on
May 29, 1919, was made by Alfred J. Ogston, Esq.,
acting British Consul in Boston, and the relic accepted for our City by its Mayor, Hon. Andrew
J. Peters.

Mayor Peters during his address made
the following remarks:—

"Standing here it will serve as a link
between the old days and the new, mutely
teaching the great virtue of reverence to
our children. It will furnish a fresh bond
of attachment between ourselves and the
people of Boston in Lincolnshire. As Mayor
of the younger City bearing that honored
name, I send back sympathetic greetings
and warm appreciation to our kindred across
the ocean who have been inspired to this
act of gracious courtesy."

The First Church in Boston, on the
corner of Berkeley and Marlborough
Streets, contains so many tablets of interest that they form almost a history
in themselves of the early days of the
Colony. The chief memorial is a recumbent statue of John Cotton which
was erected to his memory by his descendants and which was unveiled in
1907. The inscription records his birth
in Derbyshire, England, in 1585, and his
death in the Colony of Massachusetts
Bay in 1652; it also mentions that he
was a fellow of Emmanuel College, Cambridge, in 1607, that he was Vicar of
the Church of St. Botolph, Boston,
Lincolnshire, from 1612 to 1633, and
that he was Teacher of the Boston
Church from 1633 to 1652. The most
interesting feature of this memorial is
the stone pendant from the east portal
of St. Botolph's Church, which now

forms a part of the front of the pedestal upon which his statue rests. This
stone, which can easily be identified in the accompanying cut, dates from the
beginning of the fourteenth century and doubtless formed a part of the main entrance during the time Cotton was Vicar. John Cotton's body rests in a big tomb,
the First Church Vault, in King's Chapel Graveyard, but no other tablet in Boston
commemorates his valuable work for the Colony. Rev. Paul Revere Frothingham,
who is a descendant of John Cotton on his mother's side, made the address on the

occasion of the dedication of this monument and during his address referred to Cotton's great power of application as a student, evidenced by a four-hour sand glass which he turned over three times a day, whereby he figured his working hours.

While on the subject of Vicar Cotton it may be interesting to mention that, a month after sailing, his fourth child was born on the Atlantic Ocean and the parents decided, therefore, to call him "Seaborn," presumably the suggestion having come from Stephen Hopkins, one of the Pilgrim Fathers, who thirteen years before had a son born on the outward voyage of the "Mayflower," whom he named "Oceanus." John Cotton's house stood on the upper part of the present site of the Suffolk Savings Bank.

The people of Boston will always associate John Cotton with the old town in England from which he came, and they will appreciate him as much as the inhabitants of old Boston, who, it is said, believed

From a print   *Kindness Rev. Charles E. Park, Julius H. Tuttle, Esq., and Henry H. Edes, Esq.*

MEMORIAL TO JOHN COTTON IN THE FIRST CHURCH, BOSTON, MASSACHUSETTS

On the pedestal can be seen an old stone pendant, dating from the fourteenth century, from the east portal of St. Botolph's Church, Boston, England, of which Cotton was Vicar for twenty-one years. Rev. Paul Revere Frothingham, a descendant of John Cotton on his mother's side, made an interesting address at the dedication.

"The lantern of St. Botolph's ceased to burn
When from the portals of that church he came
To be a burning and a shining light
Here in the wilderness."

Another connecting link between the two Bostons has been made by the restoration of the chapel in St. Botolph's, now called Cotton Chapel, and by a memorial placed upon its walls to his memory, mainly through the liberality of his American descendants. Here is recorded a Latin inscription of his life-work written by Hon. Edward Everett of our city, whose wife, by the way, was a descendant of John Cotton; translated into English it reads as follows:—

"That here John Cotton's memory may survive
Where for so long he laboured when alive,
In James' reign—and Charles's, ere it ceased,—
A grave, skilled, learned, earnest parish priest;
Till from the strife that tossed the Church of God
He in a new world sought a new abode,
To a new England—a new Boston—came,
(That took to honour him that rev'rend name)
Fed the first flock of Christ that gathered there—
Till death deprived it of its Shepherd's care—
There well resolved all doubts of minds perplext,
Whether with cares of this world, or the next:
Two centuries five lustra, from the year
That saw the exile leave his labours here,
His family, his townsmen, with delight—
(Whom to the task their English kin invite)—
To the fair fane he served so well of yore,
His name, in two worlds honoured, thus restore,
This chapel renovate, this tablet place,
In this the year of man's recovered Grace.
1855"

The restoration of the chapel was brought about chiefly through the help of three American citizens, George Peabody, Joshua Bates and Russell Sturgis, who were at that time living in London. They found that the chapel was being used as a lumber-room and that for some time the town fire-engine had been kept there. The corbels supporting the timber ceiling of Cotton Chapel are carved with the arms of early colonists of New England.

The visitor to the First Church in our Boston will find tablets placed on its walls to John Winthrop, Thomas Dudley, Isaac Johnson and John Wilson, all founders of the church and all so well known that they need no description here. There are also other memorials to John Leverett, Sir Henry Vane, placed there by one of Vane's descendants in England, Thomas Oliver, Jeremiah Dummer, Ezekiel Cheever, John Davenport, Simon and Anne Bradstreet and Anne Hutchinson. Other tablets to distinguished citizens of this city were erected later to Edward Everett, the Emersons, Robert Treat Paine, John Quincy Adams, Rev. Nathaniel L. Frothingham and other persons too numerous to mention here. A doorway has also been erected in the church by the Colonial Society of Massachusetts to the memory of Governor Thomas Hutchinson "in grateful recognition of a long and distinguished career of public service always guided by a conscientious desire to be loyal both to the Province and to the Crown." The only statue outside of the church is that of Governor John Winthrop and it is interesting to mention to our readers that a descendant of his now lives in the house directly opposite this First Church.

Dr. Charles E. Park, the present minister of this church, and Rev. A. G. Peaston, of the Spain Lane Unitarian Chapel of old Boston, carried on a correspondence in 1915, and parts of their letters are here given:—

From a recent photograph by G. E. Hackford, Boston, England   *Kindness Ian Forbes-Robertson, Esq.*

COTTON CHAPEL (FORMERLY CALLED FOUNDERS CHAPEL) IN ST. BOTOLPH'S CHURCH, BOSTON, ENGLAND,

restored in 1855 chiefly through the help of three American citizens then living in London, George Peabody, Joshua Bates and Russell Sturgis. The memorial tablet to John Cotton, shown in another illustration, is in this Chapel.

"To the Minister and Members of
the First Church, Boston, Mass. U.S.A.

Dear Brethren:

The celebration of a century of peace between the U.S.A. and Gt. Britain, which we had hoped to commemorate suitably this month, affords us the agreeable privilege of greeting you with cordiality and affection. December 24th, 1814, will be ever memorable in this Country, not only for 'ringing in the hundred years of peace,' but as the inauguration of a sentiment of kinship, trust and good-will, which has gained strength steadily, and has made a suggestion of armed conflict between the two nations literally unthinkable.

A. G. Peaston, *Minister,*
H. Barron Clark, *President,*
F. Kime, *Secretary.*"

From an old print engraved and published by B. Howlett, London, owned by Allan Forbes

BOSTON, LINCOLNSHIRE, ENGLAND,
showing St. Botolph's Church in the background.

Formerly in the collection of J. H. Seers, Essex, England

To which Mr. Park made a reply which we quote in part:—

"TO THE MINISTER AND CONGREGATION OF THE
SPAIN LANE UNITARIAN CHAPEL,
BOSTON, LINCOLNSHIRE,
ENGLAND.

Dear Brethren:—

Your cordial communication having been received and read in Congregation, we are directed by the First Church in Boston to address you in acknowledgment of your letter, and to assure you of the lively and heartfelt gratification which your friendliness has aroused in us.

We share with you the pride and pleasure of the thought that one hundred years of unbroken peace have cemented the relations of these two countries in a union of ideals and an identity of sympathies, which we are emboldened to hope and believe, can never again be dissolved; and these feelings we believe to be by no means peculiar to us, but to be the common property of all true citizens of the United States of America.

We are deeply conscious of the significance of this Centennial, standing, as it does, almost if not quite unique in history, as the symbol of the longest peace that has ever existed between two nations in such active and constant intercourse as ours; and giving the world a notable object lesson in international comity and fellowship. . . .

The value of our own Centennial is tragically accentuated by these momentous events. Our hopes and our wishes go forth to you day and night, that you come to a peace, that shall be speedy if it may be, but that shall be honorable at all costs. . . .

On behalf of the First Church in Boston,

CHARLES E. PARK, *Minister,*
JOHN W. BARTOL,
HENRY H. EDES *for the Standing Committee,*
JOHN W. DENNY, *Clerk.*"

JAN. 25, 1915.

The First Church also sent over funds during the war to be used by this church in old Boston for the relief of soldiers' families. In 1880 Rev. Dr. Rufus Ellis, minister of the First Church, visited the old town and brought back a number of presents.

Another connecting link between old Boston and this city is a beautiful stone tracery of an ancient window which was sent as a present from St. Botolph's Church to our Trinity Church and which is placed on one side of the cloister leading from the Clarendon Street entrance. The inscription on the plate nearby reads as follows:—

Part of the original tracery from a window
of the ancient Church of St. Botolph, Boston,
Lincolnshire, England, of which John Cotton
was Vicar for XXI years until he came to
New England in MDCXXXIII.
Presented to Trinity Church by the
Reverend G. B. Blenkin, Vicar of St. Botolph's
and placed here as a precious memorial of the
Church of our Fathers, October MDCCCLXXIX.

The fragments of this window had been discarded in old Boston and an American visitor, seeing them in the corner of the church, expressed the wish that they be sent

Photographed by George B. Brayton

TRACERY WINDOW FROM ST. BOTOLPH'S IN THE
CLOISTER OF TRINITY CHURCH,
BOSTON, MASSACHUSETTS,

sent as a present by the Vicar of the English church. It is placed in the open corridor on the Clarendon Street side of the building.

over here to Trinity Church, which was accomplished in the year 1879. There was a friendly rivalry in our Boston as to which church should be favored with this gift from the old city. Rev. Rufus Ellis, pastor of the First Church, and, therefore, a successor of John Cotton, thought that his edifice was the fitting place for the tracery to be installed, while Rev. Phillips Brooks as rector of Trinity Church, the foremost Episcopal church of Boston, urged that the gift was without doubt intended for his church. After several pleasant discussions it was amicably settled, and the mediæval stone work found a final resting-place in the cloister of Trinity Church. The Rector of Trinity at the time of the receipt of this relic spoke of the great value which attaches in New England to anything associated with the name of John Cotton and added: "For ourselves and for the church which we represent we acknowledge a peculiar gratification in affixing to our new walls so welcome a reminder of our mother country and of our Mother Church, for whose prosperity and welfare we shall ever pray. . . . The gift has attracted the interest not only of our own parishioners, but of all our citizens!"

Trinity Church has five pieces of communion silver given by his "Maj^{ty}. K. George 2nd by his Exc^y. Govr. Shirley: 1742," and on each one is the English coat of arms. There is also in this church a memorial to Rev. Arthur Stanley, Dean of Westminster, a great friend of Rev. Phillips Brooks, in memory of the first sermon he preached while in America in 1878. Rev. Phillips Brooks preached several times in St. Botolph's Church and also in Westminster Abbey, London. On one occasion when he preached in St. Botolph's, all the other places of worship in the town were closed in order that their congregations might hear him.

King's Chapel possessed for a number of years some church silver, which Governor Hutchinson exchanged for a new communion service, the gift of King George III, at which time he took away the old service, sending some pieces to Christ Church, Cambridge, two of which are marked, "The gift of King William and Queen Mary to ye Reve'd. Sam'l Myles for ye use of their Maj'ties Chappell in New England, 1694." Other pieces were sent to St. Paul's Church, Newburyport. King's Chapel was founded in 1686 and the first building was the first Church of England in Boston. The corner-stone of the present building was laid on August 11, 1749, the architect being Peter Harrison, who was born in England in 1716. In 1918 a tablet was placed near the entrance of the church in his honour by certain architects of Boston. There are also many interesting tablets to the early settlers and to important members of the congregation up to the present day, including such well-known people as Oliver Wendell Holmes, Roger Wolcott, Samuel Appleton, Charles P. Curtis, Francis E. Foote, Henry Wilder Foote, Ephraim Peabody, Robert S. Peabody, Thomas Newton, one of the founders of the church, John Lowell, Kirk Boott and Arthur T. Lyman.

From a photograph   *Kindness*
Ian Forbes-Robertson, Esq.

MEMORIAL TABLET IN COTTON CHAPEL, ST. BOTOLPH'S CHURCH, ENGLAND,

placed there in memory of Rev. John Cotton, by his American descendants and others. A Latin inscription, written by Hon. Edward Everett, given in the text in English, describes the placing of this memorial, in the year 1855.

Christ Church, which is usually referred to as the Old North Church, and which is situated on Salem Street, once called Green Lane when it was the most fashionable thoroughfare in Boston, is the possessor of two flagons bearing the royal arms of King George and among other relics is the well-known "vinegar" Bible also given by this king.

The St. Botolph Club in our city possesses some interesting relics of the mother town, which are best described by quoting from the original records of the Club. A meeting of the members was held on the 25th of February, 1882, Francis Parkman, Esq., the President, presiding, at which a letter was read by the Secretary, parts of which are here given:—

*Photographed by
George B. Brayton*　　　*Kindness of the Governors
of the St. Botolph Club,
Boston, Massachusetts*

LOVING CUP, FORMERLY THE PROPERTY
OF THE CORPORATION OF BOSTON,
ENGLAND,

presented to the St. Botolph Club, Boston, Massachusetts, by Rev. George E. Ellis, whose nephew, Arthur B. Ellis, Esq., brought it to this country. It was presented to the Club on February 25, 1882, and accepted on behalf of the Club by Francis Parkman, Esq., then President. The cup is marked beneath the Borough Arms, "Richard Bell, Mayor, 1745."

"Dear Mr. Parkman:—

I herewith—through you as its President,—present to the St. Botolph Club, of this City, a massive Silver-Gilt 'Loving Cup' formerly belonging to the Corporation of our Mother-town, Boston, Lincolnshire, England. The Cup, with other pieces of Silver-plate belonging to that Corporation, was sold by auction in June, 1837, was purchased by Mr. Daniel Jackson, and by him bequeathed to his Son, Mr. George Jackson, on whose death in May, 1881, it was at the disposal of his widow.

My nephew, Mr. Arthur B. Ellis, being in Boston last summer, and having the opportunity, thinking I might wish to possess the Cup, was allowed to bring it to this country.

It seemed to me that the St. Botolph Club should fitly have the Cup in its possession and would value it though it is not requisite that they should put it to its original use. . . .

GEORGE E. ELLIS."

On motion of Mr. Bradford it was

"VOTED that the thanks of the Club be tendered to the Rev'd. Dr. George E. Ellis for his valuable gift of a 'Loving Cup,' formerly owned by the Corporation of Boston, England, which is hereby gratefully accepted upon the conditions named in his letter of the 22nd day of February, 1882.

Adjourned, T. R. SULLIVAN, *Secretary*."

This cup is marked beneath the Borough Arms, "Richard Bell, Mayor, 1745." Three years later the Club received another valuable relic of old Boston, the gift being made at a special meeting of the Club held on Monday, June 22. The President, Francis Parkman, Esq., called the meeting to order and introduced to the members Rev. William S. Key of Boston, England, who then presented to the Club on behalf of the Municipal Charity Trustees of St. Botolph's Town a casting, or reproduction, of its Borough Arms. On this occasion the cup was filled and passed round among those present, who drank suitable toasts to the two Bostons and to the mermaids that appear on the shield. After an acceptance of the gift by the President, the following votes of thanks were passed by the meeting:—

"VOTED that the cordial thanks of the St. Botolph Club be extended to the Rev. William S. Key for the kind efforts which he has made in securing this interesting gift for permanent exhibition by the Club.

Voted that we accept with warm thanks the kind and welcome gift of the Municipal Charity Trustees of the Borough of Boston, England.

Voted that the Arms of the Town of St. Botolph be placed in our Club-House as a memorial of Old Boston and a token of the cordial regard borne towards her by her namesake."

These records are signed by Arthur B. Ellis, Esq., Secretary. The discovery of this relic and its voyage to our Boston are worth describing. In 1881 Rev. William S. Key and two friends of his, sons of Rev. Rufus Ellis, former pastor of the First Church, Boston, Massachusetts, while visiting the Town Hall in old Boston, formerly the Hall of the Guild of St. Mary, where the leaders of the Pilgrim band were confined, unearthed from a pile of rubbish in the basement the original Borough Arms made of wood which used to hang over the Recorder's seat in the Hall. A year later Mr. Key received an invitation from his Worshipful the Mayor, John Cabourn Simonds, who for some time carried on an extensive business with American firms in corn and cotton-seed,

Photographed by George B. Brayton   *Kindness of the Governors of the St. Botolph Club, Boston, Massachusetts*

COAT OF ARMS OF BOSTON, ENGLAND

A replica of the old Coat of Arms which was discovered by Rev. William S. Key, in the Guildhall of Boston, England, where the leaders of the Pilgrim band were tried. The original used to hang over the Recorder's desk and was unearthed from a pile of rubbish in the basement of the building. This reproduction was presented by John Cabourn Simonds, Mayor of the old town, the St. Botolph Club accepting it at a meeting of the Club on June 22, 1885. It now hangs on the Club walls.

to attend a meeting of the Pilot Commissioners to be held in the Hall of Justice, or Court Room, where Elder Brewster and his friends had been tried. The people of St. Botolph's Town had not known of the existence of this treasure and at the meeting thanked the discoverer and suggested that a replica be made in metal and that it should be presented to the St. Botolph Club in Boston, Massachusetts, which organization, as the presiding officer expressed it, "stands for the closest relationship between our own town and its namesake beyond the Atlantic." It was necessary to determine the exact colouring to be used in reproducing the various symbolic figures and this was attained by a visit to the Herald's College in London. When finished, the Arms was exhibited in a window in the market-place of old Boston, while over the building floated the Stars and Stripes, the occasion arousing great interest. Upon its arrival at this port the Custom House authorities were in a quandary as to how to classify it and a charge would have been

Borough of Boston

James Eley, Esq. Mayor 1910-11 & 1911-12. Meaburn Staniland, Town Clerk.

Be it known that this ancient building was purchased by Frank Harrison, Esquire, J.P. a resident of this Town, from the Governors of the Boston Grammar School Foundation, and by him conveyed to the Mayor, Aldermen and Burgesses of this Borough, for their use in perpetuity, and through the liberality of the inhabitants and a substantial donation from the Bostonian Society, Boston, Massachusetts, U.S.A. a fund was raised by the Mayor, and expended in the preservation of the Building, in commemoration of the Reign of His late Majesty King Edward VII.

From the Bostonian Society Publications   *Kindness C. F. Read, Esq., and Charles H. Taylor, Jr., Esq.*

TABLET IN GUILDHALL, BOSTON, ENGLAND

recording the fact that members of the Bostonian Society, of Boston, Massachusetts, subscribed £100 towards the restoration of this building.

levied had not Oliver Wendell Holmes, James Russell Lowell and Francis Parkman, President of the St. Botolph Club, persuaded the Collector of the Port to release it. Both of these presents, together with a number of pictures of the English town, adorn the walls of the St. Botolph Club, which takes its name from the Patron Saint of the town. On every seventeenth of June the Club has a luncheon to celebrate his birthday. Members of the Club sent funds some time ago to help defray expenses for repairs to St. Botolph's Church.

The Bostonian Society, in the Old State House, Boston, Mass., is proud of the fact that a tablet in the Guildhall of old Boston records that the members of this well-known society subscribed £100 in 1915, towards the restoration of this ancient building and the following letter of thanks was sent by Hon. James Eley, Mayor of Boston, England, to Grenville H. Norcross, Esq., President of the Bostonian Society:—

"Your letter of the 22nd ult. is to hand, and I beg to thank you for your kindly thought of me. No ceremony with reference to the preservation of the Guildhall has yet taken place. I waited during last summer in the hope that some of your members might be in the old country, and I intended arrangements whereby the completion of the work and the splendid generosity of the Bostonian Society should be recognized and placed on record. However, I trust the pleasure is only deferred, and when this terrible war is over, I look forward to something of the kind. . . . The country will generally wait for the victory and deem no sacrifice too great to secure a lasting and honourable peace.

I am, Dear Sir, very truly yours,

JAMES ELEY."

The Bostonian Society, which owns a splendid collection of Boston relics of the old days, also has on view to the many visitors who go there a wooden model of St. Botolph's Church and, also, many attractive pictures of old Boston. This Society some years ago sent to the Guildhall a large picture of our Old State House. While Hon. William Bedford was Mayor of the English Boston, he carried on an interesting correspondence with the Bostonian Society and always entertained visitors from this city. There have been so many visits by our prominent citizens to the old town that it is impossible to mention more than a few. In 1895, Hon. T. F. Bayard, the first Ambassador to Great Britain from the United States, went to Boston, Lincolnshire, and distributed prizes at the old grammar school and while there attended a banquet given in his honour by the Mayor and Corporation of the town. In a speech Mr. Bayard spoke as follows:—

"This Boston—this Boston of old England—is the mother and the name giver of a younger and a stronger Boston far away across the sea. And yet the younger and the stronger Boston, the city that holds perhaps one half-million of inhabitants, owes so much, how much cannot be fully stated or measured, to the little town of twenty thousand people that preserves its existence and holds its own on this side of the Atlantic."

In the following year a party of American Congregationalists, chief of whom was Rev. Dr. Dunning of Boston, landed in Plymouth and visited the old town in Lincolnshire, being entertained while there by the Mayor and other officials. Dr. Dunning spoke of our city and of John Cotton in the following terms:—

From a recent photograph   Kindness
Ian Forbes-Robertson, Esq.

THE GUILDHALL, BOSTON, ENGLAND,

where the Pilgrim Fathers were tried. The Bostonian Society of our Boston subscribed towards its restoration in 1915 and a tablet shown in another illustration records this fact. The Boston Public Library is the possessor of part of the ancient railing that came from this building, also shown in another cut.

"Old Boston is our home, and we feel that we have come back to the land to which we belong. It was a Vicar of Old Boston that practically founded the city of New Boston. I suppose we may accept the opinion that the successors of John Cotton have preached as well as he did, for we have abundant testimony that they do."

In 1897 Rt. Rev. William Lawrence, Bishop of Massachusetts, visited the old town and from the pulpit of St. Botolph's Church referred in these words to the ties that united the two Bostons:—

"You little realize what it is for one born in Boston, in the United States, a citizen of Boston, the Bishop not only of Boston, but of the State, of which Boston is the capital—you little realize, with what deep emotion he comes here and looks in the faces of you who are citizens of old Boston, and recalls to mind what the newer Boston owes to you, with what sympathy it turns towards you, and with what sincerity it tells you that we are brethren—brethren not only in Christ and in the Church—but brethren in race, in blood, in free institutions—brethren as sons of England."

THE PULPIT IN ST. BOTOLPH'S
CHURCH, BOSTON, ENGLAND,

from which Rev. John Cotton preached before he came to New England.   He was Vicar
of this English church for twenty-one years.
Once when Rev. Phillips Brooks preached
from this pulpit, all the other churches in
old Boston were closed so that the congregations could listen to his excellent sermon.

Another visit was that of Rev. George W. Shinn, Rector of Grace Church, Newton, who journeyed there in 1905 to inspect the plan of St. Botolph's Church with the idea that some church in this country might copy the old church "where Cotton served so long and at whose altars so many of the colonists to America had worshipped." In 1909, on the sexcentenary of the founding of St. Botolph's Church, many Americans attended unofficially the celebration, although the Mayor of our city and other distinguished persons who had been invited were unable to be present.

It has often been supposed that our city was named by, or for, John Cotton but this is not so, as Cotton came to this country three years after our city had been changed from Trimountain to Boston.   There have been many legends concerning its name; some historians believe our Boston was so named as a compliment to Isaac Johnson of old Boston, who came here in 1630; other historians believe it was so called to encourage John Cotton to come to this country and assist the colony, while Hon. R. C. Winthrop stated that "The name of Boston was especially dear to the Massachusetts colonists from its associations with St. Botolph's town and this was probably really the reason for its selection." In speaking of the early settlers, Governor Hutchinson mentioned that "Lincolnshire contributed greatly to the new plantation and more of our principal families derive their origin from thence than from any part of England, unless the City of London be an exception." The writer of "Pilgrim Fathers of New England" makes the statement that "probably there is no town in England that has sent forth so many of its best and worthiest citizens to the great work of colonizing America than this town of Boston." As a proof of this statement, we may mention the names of some of the early settlers in our city who lived in the English Boston or nearby: Isaac Johnson and John Humphrey, brothers-in-law of the third Earl of Lincoln, who was a leader of the Puritan party and who lived at Sempringham, not far from old Boston; Thomas Dudley who was steward or manager of the Earl's estate lived in or near Boston; also Simon Bradstreet who was a member of his

household. To our town also came John
Leverett, whose father, Thomas Leverett,
had been an Alderman of Boston in Lincolnshire; Richard Bellingham, who had held the
position of Recorder there as already mentioned, and Atherton Hough, who had been
Mayor of the city in 1628. William Coddington, one of the early governors of Rhode
Island, was born in Boston, England, in 1601.
The English town, as we have seen, furnished,
therefore, four governors of Massachusetts
and one of Rhode Island.

Few places in England possess a more
impressive history than Boston. Its records
go back to the middle of the seventh century
when Botolf, a Saxon monk, often called "the
Saint of seafaring men," founded a monastery
on the site of an inconspicuous village called
Icanhoe in 654. The word "Boston" is
usually held to mean Botolf's ton (or town).
As early as 1270 the form Botolfston is found
in an English poem and in the fourteenth
century such names as "Botolestone" and
"Botolf's tune" occur. Still later, Lambarde,
about the year 1577, states that the place was
then called Bostonstow, though "commonly
and corruptly called Boston." Towards the
end of the ninth century the Danes invaded

*From an enlargement in the St. Botolph Club, Boston,
Massachusetts*
Kindness of the Governors of the St. Botolph Club

FIGURE OF ST. BOTOLPH ON ST.
BOTOLPH'S CHURCH, BOSTON,
ENGLAND

the place and the followers of St. Botolph and his buildings were swept away. In
1309 the church, which tradition says was built on wool-packs, was rebuilt, largely
through the efforts of Margaret Tilney, to whom a memorial has been placed in the
church. The tower which is usually known as "Boston Stump" can be seen forty
miles out to sea, and the many American visitors there are never tired of speaking
of the impressiveness of the old church, with its high tower, on the banks of the river
Witham. The church has some peculiar architectural features. It has a narrow
winding stone staircase composed of three hundred and sixty-five steps, the exact
number of days in a year; seven doors, being the number of days in a week; is lighted
by fifty-two windows, the number of weeks in a year. The clerestory roof is supported on twelve massive stone columns, the number of months in a year; while,
in order to reach the library located over the South porch, which contains official
relics of Rev. John Cotton's family, among them being the baptismal registers of

From an old print owned by Allan Forbes

BOSTON, ENGLAND, FROM THE TOWER OF ST. BOTOLPH'S CHURCH

From an old print engraved by J. Walker from a drawing by W. Brand, published 1795, London   *Owned by Allan Forbes*

BOSTON, ENGLAND

his children, the visitor has to climb twenty-four much worn stone steps,—the same number as the hours in a day. To reach the roof of the chancel one must climb sixty steps, the exact number of minutes in an hour and seconds in a minute. At the left as one enters the door of St. Botolph's Church there is a heavy oak chest, iron-bound and with a heavy padlock attached, which is filled every Saturday night with four-pound "quartern" loaves purchased out of the income derived from legacies left by different benefactors who made the bequests between the years 1600 and 1755 A.D. and on Sunday, at the close of morning service, the loaves are distributed to a number of deserving women. This chest was discovered in the belfry of the church by Hon. Edward Everett while he was Minister to England on a trip made to Boston, during which he ascended the "Stump," or tower of the church, and espied the chest from his high position. The Vicar was much surprised to hear of his discovery and immediately had it brought down, thoroughly overhauled and put to its present use.

Boston is about four miles from the sea and a lantern in the top of the tower formerly acted as a guide to mariners. It was

From a photograph   *Kindness Fred H. Kimball, Esq.*

STATUE OF ANNE HUTCHINSON IN THE STATE HOUSE, BOSTON, MASSACHUSETTS

Anne Hutchinson, who was Anne Marbury before her marriage, was the daughter of a minister at Alford in Lincolnshire. She was the first woman to be conspicuously connected with public life and the placing of her statue recently in the State Capitol in a sense marks the advent of woman suffrage in Massachusetts. While in our Boston, her opinions seem to have been favored by Rev. John Cotton.

this lamp in the old tower that is said to have ceased to burn when Cotton left his home for the wilderness of New England. Old Boston was once a large seaport

Photographed by George B. Brayton

TABLET ON BOSTON COMMON RECORDING ITS PURCHASE FROM WILLIAM BLACKSTONE,
FIRST SETTLER IN BOSTON, MASSACHUSETTS

He died in Attleboro, Massachusetts, in that part of the city now Lonsdale, Rhode Island, a picture of the
monument near his grave being shown on page 45.

This tablet stands near the corner of Tremont and Park Streets, the inscription reading:—

In or about
the year of our Lord
One thousand six hundred
thirty and four
the then present inhabitants
of s^d Town of Boston of whom
the Honble John Winthrop Esqr
Gov^{nr} of the Colony was chiefe
did treate and agree with
Mr. William Blackstone
for the purchase of his
Estate and rights in any
neck of Land called
Boston
after which purchase the
Town laid out a plan for
a trayning field which ever
since and now is used for
that purpose and for
the feeding of cattell

The deposition of John Odlin and others concerning the sale of Blackstone's land known as Boston
Common.

THE OLD STATE HOUSE, BOSTON, MASSACHUSETTS

It stands at the head of State Street, on the site of the original town-house, and has witnessed many important historic events. The significance of the Lion and the Unicorn is explained on the copyright page.

and in the first part of the fourteenth century was one of the ten most important ports of the Kingdom, during the reign of King John even rivaling London. It was made a staple port in 1369, being the principal place in the east of England for the export of wool to Flanders and for the import of woolen cloth from there.

The May Sheep Fair is one of the most important yearly events held in Boston. From early historic times Lincolnshire has been famous for the number of sheep raised there and for the superior quality of the wool and mutton. Fabulous prices have been paid by well-known sheep herders, farmers and exporters for Lincolnshire rams and ewes, for shipment to Argentina and other South American countries, as well as to Australia, New Zealand and other parts of the world, the purchase price for one ram often reaching $5,000. The exact date when the great sheep fair was started is lost in the mazes of early history, but there is a definite record in the year 1623, which mentions the price of pens for the accommodation of the animals while on sale. The importance of this fair has steadily increased and at the present time it ranks as one of the most important in England, occasionally assuming such large proportions that at times forty thousand sheep have been known to change hands in less than three hours. A scene at the fair is shown in the frontispiece.

The fens stretched out towards the sea, even after the Normans had conquered the territory, and it is said that the natives sometimes went out on stilts to meet the foe in order to be able to retreat in safety across the marshes to their strongholds after an attack. It may be interesting to New Englanders to know that eight miles from the town is a place called "Bunker's Hill," and also that a mile or so away is a small village called "New York" which recalls the remark of a New York driver in "Martin Chuzzlewit" who said "it brought Old York home to him quite vivid on account of its being so exactly unlike in every respect."

ATHOL, MASSACHUSETTS

THE Scotch tartan of the Murray clan was used in the decorations for the one hundred and fiftieth anniversary of the incorporation of the town of Athol, Massachusetts, which was named in honour of Col. John Murray who was the founder of our town and who gave it its name for Blair Atholl, his native town in Scotland. At this celebration, which was held in June of the year 1912, the committee used letter paper on which appeared in colours this attractive tartan. John Murray was probably a distant relative of the Duke of Atholl, head of the great Murray clan, but he was not his son as many people have supposed. The present Duke, the eighth in line, is a typical Highland Chieftain. He served in the Nile expedition; in the South African War; commanded a Scottish cavalry regiment in the Great War and later took part in the fighting at Gallipoli. He and his family have taken the greatest interest in the Massachusetts Athol, which, by the way, has always been wrongly spelled with only one "l." The interchanges began in 1904 with an interesting correspondence between Lodge St. John's No. 14 of Dunkeld (near Atholl), in Perthshire, Scotland, of which the late Duke was a member, and F. E. Wing, Esq., one of Athol's foremost citizens and Worshipful Master of Star Lodge in his town. This friendship resulted during the same year in the gift of a gavel, by the Duke of Atholl, to the Massachusetts Lodge, copied from the one used in the Scotch Lodge and made from one of the larch trees which abound in the Duke's private park and which were planted by the Duke himself. This gavel was pre-sented at one of the meetings of the Lodge

From a photograph   *Kindness F. E. Wing, Esq.*

HIGH SCHOOL BUILDING, ATHOL, MASSACHUSETTS,

showing the colours of the Duke of Atholl, of Blair Atholl, Scotland, flying at half mast at the time of the death of one of the Dukes in 1917. The colours were a present from this Duke some years before.

and is still used on all important occasions, the inscription thereon reading as follows:—

> Gavel made of larch grown on the Atholl Plantation Scotland: pre-sented by John 7th Duke of Atholl K. T. to the Star Lodge of Free and Accepted Masons, Athol, Massachusetts, U.S.A.: Frank E. Wing, Worship-ful Master: 1904.

During the following year the distinguished Scotchman was elected an honorary member of Star Lodge and was invited to visit the town on several occasions, one being the one hundred and fiftieth anniversary of Athol. In 1911 the Duke sent Mr. Wing a flag similar to his private colours flown over his castle, the pattern consisting of alternate horizontal stripes of orange and black. It is interesting to mention that this flag, by order of the Board of Selectmen and School Committee, was flown at half mast from the High School building of our Athol when the Duke died in the year 1917. At the same time, at the suggestion of Mr. Wing, the Selectmen sent the following cable to the Duke's son: "Town of Athol, Massa-chusetts, mourns death of His Grace, your father. Athol colors half staff one week." A reply cable in these words was received and entered upon the records of Athol: "Atholl men this side, family and self, deeply touched that you share in our sor-row." Cables were also exchanged in 1914 at the time of the Duke's Jubilee cele-bration of accession to the title.

The Scotch godmother of our Athol, a name which is understood to mean "pleasant land," is situated among the hills of Perthshire on the southern slope of the Grampian hills, the river Tay flowing through the district. In the picturesque

From a recent photograph by Valentine & Co., Dundee, Scotland   *Kindness Ian Forbes-Robertson, Esq.*

BLAIR CASTLE, BLAIR ATHOLL, PERTHSHIRE, SCOTLAND,

the residence of the Dukes of Atholl.   The Massachusetts town of Athol was named for this Scotch town by Col. John Murray, who was probably a distant relative of the Dukes of Atholl, who have always shown a great interest in the New England town.

pass of Killiecrankie, nearby, Claverhouse fell in 1689, though victorious over the troops of King William.

The Duke of Atholl, grandfather of the present Duke and head of the Murray clan, was a great Scottish chieftain, having the title of Marquess of Tullibardine. In 1839 for the Eglinton Tournament he formed a Guard of Honour composed of Atholl men in Highland uniform and armed with Lochaber axes and swords, like the Yeomen of the Guard.   Three years later, on Queen Victoria's first visit to Scotland, two hundred and fifty men formed a Guard of Honour to her at Dunkeld and, in commemoration of the event, Her Majesty presented the Atholl Highlanders with Colours, which was practically a recognition of the body as a unit, a picturesque relic of bygone days.   Since then they have been armed with rifles.   Drills are still held for ceremonial purposes and their execution is said to be very fine.   Every man of this body who could enlist in the Great War did so. This Atholl "army" used to drill in front of Blair Castle and is described as speaking Gaelic fluently.   It was customary for it to conduct a wild dance on drill days, known as the "Ram's Reel." The thrill of the Atholl pipes is well described in these lines written by James Hogg of Perthshire:—

> "A' the din o' a' the drummers
> Canna rouse like Atholl cummers [noise of the pipes].
> When I'm dowie, wet, or weary,
> Soon my heart grows light and cheery,
> When I hear the sprightly nummers
> O' my dear, my Atholl cummers.
> When the fickle lasses vex me,
> When the cares o' life perplex me,
> When I'm fley'd wi' frightfu' rumors,
> Then I cry for Atholl cummers."

Another event of interest in connection with this Scotch town was the visit of Robert Bruce to Blair Castle; his hosts enjoyed his visit so much and were so anxious to prolong his stay, that they sent a servant to persuade his coachman to remove a shoe from one of the horses in order to retard his departure. At another time King George IV was a visitor to Scotland; it is said that he appeared at a ball given by the Duchess of Gordon with his shoes tied with silk ribbons instead of the usual buckles, thereby causing ruin to all persons engaged in the buckle trade.

Another story is told of two Scotchmen who, having just decided to fight a duel, repaired at once to the appointed place. Upon reaching their destination, one of them scribbled these words on a card which he handed to his rival: "Naething should be done in a hurry but catching fleas." The recipient of the card burst out laughing and the two departed good friends. Another anecdote is related of an old Scotch woman, who, unfortunately, had been indulging in too much liquid refreshment. She was, as a result, brought before a magistrate, who asked her if she knew where all drunkards go. "Yes," she replied, "where they get the best whiskey."

Colonel Murray came to America before the Revolution, settling in Rutland, but when the war broke out, his property was seized, as he remained loyal to the King. He went to Halifax by way of Boston with the royal army and became a resident of St. John, New Brunswick, where his descendants still possess many relics of his early days in Athol, including the deeds to his lands in this town and also in Rutland and Lenox. There is a portrait of him in the Hazen family of St. John. There was a hole in this painting and there is a tradition in the family that a number of persons who searched for the Colonel after his flight from Massachusetts became vexed because he had escaped and so pierced the canvas with their bayonets, vowing they would leave their mark behind them.

Athol, formerly called Pequiog, is supposed to resemble in scenery Blair Atholl and this fact may have been an added inducement to Colonel Murray to give his new abode the name of his ancestral home in Scotland. The township was first laid out in 1732 by the General Court, the incorporators including the well-known names of Oliver, Lee and Lord, other early settlers being the families of Field, Kendall, Goddard, Bancroft, Fay, Twichell and Wheeler. Rev. James Humphreys was the first minister of the town and he arrived on horseback, to assume his new duties, with his sermons and his goods in his saddle-bags.

ATTLEBORO, MASSACHUSETTS

ATTLEBORO, Massachusetts, derived its name from the market town of Attleborough, County Norfolk, England, whence some of the early inhabitants of the Massachusetts city emigrated to America, giving their settlement this name in remembrance of their native place. This origin of the name is further confirmed by the fact that in the English town there is a river called Bungay of about the same size as the one of that name in Attleboro, Massachusetts. The name of the Massachusetts city was formerly spelled the same as the town in England from which it took its name, but to conform, apparently, with the American idea of time saving and efficiency the final "ugh" was left off some time ago.

The first inhabitant within the original limits of Attleboro was the celebrated William Blackstone, who was also the first settler and sole proprietor of "Shawmut," now Boston. He was a graduate of Emmanuel College, Cambridge University, and had been a clergyman in England, emigrating about the year 1625 to this country that he might enjoy his own religious opinions here unmolested. He even found Governor Winthrop's colonists too intolerant, so he sought another retreat, selling his right and title to his old home on "Blackstone's Neck," as the Peninsula of Boston was then called, to the new inhabitants, each one paying him six shillings and some of them more, amounting in all to £30. With the purchase money he bought a "stock of cows" which he took with him to his new home on the banks of the Pawtucket River, now called Blackstone River in his honour. The Valley of the Blackstone has become justly celebrated as a manufacturing district, and contributes, by the advantages of its water-power, to the wealth and industry of New England. The place where he settled was within the ancient limits of Attleboro, in that part called "The Gore," now Cumberland, Rhode Island, where he died in 1675. His house he called "Study Hall," and the eminence on which it was built was named "Study Hill," being so called to this day. The site of his dwelling and grave is now occupied by the Ann and Hope Mill of the Lonsdale Company, there being a monument in the mill yard in line with his grave, erected by his descendants in 1889, a picture of which is shown on the next page. Blackstone is best known through his connection with Boston, though he lived in the latter place but ten years as compared with forty years in Attleboro. He was fond of study and contemplation, and preached sometimes for Roger Williams at Providence. He was also skillful in horticulture and woodcraft, caring more for solitude than for society. The library of one hundred and eighty-four volumes in his wilderness home was remarkable for those early days in this country. He was a man of many eccentricities and among other things is recorded as keeping a trained bull which he is pictured as riding up and down the sandy shore of Charles Street in Boston. Later, after he had moved from the latter city, he used to visit his friends in Providence, similarly mounted, such animals being used quite frequently in those days for carrying burdens of all kinds.

The original purchaser of Attleboro land was Captain Thomas Willett, an Englishman who had lived with the Pilgrims in Holland and who became the successor of Miles Standish as the Commander of the Military Company of New Plymouth. Captain Willett was

From a photograph

WILLIAM BLACKSTONE MEMORIAL IN LONSDALE, RHODE ISLAND,

formerly part of Attleboro, Massachusetts, now part of Cumberland, Rhode Island. It is placed in the yard of the Ann and Hope Mill of the Lonsdale Company in line with his grave. The above mill now occupies the site of Blackstone's home where he spent forty years of his life. While he is best known on account of his connection with the early history of Boston, Blackstone lived a far greater length of time within the original limits of Attleboro.

the best kind of diplomat, an able man of justice who inspired confidence among all, including the Indians, with whom he was always on friendly terms. By authority of the Court of New Plymouth in 1666 he obtained the Rehoboth North Purchase, which became Attleboro, buying the land from Massasoit's eldest son, Wamsutta, who was then the reigning sachem of Pokanoket. He was honoured by selection as organizer of the new government after New York had been surrendered by the Dutch, was chosen the first English Mayor of the American metropolis and re-elected to that position. He afterwards returned to Swansea, near Attleboro, where he died August 11, 1674. His great-grandson, Col. Marinus Willett,

ST. MARY'S CHURCH, ATTLEBOROUGH, ENGLAND

A stone which once formed a capital in this church was obtained through the efforts of the late Major Everett S. Horton, and placed in the ladies' parlor of the Second Congregational Church of Attleboro, Massachusetts.

a distinguished officer in the Revolutionary War, was also a Mayor of New York City.

The first actual settlement within the bounds of the original town of Attleboro was in the neighborhood of the Baptist meeting-house and was begun by John Woodcock and his sons soon after the first division of lands. In May, 1676, while his sons were at work in a cornfield near the house, they were surprised by Indians, and one son, Nathaniel, was killed.

Attleboro was incorporated as a township October 19, 1694, but the first town meeting on record appears to have been held in 1696 at which time John Woodcock and John Rogers were chosen to manage the affairs of the township, other names identified with the early history of the town being Daniel Sheppison, John Callendar, John Lane, George Robinson, David Freeman, Anthony Sprague and Daniel Jenks.

One Thomas Doggett came to this country from Attleborough, England, and he is supposed to be a brother of John, the first ancestor in this country of the Daggetts (the present way of spelling the family name) of Massachusetts and Connecticut. This John Doggett came over in Winthrop's fleet in 1630. Another early settler who came from Attleborough, England, was John Sutton, whose daughter Anne became the wife of John Doggett. Thomas Mayhew, who was listed as "a merchant," was born in Southampton, England, and was also one of the early settlers of Attleboro. That the Daggett family still takes an important part in the activities of the city is shown by the fact that Mrs. Homer Daggett, wife of a direct descendant of John Doggett, ran for election as Mayor in 1920.

The jewelry industry, now the most important in the city, had its commencement in 1780 when a Frenchman, who was called "the foreigner," very likely because his real name was too difficult of pronunciation, began to make jewelry. The first shop erected expressly for the manufacture of jewelry, the forerunner of over one hundred concerns of today, was that of Col. Obed Robinson. His partners were Otis Robinson and Milton Barrows, the latter being the great-grandfather of those now carrying on the business of H. F. Barrows Company. Other men prominent in establishing this industry were Freeman, Bates, Simmons, Dean, Bliss, Sturdy, Whitney and Richards.

Attleboro became a city in 1914, Hon. Harold E. Sweet being the first Mayor.

The original post-office is still in existence and is located in the drawing-room of the Holman homestead on Pleasant Street. The "post-office" was merely an old-fashioned table into the drawer of which the stage-coach driver of long ago hastily dropped the town's letters. The residents walked to the homestead or drove to the door and made their way to the "post-office room" unheeded. There were no clerks nor locks and each caller sorted the mail in search of his own.

The most tragic encounter of the whole Indian War, Pierce's Fight, took place in old Attleboro. Sixty Plymouth colonists were surprised and almost annihilated on March 26, 1676, and later the same day the remainder were massacred at the spot, a few miles distant, called to the present time "Nine Men's Misery."

The first religious meetings on record date back to 1704 and the first minister called was in 1707. The First Church of Christ, Congregational, of Attleboro, is still active at Oldtown, and the present pastor, Rev. John Whitehill, who is in his fifty-third year of service there, was born at Paisley, Scotland, August 11, 1833, coming to this country when a child.

There have been no official letters or visits exchanged between the English town and its namesake in Massachusetts but there is now in the Second Congregational Church, Attleboro, a stone which once formed a capital in St. Mary's Church, Attleborough, England. This was obtained at the instigation of the late Major Everett S. Horton, who was very much interested in the erection of the new Second Congregational Church. He conceived the idea of having Mr. Louis J. Lamb, who was about to start on a trip to England, obtain some sort of memento in the old town to have a place in the new building, which was then under construction in Attleboro, Massachusetts. Mr. Lamb readily pledged hearty co-operation and a copy of the letter regarding the finding of this stone now hangs in the ladies'

From a photograph   Kindness Rev. J. Lee Mitchell, Ph.D., and Mrs.
                                                         Walter M. Kendall

SECOND CONGREGATIONAL CHURCH, ATTLE-
BORO, MASSACHUSETTS,

in which there is a stone from St. Mary's Church, Attleborough, England, which was obtained through the efforts
of the late Major Everett S. Horton.

parlor of the Second Congregational Church and is interesting
enough to be repeated here:—

"ROYAL HOTEL

ATTLEBOROUGH, NORFOLK, ENGLAND
August 22d, 1902

Mr. EVERETT S. HORTON,
Attleboro, Mass. U.S.A.

My dear Major:

Have had your commission to
find you a stone in Attleborough,
England, in mind ever since leaving
home in May and as soon as we arrived here today made inquiries for a
builder and were introduced to Mr.
John Harrison, leading contractor
and builder in this vicinity. We
told him our errand—that we wanted
to secure if possible a stone in some
way identified with the Old Parish
Church or other public building in
town to be placed in a new church
now building in Attleboro, Mass.,
U.S.A. He was immediately interested and said 'A few years since
while I was employed in making some
repairs on the old church, it became
necessary to clear out a lot of refuse
stone and other material which had
been left under a portion of the
church at the time it was "restored"
about one hundred years ago. There
was one piece so shapely and well
adapted to the purpose that I saved
it and took it home to make a base or pedestal for my flower vase in front garden and
I should think it would answer your purpose.'

We went to his house and viewed the stone and I assure you it did not take long to
secure it and arrange for its shipment to you via Cunard Line from Liverpool to Boston
and you should receive it about the middle of September.

We had found just what we wanted—a good shaped, fair sized stone and withal with
a history—for the Old Parish Church is said to be about 600 years old and as the stone
gives evidence that it has been cut and fashioned something after the style of a capital
for a column, it is probable that it was originally part of the ornamental architecture of
the building. We believe you and the 'White Church' friends will be pleased with it.

Attleborough, England, is very unlike its younger namesake in Massachusetts but it
is a quiet, thrifty little English village with three public houses, Post-Telegraph and
Telephone office, Railway Station, several stores and the usual adjuncts of a trading centre
in rural England. The inhabitants and the homes give evidence that no extreme poverty
prevails and the few people whom we have met are very cordial and interested to hear

about the other Attleboro beyond the sea. I know you would enjoy a visit here. Will tell you more about it on our return.

With cordial remembrances of our entire party,

Yours very truly,
Louis J. Lamb."

It is interesting to record that this letter is framed in a piece of wood which came from England as part of the crate around the stone. The stone now occupies a niche at the right of the entrance of the Second Congregational Church, bearing the following inscription:—

COURTESY OF
MR. JOHN HARRISON,
ATTLEBOROUGH, NORFOLK, ENGLAND
MR. L. J. LAMB,
ATTLEBOROUGH, MASSACHUSETTS, U.S.A.
PRESENTED BY MAJOR E. S. HORTON

From a photograph   *Kindness Rev. J. Lee Mitchell, Ph.D., and Mrs. Walter M. Kendall*

STONE IN SECOND CONGREGATIONAL CHURCH, ATTLEBORO, MASSACHUSETTS,

formerly a capital in St. Mary's Church, Attleborough, England.

In writing about this Attleboro church, it is amusing to note that in 1868 a clock which struck every five minutes was installed in the vestry, the purpose of this being, apparently, to discourage any long speeches.

The late Major Horton exchanged many gifts with Mrs. John Harrison of Attleborough, England (wife of the gentleman mentioned in Mr. Lamb's letter, who provided the stone sent to Attleboro, Massachusetts), sending her pictures of the Massachusetts city and articles of jewelry for the manufacture of which our Attleboro is justly famous, receiving pieces of crockery which had been in the Slade family of Attleborough, England, for many years, also a sampler and a quilt made by a woman of that town who had reached the age of one hundred and four years.

The Angle Tree Stone which was erected at the time of the settlement of a long controversy in regard to the Plymouth and Massachusetts Bay Colonies' boundary line between Attleboro, Dorchester, Stoughton, Norton, Easton and Wrentham is of historic interest to visitors.

On January 4, 1921, the Attleboro Community Fellowship, which takes a very active interest in the affairs of the Massachusetts city, passed a set of resolutions to encourage the interchange of correspondence between citizens of their city and Attleborough, England. The reasons given in the preamble for favoring these resolutions were that history may and should be made humanly interesting and helpful; that this is a time when New England towns are making considerable study of their Old World pioneer inheritances, and as the history of the American Attleboro connects at the beginning with Attleborough, England, it is fitting that communications be exchanged in order to add to the proud fund of historic data already collected.

The town of Attleborough, England, lies in the southern part of County Norfolk, and is a pleasant little place situated in the midst of a level bit of country, its most important feature being St. Mary's Church, which was built centuries ago and which contains some very interesting architectural features, the window tracery being extremely beautiful. Attleborough shared with other towns of the county a custom which allowed any person out of a home to seek refuge in the church porch until other lodgings could be found, showing that housing conditions in the early days sometimes resembled the present condition in New England. In legendary history, St. Edmund, King of East Anglia, is said to have gone to Attleborough and remained there an entire year, engaged in the pious duty of committing the psalter to memory. Although surpassed in commercial pursuits by its Massachusetts namesake, the town of Attleborough still has a charm of its own which the younger place can never hope to attain.

BIDDEFORD, MAINE

A MEMORIAL tablet has been placed at Winter Harbour, now known as Biddeford Pool, near the mouth of the Saco River, on the spot where the well-known English explorer Captain Richard Vines and his adventurous crew of sixteen spent the winter of 1616–17, even before the settlement of Plymouth. After landing they proceeded about eight miles up the Saco River which carried them to the Great Falls, as they called them, which now furnish power to the cotton mills of the Pepperell Manufacturing Company and the York Manufacturing Company, both well known throughout the world, also to several other thriving industries of Biddeford, including the Saco-Lowell machine shops which have sent to many foreign countries the most modern mill equipment. Vines and his men returned to England in the year 1617 with favorable reports and continued to make voyages to this country for a number of years, transporting colonists, so that as early as the year 1620 there were a number of families, including that of Richard Vines, in this very early Maine settlement. For his services this explorer received from Sir Ferdinando Gorges a grant of all the land within the present limits of Biddeford, the original deed, dated February 12, 1629, being now in the possession of the Maine Historical Society.

Two earlier English explorers of this territory were Martin Pring, mentioned in Part I, and Captain George Weymouth who, two years later, in 1605, took possession of these lands in the name of King James I.

Biddeford, Maine, probably owes its name to John Parker and others who came from Bideford, England, about the time of the town meeting, November 14, 1718, when the settlement on the west side of the Saco River was set off from Saco, on the east side, under the name of Biddeford, the name being spelled, it will be noticed, differently from that of the mother town.

The First Congregational Church of Biddeford, Maine, was formed in 1730, and it is a tradition among some of the older residents of Biddeford that the good people of Biddeford, England, gave the Maine town a church bell which arrived in Boston, whereupon it is supposed to have passed into the hands of a Boston church for the reason that the Biddeford parish was at that time too poor to pay freight on it. Some believe it was a chandelier instead of a bell which thus went astray.

The English Bideford, meaning "by the ford," like Biddeford, Maine, is on a river near the sea, with a long bridge uniting the two parts of the town similar to the bridge between Biddeford and Saco. Visitors from Biddeford, Maine, to Bideford, England, also discover that both have a St. Mary's Church. The English town is now much the smaller of the two places, not having grown like its namesake. Bideford, which received the right to hold a market in 1271 and was made a free

From a photograph *Kindness Walter H. Bradley, Esq., and Burton H. Winslow, Esq.*

MEMORIAL TABLET AT WINTER HARBOUR, NOW BIDDEFORD POOL, MAINE,

near mouth of the Saco River, where Captain Richard Vines, the English explorer, and his adventurous crew of sixteen spent the winter of 1616–17. Vines received a grant of the lands within the present limits of Biddeford.

The words on the Tablet read as follows:—

RICHARD VINES, agent of SIR FERDINANDO GORGES, to experience and report upon the CLIMATE of NEW ENGLAND; visits the Indians in their huts, and passes the winter of 1616 at the present LEIGHTON'S POINT, territory of BIDDEFORD, while his ship lay in the nearby "WINTER HARBOR" until spring.

From "The West Coast of England," Pictorial Guide, Second Edition   *Kindness Walter K. Watkins, Esq.*

BIDEFORD, ENGLAND

Biddeford, Maine, is named for this town.

borough in 1573, is a seaport and market-town in Devonshire, England, on the banks of the river Torridge. In the sixteenth century Sir Richard Grenville did much to stimulate the commercial trade of Bideford with America.

BRAINTREE, MASSACHUSETTS

BRAINTREE, first called Mt. Wollaston, formerly included Quincy and Randolph and is one of the oldest communities in the State. The first settlement was made on Black's Creek as early as 1625, when Captain Wollaston and thirty of his followers came over from England and started a plantation here, and a tablet has recently been presented by the Quincy Chapter of the Daughters of the American Revolution to mark the establishment of this early trading-post. It is believed some of these settlers came from Braintree, England, and therefore gave the town its present name. The colony was a failure owing to the intrigues of Thomas Morton of Clifford's Inn, London, who became notorious on account of his gay May Day festival held at Ma-re-mount, of which much has been written. What we generally understand to be the "Braintree Company" that came from England to our Braintree was a group of people including James Olmstedd, J. Talcott and a Dr. Goodwyn who came over some years later, in 1632, in the ship "Lyon" under the auspices of Thomas Hooker of Chelmsford, and who settled in our Cambridge. Some confusion has therefore arisen as to these two groups of pioneers. The town of Braintree, at first often spelled Braintry, was really not permanently settled until 1634, when a number of people came over here from the counties of Devonshire, Lincolnshire and Essex. The town was incorporated in 1640 and comprised the land now included within the bounds of Quincy, Braintree, Randolph

Kindness of the Boston Post

TABLET PLACED BY THE QUINCY CHAPTER OF THE DAUGHTERS OF THE AMERICAN REVOLUTION, IN QUINCY, MASSACHUSETTS,

once part of Braintree, where Captain Wollaston in 1625 first established a trading post at Black's Creek. From him Wollaston, near Quincy and Braintree, received its name.

and Holbrook, the business center being at Quincy. Among those to whom early grants were given were Coddington, Wilson, Quincy, Hutchinson and Wheelwright. Joseph Loomys, or Lummys, who came from Braintree, England, was another early settler. He was a woolen merchant and the founder of the American branch of this family, the name now being spelled Loomis. Quincy was formed into a separate township in 1792, and is known the world over as having been the New England home of two Presidents of the United States.

The first attempt to establish an industry at Braintree was made in 1643 when Governor Winthrop brought over some workmen to start there the manufacture of iron, among the newcomers being Lionel Copeley from York County, Nicholas Bond and others. Lynn, however, began this industry before Braintree and was evidently more successful if we may judge from the words of one writer who said that in the latter town they "pounded out less iron than they hammered out law suits."

It may be interesting to mention that Captain John Smith on his map gave Quincy the name of London; and the figures of a castle and cathedral were annexed as showing the prosperity and grandeur to which he believed the town would attain.

There is also a Braintree in Vermont.

Drawn by W. Bartlett.

Engraved by H. Adlard.

BRAINTREE, ESSEX.

Photographed by Montague Cooper from an old print

Kindness Ian Forbes-Robertson, Esq.

BRAINTREE, ESSEX, ENGLAND

The English town of Braintree in Essex County was once called "Branchetreu," a Saxon name meaning "town near a river," and was once the seat of the Bishops of London. It bears evidence of having existed for generations. The earliest part of the town was located on the banks of Pods Brook in the vicinity of what is now known as Skitt's Hill; as the settlement expanded and the Romans built their great roads, the population shifted toward the intersection of the two great Roman highways. The annals of Braintree are rich in names that have become famous not only in Britain but throughout the world; among these are John Ray, the naturalist; Benjamin Allen, surgeon; Sir William Tilbury, who, though once a boot-boy in a shop near the Square, became tutor of the children of the Emperor of Brazil; and Samuel Dale, author. Braintree's taverns also have been a subject of considerable interest, and there are still left a number of them to tell of the coaching days long past; one of the most famous is "The George Inn," the sign of which stretched over the entire width of New Street. This town, with Coichester, Dedham and several others, was called one of the "clothing towns" of England on account of the fact that the woolen cloth weavers carried on their business there. Toward the end of the eighteenth century hard times overtook Braintree and in 1804 appeared these lines:—

> "We saw two large townships called Braintree and Bocking
> Where the tale of distress was of late years most shocking."

Silk mills, however, were erected there some years later, and both towns then began to prosper.

Little Square is perhaps the most typical part of old Braintree, which contains also many attractive and quaint streets. The parish church of St. Michael dates back to 1199.

BRIDGEWATER, MASSACHUSETTS

ON the roll of Mayors and members of Parliament of the town of Bridgewater in Somersetshire, England, are found the names of Allen, Bryant, Hooper and Mitchell, and because these names are familiar in the annals of Bridgewater, Massachusetts, it is supposed that it was so called for English Bridgewater in honour of that lovely village from which staunch Puritans emigrated to American shores. The town of Bridgewater, Massachusetts, was incorporated in 1656 and at first included territory now comprised by Brockton (formerly North Bridgewater), East Bridgewater, West Bridgewater and parts of the towns of Abington and Hanson. The land was originally a part of what was known as "Duxbury New Plantation," which Miles Standish and others in 1645 had received permission from the Old Colony Government to purchase from the Indians. Soon after the purchase, some of the Duxbury proprietors, of whom there were in all

Photographed by Valentine & Co., Dundee, Scotland   *Kindness Ian Forbes-Robertson, Esq.*

BRIDGEWATER, ENGLAND

fifty-four, became settlers here, and among the first to be associated with them was Deacon Samuel Edson, of Salem, the owner of their first mill, who became a proprietor and settled with the Duxbury men near the Town River, where Tavern Bridge crosses it. "And," continues the chronicler, "because this was the richest land in the whole region, some of the Duxbury people who had taken shares in the purchase settled near him, about the same time, on scattered farms from below the present village of West Bridgewater gradually extending up the river to within a mile of the head of it in Lake Nippenicket. One of the first of these was John Howard, whose house was the first tavern—for more than a century the only tavern—in the region; and for a long time the bridge nearby was the only bridge over the river. This was, therefore, the center to which all the primitive paths converged—one from the Massachusetts Bay towns on the north, known as 'the Bay path;' two others to the southeast along the river on opposite sides of it, through the wilderness which is now Bridgewater, on the way to Plymouth; and others through the woods north and south of Lake Nippenicket to Taunton on the southwest, where the first settlers went to trade and carried grist on foot."

The Duxbury settlers, who in 1651 to 1656 founded what is now West Bridgewater, in 1662 to 1665 settled the land covered by the present Bridgewater, and among the early farms were those of the Leonards, Washburns and Edsons. Until

1822 the town meetings were held in West Bridgewater and for more than half a century the church services were conducted in the same place.

The English seaport of Bridgewater lies in a romantic and historic part of Somersetshire where tales of King Alfred are still told, and where, six miles distant, the noble Saxon king in 878 took refuge from the Danes encamped near the town. This county, according to tradition, also witnessed King Arthur's desperate encounters with the Saxon hordes who invaded Britain and who were met by this famous king in that great battle in the West. The town itself grew up around the ford, which appears to have been the only one across the river Parret, as all roads led to it. "The ford," says the historian, "gave the name of Brugie, or bridge, to the village in Saxon times. When William the Conqueror, after the year 1066, parcelled England with his Norman barons, Brugie and the vicinity were given to a Baron Walter and the place began to be known as Brugie-Walter, or Walter's Bridge, which finally became Bridgewater."

In 1649 when Miles Standish and others purchased the "Duxbury New Plantation" in America, the mother town was one of the most important places in southwestern England and in that year Cromwell's army attacked the town and castle which surrendered with sixteen hundred officers and men. Portions of the old walls of the town and castle were standing until a century past. Two hundred years after Cromwell assaulted and conquered Bridgewater and after Miles Standish had made his valuable purchase of New England territory, representative citizens of Bridgewater, England, sent a letter dated September 10, 1846, to the town of Bridgewater, Massachusetts. Correspondence ensued which made it apparent that the English town presented to Parliament the first petition against the slave-trade, with successful results. In these letters appeared names common to both towns. Certain books and maps were sent to England with a letter from our Bridgewater which was drafted by Rev. Paul Couch and Hon. Jesse Perkins of North Bridgewater, Rev. Darius Forbes and Hon. John E. Howard of West Bridgewater, Rev. Baalis Sanford and Rev. Nathaniel Whitman of East Bridgewater and Rev. David Brigham and Rev. Claudius Bradford of Bridgewater. Hon. John Reed also served on the committee. There are Bridgewaters also in Maine, New Hampshire, Vermont and Connecticut.

THE CHAIN PIER AT BRIGHTON WITH CHARACTERS

Photographed by George B. Brayton from a very old print by G. Atkinson   *Owned by Allan Forbes*

BRIGHTON, ENGLAND,
showing in the distance the Chain Pier.

From a photograph   *Kindness Mrs. Mary Fifield King*

A RECENT VIEW OF BRIGHTON, ENGLAND

BRIGHTON, MASSACHUSETTS

THE ancestors of several of the first settlers of Brighton, Massachusetts, came from the vicinity of the English Brighton, called in early days Bristelmestune, Bruyton and later Brighthelmstone, named from Brighthelm, an Anglo-Saxon bishop of the tenth century. It is fair, therefore, to suppose that our Brighton, incorporated in 1807 and now a part of Boston, was named for the fashionable watering place in England frequented by King Edward VII, Queen Victoria and many other royal persons, as well as by legions of "trippers" during the summer season.

The Royal Pavilion, built by King George IV as a maritime residence when he was Prince of Wales, is undoubtedly the most interesting feature of the town and cost such a fabulous sum that Byron wrote about it the following couplet:—

> "Shut up—no, not the King, but the Pavilion,
> Or else 'twill cost us all another million."

This building is no longer a residence but is used for various purposes. Part of it serves as a museum and among other interesting objects therein is a collection of pottery decorated with American subjects, such as "The Landing of the Fathers at Plymouth," "Landing of Roger Williams at Providence," bust of George Washington, etc.

Four miles from Brighton is the pretty village of Rottingdean where Rudyard Kipling lived for some time.

Our Brighton was set apart from Cambridge in 1779, the committee appointed to wait on the Honourable General Court with the petition being Samuel Willis Pomeroy, Gorham Parsons, Stephen and Thomas Dana and Daniel Bowen.

There is also a Brighton in Maine and one in Vermont.

COVENTRY, CONNECTICUT

> "And to-day, as we look o'er that village,
> Named for the one 'cross the sea,
> It seems to extend hearty welcome
> To you, from old Coventry."

(The above is part of the last verse written by Ruth Amelia Higgins on the occasion of the two hundredth anniversary of the founding of Coventry, Connecticut.)

ALTHOUGH a small town, Coventry has had such close relations with Coventry in England, that it should be included in this book. Previous to this two hundredth anniversary celebration, William L. Higgins, who has always shown a great interest in old Coventry across the water, and who was President of the Coventry Town Committee, sent the following letter to the Mayor of Coventry, England:—

"COVENTRY, CONN. U.S.
July 6, 1912.

To THE HONOURABLE MAYOR, COVENTRY, ENGLAND.
Dear Sir:—

We are about to celebrate the 200th anniversary of the founding of this town, which according to tradition, was named after Coventry in England. In view of the fact that the first settlers in this town of Coventry were either Englishmen or of English descent, some of whom, or their ancestors, may have come from your English city, or from its vicinity, it is very probable that in selecting a name for this place, as in the establishment of laws and customs, their minds reverted to the mother country and to the town and surroundings from whence they came. We, therefore, accept the tradition as true and feel that some communication either in person or by letter from you would be most welcome to the people of this town, and very appropriate to the occasion. On behalf of this town of Coventry we therefore extend to you a cordial invitation to be present as a representative of your city at the celebrations of our anniversary, which will take place during the last week in August, 1912, known as 'Old Home Week.' In case you cannot be here, and are unable to send a representative, it will give us great pleasure to receive some kind of acknowledgment or communication from you as a memorial of Coventry in England.

Respectfully yours,

WILLIAM L. HIGGINS, *President Town Committee*
CURTIS DEAN, *Secretary Town Committee*"

We are also going to quote the reply in order to show the great interest taken by the old town in its namesake:—

"THE CHARTERHOUSE, COVENTRY
July 30, 1912.

To
WILLIAM L. HIGGINS, Esq., M.D.
President of Town Committee,
South Coventry, Conn. U.S.A.
Dear Sir:—

I was much interested to receive your letter of July 6th inviting me to the celebration of the 200th anniversary of the founding of your town and I only regret that I am unable to accept your kind invitation, but unfortunately all my days are practically taken up and mapped out up to the end of my term of office, November 1st, next.

I see no reason to doubt that the original founders of your town were connected with our city as its citizens have always been capable of adapting themselves to the needs of the age, as witnessed by their adoption of comparatively new industries such as the bicycle and motor trades, after the shrinkage in the old watch and ribbon trades introduced by the Huguenots, and this spirit of originality no doubt prompted some of our ancestors 200 years ago to seek their fortunes in the New World, and to name their town in memory of their old home.

At any rate there is a strong feeling among us that we have brothers and sisters in America, and I shall with pleasure make known to our citizens the reception of the kind wishes and sentiments of the New Coventry over the water, which are heartily reciprocated and I trust that your Town may prosper in the same way as this ancient city has done.

I am sending you a few photographs of some of the beauty spots of our ancient city, and believe me
With cordial greetings,

Yours very truly,

W. F. WYLEY, *Mayor of Coventry*"

From a print dated 1794 owned by Allan Forbes   *Formerly in the collection of J. H. Seers, Essex, England*

COVENTRY, ENGLAND

This correspondence was followed by the following resolution passed by the citizens of the Connecticut town at the regular town meeting held on the 7th of October, 1912:—

"*Resolved*, That, We, citizens of the Town of Coventry in town meeting assembled do hereby send to Coventry, England, Greeting: that we express to its Mayor and City Council our hearty appreciation of and thanks for the kind reception which our bi-centennial message received from them, and also for the numerous books, pictures, papers and other tokens of their interest and regard sent to us in return; that we sincerely reciprocate the kind wishes and sentiments expressed in Mayor Wyley's letter to us, and that we shall ever hold Coventry across the sea in affectionate remembrance and regard and rejoice in her prosperity.

Attest.

JOHN S. CHAMPLIN, *Town Clerk* "

This celebration and the correspondence that ensued created a great deal of interest in old Coventry, which, by the way, is sometimes referred to as the "town of the three spires," and an account of the proceedings was printed in the Coventry *Herald* in the English town. Many friendly letters were also received by our Coventry, which included a very impressive letter from an English workman describing his pleasure at the interchange of friendly messages between the two towns. These letters including the article in the Coventry *Herald*, together with a number of

Photographed by Ernest W. Appleby   Kindness Ian Forbes-Robertson, Esq.

THE DAVENPORT HOUSE, COVENTRY, ENGLAND

The home of the ancestors of John Davenport, who was one of the founders of New Haven, Connecticut, and first pastor of the church there.

books, pictures and presents, sent from the ancient city, are prized very highly by the town committee of our Coventry. Still another evidence of the friendship between the two countries was shown on this occasion of the anniversary of the Connecticut town, when ribbons from Stephen's Factory in the English town were worn as badges by the citizens of our town.

Some years ago Dean Beaumont of Coventry, England, visited New Haven and while there recalled the fact that their first Governor was Theophilus Eaton, who was the son of an early vicar of Holy Trinity, Coventry, England, and that the first pastor of the New Haven church was John Davenport, the son of a former Mayor of the English Coventry. Davenport with some friends visited Quinnipiac, the old Indian name for New Haven, and founded a colony there in the year 1638. Both had been students at the Coventry Grammar School. Canon Beaumont at one time was able to save an historic building in New Haven, whereupon he was made a corresponding member of its Historical Society. While a guest of the town, Beaumont was received with much courtesy by Professor Dexter of Yale University, whose wife was a descendant of Davenport, and who had several times visited the old town in search of historical information respecting the founders of her city.

There are at least five Coventrys in America, four of which are situated in Connecticut, Pennsylvania, Rhode Island and Vermont, the Connecticut Coventry being incorporated in 1712. The early petition to the Court gave a list of six families most of whom are said to have come from Hartford, Connecticut, and Northampton, Massachusetts. One of the interesting objects in connection with the early history of the Connecticut Coventry was the will of the Indian sachem "Joshua," which is preserved in the State Library at Hartford. The redskin made careful provisions for his children and their bringing up, recording his wishes in these words:—

"Further my Will is that my Children be brought up the first four years with Trusty and their mother to teach them English . . . and at the expiration of the said four Years I desire that my Children may be kept at the English Schoole."

He especially desired that they should be kept apart from the Connecticut Indians, and made the further request that he be buried at "Saybrook in a Coffin after the English manner."

The town is best known as the birthplace and home of Nathan Hale who was shot as a spy in the Revolutionary War, his last words, "My only regret is that I have but one life to lose for my country," being known the world over. A beautiful monument has been set up to his memory in the Nathan

Photographed by Ernest W. Appleby   Kindness Ian Forbes-Robertson, Esq.

EFFIGY OF PEEPING TOM, KING'S HEAD HOTEL, COVENTRY, ENGLAND

Hale Cemetery in Coventry, other memorials also having been erected in the east corridor of the State Capitol, Hartford, Connecticut, on the front lawn of the Wadsworth Athenæum, Hartford, Connecticut, in City Hall Park, New York, and on the Yale Campus, New Haven. The town of this name in Vermont was named for the Connecticut town in honour of Major Elias Buel, whose father, Captain Peter Buel, was one of the first settlers in the latter place.

To the reader the English Coventry, of course, suggests Lady Godiva and the "Peeping Tom" incident. Tradition has been heaped upon tradition until the story has assumed large proportions and today in the English town there is an effigy of the curious one—who was a tailor—in the wall of the King's Head Hotel on Hertford Street. For his rashness, according to Tennyson,—

> "His eyes, before they had their will
> Were shrivell'd into darkness in his head,
> And dropped before him."

It must be remembered, however, that Lady Godiva was a real person, the wife of Leofric, mother of Ælfgar, Earl of East Anglia, and that her remains were buried in the monastery at Coventry.

The town itself has been the scene of many charming stories and a modern chronicler well described its place in British history in these words: "It is a typically English city, whose history might serve as the 'abstract and brief chronicles' of the time. A thoroughly corrupt borough in the worst days of municipal corruption, rigidly Puritan under the Stuarts, loyal under Elizabeth, steady for hereditary right at Mary's accession—but Protestant, as witness its martyrs—Lollard in the heyday of Lollardry, patriotic and tolerant throughout the Hundred Years' War—as England was, so was Coventry. In art and letters, also, the city recalls what is most characteristic in the achievements of the English people. Here flourished mediæval architecture, an art wherein Englishmen have excelled greatly; . . . while chance and the sojourn of George Eliot, have given the city associations with the literary outburst of the Victorian time."

A part of the old wall begun in 1356 still remains; it is recorded that Charles I made a breach in this wall in 1642 and that some years later another breach was ordered by Charles II in revenge for the repulsing of his father's forces. Many have believed that the famous Mother Shipton foretold the final destruction of this wall when she prophesied that a pigeon should pull it down, which turned out to be true, for the walls were eventually taken down during the Mayoralty of Thomas Pigeon.

There are many old landmarks in Coventry and among other attractive features are "the three tall spires" shown in the cut, which lend a dignity to the view as one approaches the city. One of these spires is that of St. Michael's, said to be one of the finest specimens of the florid or perpendicular style of architecture in England.

Coventry is the center of many industries such as woolens, hosiery, textiles, watches, iron and brass foundries, printing, motor and cycle manufacturing. It is well described by Michael Drayton, Poet Laureate in 1626, in these lines:—

> "Now flourishing with fanes [temples] and proud pyramides [spires]
> Her walls in good repair, her ports [gates] so bravely built,
> Her halls in good estate, her cross so richly gilt
> As scorning all the Towns that stand within her view."

In ancient documents the town was called Coventree, sometimes Coventria, both names probably being derived from a convent established there in the seventh century of which St. Osburg was the Abbess. When Queen Elizabeth visited Coventry, the Mayor is supposed to have received his Sovereign with these words:—

> "We men of Coventree
> Are very glad to see
> Your Gracious Majestie.
> Good Lord, how fair ye be!"

To which the Queen is said to have replied:—

> "Our gracious Majestie
> Is very glad to see
> Ye men of Coventree.
> Good lack, what fools are ye!"

In St. Michael's Cathedral is the burial-place of Ann Sewell, wife of William Sewell, who is an ancestor of many of the family of this name in New England. The famous Mrs. Siddons was married in Holy Trinity Church. John Davenport was born in Coventry in 1517 and his house is still standing. The town quite recently commemorated the centenary of George Eliot.

DOVER, MASSACHUSETTS

FORTY–FOUR American and Colonial Dovers, including the Maine and Massachusetts Dovers and possibly the New Hampshire Dover, were represented at the great pageant held in Dover, England, in 1908. The chorus sang the following two verses, one expressing the pleasure of Dover, England, in receiving so many of her offspring, the other being an ode to the famous English port:—

> "And ye that hearken the while we sing,
> Look up, and behold a wondrous thing!
> For these her daughters from oversea,
> That follow in Dover's company,
>   Forty and four
>   The wide world o'er,
> And mothers of mighty sons to be—
> These from the ends of the earth who came,
> Share her honour, and bear her name—
> With home-felt rapture around her throng,
> And thrill to the close of her triumph-song!"

.   .   .   .

> "Oh, fair and majestic haven, couched under the seacliffs white,
> That title upon thee graven, Invicta, was thine of right.
> For one with the waves thy glory, and one with the winds thy might,
> And the web of thine endless story is woven by day and night,
> Of ocean's infinite yearning, criss-crossed with the to-and-fro
> Of a thousand keels returning, a thousand that outward go!
> From the frowning towers above thee, to the fringing foam below
> To think of thee is to love thee, as all that have known thee know."

The scene of this pageant must have been very inspiring, for nearby was the historic Dover Castle, shown in the cut on the next page, and also Shakespeare Cliff, which was chosen by Shakespeare for his famous scene between Edgar and Gloucester in "King Lear." A monument is to be raised on the Cliffs to the men who fell during

View of Dover from the South Pier Head.

DOVER, ENGLAND,

from the South Pier Head, showing Shakespeare Cliff and Dover Castle.

From a rare print dated 1810, published by Horn & Adlard, Dover, England
Engraved by Rob. Havell & Son

Owned by Allan Forbes

EMBARKATION OF HENRY VIII AT DOVER IN 1520
The original of this picture hangs in the Royal Apartments at Windsor Castle. It can be seen that even in those days Dover ranked high among the important ports of the world.

the Great War while serving in the splendid "Dover Patrol," whose duties were shared by many Americans. A similar monolith will be erected near Cape Blanc Nez in France and also on some government land overlooking New York Harbour, the cost of the latter having been defrayed by subscriptions to the Dover Patrol Memorial Fund Committee, the presentation of which was made on April 21, 1920, to our Secretary of War by Major Evelyn Wrench, Hon. Secretary of the London Branch of the English-Speaking Union. The memorial will testify to the spirit of co-operation which existed between the American and British navies during the late war.

Most of the travelers to Dover in the past have thought first of all of the channel passage, whether it was to be rough or smooth, but it is inevitable that tourists should in the future take more interest in this town, which is a prosperous port, an important garrison town, a naval depot, a popular watering place and a busy commercial center, with a population of about forty-two thousand. It is only twenty-two miles to France, and on a clear day the coast is clearly discernible, as Wordsworth described in these words:—

> "And saw, while sea was calm and air was clear,
> The coast of France! the coast of France how near!"

It was from Dover that the first successful start was made to cross the Channel in a balloon, on January 7, 1785, and in this port on July 25, 1909, landed M. Blériot, the first to cross these waters in a monoplane.

Dover, situated in County Kent on the river Dour, is one of the historic Cinque Ports, and furnished five ships which helped considerably in defeating the Armada.

Photographed by The View & Portrait Supply Co., 15, Lisle St., Leicester Sq., W.   *Kindness Ian Forbes-Robertson, Esq.*

DOVER CASTLE, DOVER, ENGLAND

The Massachusetts town has taken a great deal of interest in the English Dover and, about the year 1845, officially appointed the Rev. Dr. Sanger in town meeting to write a suitable reply to a letter of greeting sent from this channel port, but as the subject did not appear in the Town Warrant, there is no record of this interesting event. Again in 1898, when the Dover First Parish celebrated the one hundred and fiftieth anniversary of its organization, fitting reference was made to the mother town. In 1918, H. J. Taylor, Esq., of Dover, England, a member of the British American Fellowship Committee, sent Dover an invitation to have any of its men serving in the war visit the English seaport and so far as possible notices were sent to all Dover boys informing them of this invitation.

In 1920 various publications giving the history of Dover were sent to the mother town and were acknowledged for the corporation by the town clerk, Reginald E. Knocker, Esq. In exchange, the Dover, Massachusetts, Public Library received "Annals of Dover" by J. Bavington Jones; "Dover and the Great War;" and "Dover, England's Gate" by Walter Emden, late Mayor of Dover, all volumes being highly prized by the library.

Dover, Massachusetts, was incorporated as the Springfield Parish of Dedham in 1748, as the District of Dover in 1784 and as the town of Dover in 1836.

There is also a Dover in Vermont.

EXETER, NEW HAMPSHIRE

THE beginnings of Exeter, New Hampshire, date back to the year 1638 when Rev. John Wheelwright, being denied by the Massachusetts Bay Colony freedom in religious matters and having incurred the displeasure of the authorities, was banished from the Colony in 1637. With a small band of followers and companions he turned to the North and was given by the Indian sagamore and his son, by deeds dated 1638 which are still preserved, title to a tract of land about the Falls of the Squamscott. The name of Exeter was given to this settle-

ment in honour of Godfrey Dearborn of Exeter, England, who had accompanied Rev. Mr. Wheelwright in his exile. There is on record an estimate of the prowess of Rev. Mr. Wheelwright on the football field, written by Oliver Cromwell who often played against him while they were fellow-students at Cambridge University, and who declared later that he used to be more afraid of meeting Wheelwright at football than he had been since of meeting an army in the field. After graduation Wheelwright took holy orders and later became allied with the Puritan movement and was silenced for non-conformity. In 1636 he landed in Boston and soon after became pastor of a new church gathered at Mt. Wollaston, now Quincy. After falling under the ban of the Massachusetts Bay Colony and settling in this New Hampshire territory, now Exeter, one of the first deeds accomplished was the founding of a church which still remains the Town Church. Rev. Samuel Dudley, son of Governor Thomas

From a photograph   Kindness Edmund S. Boyer, Esq., and Joseph S. Ford, Esq.

REPLICA OF THE COAT OF ARMS OF EXETER, ENGLAND, IN THE ADMINISTRATION BUILDING OF PHILLIPS-EXETER ACADEMY, EXETER, NEW HAMPSHIRE,

procured by Joseph S. Ford, Esq., at the suggestion of the President of the Board of Trustees of the Academy, S. Sidney Smith, Esq. The present was sent in 1915 by A. Wheaton, Esq., of the English Exeter, and with it came a copy of the exemplification of the coat of arms given by Queen Elizabeth, dated August 6, 1564, the town being spelled Exceter at that time. The building in which it is placed is shown in the accompanying cut.

ADMINISTRATION BUILDING OF PHILLIPS–EXETER ACADEMY, EXETER, NEW HAMPSHIRE,

in which there is a reproduction of the coat of arms of Exeter, England, shown in another illustration.

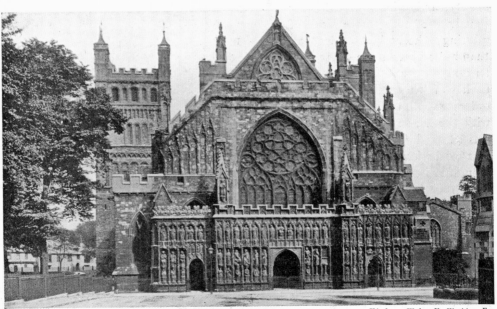

EXETER CATHEDRAL, EXETER, ENGLAND

From " The West Coast of England" Pictorial Guide—Second Edition   *Kindness Walter K. Watkins, Esq.*

THE EXE BRIDGE, EXETER, ENGLAND

Dudley, a native of England, was pastor of this church for thirty-three years. Another man who added to the fame of Exeter was John Phillips, who, born in Andover, Massachusetts, moved to Exeter in 1741. He taught for a time, then engaged in trade in which he was very successful. He gave liberally to the cause of education, contributing to Dartmouth College and, joining with his brother, Samuel, founded Phillips-Andover. He later founded and organized Phillips-Exeter Academy in 1783, remaining for twelve years as its head. Daniel Webster, Edward Everett and General Lewis Cass (who was born in Exeter in a house which is still standing) are three well-known graduates of this Academy. The Gilman, Ladd, French and Folsom families are others who have done much for the development of the town from its earliest days down to the present time. William H. Folsom who pitched the first curved ball for Harvard University was a native of Exeter.

In 1915, through the efforts of Mr. Joseph S. Ford, at the suggestion of the President of the Board of Trustees of the Academy, S. Sidney Smith, Esq., of New York City, a replica of the City Arms of Exeter, England, was sent to the New Hampshire town by Mr. A. Wheaton, book publisher in the English Exeter. This now hangs in the Administration Building of Phillips-Exeter Academy. An exemplification of the coat of arms, as granted by Queen Elizabeth, dated August 6, 1564, and verified as a copy by Mr. H. Lloyd Parry, Town Clerk, was sent from England as descriptive of the replica and is now preserved in the Library of the Academy. At the time the original document was written the manner of spelling the name of the town in England was "Exceter."

Exeter, England, is situated in the county of Devon, on the river Exe, which plainly shows whence came its name. This old English town is famous for the number of sieges it sustained as the chief place in the southwest of England. In early times it was called Caer Isc by the Britons, while later the Romans called it

Isca Damnoniorum. On an eminence near one of the railway stations may be seen the ruins of Rougemont Castle, built by William the Conqueror, which was so named for the colour of the rock on which it was built. Exeter's principal edifice is the cathedral, begun in 1100, which is famed for the beauty of its design and the richness of its decorations. In the chapter-house of the cathedral is preserved, among other valuable ancient manuscripts, Leofric's famous book of Saxon poetry.

The city has some shipping trade, communication with the sea being furnished by the ship-canal originally cut in the reign of Elizabeth in 1564. This waterway is an interesting work, being the first one carried out in the United Kingdom for the purpose of enabling seagoing vessels to pass to an inland port.

FRAMINGHAM, MASSACHUSETTS

FRAMLINGHAM, England, which is spelled with an "l," is a small town near Ipswich as shown in a letter written in 1900 by Rev. J. Holme Pilkington, Rector of Framlingham, to Peter N. Everett, Esq., Secretary of the Bicentennial Committee of Framingham, Massachusetts:—

"A remark in an Ipswich paper a week or two back, will, I think, give you a good idea of our present condition. It says 'Framlingham went to sleep in the time of Queen Elizabeth, and has not woke up yet. You may make as much noise as you like, you will never wake it now.' I am afraid there is much truth underlying the sarcasm."

Another note written in 1900 describes Framlingham as a "small town of rather more than two thousand inhabitants. Though a small and (except locally) unimportant place now, it has great and interesting historical associations and the imposing ruins of Framlingham Castle testify to its ancient grandeur. I expect the American daughter has altogether eclipsed her English Mother."

There have been a few interchanges of presents which have been sent chiefly by the Rector, as the town does not boast of a Mayor. The most interesting report, however, of the old town has been written by Mr. John M. Merriam and we believe we cannot do better than quote parts of his account of his visit to Framlingham, which he has kindly furnished for this article:—

"It was an unusual pleasure which fell to our lot May 26, 1914, to visit the Town of Framlingham, in England, and it has been a continuing pleasure since our return to our home in Massachusetts to study, so far as we have been able, the history of this old Mother town.

These two far distant Towns are connected through the life of Thomas Danforth. When the Pilgrims were endeavoring to preserve their frail settlement on these Massachusetts shores in 1622, a son was born to Nicholas Danforth in Framlingham, England. The father, Nicholas, was a man of position in his community, in England, being a Vestryman in the established church. According to the custom of the church the son was baptised at the old Font in front of the Altar and this font is still in use, and the record of his baptism is preserved in the Parish records which can still be examined in consecutive order from the century preceding his birth to the present time. The father moved from Eng-

From a picture owned by John M. Merriam, Esq., of Framingham, Massachusetts

FRAMLINGHAM CHURCH, FRAMLINGHAM, ENGLAND

The Rector of this church, Rev. J. Holme Pilkington, sent letters at the time of the Bicentennial celebration of the incorporation of Framingham, Massachusetts, in 1900.

land in 1634. He had lost his wife in 1629 and he brought with him the six children she had left. He was among the early settlers of Cambridge. The son, Thomas, was destined for important service in this new land. . . . According to Governor Hutchinson, he had a 'great share in managing the public affairs in the most difficult times.' For his public service, and for money spent by him in the public interest, several grants of land were made to him which were known as 'Danforth Farms' and this territory was incorporated in 1700 as Framingham in remembrance of the town of his birth. Danforth had died in the preceding year, November 5, 1699. The name was in use before the incorporation of the town and occurs in Danforth's own letters, spelled Framingham. Our Town Historian, Rev. Josiah H. Temple, gives a few references in our Colonial records in which the English spelling Framlingham was followed. I have found a further instance of this spelling in Cotton Mather's Diary, where he records, August 14, 1718, 'Divisions and Confusions in the Church at Framlingham call for my best endeavors to bring them to a period.' This will suffice to show the connection historically of Framlingham, England, and Framingham, Mass.

A branch railroad leaves the main line about eighty miles from London, and ends at the little Town of Framlingham, a township of some two thousand people in the northern part of Suffolk County near the line of Norfolk.

. . . The oak seems to have flourished near Framlingham. Probably many of these giants of the forest went into the frigates and merchantmen which have carried the English flag to all the seas of the world.   One of these old giants was known as the 'Framlingham Oak,' an account of which is given in the 'Library of Entertaining Knowledge.' This tree was used in the construction of the 'Royal Sovereign.'   It yielded, so we read, four square beams, each one forty-four feet in length, the largest one of which was four feet nine inches square.   These old English oaks were very dear to the English people, as some of their old songs abundantly prove.   Listen to the words of the familiar song 'Hearts of Oak.'

'Hearts of oak are our ships.
Jolly tars are our men.
We always are ready,
Steady boys, steady,
We'll fight and we'll conquer
Again and again.'

'They swear they'll invade us, these terrible foes,
They frighten our women, our children, our beaux,
But should their flat bottoms in darkness get o'er
Still Britons they'll find to receive them on shore.'

Let us now turn to the history of Framlingham.   It is a town of great antiquity beginning possibly with the Roman occupation.   The ruins of a castle of very considerable proportions crown the highest land, and with the old church nearby, are the principal objects of interest.   This old Castle is among the prominent ones of early England.   All it needs is the genius of another Scott to cast around it romantic interest similar to that of Kenilworth.   This Castle was the home of perhaps the foremost family in England, the Howards, famous for many generations as the great House of Norfolk.   It was this family which furnished Thomas Howard, the second Duke of Norfolk, the English leader of the battle resulting in the defeat of Scotland at Flodden Field.   Closely connected with the same family were those unfortunate royal cousins, Anne Boleyn and Catherine Howard, wives of Henry VIII, who lost their heads at the command of their husband and king. Another Howard was their powerful uncle, Thomas the Duke of Norfolk, who was saved from death at the block by the death of the king himself the day before the time appointed for the execution. . . . The present representative of the Howard family in England is the Duke of Norfolk, often called the premier duke of England, as his title can be traced to the earliest sources of all present titles.

Among the paintings of the last century is one of Framlingham Castle bearing date 1828, by John Sell Cotman, A.W.S.   A friend recently gave to me a portfolio of copies of English oils and water colors, and in it I was delighted to find a copy of Cotman's painting, which shows the castle as it stood eighty-six years ago. . . .

The author, Richard Green, gives two possible sources of the name Framlingham; one from the Saxon words Friendling and Ham—a stranger's home, or a habitation of strangers; and the other from the name of the stream Fromas.   The name antedates the Domesday Book of William the Conqueror when it is written 'Framincham.'   It became a family name in 1330 as there is record of John de Framlingham, a Rector of Kelsale, and in 1540 Henry VIII conferred a grant of land to Francis Framlingham, who held the same from Thomas Howard, third Duke of Norfolk, as 'Lord of the Manor of Framlingham ad Castrum.'

In this history of Green's the Castle is called a 'pile of unknown antiquity.'   An early description by Dr. Henry Sampson, the Rector of Framlingham in 1650–1660 is this: 'Framlingham Castle is a very ancient structure, and said to have been built in the time of the Saxons.   It was one of the principal seats of St. Edmund the King and Martyr. When he fled from Dunwich, being pursued by the pagan Danes, he took refuge in this Castle but being hard besieged, and having no hope of rescue, he fled from thence, and

From a print dated 1813, owned by Allan Forbes *Formerly in the collection of J. H. Seers, Essex, England*

FRAMLINGHAM CASTLE, SUFFOLK, ENGLAND
Framingham, Massachusetts, is named for Framlingham, England.

being overtaken by his enemies, was beheaded at Hoxon, from where long after his corpse was removed and reinterred at Bury, called since Bury St. Edmunds.'

Dr. Henry Sampson gives the interesting description of Framlingham Castle. 'This castle was given by King Edward I to his second son, Thomas of Brotheron, Earl of Norfolk and Marshall of England, who repaired it, as appeareth by his arms in diverse places thereof.'

But the chief interest in Framlingham Castle is in its association with Mary, who became Queen of England upon the death of her younger brother, Edward VI, in 1553. When he died Mary was at Hunsdon in the north of England, and the message came to her that her right to succeed was disputed and that she was destined for imprisonment in the Tower of London. She turned as a fugitive toward Kenninghall in Norfolk County, where at one time she had lived. . . . Kenninghall was unfortified, but only twenty miles away was Framlingham Castle, encircled with moats and completely fortified, and here she determined to make her stand as England's Queen. Directly Mary stood within the magnificent area formed by the circling towers of Framlingham Castle, she felt herself a sovereign; she immediately defied her enemies, by displaying her standard over the gate-tower, and assumed the title of queen-regent of England and Ireland.

With the arrival of Queen Mary, Framlingham Castle became and remained for a few days the seat of Government. Mary appointed a privy council who came to her assistance at Framlingham and royal proclamations were issued from this Castle. . . . On the last day of July, Mary began her triumphal march from Framlingham to London. The opposition to her succession to the throne had been overcome, influential leaders had come to her support, an army had been placed at her command, ships sent to Yarmouth in order to besiege, the Framlingham Castle had surrendered upon her order, money had been supplied, and she had organized a Government. This event in the life of Queen Mary is thus summed up by the historian Knight;—'Here Mary remained till the last day of July. She entered the gates of Framlingham after a hurried ride of secrecy and fear. She went forth surrounded with armed thousands in the state of a Queen.' . . .

The old church at Framlingham, as well as the Castle, is of unusual interest; it is situated near the entrance to the castle. In this Church are the tombs of Henry Howard, Duke of Norfolk, and his son the Earl of Surrey.

In the same corner of the Church is the tomb of Henry Fitzroy, the natural son of King Henry VIII, known in history as the Earl of Richmond. This King wrought speedy punishment upon his wives, Anne Boleyn and Catherine Howard when slander impeaching their fidelity was brought to him, but he saw no wrong in his own association with Lady Elizabeth Talbois, resulting in the birth of this son in 1519. This boy lived only seventeen years, but before his death he married Mary Howard, the sister of the Earl of Surrey. This boy was not only acknowledged by his father, but had all the favor and training which could have been given him as the legitimate Prince. Froude states that he was 'a gallant high spirited boy,' that his 'beauty and noble promise' were at once 'his father's misery and pride,' and adds 'if this boy had lived he would have been named to follow Edward VI in this succession and would have become King of England.' To what strange fancy are we led as we pause at the tomb of this boy in the Framlingham Church and conjecture how his life, had it been spared, might have changed the whole course of English history.

But our most pleasant recollection of Framlingham centers around the Rectory occupied by the Rev. James Holme Pilkington. Our letter of introduction from Mr. Peter N. Everett in the name of the Selectmen of Framingham secured a very cordial welcome from the Rector and his wife. He recalled his correspondence with our Bicentennial Committee in 1899 and 1900, parts of which have already been quoted, and expressed an interest in our populous community, which in commercial prosperity has far outstripped the English town. We were made welcome in his home, learned from him something of the history of the Castle and of the Church, saw the old Parish register, partook of tea at his table, and walked about his beautiful grounds. It was a welcome many miles from home, and in a strange land, from one we had never met before, but it had the warmth and sincerity as from an old friend. The hospitality of our host expressed to us a bond of real kinship between the English Framlingham and the American Framingham."

The English Rector in one of his letters to Mr. Everett wrote:—

"I am sending by this post a packet containing the guide to Framlingham which I promised, and also a small local Almanack containing a short retrospect of the past year, with three or four back numbers of our small local paper. You will see, as you doubtless already know, that we are very much behind you in the matter of journalism. I am unable to send you a facsimile of our official seal, as Framlingham does not possess such a thing. We are under the rule of Parish Council, which are *seal-less* corporations."

There is only one Framingham in the United States.

GREENWICH, CONNECTICUT

THE town of Greenwich in the county of Kent, England, from which Greenwich, Connecticut, received its name, is celebrated as the home of many distinguished individuals. Dr. Johnson lived there for a short time and liked the town, although he and his companion agreed that they liked London much better. He must have enjoyed the place a great deal, however, for he described it in the following lines:—

> "On Thames's banks in silent thought we stood,
> Where Greenwich smiles upon the silver flood;
> Pleased with the seat that gave Eliza birth,
> We kneel and kiss the consecrated earth."
>
> (Eliza refers to Queen Elizabeth.)

Greenwich has been spoken of as the "marine residence" of the kings and reached its zenith at the time of Charles I. During the reign of Henry VIII many tilting tournaments were held there, the King himself being most skillful at this ancient sport. Besides excelling in tilting, he was also good at other games, for we are told that once on a visit to France he defeated a huge German in a combat with battle-axes, being beaten, however, by Francis I of France in wrestling. King Henry's brother-in-law, Charles Brandon, whose marriage took place at Greenwich in 1515, was also an expert at the tilts, and at one tournament held in France he won over all comers in a contest in which pointed spears were used. The following extract from a challenge issued in 1606 well expresses the romance and excitement attending one of these tournaments:—

"To all honourable men at arrmes, and knights, adventurers of hereditarie note and exemplarie noblesse that for moste maintainable actions do wield eyther sword or lance in quest of glorie."

At another meeting it is said that three hundred spears were "shivered" in one day's sport.

Henry VIII was born in Greenwich and lived there the greater part of his early life, in the gay days of the town. It was there that he resided after his marriage in 1509 to Catherine of Aragon, with whom he lived happily for several years. While she was in the good graces of the king, Catherine took an active interest in the affairs of the nation. It is told of her that when business was dull in Bedfordshire, the center of the lace industry, she burned her lace, ordering more to be made, and, in recognition of this royal patronage, as late as the nineteenth century the lace makers kept "Cattern's Day" as a holiday of their craft. It was from Greenwich that this unfortunate wife had to depart in 1531 to give place to Anne Boleyn, and from that time on, the cruel career of King Henry is only too well known. Queen Elizabeth, who was a daughter of King Henry VIII and Anne Boleyn, was

GREENWICH HOSPITAL

GREENWICH HOSPITAL, GREENWICH, LONDON, ENGLAND,
NOW THE ROYAL NAVAL COLLEGE

Greenwich is now part of London.   Many important events in England's history took place there.

born at Greenwich and raised the village to the position of a town. It was during the reign of this queen that Drake circumnavigated the globe and after this event sailed up the Thames in front of her Greenwich Palace to receive honours from Queen Elizabeth, who dined on board Drake's vessel and knighted the famous explorer.

The Royal Naval College is a feature second only in importance to the Royal Observatory. Before being taken over for the present purpose, this splendid range of buildings was known as Greenwich Hospital, and it is interesting to know that its pensioners were benefited indirectly by the well-known pirate Captain Kidd, whose property was sold after his execution in London and £6472 therefrom given to the hospital. There is a "Nelson" room in this College, containing some fine paintings of that great seaman's victories. On the site of this building once stood the Royal Palace in which Henry VIII, Queen Mary and Queen Elizabeth were born, and Edward VI died.

Cardinal Wolsey lived in Greenwich and also the family of General Wolfe of

Canadian fame. It is from the meridian of Greenwich that geographers reckon longitude and from the Royal Observatory the hours are flashed to every part of England and Scotland by means of the "motor" clock which is one of the many extraordinary instruments of this institution.

The connecting links between old Greenwich in England and new Greenwich in Connecticut were the two brothers John Mead and Joseph Mead, who were born in Greenwich, England, now part of Greater London, and who settled in that part of Greenwich, Connecticut, now called Sound Beach, formerly named Elizabeth's Neck in honour of Queen Elizabeth, and later Greenwich, to commemorate the birthplace of these two Meads. The two brothers were buried in the old cemetery in Sound Beach, having lived in that Connecticut town for the greater part of their lives, except during the time of the controversy between the English and the Dutch over the sovereignty of the settlement, when they temporarily moved to Hempstead, Long Island.

John Mead made his first purchase of land in Greenwich in the year 1660 and from then to the present time this name has been one of the most important in the town. Eleven out of twenty-three subscribers towards the Greenwich Library were members of the Mead family. The following story is told in Greenwich of this early settler:—

One day when he was riding on horseback Mead overtook a man walking along the road with a heavy bundle and asked him whether he couldn't carry it for him. "No," was the reply, "you don't get my bundle, for I can read men's thoughts." This, of course, irritated Mead. In a short time they came to a river which had to be forded, whereupon the horseman offered to take the suspecting traveler over the stream on his horse; the offer was accepted, and Mead, on reaching the deepest part, precipitated his passenger into the water, telling him it would teach him a good lesson.

Joseph Mead, the brother, was one of the "Twenty-seven Proprietors of 1672" of the Town of Greenwich; other important names were Peck, Lockwood, Reynolds, Close, Ferris and Palmer.

Two other early settlers were George Hubbard and Robert Husted, both well-known names in our Greenwich. The former was probably born in Somerset, England, coming to this country about 1635 and buying land in the town in the year 1659; the latter sailed from England for Massachusetts in 1635, moving to Stamford, Connecticut, several years later. He was a witness in 1640 to the Indian deed to Greenwich, conveying part of the town to Robert Feaks and Captain Daniel Patrick, who landed at Greenwich Point as agents of the New Haven Colony for the purpose of acquiring that property at Greenwich. It may be interesting to mention that Feaks' wife was the widow of Henry Winthrop, son of Governor Winthrop of Massachusetts. These two men at once settled at Greenwich, where they died a few years later.

The early settlers had much trouble with the Indians, but finally made an agreement with the Dutch providing that their combined forces should be used in case of Indian attacks.

The early town of Greenwich, or Old Town, as it was called, included the territory between the Mianus River on the west and the town of Stamford on the east. The town soon spread westward beyond the river, this settlement being known in 1669 by the curious name of Horseneck, so called because its shape was said to resemble a horse with his neck outstretched. This name was used until 1849, although the consolidation of the two towns took place in 1705. The patent for the town was granted only on the condition that an orthodox church should be maintained and the first church stood near the Greenwich Cove.

In the year 1673 postal trips on horseback were inaugurated over the trail that was at first known as the Westchester Path, later called the Country Road, then the King's Highway, Post Road, Turnpike Road, and finally the Post Road again, by which name it is now known. The messenger allowed people to travel with him. A weekly packet service between Greenwich and New York was also established as early as 1696, to carry produce and passengers.

No visitor should go to Greenwich without visiting the scene of General Israel Putnam's famous ride of the Revolutionary War. The centennial of this event was held at Greenwich on February 26, 1879, and on that occasion there were present as guests a great-grandson of Putnam and also a grandson of Thomas Merritt of Canada, the Tory who chased the General to the brow of the hill, down which he galloped his horse, "daring to lead where not one of many hundred foes dared to follow."

The history of the nearby city of Stamford is closely connected with that of Greenwich, as the latter place was in the early days part of the former.

There is also a Greenwich in Massachusetts.

HAVERHILL, MASSACHUSETTS

"Graceful in name and in thyself, our river
　　None fairer saw in John Ward's pilgrim flock,
　　Proof that upon their century-rooted stock
The English roses bloom as fresh as ever.

Take the warm welcome of new friends with thee,
　　And listening to thy home's familiar chime
　　Dream that thou hearest, with it keeping time,
The bells on Merrimac sound across the sea.

Think of our thrushes, when the lark sings clear,
　　Of our sweet Mayflowers when the daisies bloom;
　　And bear to our and thy ancestral home
The kindly greeting of its children here.

Say that our love survives the severing strain;
That the New England, with the Old, holds fast
The proud, fond memories of a common past;
Unbroken still the ties of blood remain!"

THE above lines were written by the poet John Greenleaf Whittier, at the time that Hon. Daniel Gurteen, Jr., Chairman of the Local Board of Haverhill, England, and his daughter, Miss Grace Gurteen, officially visited our city of Haverhill, in 1890, on its two hundred and fiftieth anniversary. Mr. Gurteen and his daughter called on Mr. Whittier at his home in Danvers and it was there that he wrote these impromptu lines, which he dedicated to the young English woman. The English Chairman in the following letter had been officially asked by the Mayor of Haverhill, Massachusetts, Hon. Thomas E. Burnham, to represent his town at this celebration:—

"MAYOR'S OFFICE, HAVERHILL, MASS.
March 15, 1890.

To THE CHAIRMAN OF THE LOCAL
BOARD,
Haverhill, England.

Sir:—

In the year 1640, Rev. John Ward, born in Haverhill, England, penetrated with a small band of followers into what was then a wilderness, and formed a little settlement on the banks of the Merrimac River, in what is now Essex County, Massachusetts. In honor of their devout pastor they named the settlement Haverhill for his home in England. . . .

This year, on the second and third of July, we propose to have a celebration of the quarter-millennial anniversary of the settlement of our city, and recognizing the ties that bind us to your own ancient town, and feeling that it would

From a photograph   *Kindness John G. Moulton, Esq.*

ADDRESS FROM HAVERHILL, ENGLAND, TO
HAVERHILL, MASSACHUSETTS,

brought to this country by Hon. Daniel Gurteen, Jr., Chairman of the Local Board of the English town, on the occasion of the two hundred and fiftieth anniversary of our town, in 1890. It is now in the Haverhill (Massachusetts) Public Library.

Another document sent by the English town twenty-five years later hangs in the Mayor's office in the City Hall of our Haverhill.

Photographed by J. H. Godden   Kindness Ian Forbes-Robertson, Esq.

SHIELD SENT BY HAVERHILL, MASSACHU-
SETTS, TO HAVERHILL, ENGLAND, IN 1890,

where it now hangs in the Town Hall. It is made of
wood from an old oak tree that grew on the place in
Haverhill where Whittier was born.

afford real pleasure not only to myself but to the people whom I have the honor to represent to have Old Haverhill over the sea represented on that occasion, I take great pleasure in extending to you the freedom of the city during that event, and in inviting yourself and lady to be the guests of the city on that occasion.

Hoping that you will favor us with your presence, and that we shall receive an early acceptance of the formal invitation that will be forwarded to your Honor in a few days,

I am yours truly,

THOMAS E. BURNHAM,
Mayor of Haverhill, Mass. U.S.A."

The Englishman brought with him the following congratulatory address, very attractively gotten up and signed by the town officers, ministers and citizens of his town; it is now in our Haverhill Public Library:—

"TO THE HONOURABLE THE MAYOR, THE CITY COUNCIL AND CITIZENS OF HAVERHILL, MASSACHUSETTS, IN THE UNITED STATES OF AMERICA:

We, the undersigned local authorities, public officers, and citizens of the ancient mother town of Haverhill, in the counties of Suffolk and Essex, in England, desire to convey to you our friendly greeting and hearty congratulation upon the celebration of the 250th anniversary of the settlement, in the year A.D. 1640, by John Ward, a native of this place, and others who accompanied him from the Old World to the New. We thank you for the opportunity of being represented on this auspicious occasion, not merely as an acknowledgment of the natural tie which exists between our respective communities, but also as a proof of the kindly spirit which prevails on your side towards us here. We assure you that your good will is most cordially reciprocated, and that we highly appreciate the kind invitation extended to us through our representative; and we trust that his visit may still further promote friendly relations of an abiding kind. We rejoice with you at the continued progress of your city, and earnestly hope that it is destined to enjoy still greater prosperity, so that its future may be even brighter than its past, and that it may steadily grow in everything conducive to the welfare of its citizens and the advancement of our common civilization.

Dated this 27th day of May, 1890."

In recognition of the courtesy shown by the English town and in memory of the visit of Mr. Gurteen and his daughter, our city of Haverhill sent to the English town a medallion, a shield in the form of the coat of arms of the Commonwealth of Massachusetts, carved in wood from an old oak tree that grew on the place in Haverhill where Whittier was born, with the city seal in the center and smaller carved medallions in the corners. It now hangs in the Town Hall of the English Haverhill. An album was also sent to Mr. Gurteen containing photographs of some of the prominent citizens of the Massachusetts city. Hon. William H. Moody, afterwards Secretary of the Navy, Attorney-General and Justice of the Supreme Court of the United States, was one of the Committee appointed to present these gifts. These presents were received with a great deal of ceremony at a large reception held in the Town Hall and acknowledgment was sent to our city later. Details of these English proceedings and of the Haverhill celebration are given in "The Story of a New England Town" published in 1891, which gives all the correspondence and an account of Mr. Gurteen's visit, with copies of articles from the papers of Haverhill, England. The Haverhill Public Library treasures several autographed letters of Mr. Gurteen which were sent to residents

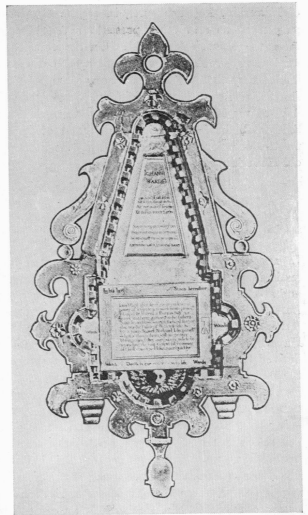

From a photograph   *Kindness John G. Moulton, Esq.*

MEMORIAL TABLET IN THE PARISH CHURCH, HAVERHILL, ENGLAND,

erected to Rev. John Ward, grandfather of Rev. John Ward who was the first minister of Haverhill, Massachusetts. A drawing made from the original tablet is owned by the Haverhill, Massachusetts, Public Library, and is loaned to the Haverhill Historical Society. The inscription is in the text.

Haverhill, Massachusetts, was so named in honour of Rev. John Ward, who, born in the town of the same name in England, settled on the banks of the Merrimac soon after 1640.

of Haverhill, Massachusetts, in 1891 and 1892, and it also has received news-papers, books and other presents which have come across the ocean as gifts from the English Haverhill. On the occasion of the two hundred and fiftieth anniversary, cables were interchanged between the two Haverhills and at the anniversary banquet an address was made by Hon. Leverett Saltonstall of Boston, a descendant of Richard Saltonstall, who was very active in the early days of our Haverhill and who was descended from Rev. John Ward, Nathaniel Saltonstall having married a daughter of John Ward. Whittier wrote a poem for the occasion which was read at the literary exercises, in which he alluded to old Haverhill, as follows:—

> "We see, their rude-built huts beside,
> Grave men and women anxious-eyed,
> And wistful youth remembering still
> Dear homes in England's Haverhill."

In 1915 when our Haverhill commemorated its two hundred and seventy-fifth anniversary, there was another exchange of greetings between the two Haverhills and at this time the English town sent a very attractive document which has been framed and which now hangs in the Mayor's Office, City Hall. Hon. Albert L. Bartlett was Mayor of our Haverhill at that time and wrote an account of old Haverhill in which we have found much of interest. The first part of the name is derived from the Anglo-Saxon "hoefer" meaning a "he-goat." In the old records the name is spelled "Haverell" or "Haverhull." The town is situated partly in Essex County and partly in Suffolk County, about fifty-five miles northeast of London and not far from Cambridge, High Street which runs through the town being part of an old Roman road connecting Cambridge and Colchester. Into this settlement the Huguenot, or Flemish, exiles brought the art of weaving three hundred and more years ago and on their hand looms was first woven the coarse homespun cloth of linen and wool. From these humble beginnings, however, have grown the present mills, employing many hundreds of operatives. The town is partly a manufacturing and partly an agricultural center and withal a market town; its annals, although interesting, contain no events of national importance. Messrs. Gurteen and Sons are the leading manufacturers of the English town, employing in their textile plant more than half of the population of forty-five hun-dred persons living there. The Town Hall was built in 1883 by the late Daniel Gurteen to commemorate his golden wedding and it was in this hall that the gifts sent to Haverhill, England, in September, 1890, were exhibited. Unfortunately the early records of the town perished in the fire of 1665.

In 1881 Rev. F. T. Ingalls, a native of Haverhill, Massachusetts, visited the English Haverhill and wrote a letter describing the place, which was published in one of the newspapers of our city.

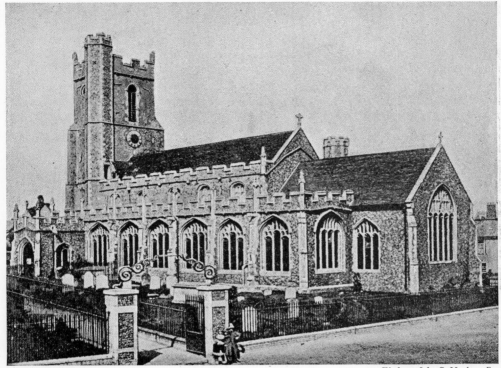

From a photograph   *Kindness John G. Moulton, Esq.*

PARISH CHURCH, HAVERHILL, ENGLAND,

in which the original tablet, shown in another illustration, has been placed in memory of Rev. John Ward, grandfather of Rev. John Ward, first minister of Haverhill, Massachusetts. This picture is in the Haverhill Public Library, Haverhill, Massachusetts.

The Indian name for the site of our city was "Pentucket" and when it was settled in 1640 it was named Haverhill in honour of its first minister, Rev. John Ward, mentioned above, who was born in Haverhill, England, in 1606, and who was the son of Rev. Nathaniel Ward, first minister of our Ipswich. The home of John Ward, afterwards owned by the Saltonstalls, and the first framed house in the town (now a city), is still preserved on the exact spot on which it was originally built in the sixteen hundred and forties, on the grounds of the Haverhill Historical Society. Over the mantel of the old house is a tablet which gives the history of the house and of the Saltonstall family and which also commemorates the fact that it was given to the Historical Society in memory of that family. In the Historical Society is a painting of the memorial tablet to John Ward's grandfather copied from the original in the Parish Church in Haverhill, England, the wording being as follows:—

From a photograph   *Kindness George Francis Dow, Esq.*

WITHERSFIELD ROAD, HAVERHILL, ENGLAND

John Warde after he with great evidence &
power of ye spirit & with much fruit preached
ye gospel at Haveril & Bury in Suff[k] 25
yeares was heere gathered to his fathers
Susan his widdowe married Richard Rogers
that worthie Pastor of Wethersfielde.   He
left 3 sonnes Samuel Nathaniel John preachers
who for them & theirs wish no greater blessinge
than yt they may continue in beleeveing
and preaching the same Gospel till ye comming
of Christ   Come Lord Jesus come quicklye

There is also a Haverhill in New Hampshire which took its name from Haverhill, Massachusetts, for the reason that the first white persons who permanently occupied its territory came from that town about 1761.

HULL, MASSACHUSETTS

HULL, Massachusetts, was undoubtedly named for Hull, England. It will be remembered that the passengers on the "Mary and John" were put ashore here at Nantasket Point, her captain leaving the "Godly families from Devonshire and Dorsetshire" to shift for themselves. Roger Clap later on took some of his shipmates up the river to Watertown. Among the first permanent settlers of our Hull was John Prince, an exile in Cromwell's day.

Hull, England, officially known as Kingston-upon-Hull, is the third port of the United Kingdom, and was founded by King Edward I in 1296. From 1598 to 1865 this seaport engaged in the whale fishery, and has the distinction of being the first port to dispatch to the fishing grounds a steam-whaler, which was called the *Diana*.

This city has several features of historical interest, mainly connected with the struggle for civil and religious freedom in the seventeenth century. At the opening of the contest between Charles I and his parliament the King failed in his attempt to win over the city of York and, indeed, narrowly escaped capture. He fled in haste to Hull, confidently expecting its gates to open to him and to have there a base for further operations. A severe blow was dealt at the royalist cause when the citizens stoutly refused entrance to him, closed the gates, and declared for the Parliament.

James II, perhaps in revenge for his father's rebuff, took from the city its charter and everything else he could lay his hands on, just as he did from London, when the Lord Mayor of that City was so overcome that he fell upon his knees crying cynically, "Will your Majesty please leave us the Thames?" This, like all James' arbitrary acts, was reversed when William of Orange ascended the throne with Queen Mary.

It is not as widely known as it should be how closely Hull was associated with the Pilgrim Fathers. The earliest exiles for religious liberty were drawn from Gainsborough and its neighborhood, little more than thirty miles from Hull. Their immediate objective was Holland, for which country there were two possible places of embarkation—Boston and the estuary of the Humber. In 1609 they made the attempt by Boston, were betrayed by a ship's captain, arrested and cast into prison. Being eventually liberated, they repeated the venture the following year, led by John Bradford, the future Governor, and Elder Brewster. This time they were, at least, partially successful. Their leaders escaped from a creek opposite Hull and the rest followed later in separate groups, mostly from the same estuary.

Amongst the most courageous and determined of the Pilgrims who twelve years later sailed from Delfshaven were those who had come from the Gainsborough district.

From Hull sailed the Rev. Ezekiel Rogers, Rector of the nearby village of

Photographed by Turner & Drinkwater   Kindness Ian Forbes-Robertson, Esq.

HULL, ENGLAND,

showing Princes Dock. Hull is the third port of importance in the United Kingdom.

Rowley, who is described under our article on that place. Along with Rogers sailed the greater portion of his congregation. William Penn also made Hull his port of departure.

Andrew Marvell, patriot, wit and satirist as well as earnest Puritan, whose statue now occupies an honoured place in the city, was the son of a Puritan clergyman of Hull. He became Latin Secretary to Cromwell, along with John Milton, and represented Hull in Parliament from 1660 to the end of his life in 1678.

In still later days Hull was the birthplace and home of William Wilberforce, whose name will ever be associated with the abolition of slavery in the British dominions. His residence, once the home of a Puritan Mayor of the city, is still preserved in its original state. It is now used as a museum and is full of deeply interesting mementos both of the slave trade and the city's history. Wilberforce's memorial—a lofty pillar on a massive pediment crowned with his statue—is in the very heart of the city.

In prehistoric times the district embracing Hull was inhabited by a race of Celts called "Dolicho-Cephaloid," these Greek words merely meaning "Long-Heads," still a characteristic of Yorkshiremen. Then came the Brigantes, or highlanders, named in Juvenal as the most numerous and important of the British tribes, which were the last of the ancient Britons to submit to the Romans.

At a meeting held in Hull, England, recently, a fund, the equivalent of about one hundred and fifty dollars, was raised for the erection of a monument at Killing-holme to commemorate the spot whence most of the Pilgrims left for Holland.

IPSWICH, MASSACHUSETTS

" I love to think of old Ipswich town,
 Old Ipswich town in the East countree,
Whence, on the tide, you can float down
 Through the long salt grass to the wailing sea,
Where the ' Mayflower' drifted off the bar,
 Sea-worn and weary, long years ago,
And dared not enter, but sailed away
Till she landed her boats in Plymouth Bay.

I love to think of old Ipswich town;
 Where they shut up the witches until the day
When they should be roasted so thoroughly brown,
 In Salem village, twelve miles away;
They've moved it off for a stable now;
 But there are the holes where the stout jail stood,
And at night, they say, that over the holes
You can see the ghost of Goody Coles.

I love to think of old Ipswich town;
 That house to your right, a rod or more,
Where the stern old elm trees seem to frown
 If you peer too hard through the open door,
Sheltered the regicide judges three
 When the royal sheriffs were after them,
And a queer old villager once I met,
Who says, in the cellar, they're living yet.

I love to think of old Ipswich town;
 There's a graveyard up on the old High Street,
Where ten generations are looking down
 On the one that is toiling at their feet;
Where the stones stand shoulder to shoulder, like troops
 Drawn up to receive a cavalry charge,
And graves have been dug in graves, till the sod
Is the mould of good men gone to God."

(The above are some of the verses of a poem written by James Appleton Morgan, entitled "Ipswich Town.")

THERE are probably few residents of Ipswich, Massachusetts, who are aware of the fact that the clock now in the Chapel of the First Church, marked "Moore, Ipswich," was a present sent by the English town from which Ipswich got its name. It was sent over, together with some photographs of old Ipswich, by Sir Daniel Goddard of the Congregational Church of Ipswich, England, just

Photographed by George G. Dexter, Ipswich, Massachusetts
Kindness Francis R. Appleton, Esq., Joseph I. Horton, Esq. and the late
T. Franklin Waters

CLOCK PRESENTED TO THE FIRST CHURCH
OF IPSWICH, MASSACHUSETTS,

by Sir Daniel Goddard of the Congregational Club of
Ipswich, England, in 1884.

after the celebration of the two hundred and fiftieth anniversary of the incorporation of the Massachusetts town held in 1884, and with it came a cable of congratulations given below. Sir Daniel Goddard, M.P., was a guest of the town, and only a short time ago Hon. William F. Paul, formerly Mayor of old Ipswich, sent to the Historical Society of the Massachusetts town several volumes of illustrations of ancient buildings of his town and an elaborate portfolio containing a copy of the proclamation of King Edward VII. In return the new Ipswich sent a history of the town written by the late Rev. Thomas Franklin Waters, A.M., President of the Historical Society. On the anniversary of the Massachusetts town, above referred to, in 1884, a letter was read from the Mayor of Ipswich, England, part of which is as follows:—

"I regret it is not in my power to be present at the celebration of the two hundred and fiftieth anniversary of the incorporation of the town of Ipswich, Mass., as my mayoralty duties entirely prevent my being absent from home for any long period during my year of office. I should have returned thanks for old Ipswich among some of the descendants of those who emigrated from their native land in order that they might have freedom to carry out their political and religious opinions, which was denied them in England. . . . Wishing that your enterprising town may increase and prosper, and ever be celebrated for its civil and religious liberty.

Yours faithfully,

JOHN MAY, *Mayor of Ipswich, England.*

To JOHN HEARD, Esq., of the Committee of Arrangements."

The following was the cable received from the Corporation of Ipswich, conveying congratulations:—

ST. MATTHEW'S GATE, IPSWICH, SUFFOLK, ENGLAND

"Aug. 15, 1884.

The Corporation of Ipswich, England, send their hearty congratulations to the Corporation of Ipswich, Mass., on the celebration of the two hundred and fiftieth anniversary of their incorporation, and wish them continued prosperity.

MAYOR OF IPSWICH, ENGLAND."

This letter and cablegram were both read at the celebration, an answering cable being sent as follows:—

"The town of Ipswich, celebrating its two hundred and fiftieth anniversary, sends thanks to Mother Ipswich for her kindly greeting and best wishes for her continued prosperity."

The most recent visitor from the English Ipswich was Rev. John A. Patten, minister of the Tacket Street Congregational Church, of which one of the congregation is Arthur Goddard, son of Sir Daniel, who has always taken such a great interest in the New England Ipswich.

The English Ipswich was a great coaching center and the Bull Inn, Whitechapel, London, was one of the taverns at which the Ipswich coaches put up for the night. It was from there that Mr. Pickwick set out, who quotes Tony Weller as saying just before the coach left the courtyard, "Take care o' the archway, gen'l'men." This Inn for a long time belonged to the Nelson family, which was a noted race of inn and coach proprietors, and at one time was managed by Mrs. Ann Nelson upon the

From a photograph by W. Downes   *Kindness Ian Forbes-Robertson, Esq.*

GREAT WHITE HORSE HOTEL, IPSWICH, ENGLAND,
of Pickwick fame.   A model was sent to the Chicago Exposition.

death of her husband.   In her coaching speculations she was usually associated with
a pastry cook who owned a little shop adjoining the gateway of the "Bull," and
who often complained of being interrupted in his work when a new hand on one of
the coaches sent the nose of one of his leaders through his shop window, the gate
being very narrow and Mrs. Nelson's coachmen not being very deliberate.   This
woman coach proprietor was a martinet, and spared neither herself nor her servants,
up to her seventieth year being the last up at night and the first up in the morning.
Her team of "Ipswich Blues," as they were called, was famous even after an opposition coach was started.   The proprietress insisted on rigid punctuality, and if a
coachman brought one of her crack coaches into the yard five minutes late, he
received a severe reprimand; if he were ten minutes late, he was fined half a crown;
and if he were one-quarter of an hour late, he stood a good chance of being dis-
missed from service.   Once when she was called into Court, the Chairman of the
Bench said to her, "I understand that you give your coachmen instructions to race
the rival coach."   "Not exactly," she replied.   "My orders to them are simply
that they are to get the road and keep it."   Towards the year 1830, there was a
whisper of coming changes, and the coachmen and travelers talked in the stable-

yard and in the cozy rooms of the "Bull" of men with strange instruments encountered along the road; "chaps with telescopes on three sticks and other chaps with chains and things measuring the fields." The Eastern Counties Railway was being projected to run from London to Colchester, Norwich and Yarmouth, and the days of the coaches were to be no longer.

Ipswich is the front door of East Anglia, which means the eastern part of England. It was here that Daniel Defoe, the author of "Robinson Crusoe," stayed for a short time, mentioning that he found "very agreeable and improving company almost of every kind." Here is the Great White Horse Tavern where Pickwick accidentally encountered the elderly lady in the yellow curl-papers; his bedroom No. 36 is still preserved, and although the Tavern has been much changed, over the entrance still stands the "white painted stone statue of some rampageous animal with flowing mane and tail, distantly resembling an insane cart-horse." Dickens does not give a very favorable description of this Tavern, for he stated that

"the Great White Horse is famous in the neighborhood in the same degree as a prize ox, or county paper-chronicled turnip or unwieldy pig—for its enormous size."

This amusing account of the place, however, made it all the more popular. King George II visited this noted Tavern in 1736, as also did Louis XVIII, King of France, as he passed through the town. It may be interesting to Americans to know that a model of this building was exhibited at the Chicago World's Fair. The greatest treasure, however, possessed by Ipswich is "The Ancient House," in the Buttermarket, in which King Charles II sought refuge when he was fleeing from the Parliamentary Army. Cardinal Wolsey was born in Ipswich, and connected with the town are the names of Clara Reeves; Gainsborough, the artist, who lived there for some time; also David Garrick, the actor, who made his début there in 1740. The Duke of Buckingham, known as the "Great Duke," visited the town, which is really most attractive, but his account of it was not very inspiring, for he wrote that it "was a town without inhabitants, a river without water, streets without names, and where the asses wore boots." It used to be called Gippeswiche from the river Gipping and "Wick" meaning creek or haven for ships.

Captain John Smith mentioned our Agawam as early as 1614, stating that Prince Charles changed its name to Southampton and this name actually appears on Smith's map. The first real history of our Ipswich, called on the seal of the town "Birthplace of American Independence," began in 1620 when we learn that some of the Pilgrim colony, before settling here "urged greatly the going to Angoan, Anguum or Angoum, meaning 'Agawam' a place twenty leagues off to the northward which they heard to be an excellent harbour for ships, better ground and better fishing." Of course, in respect to the harbour they were very much mistaken. Ten years later a messenger was sent to Agawam with a message saying "a war-

From a photograph by W. Downes   *Kindness Ian Forbes-Robertson, Esq.*

THE ANCIENT HOUSE, IPSWICH, ENGLAND,
in which King Charles II sought refuge when he was fleeing from the Parliamentary Army. It is one of
the chief objects of interest in the town.

rant shall be presently sent to Agawam for those planted there, to come away."
Three years later we learn that the Court of Assistance ordered that a plantation
be begun here as it was the best place in the land for tillage and cattle, lest an
enemy finding it should take possession from them. John Winthrop, Jr., was
instructed to undertake the settlement and it was suggested that twelve men
should go with him to assist him. In 1634, Rev. Nathaniel Ward, the son of John
Ward, of Ipswich, England, and his friends, came to the town and ordered the
name changed to Ipswich, after the town of the same name in England, in honour
of Ward and also "in acknowledgment of the great honour and kindness done to
our people who took shipping there." The Court believed that the town was large
enough to give up the Indian name. Another reason for the change in name was
the resemblance of the approach to our Ipswich to the territory near old Ipswich
on the river Orwell.

Nathaniel Ward bore one of the best known names in the early history of New
England, having been born in Haverhill, England, in 1570, where his father
had been a clergyman. It is interesting also to mention that he was granted six
hundred acres of land by the General Court in Haverhill in Massachusetts, then
called "Pentucket," where his son was later a minister. He wrote several books,
the best known being called "The Simple Cobler of Aggawam in America," which
was meant to be a lesson to the early colonists and to accomplish his purpose he
chose to write about the cobbler, describing him as

"willing to mend his Native Country, lamentably tattoed, both in the upper leather and
sole, with all the honest stitches he can take."

Nathaniel Rogers, who was also born in Haverhill, England, was another prominent person in the early history of our Ipswich. The Rogers family held a place
of great distinction both in this town and in the Colony, John Rogers, the son of
Rev. Nathaniel Rogers, becoming President of Harvard College while the grandson
of Rev. Nathaniel, also named John, was a minister at Ipswich. Therefore, grandfather and grandson between them held the pastorate of the Ipswich Church for
seventy years.

The Ipswich Historical Society has erected tablets in a small triangle in the
South Common, in memory of Nathaniel Ward, Nathaniel Rogers and Richard
Saltonstall, another early settler, and two of the inscriptions on the south side of
the tablet, which stands in front of the South Church, read as follows:—

ON THE EAST SIDE OF THE COMMON
WAS THE HOUSE OF
REV. NATHANIEL WARD
1634   MINISTER OF IPSWICH   1637
AUTHOR OF
"THE SIMPLE COBLER OF AGGAWAM"
COMPILER OF
THE BODY OF LIBERTIES

Photographed by George G. Dexter *Kindness Francis R. Appleton, Esq., and Joseph I. Horton, Esq.*

TABLET ON THE SOUTH GREEN, IPSWICH, MASSACHUSETTS,

placed there in memory of Ezekiel Cheever, first master of the Grammar School; also as a memorial of Rev. Nathaniel Ward's first house nearby, and also to commemorate the early houses of Richard Saltonstall and Rev. Nathaniel Rogers, both early settlers in this New England town.

THE RESIDENCE OF
RICHARD SALTONSTALL
WAS ON THE SOUTH SIDE OF THE COMMON
AND THAT OF
REV. NATHANIEL ROGERS
PASTOR OF IPSWICH CHURCH
1638–1655
WAS ON THE WEST SIDE

The oldest house in the town, now known as the Burnham House, was built in 1640 by Thomas Hart of England, soon after his arrival in this country. Several of the old rooms are still in their original condition and afford much interest to the sight-seer who stops here.

One of the streets of Ipswich which leads from the town to Castle Hill, the place originally granted to John Winthrop, Jr., now owned by Richard T. Crane of Chicago, is called "Argilla Road," after the estate in England owned by the Symonds family which settled here. The present High Street was once called Pudding Street, the origin of its name being told in a legendary poem written by J. K. F.:—

"I can remember very well
A tale the old folks used to tell,
Of how a street, well known to fame,
Received its somewhat curious name.
The oven, then, so long ago,
Was built outside the house, and so
While the good wife was getting dinner,
There came along a tramping sinner,
Who, having not the fear of man,
Opened the oven door and ran.
The pudding had so much of heat,
He quickly dropped it in the street,

And fearing in that place to stay,
Kicked it before him on his way.
The pudding bag, so stout at first,
By violence at last was burst,
And ever since that wicked feat,
The thoroughfare is Pudding Street."

Another fact of interest to Americans and Britons alike is that the ancestors of the late Joseph H. Choate lived in Ipswich, Massachusetts, a member of the family still residing here near the town on Hog Island, often referred to as Choate Island, which is also owned by Richard T. Crane of Chicago.

The town of Ipswich is responsible for the settlements of Chebacco, which when incorporated was called Essex; and Hamilton, which was first called "The Hamlet."

LANCASTER, MASSACHUSETTS

IN 1913 the mother town of Lancaster sent the following message of good wishes to her daughter on this side of the ocean:—

"TO

THE SELECTMEN, OFFICIALS AND INHABITANTS OF THE TOWN OF LANCASTER, MASSACHUSETTS.

At a meeting of the Town Council of the Borough of Lancaster in the County of Lancaster England held on Wednesday the 24th day of September 1913 the following resolution was passed unanimously:—

'That the Mayor, Aldermen and Burgesses of the Borough of Lancaster in Council assembled heartily reciprocated on behalf of the Burgesses and Inhabitants of this County Town the greetings so well expressed in the resolution of the daughter Town of Lancaster Massachusetts . . . and wish that all prosperity may in the future attend the Selectmen, Officials and Inhabitants of that Town.'

The Common seal of the Corporation of
Lancaster England was hereunto affixed
in the presence of

C. F. SEWARD, *Mayor*."

Some authorities claim that Edward Breck was the earliest settler in this Bay State town, but such is not the case, for this honour belongs to John Prescott, who was not only the earliest settler here but was also the founder of the town. Others interested in its early success were Thomas King, Harmon Garrett of Charlestown, Thomas Skidmore of Cambridge and Stephen Daye, who, it will be remembered, was the first printer in Cambridge. Prescott, however, was the only one to take up his residence here. They expressed the wish that the town should be called "Prescott" in honour of John Prescott and later suggested it might be named "West Town." The people of Lancaster have remembered the founder of their town by a slate tablet near his grave in Old Burying Field which records in the words of the late Senator George F. Hoar:—

Photographed from a print   *Owned by Allan Forbes*

SOUTH VIEW OF THE GATEWAY TOWER OF LANCASTER CASTLE, LANCASTER,
ENGLAND

The castle is the chief object of interest in Lancaster, being now used as a jail.

Here
with his children about him lies
John Prescott
founder of Lancaster and first settler
of Worcester County
born at Standish, Lancashire, England
Died at Lancaster, Massachusetts, December, 1681.
Inspired by the love of liberty and the fear of God
this stout-hearted pioneer
forsaking the pleasant vales of England
took up his abode in the unbroken forest
and encountered wild beast and savage
to secure freedom
for himself and his posterity.
His faith and virtues
have been inherited by many descendants
who in every generation have well served the state
in war, in literature, at the bar, in the pulpit, in public life,
and in Christian homes.

This tablet was set in place in time for the two hundred and fiftieth anniversary of Lancaster's incorporation, in 1903. In this cemetery are also the graves of Jonathan Fairbanks, formerly of Dedham, and his wife, who was Lydia Prescott, daughter of this first settler, their marriage being the first recorded within the limits of Lancaster. One year after the incorporation of the town came Rev. Joseph Rowlandson, then John Whiting, and later on, in 1793, Rev. Nathaniel Thayer, Edward Hamilton Sears and George M. Bartol, whose descendants have been prominent citizens of Massachusetts.

There is also a Lancaster in New Hampshire.

Tradition says that the English Lancaster was once a Roman station and later was used as a fort by the Saxons. On a hill in the town stands Lancaster Church, and near its site Agricola more than two thousand years ago planned his second

Photographed by James Macdonald

PRESCOTT TABLET IN OLD BURYING–FIELD, LANCASTER, MASSACHUSETTS,

in memory of John Prescott of Lancashire, England, founder of the New England Lancaster, and first settler of Worcester County.

year's campaign in Britain and from there also he directed the march of his Roman legions. A thousand years later came Roger of Poictou, a Norman Baron, who recognized the military importance of the town and erected there a great keep. In later years the town for two centuries was the center of Norman chivalry; it was there, too, that John of Gaunt held his Court, which in pomp rivaled that of the King himself; it was from there also that many edicts of great importance were issued, and through its castle walls rode many a gallant herald carrying tidings of peace or war. In fact few towns can claim a greater connection with royalty than Lancaster.

The Scots attacked the fortress of Lancaster innumerable times, and in 1314, after the defeat of Edward II at Bannockburn, they burned the town and succeeded in partially destroying the Castle. During the Wars of the Roses, it was alternately occupied by both parties and there not infrequently monarchs took refuge. At one period Court was held there, parts of the Castle being used as a prison. It was in 1715 that the prisoners of the Castle, climbing to the parapets, watched and cheered the Scottish Army as it captured the town. After a ceremony, during which the Stuart Pretender was proclaimed King, the soldiers dispersed to seek quarters, and a council was held that night to decide whether the prisoners at the Castle should be released. It was decided to set free those on the Crown side. On the following day the officers, after attending service at the Lancaster Church, "dressed and trimed themselves up in their best cloathes for to drink a dish of tea with the Ladys of this town." We are told that "the Ladys also here appeared in their best riging, and had their tea tables richly furnished for to entertain their new suitors." It is further related that the swains left the town very reluctantly, as they did not wish to part with their new loves. The last hostile army to enter Lancaster was that of Bonnie Prince Charlie, known as the Young Pretender, who marched through the town on November 24, 1745.

LINCOLN, MASSACHUSETTS

HISTORY tells us that the part of England between the Wash and the river Humber, whence came the pioneers of our Lincoln, was wrested from the Britons and occupied by the tribe of Angs, or Angles, from which the word "England" is derived. "Lindum Coloniae" (or "Colonia") was the name given to Lincoln by the Romans, who while possessing it surrounded the place by strong walls and made it one of the chief seats of Roman power in that section of the island. During the Saxon period it was the capital of Mercia and in 786 was subjected to assault by the Danes. Lincoln is one of the most important cities in England, so important, in fact, that at one time it rivaled London, as these lines show us:—

> "Lincoln was, London is, and York shall be,
> The greatest city of the three."

It is situated on a hill, overlooking the lowlands of England's eastern coast, and the high towers of the cathedral are most impressive. The river Witham flows by the city on its way to Boston and at one time was noted for its fish, if we believe the following lines written about the river:—

> "Wytham eel and Ancum pike:
> In all the world there is no syke" (such).

When Phillips Brooks visited Lincoln, England, he said, "Be proud of your City, and show your pride of her by seeking to become worthy of her."

From an old print owned by Allan Forbes   *Formerly in the collection of J. H. Seers, Essex, England*

LINCOLN, ENGLAND, FROM THE RIVER WITHAM

In 1896 a band of Pilgrims from the United States, headed by the Rev. Dr. Dunning of our Boston, visited Lincoln, England (which claims John Robinson as its own), and other towns associated with the Pilgrim Church, being particularly impressed by the cathedral, which is the pride of Lincoln and which Ruskin claimed was the most precious piece of architecture in the British Isles. Work on this edifice was begun in 1075 by Bishop Remigius but was not completed until the fourteenth century. The burial at Lincoln of St. Hugh of Avalon, who was made bishop in 1186, was attended by two kings and many other notables of that day. It may be interesting to remind Americans that Tennyson, the poet, was born near Lincoln and that a statue has been erected to his memory in the close of the cathedral. It is also noteworthy that there is a Bunker Hill about a mile from the city.

Our Lincoln was not set apart as a town until 1754, when the Honourable Chambers Russell, whose ancestors had come from Lincolnshire, England, persuaded the legislature to call it Lincoln after the English city. Rev. William Lawrence, the first minister, John Hoar, Edward Flint, Stephen Weston and Benjamin Brown were very helpful to the Colony in the early days. Chambers Russell was honoured by being allowed to choose the first pew in the church.

Edward Flint came over to Concord in 1636 with his family, and his will was the first one recorded in Middlesex County records, Cambridge. The family place on the Lexington road, we believe, has never gone out of the possession of a member

From a photograph by S. Smith, Lincoln, England   *Kindness Ian Forbes-Robertson, Esq.*

A VIEW ON CASTLE HILL, LINCOLN, ENGLAND

of this family. Lincoln was often called in jest "Niptown" by the surrounding communities, which claimed that it was made up by "nipping off" the best parts of three or four other towns.

There are also places by the name of Lincoln in Maine, New Hampshire, Rhode Island and Vermont.

LONDONDERRY, NEW HAMPSHIRE

AT the one hundred and fiftieth anniversary of the founding of this New Hampshire town, Rev. Dr. William McClure of Londonderry, Ireland, was invited to attend the ceremony and the following reply was received by R. C. Mack, Esq., Secretary of the Celebration Committee:—

"LONDONDERRY, IRELAND, JUNE 3, 1869.

My dear Sir:—

I have been from home some time, attending the meetings of the General Assemblies in Edinburgh. This must be my apology for not writing to you sooner. However delightful it would be to be present at your one hundred and fiftieth anniversary, I must

IRISH JAUNTING CARR.

From a print dated 1814

AN IRISH JAUNTING CAR

deny myself the pleasure.   My occupations at home are so pressing and numerous that I cannot leave. The citizens of the parent Londonderry, in Ireland, will be greatly interested in your proceedings, and we trust everything will go on prosperously and well.   I will be very glad to have, either by letter or newspaper, an account of the ceremonies.

Very sincerely yours,

WILLIAM McCLURE."

Invitations were also sent to the Mayor and Aldermen of Londonderry, Ireland.

In April, 1719, sixteen Scotch-Irish families came over from the north of Ireland and they were followed within a short time by many others, their reason for migrating to this country being to secure more religious liberty.   It can, therefore, be said that they played the same part in Ireland that the Puritans did in England in relation to the new country.   The newcomers spent their first winter in the harbour near Portland, Maine, where they suffered great hardship, as their vessel was frozen in the ice and it was difficult to procure supplies.   When spring came, however, they wandered to the territory called by them "Londonderry" from the town of the same name in Ireland, so well known to them.   The first thing they did was to purchase from John Wheelwright the title to these lands that had been purchased by his family from the Indians a long time before; it was in this way that they became possessors of this territory which was at that time called "Nutfield,"

LONDONDERRY, IRELAND

From an old print owned by Allan Forbes

Formerly in the collection of J. H. Seers, Essex, England

on account of its many chestnut-trees. The name Londonderry was given in 1722. The early days brought many hardships to these settlers. They were once attacked by an armed party in the hope of dispossessing them by force from the newly acquired property. At the time of this raid they were attending church services and it is said that the gallant Londonderry clergyman threw off his coat and offered to lead the attack should the enemy persist in trying to drive out the congregation. It is also said that the first minister, Rev. Mr. MacGregor, always carried his loaded gun into the pulpit and it is believed that this weapon is still in the possession of one of the citizens of the nearby city of Manchester, New Hampshire.

It may be interesting to give the names of some of the distinguished families of our Londonderry. Among them were the Morrisons, MacGregors, McKeans, Duncans, Greggs, Bells, Pattersons and Dinsmores. It is also worthy of mention that the well-known Elias Hasket Derby, who was born in Salem in 1803, lived for some time in this town.

Among the articles on exhibition at the time of the anniversary in 1869 were plates brought over from Ireland in 1720 by some of the early emigrants, who soon after leaving the Irish coast were captured by pirates. A daughter was born to one of these emigrants on board the pirate vessel and these plates came into her possession and at the time of the celebration belonged to one of her descendants. There was also a powder-horn used at the siege of Derry, in Ireland, which was brought over by Rev. Mr. MacGregor. These early emigrants are said to have introduced the potato into New England in 1719. The people of Londonderry are also responsible for the settlement of a number of other towns in New Hampshire, New York, Michigan and Nova Scotia. Londonderry in Vermont, formerly called Kent, owes its name to the original settlers most of whom came from Londonderry, New Hampshire, and it can, therefore, be said that the town owes its name, indirectly, to the Irish city.

The ancient city of Londonderry, the capital of County Londonderry, Ireland, is situated on the river Foyle, about ninety-five miles northwest of Belfast. It was formerly called Derry,—a name derived from Doire, meaning the "place of oaks." The city owes its origin to the monastery which was founded there by Columba in 545. Like all towns of the British Isles, Derry suffered by the inroads of the Danes and was burned more than once by these invaders, but they were finally expelled by Murtagh O'Brian in the early part of the twelfth century. Its chief historic interest, however, centers around the "siege of Derry" in 1690, when the Irish Protestants successfully defended the town against the forces of James II. George Walker, the rector of Donaghmore, who with Major Baker had been chosen to govern the town, won lasting fame for himself by his bravery and hopefulness during this siege, and the famous reply of "no surrender" which was made to the enemy became the watchword of the men of Derry and has been accorded a place of honour in the annals of history.   When the plucky garrison had almost reached its last extremity on the 30th of July, some ships broke through the obstruction across the harbour and brought relief to the suffering town.   King William, as a recognition of the importance of the work of the inhabitants of "Old Londonderry" in this memorable siege, caused an act to be passed whereby those who participated in the defense of the city, bearing arms, were thereafter to be exempt from taxation throughout the British dominions.   Some of the settlers of Londonderry, New Hampshire, were entitled to such exemption and availed themselves of their right until the Revolution.   On the Royal bastion from which the men of Derry defied the enemy stands a tall column bearing a statue of Walker, in commemoration of the siege.   The anniversary of the relief is still celebrated.

The ancient rampart, with its gates and bastions, which surrounds a section of Londonderry, and a few ancient houses with high, pyramidal gables, give the town an atmosphere of antiquity in spite of its numerous modern features.   The industries carried on there include the manufacture of linen, shipbuilding, iron foundries and fisheries.   It is interesting to recall that the Cathedral, completed in 1633, was built by money subscribed from London.   The town was a great port of emigration to the United States in the days before the transatlantic steamers came into operation, the emigrants sailing in "clippers" owned by Derry merchants.

LYNN, MASSACHUSETTS

IT is interesting to notice that the first visitor to England, according to some writers, from the territory that is now called Lynn, was probably Montowampate, the Indian chieftain, who lived here peacefully for some time with the new settlers, but, having been defrauded of twenty beaver skins by a trader in England, he journeyed to London in 1631, armed with a letter from Governor Winthrop to Emmanuel Downing of London.   The redskin was received with much respect and was given the money for his furs, but not liking the English bill of fare, it is said that he returned to his native hunting ground to enjoy his clams and succotash.   The first settlement in the town, which was called "Saugus" or "Saugust," was made nine years after the landing of the Pilgrims, and the first five men to whom is given the honour of making the settlement are Edmund and Francis Ingalls, William Dixey and John and William Wood.   These pioneers were with Captain John Endicott's colony, which came to Salem in 1628 and, as it has been expressed, "strayed over" to Lynn the following year.   They set out, we are told, from Salem with leave to go "where we would" and having discovered "a faire playne" lying between Salem and Charlestown, called Saugus, they took "peaceable possession."   The organized settlement did not take place, however, until two years later.   Edmund Ingalls came from Lincolnshire, England, in 1629, and was drowned in 1648, when he and his horse fell through the old Saugus Bridge.

Some of the names connected with the early history of Lynn were Breed, Newhall, Mansfield, Burrill, Hood, Alley, Lewis, Fuller, Baker, Dexter and Bassett. In 1636, Rev. Samuel Whiting, who has been called the "Father of Lynn" and the "Angel of Lynn," was installed minister of the little church at Saugus. He was born in Boston, England, and was the son of Sir John Whiting, who was twice Mayor of that town. Samuel's brother, John, was Mayor of Boston, England, in 1626, 1627, 1644 and 1645, that being the only instance of any man having been Mayor four times previous to the Municipal Act of 1835. Another brother, James, also was Mayor of Boston, in 1640. Rev. Mr. Whiting was Rector of St. Margaret's Church, Lynn Regis, and also of Skirbeck Church, Boston, England, but on account of his non-conformist tendencies he decided to come to this country, bringing with him his second wife, who was a daughter of Oliver St. John, Chief Justice of England at one time, and a cousin of Oliver Cromwell. In honour of this preacher the name of the town during the next year was changed from Saugus to Lynn, by order of the General Court, being recorded in these words, "Saugust is called Lin." Whiting on the voyage over said, "I would much rather undergo six weeks' imprisonment for a good cause, than six weeks of

From a photograph   *Kindness Rev. William Appleton Lawrence, John Albree, Esq., and Walter R. Whiting, Esq.*

SHAFT OVER THE GRAVE OF REV. SAMUEL WHITING, THE FIRST MINISTER OF LYNN, MASSACHUSETTS, IN WEST LYNN CEMETERY, LYNN, MASSACHUSETTS

Rev. Samuel Whiting had been rector of St. Margaret's Church, Lynn Regis, England, a picture of which is shown in another illustration.

Photographed by Amy E. Purdy, The Studio, King's Lynn   *Kindness Ian Forbes-Robertson, Esq.*

ST. MARGARET'S CHURCH, LYNN REGIS, ENGLAND,

the church of which Rev. Samuel Whiting was Rector before coming to the New England Lynn. A stone from this church was sent, in 1880, to St. Stephen's Church, in Lynn, Massachusetts.

such terrible sea-sickness." He lies buried in the old Western Burying-ground, Lynn, and a granite memorial shaft has been erected over his grave by Hon. William Whiting of our Boston. There are many of his descendants in different parts of this country. The Whiting family has been prominent in the history of old Boston and the neighborhood not only for generations but for centuries, for in a document known as the Subsidy Roll of Edward III (1333) occurs the name of William Whytynge.

There have been many interchanges between the two places, and it is evident that the people of old Lynn were in sympathy with their kinsmen in the New World from the very first, for in the records of St. Margaret's Church in 1653 is the following entry:—

"Collected for the natives and distressed people of Newe England, and that from house to house within the parrish, and paid unto Mr. Joshua Green, ald'n. the 20th of Nov. 1653, £25: 13: 00"

The corner-stone of the present St. Stephen's Memorial Church, formerly called St. Stephen's Church, and still before that, Christ Church, was laid in the year 1880. Several years previously Rev. Louis De Cormis, the Rector of the Parish at

From a photograph   *Kindness Rev. William Appleton Lawrence*

ST. STEPHEN'S CHURCH, LYNN, MASSACHUSETTS,
which has a stone sent from St. Margaret's Church, Lynn Regis, England.

that time, suggested that a block of stone from one of the churches in Lynn, England, might be sent and inserted in the wall of his church and suitably inscribed. It was, therefore, decided that Hon. Roland G. Usher, a former Mayor of our Lynn, should take a letter from Rev. Mr. De Cormis to the English Rector, containing this suggestion. Part of this message read as follows:—

"LYNN, MASS. UNITED STATES
Oct. 29, 1879.

Rev. and Dear Brother:—

The recent celebration of the two hundred and fiftieth anniversary of the founding of our City, in bringing to mind the history of our name and the home of our first settlers, has generally revived and increased our attachment for the old parent city of Lynn, England; and I think you will understand how natural the desire is to increase it in the coming years, and especially to link our religious life as firmly as we can with that of our forefathers in the great English Church. To this good end, I am about to ask a very special favor of you. St. Stephen's Episcopal Church here is about erecting an elegant and commodious Church building, and it has occurred to many of us, that if we could secure a block of stone from the structure of one of the old churches of Lynn, England, to be inserted into one of our walls, with an inscription plate upon it, it would be a very beautiful and desirable thing to do."

Kindness Rev. William Appleton Lawrence

STONE SENT BY ST. MARGARET'S CHURCH, KING'S LYNN,

of which Rev. Samuel Whiting, Lynn's first minister, was rector before coming to New England. This relic is now in St. Stephen's Church, Lynn, Massachusetts, having been procured from the English Church in 1880 by Hon. Roland G. Usher, and Rev. Louis De Cormis, once a minister of this church in our Lynn.

A reply to this letter, dated June 28, 1880, read as follows:—

"Rev. and Dear Brother:

My thanks are due to you for kindly introducing to me so pleasant and friendly a man as the Honourable R. G. Usher, and also for the kind and brotherly greeting contained in your letter. . . . Mr. Usher and I have selected a stone for your interesting purpose, from such fragments as were available in our grand old church. My only regret is that all the pieces were so small. I hope, however, that our inability to find a piece of stone better adapted for your wishes will not materially lessen the satisfaction of yourself and your Church people on the receipt of a relic which it has been a real pleasure to me to send.

JOHN DURST, *Rector of North Lynn and Vicar of King's Lynn, England"*

The stone, quarried during the eleventh century, was carefully selected by the English Rector and Mr. Usher from this building, which is the old parish church, and sent to this country where it now occupies a place of honour in St. Stephen's Memorial Church in our Lynn, and makes a very tangible link between the new and the old Lynn. It forms a part of a window-jamb and bears the following inscription on one side:—

ST. MARGARET'S CHURCH, LYNN, ENGLAND
TO
ST. STEPHEN'S CHURCH, LYNN, MASS. U. S. A.
28TH JUNE, 1880

The other side was left untouched as it had been for years. An inscription is also cut on a stone panel just below the shelf on which the stone is placed, as shown in the illustration on this page. At the laying of the corner-stone, Mr. Usher said in part:—

"It comes as the expression of the interest and good will of the people of St. Margaret's—as a link to connect our Lynn with old King's Lynn in England. . . . we pray

that the record for the ages to come of St. Stephen's Memorial Church, may be for use-
fulness and influence equal to that of St. Margaret's."

A formal resolution of thanks was adopted and sent across the water. A Centennial Memorial of Lynn, Massachusetts, was also sent over about this time, by
Mr. Usher, to the English Lynn.

The good will between the two places had been manifested also during the
celebration of the two hundred and fiftieth anniversary of Lynn, Massachusetts,
held in June, 1879, at which time an invitation was sent by Mayor George D.
Sanderson to Mayor Thomas A. Seppings of Lynn Regis to be present. Although
unable to accept, the English Mayor replied most cordially, sending his congratulations and best wishes to our city. Another letter was received from Rev.
Edward J. Alvis, Vicar of East Winch and a native of old Lynn, who also sent an
interesting engraving of his town. Another resident of the English town, John
Coulton, sent a poem written by himself and dedicated to our Lynn, which was
read at the anniversary, the last stanza of which was:—

> "For each a happy future is in store,
> If wisdom's counsels shall unite the nations
> Firmer in friendship for our feuds of yore—
> Alone, unrivall'd in our lofty stations
> Old England new in brighter destinies,
> New England old in hallow'd memories."

Still another letter was received from Robert Brooks in which he said in part:—

"Many of us when youths at school, scanning the map of the 'Young Giant' your
country, have had our eyes drawn to 'Norfolk' and to 'Lynn' in a far distant land,—the
names of our county and loved old town—we have wondered how it was, and at times with
anxiety have wished to learn something of your history. At last kindly words 'have
come across the sea.' You tell a tale of affection for one you were pleased to honour,—
'A beloved clergyman' who once claimed our home as his; in honouring him you honoured
us. We now, in no formal words, *Thank you.*"

Another occasion of interest was the celebration by the Lynn Historical Society,
called "King's Lynn Night," which was observed a few years ago with appropriate
exercises, including lectures on historical subjects pertaining to the old Lynn, stere-
opticon views of the places of interest and a description of the town by some of the
citizens of new Lynn who had visited there. In the records of this society mention
is made of a Queen Victoria Medal which was presented to the organization in
1899 through Mayor Walter S. Ramsdell, having been sent from old Lynn accompanied by a letter from the Mayor. At this time it was also mentioned that St.
Stephen's Church had been sent some small organ pipes from St. Margaret's Church,
but as no inscriptions were placed upon them they cannot be identified.

The first offspring of our Lynn was Reading, which became a separate township
in 1644 and which is dealt with later on in this volume. Nahant was granted in
1622 by the Council in England to Captain Robert Gorges, who in turn gave part

From an old print owned by Allan Forbes

Formerly in the collection of J. H. Seers, Essex, England

LYNN REGIS, NORFOLK, ENGLAND

Lynn, Massachusetts, is named for this English city.

of the island and Saugus to John Oldham. Still later Nahant was purchased for the price of a suit of clothes by Thomas Dexter, who was then a farmer and who was one of the "ten men of Saugust" to found Sandwich in 1639. Even to this day the seal of Nahant depicts Dexter offering his suit of clothes to the Indian in exchange for the lands. In these early days and for many years there was a fence across Lynn Neck to keep in the cows and sheep that were pastured in Nahant by the people of Lynn. It may be interesting also to record that in 1803 there were only five houses in Nahant, the Johnson family owning one of these. It is said that the wolf-pits of 1630 in the Lynn Woods are the oldest unchanged works of man in the Colony.

The English town now called Lynn, on the river Ouse, was once named Bishop's Lynn, but was later changed to Lynn Regis, or King's Lynn, during the reign of Henry VIII. It is situated in the county of Norfolk and is especially famous for its fine churches, its Custom House and its Guildhall; it also has an excellent public library, the gift of Andrew Carnegie. Through the fourteenth century the town was given over almost entirely to religious orders, and many monasteries were built there, chiefly by the Franciscans, Augustinians and Dominicans, the best known of all these scholarly monks being John Capgrave, who wrote much poetry. Daniel Defoe visited the town in 1722 and described it as a "rich and populous port-town."

Lynn rose rapidly from a marsh town to a seaport, still being an important port, as expressed in the following lines:—

> "Rising was a sea-port town
> When Lynn was but a marsh;
> Now Lynn it is a sea-port
> And Rising fares the worse."

The derivation of the name is from the Celtic "lyn," meaning a "lake," which referred to the sea which covered a large part of the immediate district called Marshland, now reclaimed. One of the chief events in the history of the borough was the Siege of Lynn, which occurred in the time of the conflict between Charles I and the Parliamentary forces. The town, which sided with the Royalist cause, was fortified and awaited the attack by the Earl of Manchester. While divine worship was being held one day a cannon ball was sent through the church, scattering the congregation. This did not daunt them, however, for they said, "As soon might the Earl of Manchester raise his good father from the dead as force his entrance into Lynn." No help, however, came to the men who held the town and they were finally forced to surrender to the Parliamentary troops.

It is told that Oliver Cromwell, when a child, fell into the Ouse and was pulled out by a Royalist parson who was fishing nearby. Years later when Oliver the Protector revisited the scenes of his youth with his triumphant army, he met his rescuer and asked him if he remembered the occurrence. "Truly do I," was the prompt reply, "and the Lord forgive me but I wish I'd let thee drown."

Lynn's church was founded by Herbert de Losinga, the first Norman bishop of East Anglia, and is famous for two fine sepulchral brasses, one of which shows a wonderful feast, among the delicacies on the table being a peacock "that noble bird, the food of lovers and the meat of Lords." An attendant is shown bringing in the peacock, and one of the guests is depicted in the act of straddling the table in his desire to obtain possession of it, while his neighbors remonstrate with him on his bad manners. The famous navigator George Vancouver, for whom Vancouver Island was named, was born in the English Lynn.

Some one who visited the town remarked, "There's a bit o' life sometimes there," explaining further that he liked it very much as compared to the quiet country, which he said was like "living in a teapot and 'peekin' at the world through the spout."

Among the important people of our Lynn should be mentioned Joseph Rednap, the cooper, who established his business here in 1634; Francis Ingalls, who established in the town the first tannery; Philip Kertland, a shoemaker, John Adam Dagyr, who was called the "celebrated shoemaker of Essex," and who added a new chapter to the shoe industry by introducing the more skillful French method of making shoes, making footwear, it is said, for the brides of Boston. In these early days shoemaking was carried on in the homes. To the town also came from London William Rose, who understood the art of manufacturing morocco and who, it is claimed, was the first to set up this business in the town.

The dies for the Pine Tree shillings were made at the Saugus Iron Works by Esther Jenkes, the wife of the Superintendent. These works were established in 1642 near the present site of Pranker's Mills and they laid the foundation for the iron industry of the United States. The first Superintendent was Joseph Jenkes, who on May 14, 1646, received, for a water wheel which he designed, the first patent granted on the continent of North America. Jenkes was also the inventor of the American scythe. In the Public Library of Lynn is exhibited an iron kettle which is supposed to represent the first iron casting made in the New World.

In the early days the preachers frequently timed their sermons with an hour glass and on one occasion a minister is said to have remarked, "I know you are good fellows; stay and take another glass."

MALDEN, MASSACHUSETTS

WE believe we can do no better than reproduce a letter written by Hon. Charles L. Dean, Mayor of Malden, Massachusetts, to His Worship Edward A. Fitch, Mayor of Maldon, Essex, England, in reply to one received from Mr. Fitch on the occasion of the two hundred and fiftieth anniversary of the incorporation of our Malden. With this letter from the English official came a short account of his old borough, with a request for information in regard to our Malden. This letter runs as follows:—

"MALDEN, MASS. May 13, 1899.

Dear Sir;—

Your valued communication of April 22nd duly received, also a copy of your book entitled Maldon and the Blackwater. I appreciate your kindness and am grateful for the trouble you have taken. I regret that you will not be able to be with us on our birthday, but you may be assured that the people of Malden in New England will not forget the old mother on the Blackwater at that time.

Our historian has given me the following items of information in regard to the old settlers and I hope that you may be able to trace some of them as coming directly from your borough.

A leader in the settlement of our town was Joseph Hills, who was married at Burstead Magna, Billericay, in 1624. He was of your parish of All Saints in 1631, and the births of his children are recorded there. In 1638 he came to New England with others. His son-in-law, John Wayte, who was a leading man here, was from Wethersfield, Essex. Another of our early settlers, Richard Pratt, is said to have been a son of John Pratt of your borough, where he was baptized in 1615. The authority for this statement is not known. Salmon, History of Essex, 424, says that John Pratt, an alderman of Maldon, was buried in All Saints in 1619. Thomas Ruck, an early landholder but not a settler, is said to have come from Maldon.

It may interest you to know that out of the little settlement of 1649, which was named Maldon (now changed to Malden) have grown three cities with an aggregate population of about seventy thousand people.

Again expressing our regret that you will not be able to be present at our anniversary exercises, I am, with kind regards,

Very truly yours,

CHARLES L. DEAN, *Mayor*."

The territory now included in Malden, Everett and Melrose originally belonged to Charlestown and in 1634 it was known as "Mystic Side." The settlement of Malden was actually made in 1640, but the town was not incorporated until 1649, when the following record appears: "In answer to the peticon of seull inhabitants of Misticke side their request is graunted, viz, to be a distinct towne of themselves & the name thereof to be Maulden." The name has been spelled Maldon, Mauldon, Maulden and Malden. The town became a city in 1882. The first minister of the settlement was Marmaduke Matthews, who came from South Wales.

At the two hundred and fiftieth anniversary of the incorporation of the town, St. Paul's Church exhibited a number of seals of England, and a sermon was at

From an old print owned by Allan Forbes

Formerly in the collection of J. H. Seers, Essex, England

MALDON, ESSEX, ENGLAND,

the town from which Malden, Massachusetts, derived its name.

Photographed by Hazeltine Frost, Glendale Studio, Maldon   *Kindness Ian Forbes-Robertson, Esq.*

ALL SAINTS CHURCH, MALDON, ESSEX, ENGLAND

In the graveyard of this church lie the remains of Lawrence Washington, the great-grandfather of George Washington, and his burial record is in the register of the church.

that time preached by Rev. William Cunningham, Vicar of Great St. Mary's Church, Cambridge, England.

Maldon, England, is in Essex County, about thirty-eight miles from London. It is said that once it had the distinction of being the real Camulodunum where King Arthur held his court, about which cluster the finest tales of chivalry ever recorded. While Maldon does not insist on this ancient claim, it can still boast of being the oldest chartered city in the county of Essex. In the Saxon Chronicle there are two references to Maldon. In 913 King Edward the Elder, while fighting the Danes, encamped there with his forces, during the construction of a fortress, and there he fought a great battle, driving the enemy out of the town and slaying them by the thousands. In 920 Edward rebuilt Maldon and raised and garrisoned a castle there.

The death of a Saxon hero during this early conflict brought forth one of the gems of old English poetry,—" Brihtnoth's Death,"—that, even though imperfectly preserved, dramatically relates the story of the Battle of Maldon. Many times did the Northmen invade the East Anglian shores, but after centuries under the conflicting rule of four nations, Maldon passed through a period of peace sufficiently extended to enable the people to build churches. Before the Norman Conquest beautiful St. Mary's was erected, the tower of which fell in the seventeenth century, being rebuilt at the time of the emigration of the men who carried the name of Maldon into New England.

Though a borough at the time of the Conquest, it is thought that the town's corporate existence must have begun under Saxon rule. The first recorded charter was granted in 1154 by Henry II. "Bloody Mary" gave a second charter in 1553 and in 1810 the present charter was granted.

The three lions depicted on the shield of the old borough appear in the town and city seal of Malden, Massachusetts. American travelers through Essex County, England, invariably visit the old churchyard of All Saints, Maldon, where rest the remains of George Washington's great-grandfather, Lawrence Washington, who held the living of Purleigh. His burial record is also in the register of All Saints, Maldon.

MANCHESTER, NEW HAMPSHIRE

THE one hundredth anniversary celebration of the naming of the city of Manchester, New Hampshire, was held in 1910, and on this occasion the Lord Mayor of Manchester, England, sent the following letter to Isaac Huse, Esq., President of the Manchester Historic Association:—

"*My dear Sir:*—

Your interesting letter of the 18th May, informing me that one hundred years ago your town adopted the name of Manchester in the hope that it would attain a position of importance in manufactures and population, has given me great pleasure and I trust that your Centenary proceedings will prove a great success.

Your expressions of goodwill towards us are much appreciated and reciprocated.

I am, yours faithfully

CHARLES BEHRENS,
Lord Mayor."

The City Library in Manchester, New Hampshire, has exchanged reports and letters with the library in Manchester, England, and also contains about three hundred books, pamphlets, reports and histories relating to the antiquities of the English city and a description of the cotton industry for which that place is famous. Most of this collection came originally from the library of the late G. H. Adshead, Esq., of Manchester, England, being purchased from his nephew, Hon. John Hyde of Washington, D.C. At the time of the semi-centennial celebration in 1896 Charles K. Walker, superintendent of the City Water Works, procured a photograph of

Photographed by Fred T. Irwin *Kindness Miss F. Mabel Winchell*

CITY HALL, MANCHESTER, ENGLAND,

from a picture in the office of the Water Works of Manchester, New Hampshire, procured by Charles K. Walker, Manager of that Department at the time of the semi-centennial of the city.

the City Hall of Manchester, England, which together with a photograph of the City Hall of Manchester, New Hampshire, may now be seen in the office of the Manchester Water Works Department.

The early history of this important New England city is of great interest:—

On June 13, 1810, John Langdon, Governor of New Hampshire, affixed his seal to a bill by which the name of the town of Derryfield was changed to Manchester, the exact phraseology of the essential part of the bill being as follows:—

"BE IT ENACTED BY THE SENATE AND HOUSE OF REPRESENTATIVES IN GENERAL COURT CONVENED:

That said town of Derryfield shall forever hereafter be called and known by the name of Manchester, any law, usage or custom to the contrary notwithstanding."

The reason for this form of expression may perhaps be found in the fact that the place now designated as Manchester had already borne several different names. There is a tradition that the territory was originally called by the Indians Kaskaashadi, "the place of broken water," referring to the falls of Amoskeag. If this was the case this name must have given way to Namaoskeag, meaning "a great place for fish." The white settlers in this locality called it Nutfield, or the Chestnut

From "The Centennial Celebration of Manchester, N.H."
OLD DERRYFIELD MEETING HOUSE
Manchester, New Hampshire, was at one time called Derryfield because the people of Derry used to
pasture their cows there.

Country, on account of the abundance of chestnut trees, Tyng's Township being
another name, meaning the land granted to Tyng and his men. Still later it was
called by the derisive name of Harrytown, a shortened form of "Old Harry's
Town," and in 1751 it was called Derryfield, because the people of the nearby
town of Derry were accustomed to pasture their cows there. These names did
not all apply to precisely the same district, nevertheless they were all, excepting
possibly the first, applied at some time to the whole or a part of the territory which
in 1810 by act of legislature acquired the name of Manchester. The early settlers
were either the families of the Scotch-Irish, who had come to this part of New
Hampshire in 1719, or the descendants of the English Puritans.

The name of Manchester was given to the town as a compliment to Judge
Samuel Blodget, who had built a home for himself near Amoskeag Falls in 1793
and who became the pioneer of internal improvements in New Hampshire. He
was the first to realize the value of the water power at Amoskeag and for its development he worked incessantly, finally achieving his triumph in 1807, when he rode
through the canal amid the applause and praise of the people who had gathered on
the banks to witness the event. On the occasion of a visit to England in 1787 he
prophesied that his home town would some time surpass old Manchester as a man-

From an old print owned by Allan Forbes   *Formerly in the collection of J. H. Seers, Essex, England*

MANCHESTER, ENGLAND

ufacturing center but at the time that Manchester received its name there was little to indicate that Judge Blodget's prophecy would ever in any measure be fulfilled. In an address delivered at the centennial celebration of the naming of Manchester it was said that in the year 1810 there seemed to be but two facts that made the place in any way notable; one was the existence of the Amoskeag Falls with their fisheries and possibilities while the other was that the town was the home of Major General John Stark, the Revolutionary hero, who was then passing a peaceful old age on his estate near the Falls.

In 1814 the navigation of the Merrimack was fully opened and the river became a considerable water highway whose traffic continued for some years after the opening of the Concord railroad in 1842. The manufacture of cloth near the Amoskeag Falls was begun before Manchester was so named and, in the year of its naming, a company was formed known as the Amoskeag Cotton and Wool Factory. This company, however, had little capital or machinery and its output was small. In the year 1831 the present Amoskeag Manufacturing Company was chartered with a capital of a million dollars, a large sum for that time, and Samuel Blodget's dreams of the future began in some degree to be realized. The new company was organized "for the purpose of taking over the old company, developing water power, acquiring and selling land, selling sites and power to other manufacturing concerns, building and operating mills of its own and so bringing about the growth of a flourishing manufacturing town worthy the name it had been given." Other prominent companies here are the International Cotton Mills, the largest producers of cotton duck in this country, and the W. H. McElwain Company, makers of shoes. In connection with all these industries it has been humorously remarked that if one of the old Indian chieftains should come down the Merrimack in his canoe in quest of clothing, he could obtain a complete outfit of apparel made in Manchester and could even put the finishing touch to his modern equipment by placing between his lips a Manchester-made cigar.

It is an interesting fact that Manchester, England, obtained a city charter only eight years earlier than Manchester, New Hampshire, and that the English town did not receive the title of city until its namesake had enjoyed that honour for seven years. Old Manchester, however, had had a long history before it could be called a city. On the banks of the river now known as the Irwell in that part of England called Lancashire the ancient Romans had a camp, or "castrum," named Mancunium. The Saxon records show that about the year 923 King Edward sent a number of his Mercian troops to repair and garrison the fortress of Manig-ceaster. The place was mentioned in the Domesday Book as one of four in southeast Lancashire. It is known that woolen manufacture was carried on there in the thirteenth century and in 1552, in the reign of Edward VI, laws were passed by Parliament regulating the length of Manchester cotton, which, notwithstanding the name, was probably woolen. In 1650 the cloth manufactures of Manchester ranked among the first in England in extent and importance, and its people were described as "the most industrious in the northern part of the kingdom." The inadequate supply of cotton goods about the middle of the eighteenth century stimulated efforts for increasing the means of production and the machines successively invented by Arkwright, Hargreaves and others furnished this means; the efficiency of these machines was greatly increased by the perfection of Watt's steam-engine. The English city has long been known as the center of English cotton manufacture and, if the entire population of the urban district were included, greater Manchester would probably rival London in the number of its inhabitants. To such a Manchester, it may well be believed, there is "none like nor second."

In 1783 the English Manchester, with Salford on the other side of the river, had a population of 39,000 mainly given over to the manufacture of cloth, and it may, therefore, be interesting to note that the late Hon. Edwin F. Jones found in this fact a literal fulfillment of Samuel Blodget's prophecy. "Our Manchester," said he, speaking in 1910, "is the Manchester of America! and it is today larger and more prosperous than was the original Manchester when Judge Blodget returned from England in 1787."

The early emigration to the American colonies from Manchester and the districts nearby was very small, the names of Henry Dunster, Samuel Gorton, Obadiah Holmes and the ancestors of the Sewell and Dana families being the only ones we are able to trace to New England. Some of the Saltonstall family are well known in the English Manchester, several having died at Holme Hall.

Manchester, Massachusetts, was named perhaps for Manchester, England, but more probably for the Earl of Manchester who had an official connection with the colonies. We are sure, however, that those who settled in the Massachusetts town came from the eastern counties of England.

There are also places by the name of Manchester in Connecticut, Maine and Vermont.

MEDFORD, MASSACHUSETTS

MEDFORD, one of the earliest permanent settlements of the Massachusetts Bay Colony, unlike all others, was the proprietary of the "Governour" of the colonizing company and to Matthew Cradock the large city of today owes its name. Those early explorers, Captain John Smith and Bartholomew Gosnold, may have seen or looked from its hills, but the first recorded visit of white men was by an exploring party from Plymouth in September of the year 1621, consisting of "Standish the stalwart, with eight of his valorous army, led by their Indian guide . . ." as expressed by Longfellow. They encountered some redskins and with inducements of trade and promises to come again they returned to Plymouth. It was, however, left to others to become Medford's first settlers, nearly seven years later, the company comprising fishermen, farmers and mechanics in the employ of Matthew Cradock, a wealthy merchant, who, besides his associated interests in the "London Company of Massachusetts Bay," ventured to a certain extent on his own account. These Englishmen coming to Salem in the migration of 1628, or earlier, soon found their way to the Mistick Valley and made a permanent settlement "four miles along the river." Title to this territory was later confirmed to Cradock by the General Court, thereby making it his proprietary. It was then known by the various names of "Mr. Cradock's Farm," "Mistick" and "Medford." It was also styled a "plantation," but was never called a town until a half-century had passed. Cradock has been called "the Father of our Medford," although curiously enough he never came overseas, his business here being conducted by agents. He was the first president of the trading company chartered by King Charles I, his official title being "Governour." He suggested the transfer of the Colony's government to these shores but resigned his important office to Winthrop, who brought the charter with him, and coincident with this charter are our present titles of Governor and General Court. Cradock had a country seat at a little hamlet in Staffordshire, England, called Medford, the English name having been spelled at different times Medford, Metford, Mepford, Mefford and, at the present time, Meaford. It is considered by careful historians that he gave the name of his English possession to this new venture in the Bay

From a picture published by T. G. Adie & Co.   *Kindness Ian Forbes-Robertson, Esq.*

MEAFORD, STAFFORDSHIRE, ENGLAND

Medford, Massachusetts, was named for this small English **hamlet** which was the country-seat of Matthew Cradock, "Governour of the London Company of Massachusetts Bay." Though he never came to New England, he was founder of our Medford and until his death was its sole proprietor.

Colony and that his agent gave it to the General Court, the clerk of which spelled it Meadford; thus it appears in the earliest records of the town at the time of its incorporation half a century later. It is also spelled in this way by Dudley in his letter to the Countess of Lincoln, from which shire, as well as from Suffolk and Essex, came these early Medford settlers. Cradock's business interests were none too well managed by his agents, although at first they were considerable, as seen in Wood's "New England Prospect:"—

"Mistic . . . is seated by the water-side very pleasantly; there are not many houses as yet. . . . On the east side is Mr. Cradock's plantation where he hath impaled a park where he keeps his cattle till he can store it with deer. Here, likewise, he is at charges of building ships. The last year one was upon the stocks of an hundred tons; that being finished they are to build one twice her burthen."

After Cradock's death, his great farm passed into various ownerships. Several sons of Thomas Brooks settled here, one branch of the family still remaining in possession of the ancestral acres over which Standish marched and where died Nanepashemit, the Indian king. Other descendants were John Brooks, seven years Governor of Massachusetts, Peter Chardon Brooks, and Rev. Charles Brooks, the first historian of Medford.

"Mistick" was the Englishman's way of pronouncing the name of the river which the Indians called "Missi-tuk," meaning "the great tidal river;" Mystic it is still called, but there is nothing mystical or mysterious about it. This river, often called Medford River, was a highway of trade, and on its banks, between 1802 and 1873, were built five hundred and sixty-seven vessels,—all in Medford,— a remarkable record. The names of some of the people who have contributed to make this industry so famous are Magoun, Turner, Lapham, Hastings, Sprague, James, Fuller, Rogers, Stetson, Waterman, Ewell, Curtis, Foster and Taylor. One of the first ships launched in this country was the well-known "Blessing of the Bay" which was built in 1631 at "Ten Hills Farm," the property of Governor Winthrop, part of which was within the present limits of Medford. Of "Medford," the first recorded mention was in September, 1630, when a tax of three pounds was levied for military instruction.

Fifteen other Medfords in as many States, all more or less traceable to ours, bear the name of that little hamlet on the river Trent in Staffordshire, in old England, the country home of Governor Matthew Cradock.

NEWBURY, MASSACHUSETTS

"They came, so simply the quaint records tell,
'From England's stately homes' they loved full well,
'For conscience and religion's sake,' to dwell
'Amid this wilderness,' by God's good grace,
To rear in Quascacunquen, Newbury's race.
This goodly land, sea-fronting levels wide,
Their earnest gaze espied,
Ripe for the planting of a continent."

THE above is an extract from an ode written by Mrs. Louisa P. Hopkins on the occasion of the two hundred and fiftieth anniversary of the founding of Newbury, Massachusetts. It is not strictly correct to state that these Newbury settlers came to this country for "religion's sake," for they came really for farming and stock-raising. Many of them did not separate from the Church of England before sailing and some of their grandchildren even returned to this form of worship and built Queen Anne's Chapel in 1711, stating that they were of "the pure Episcopal Church of England." At this same anniversary celebration Dr. Samuel C. Bartlett in his address called attention to the words of Judge Samuel Sewall, who was born a few years after the settlement of our Newbury. These words were later changed into verse by John Greenleaf Whittier and were published in the history of the town issued by the Towle Manufacturing Company. We quote the first part:—

"As long as Plum Island, to guard the coast
As God appointed, shall keep its post;
As long as the salmon shall haunt the deep
Of Merrimac River, or sturgeon leap;

As long as pickerel, swift and slim
Or red-backed perch, in Crane Pond swim;
As long as the annual sea-fowl know
Their time to come and their time to go;
As long as cattle shall roam at will
The green, grass meadows of Turkey Hill;
As long as sheep shall look from the side
Of Oldtown Hill on marshes wide,
And Parker River and salt-sea tide;
As long as a wandering pigeon shall search
The fields below from his white-oak perch,
When the barley harvest is ripe and shorn,
And the dry husks fall from the standing corn;
As long as Nature shall not grow old,
Nor drop her work from her doting hold,
And her care for the Indian corn forget,
And the yellow rows in pairs to set;—
So long shall Christians here be born,
Grow up and ripen as God's sweet corn!"

This prediction of the prosperity of our Newbury has materialized, for from this early settlement also started West Newbury, the city of Newburyport and other nearby towns.

The people of Newbury have long taken a great interest in their mother town in England and just previous to the two hundred and fiftieth anniversary, on motion of Mayor Benjamin Perley Poore, the Committee on Literary Exercises was empowered to invite the Municipal Authorities and other delegates from Newbury, England, to participate in the celebration. The following answer was received:—

"Borough of Newbury, Berks.

To wit:

At a meeting of the Mayor and Corporation of the said Borough held at the Council Chamber of and in the said Borough on Tuesday the thirteenth day of January, one thousand eight hundred and eighty five, it was unanimously Resolved—That this council desires to express to the Mayor and Citizens of the Town of Newburyport, Massachusetts, in the United States of America, its hearty congratulations in the approaching celebration of the two hundred and fiftieth Anniversary of its Incorporation, recognizing its Municipality as in some sort the offspring of this Ancient Borough, the past history of which is so largely interwoven with that of the Parent Country. That they desire to greet with hearty goodwill and sympathy the Municipality of Newburyport, and to rejoice with them on the remarkable progress and prosperity which, by the blessing of Providence, and the efforts of those enterprising men who in the Seventeenth Century left their native land to found a new home in the Western Continent, has attended their Corporate existence for so long a period. That it is peculiarly gratifying to the Corporate Body and to the Inhabitants of this Borough to know that a former Minister of this Town—the Rev'd. Thomas Parker, was one of the original Settlers at Newburyport, in the year 1634; and that the name of a Rector of this Parish—the Rev'd. Benjamin Woodbridge, occupies the first place on the List of Graduates of Harvard University, and very sincerely do they trust that the town of Newburyport may continue to flourish and contribute many illustrious names to the Roll of American Worthies.

RESOLVED FURTHER:—That a Copy of these Resolutions, suitably engrossed, be sealed with the Common seal of the Corporation, signed by the Mayor, and forwarded to the Mayor of Newburyport by the Town Clerk.

WILLIAM HALL, *Mayor* (SEAL)

H. Burke Godwin, Town Clerk."

The English town sent another letter a short time later, which was elaborately engraved on parchment and which has been placed in the archives of the City of Newburyport. Another evidence of the interest taken by the English town in her namesake occurred in 1911 when at the suggestion of Walter Money, the historian of Newbury, England, Alfred Camp, Mayor of that town, sent a copy of the charter of incorporation of the Borough of Newbury, which was granted by Queen Elizabeth and which is now a valued relic in the Historical Society of Old Newbury, Massachusetts. This interesting record is dated 1596 and appoints Bartholomew Yates as the first Mayor of the town. With this present also came a letter from Mayor Camp, part of which is as follows:—

"MARCH 16, 1911.

MUNICIPAL BUILDINGS
NEWBURY

As you observe, the possession of this photographic copy will be our Historical link between our ancient Borough and your own Newburyport, and I trust while being so, it will also be a worthy addition and adornment to your Museum collection. Wishing Newburyport all prosperity in its future career, and in emulation of the best traditions of the old Borough and Country,

Believe me,

Yours very sincerely,

ALFRED CAMP, *Mayor*."

A few years ago, Rev. Glenn Tilley Morse, Rector of All Saints Church, West Newbury, and President of the Historical Society of Old Newbury, visited the old town in England and there met Mr. Money and officials of the town. When Mr. Morse built his church, he wrote to the Rector of St. Nicholas Church in Newbury, England, and asked him if he would send him a stone or some present to place in his church here. The war started soon after, which prevented at that time the carrying out of this suggestion, but in February, 1920, Mr. Morse received from him a Bible which had been used for many years in the Lady Chapel of St. Nicholas Church. Mr. Morse, as can be seen by the photographs of both churches, followed the perpendicular Gothic style of architecture of the Newbury church when he superintended the building of his church in West Newbury in 1912. Mr. Morse has taken a great interest in the old town as his ancestors were among the early settlers. Another visit we should mention was made by Rev. Mr. Titmarsh, pastor of the Congregational church in Newbury, England, who came to Newbury, Massachusetts, at the time of the International Conference of Congregational Churches, which was held in Boston in 1899, and while here he preached at the First Church in Newbury and also spoke before the Historical Society, where he told them all about his town.

From a print   *Kindness Rev. Glenn Tilley Morse*

ALL SAINTS CHURCH, WEST NEWBURY, MASSACHUSETTS

This church was built in 1913–14 under the supervision of its Rector, Rev. Glenn Tilley Morse, who followed
the character of St. Nicholas Church in Newbury, England, shown in another illustration.

The earliest commemoration of the settlement of our Newbury of which we have
any knowledge was the first Centennial held in 1735 which, according to tradition,
took place in Col. Joseph Coffin's front yard. Another celebration in the town
took place in 1759, when the British and Colonial Arms were triumphant at Quebec. The citizens on this occasion are said to have roasted an ox in the west yard
of Mr. Lowell's meeting-house, when they doubtless sang these and other words:—

> "With true British valour we broke every line
> And conquered Quebec in the year fifty-nine."

The lands near Newbury had for some time attracted the attention of the English, for we read that one William Wood returned to the old country in 1633 after
a four years' residence in Massachusetts, and published in London a book giving
a "description of that part of America commonly called New England," and in this
review of all the settlements he reserved his choicest words for the last. "Agawam"
he says, "is the best place but one, which is Merrimack, lying eight miles beyond

From an old print   *Brought from Newbury, England, by Rev. Glenn Tilley Mor..*

ST. NICHOLAS CHURCH, NEWBURY, ENGLAND

The character of this church was copied by Rev. Glenn Tilley Morse, when All Saints Church in West
Newbury, Massachusetts, was built in 1913.

it, where is a river twenty leagues navigable.   All along the river are fresh marshes,
in some places three miles broad.   In this river is sturgeon, salmon and bass, and
divers other kinds of fishes.   To conclude, the country hath not that which this
place does not yield."   His Merrimack was our Newbury.

It takes but little imagination to see the first little band, consisting of about
twenty-three men and their families, as they sailed from Ipswich one morning in
the spring of 1635, wending their way through Plum Island Sound and up the
Parker River to a spot on its northern bank one hundred rods below the present
bridge, where Nicholas Noyes was said to be the first to leap ashore.   This spot is
held quite sacred by the people of Newbury, who placed there a stone, shown in
the illustration on the next page, the inscription upon which reads as follows:—

1902
LANDING PLACE
OF THE
FIRST SETTLERS
1635

From a photograph by Noyes, Newburyport   *Kindness Miss Harriette E. Jones and Rev. Glenn Tilley Morse*

STONE MARKING LANDING PLACE OF THE FIRST SETTLERS, 1635, ON PARKER
RIVER, NEWBURY, MASSACHUSETTS

It is placed not far from the Ship Monument.

Rev. Thomas Parker and James Noyes were also with these pioneers and were
chosen pastor and "teacher," respectively, of their church.   Farther up the river,
on Oldtown lower green, has been placed another monument, surmounted by a
model of a ship of the old days, erected in honour of these early settlers, the inscription being as follows:—

> To the men and women
> who settled in Newbury
> from 1635 to 1650 and
> founded its municipal
> social and religious life,
> this monument is dedicated
> 1905

Rev. Benjamin Woodbridge, a settler in the town, has the honour of having ranked
first in the first class graduated from Harvard College.

Curiously enough, Newbury in Massachusetts was formerly called Old Newbury,
although before this it was named Oldtown and still before that Wescussacco; its
present name of Newbury was given in the year 1635.   In this year the General
Court of the Colony of Massachusetts Bay appointed a board of commissioners to
set out the bounds between Ipswich and Quascacunquen and at the same time
ordered that the new plantation should be called Newbury from the old town in

Berkshire, England, where Rev. Mr. Parker had preached before coming to this country. The list of names identified with the early history of Newbury is a long one and includes Daniel Pierce, Thomas and James Noyes, Henry Sewall, Caleb Moody, Anthony Morse, Captain Stephen Greenleaf, Richard Dummer, Colonel Kent and Edward Rawson; while those names later identified with the town were Adams, Chase, Poore, Hale, Lunt, Somerby, Lowell, Little, Sawyer, Bartlett, Brown, Jaques, Knight, Emery and Titcomb. Newburyport was not incorporated until 1764, this step being taken chiefly on account of the need for public school accommodations in that part of the township. The best-known names in this flourishing city are Lowell, Dalton, Tracy, Jackson, Todd, Cushing, Sawyer, Coffin, Jones, Wheelwright, Huse, Cary, Greenleaf, Hooper and Moseley; while those who were best known in West Newbury soon after its settlement were Moses and Joshua Brown, Josiah Bartlett, Benjamin Perley Poore, also the Ordway, Chase, Johnson, Dole, Greenleaf, Little, Smith, Bailey, Emery, Rogers, Felton and Morse families. Timothy Dexter, who originated the well-known T. D. pipe,

Photographed by Noyes, Newburyport   *Kindness Miss Harriette E. Jones and Rev. Glenn Tilley Morse*

SHIP MONUMENT PLACED ON THE OLDTOWN LOWER GREEN IN NEWBURY, MASSACHUSETTS,

in honour of the early settlers. Their leader was Rev. Thomas Parker, who had previously preached in Newbury, England, and it was out of respect to him that this name was given to the Massachusetts town. The names of all the earliest settlers are on the other side of this memorial.

was one of the curious characters of Newburyport in recent times. At the time that he wrote his book "A Pickle for the Knowing Ones," there were so many discussions in regard to proper punctuation that he left out all marks of punctuation in the body of his book but at the end printed several pages of periods,

Photographed from an old print in the Marine Museum, Boston, Massachusetts · *Kindness Robert B. Smith, Esq.*

NEWBURYPORT, MASSACHUSETTS, IN 1847, FROM SALISBURY
Newburyport was at one time a part of Newbury.

commas, etc., which he declared the reader could insert as he desired. It is a curious fact that from near Indian Hill Farm, West Newbury, can be seen many towns which bear the same names as English ones, such as Newbury, Salisbury, Gloucester, Hampton, Exeter, Amesbury and Andover; in fact almost all of the names in this region betray the origin of its colonists. Settlers from Newbury also helped found the towns of Nantucket, Concord, New Hampshire, Andover, Haverhill, Salisbury and Hampton.

There is also a Newbury in New Hampshire and one in Vermont.

St. Paul's Church in Newburyport used to own some silver plate that was sent over by King William and Queen Mary, but this was stolen from the church in 1887 and has never been recovered, though duplicates have been made. Another fact of interest is the bell presented by the Bishop of London in 1718 to Queen Anne's chapel, situated on the road between West Newbury and Newburyport.

Newbury, England, is on the river Kennet, a branch of the Thames, and was once known as "New Bourg," being situated on the road between London and Bath. The town was formerly noted for the manufacture of cloth, an industry which started during the reign of Henry VIII. In this trade the most prominent character seems to have been "Jack of Newbury," as he has been called, who, according to tradition, proved himself a hero during the battle of Flodden Field

From a pamphlet printed by the Towle Manufacturing Company, Newburyport, Massachusetts
NEWBURY STREET, NEWBURY, ENGLAND

when he and his brother warriors fought so bravely that they have gone down in history in these words:—

"The Cheshire lads were brisk and brave,
And the Kendall Laddies as free,
But none surpassed or I'm a knave
The Laddies of Newberrie."

Another interesting event in the town's history has been handed down to us. In the year 1811, Sir John Throckmorton made a bet of one thousand guineas that John Coxeter, an experienced weaver, could produce a finished woolen coat from the raw material on the sheep's back all within the space of twenty-four hours. This he succeeded in doing, much to the surprise of those who lost their money by betting against Sir John, and the winner of the wager sat down to dinner that same evening wearing the garment. It still exists and has been sent to a number of exhibitions, including the International one in 1851; also a painting recording this episode was made at the time and is now in the possession of one of the family.

In the old days the people of Newbury often journeyed by stage to Bath where they would spend their holidays and as it was possible to carry very little baggage on the coach with them, it is said that the women usually had to wait indoors several days after their arrival until their fine dresses came up later by wagon. In

From a photograph   *Kindness S. C. Reed, Esq.*

JACK OF NEWBURY'S HOUSE, NEWBURY,
ENGLAND,

the old Cloth Hall, now used as a museum. One of the most prominent characters in the cloth trade was "Jack of Newbury." A picture of this ancient house hangs, with other photographs, in the Public Library of Newburyport, Massachusetts.

Newbury is a parish called Speenhamland and it was there that the well-known Pelican Inn, so noted for its good dinners and high prices, received the many stage-coach travelers, one of whom wrote these amusing lines:—

"The famous inn at Speenhamland
    That stands below the hill,
May well be called the Pelican
    From its enormous bill."

In ancient times the Newbury church appointed officers called "dog rappers," whose duty it was to drive dogs out of church should they wander within its doors, the whips carried by these officials being used by the church wardens as symbols of service. Another event in the early history of Newbury was the siege of the castle in the year 1152 by King Stephen. There is practically nothing left of the fortress, though a picture of it on the seal of the old town still reminds us of its previous existence. This castle was defended during the siege by John Marshall, the representative of Matilda, who was the daughter of Henry I. Marshall, in command of the castle forces, pretended that he was desirous of consulting Matilda in regard to surrender and arranged with the enemy to grant an armistice, giving his little son as a hostage; but, in the meantime, he secretly endeavored to get provisions. His scheme was discovered by King Stephen, who ordered that the boy should be thrown by a sling against the castle walls. Fortunately the King relented. Several times as he was about to murder the hostage he changed his mind and finally promised to spare his life. A few days later the two were seen playing some game together, the King having become very fond of the boy.

Near Newbury is the Falkland memorial which was built in 1878 to commemorate Lord Falkland and those of his friends who died on the field of Newbury while fighting on the King's side. The old Cloth Hall, now a museum, is an interesting example of mediæval architecture. Another object of interest is the market-place containing the municipal buildings and a statue of Queen Victoria presented to the borough by the well-known circus king, George Sanger, who was born in the town. Horse races were also held in the town as early as the time of King Charles II. The Mortimer family owned much land there at one time.

NEWCASTLE, NEW HAMPSHIRE

ALTHOUGH Newcastle was probably not directly named for Newcastle, England, yet the town, with its narrow rambling streets and small low houses, reminds one so much of the English fishing villages of Cornwall and Devon from which many of the early settlers of the Island came, that we are going to include in this book a number of interesting connections between the New Hampshire town and the mother country.

In 1873, the postmaster of Newcastle, New Hampshire, Mr. H. M. Curtis, received a letter written by Mr. Henry Starr of London, informing him that one of his friends, a certain Captain Bokenham, of Hertfordshire, England, had in his possession some of the early records of this New Hampshire town. The inhabitants were very much astonished and were very skeptical as to the authenticity of these documents, but finally decided to inquire what expense there would be in getting them back. Much to the surprise and delight of the people of Newcastle the reply was the volumes themselves, which came by the next English mail and proved to be the records from the date of the incorporation of the town in 1693 to the year 1726, in perfect preservation and written in the handwriting of Francis Tucker, Theodore Atkinson and Sampson Sheafe, three of the earlier officials of the town. It is a curious fact that Captain Bokenham, in whose house the records were found, had no idea how they came there and no definite conclusion has ever been arrived at. These records were all the more valuable owing to the fact that the early records of the neighboring city of Portsmouth had been destroyed by fire. The town of Newcastle at the next annual meeting, held in 1874, passed a vote of thanks to the gentlemen who had discovered and given the records and this vote was engrossed on parchment and sent to London.

An interesting custom adopted at the early town meetings was described by an inhabitant, who stated that the voters used to deliberate with their hats on, as they wished to copy the British Parliament. Another custom in the early times was for all the inhabitants of the Province to assemble at the fort and to fire a salute whenever any important news came from England.

The town of Newcastle, at first called "Great Island," was not incorporated until 1693, although it was settled before the neighboring city of Portsmouth, and for the first seventy-five years it was the capital of the Province of New Hampshire and also the place of residence of the Governors. The chief industry of the town used to be, and still is to a certain extent, its fisheries, and in the old days one of the principal

From a photograph *Kindness William D. Turner, Esq.*

A STREET IN NEWCASTLE, NEW HAMPSHIRE

This attractive fishing village, with its narrow, winding streets and quaint low houses, is much like some of the English fishing villages of Cornwall and Devon.

town officials had the title of "culler of fish and staves." It is also a well-known fact that the States of New Hampshire and Maine both owe their discovery and early settlement to the fishing industry carried on by the English from their own harbours. Many distinguished families have lived in Newcastle and among the most prominent in Colonial days were the Sheafes, Atkinsons, Jaffreys, Vaughans, Waltons, Jacksons, Wentworths, Frosts and Odiornes. In mentioning the Sheafes it might be well to record that a member of the family owned the original settlement of Newcastle and that the family has been very prominent both in New Hampshire and in Massachusetts. Their ancestors came from Kent, England, and there is in that county an interesting inscription on a family monument reading as follows:—

Here are buried under this stone,
Thomas Sheff and his wife, Marion;
Sometyme we warr as yee now bee
And now we are as bee shall yee;
Wherefore of your charite,
Pray for us to the Trinite.

Obyt. Mccclxxxxiii

From *"Newcastle" by John Albree, 1885*   *Kindness William D. Turner, Esq.*

NEWCASTLE, NEW HAMPSHIRE

It was formerly called "Great Island" and was for seventy-five years the capital of the Province of New Hampshire and seat of the Royal Governors. "Little Harbour" is seen on the right. The river Piscataqua runs past both sides of the island, which is connected with Portsmouth only by a causeway.

Governor Wentworth's mansion is at Little Harbour and here have lived many of the family, so prominent in the history of the State. Here Samuel Wentworth, ancestor of three Governors and one of Newcastle's most respected citizens, kept a tavern called "At Ye Sign of Ye Dolphin." We wish that we had more space to describe others of the bygone days.

The people of Newcastle were very independent, and it was said that the only time citizens of Portsmouth took any interest in them was just before election, for the Island vote was so influential in the state elections that there was a prophecy "as goes Newcastle, so goes the State."

It has been said that a Newcastle sailor, as soon as he was able, always returned to his birthplace like the Kentites of the old days. It has also been claimed that the natives were so attached to their home that when a woman native of the town married a man who did not live on the island the husband always had to move his residence and business to her place of abode.

There are said to be many unmarked graves on the island, and one of the farmers, who did a great deal of plowing with his yoke of oxen, said that he was always in fear lest his cattle should stumble into one of the ancient graves, an accident which he admitted had often happened. He used to boast that he knew where many of the family burial places were, although they were not marked. "I've been in them," he said. "In old times they didn't dig very deep, and when the coffin gets empty and the wood thin and a heavy ox steps on the right place down he goes." Another citizen of the town asked a friend of his how he could find out his family history. "By running for office" was the amusing reply.

The most important visitor to Newcastle was George Washington who visited there in 1789; naturally, the natives immediately took him fishing, but, of course, catching a fish was out of the question on account of the din of the brass band. A bright fisherman, however, anticipating this possibility, had tied a fish to the end of his line and "the Father of his Country" hauled up a large cod which should have been mounted and placed among other Newcastle antiquities. Washington was entertained at the Wentworth mansion and a salute in his honour was fired from Fort Constitution. This fort was occupied by many of our soldiers during the Great War.

There is also a Newcastle in Maine.

Newcastle, in Northumberland, claimed a number of ships by the name "Mayflower." The inhabitants of this part of England took no active interest in the Puritan movement.

NEW LONDON, CONNECTICUT

"WHEREAS, It hath been a commendable practice of the inhabitants of all the colonies of these parts, that as this country hath its denomination from our dear native country of England, and thence is called New England, so the planters, in their first settling of most new plantations, have given names to those plantations of some cities and towns in England, thereby intending to keep up and leave to posterity the memorial of several places of note there, as Boston, Hartford, Windsor, York, Ipswich, Braintree, Exeter. This court considering that there hath yet no place in any of the colonies been named in memory of the city of London, there being a new plantation within this jurisdiction of Connecticut, settled upon the fair river of Monhegin, in the Pequot country, it being an excellent harbour, and a fit and convenient place for future trade, it being also the only place which the English of these parts have possessed by conquest, and that by a very just war, upon the great and warlike people, the Pequots, that therefore, they might thereby leave to posterity the memory of that renowned city of London, from whence we had our transportation, have thought fit, in honor to that famous city, to call the said plantation New London."

THE above was the vote passed by the General Court on March 24, 1658, granting permission to the early settlers to use the name "New London." It had been the wish of these pioneers that their adopted town should bear the name of London, but there was a difference of opinion, some of the colony preferring the name of Faire Harbour. They persisted, however, in calling it by its earlier Indian names of Pequot and Nameaug until they finally had their wish gratified by being allowed to use the name they desired. It was quite natural that they should also want the river, which had been called up to that time "Monhegin" (often spelled Mohegan) changed shortly after the naming of the town (now a city) to the Thames for the English river so well described by Pope in these words:—

> "My eye descending from the hill, surveys
> Where Thames among the wanton valleys strays.
> Thames, the most loved of all the ocean's sons.
> By his old sire to his embraces runs."

From the time that Block explored this coast and named the island "Block Island," probably no civilized person landed on the shores of New London until Captain John Endicott went there in 1636, as he was returning to Boston from an expedition against the Indians, when he landed at Groton on the opposite side of the Thames. A year later the Stoughton expedition pitched camp at New London and built the first English house ever erected in the place.

The settlement was formed in the year 1646 by the son of Gov. John Winthrop of Massachusetts, who bore the same name as his father. He was assisted by his friend Rev. Thomas Peters, a brother of the well-known Hugh Peters of Salem. The Massachusetts Court gave these two men authority to govern the plantation, although it was soon after decided that it did not come under the jurisdiction of Massachusetts, but belonged to Connecticut. We think it may be interesting to sketch the career of young Winthrop who, we are told, was a pioneer, traveler, scholar, statesman, lawyer, magistrate and physician. We first hear of him as advising his father to come to this country and it is very probable that he influenced his parent's decision. He was born in 1606 in the home of his ancestors in Groton, England. In 1631 he was married and sailed for Boston the latter part of the same year, whereupon he busied himself with the founding of Ipswich, as we have described in our story on that town, where he lived until he took up his residence in New London in the year 1647. In the meantime he made a trip to England in 1635, where he married again, returning to this country in the same year with a commission from Lord Saye and Sele, Lord Brooke and Sir Richard Saltonstall and others "to begin a plantation at Connecticut and be Governor there." This settlement he called "Saybrook" in honour of the two Lords who gave him the grant. It is also interesting to note that while forming this colony he coasted along the shore and visited the mouth of the Thames River, which he liked so much that he finally was induced to start a settlement at New London. He moved, however, none too soon to the Connecticut River, for hardly had his vessels appeared than the Dutch likewise hove in sight, but as the English flag and the English cannon had just been placed there ahead of them, they prudently turned back their prows towards New York. Winthrop remained "Governor of the river Connecticut, with the places adjoining thereunto" for the space of one year as commissioned by the patentees, then returned to the town of Ipswich which he had previously founded in the Bay Colony. Some years later he went abroad, returning in 1643 with workmen, tools and stock with which to take up the busi-

From a picture published by H. D. Utley, New London, Conn.   *Kindness Ernest E. Rogers, Esq.*

OLD TOWN GRIST MILL, NEW LONDON, CONNECTICUT,

established by John Winthrop, the younger, when he was chief magistrate of New London in 1650.   It was used continuously until a few years ago.   It is now owned by the city and is kept intact as an historic building.

ness of smelting and refining iron at Lynn and Braintree, which, for a time, was prosecuted with zeal and success, thereby earning him the distinction of being the first person in the United States to engage in that business.   In 1644 he obtained from the General Court of Massachusetts this grant "1644, June 28.   Granted to Mr. Winthrop, a plantation at or near Pequod [New London] for iron works." As we have noted, he began the settlement of New London in 1646, establishing a town government the next year.   His family also moved there the same year and has been represented in the community ever since.   He was Governor of Connecticut by election in 1657 and in 1659 and every year after that until the time of his death in 1676, an honour conferred upon no other Governor of the State.   Still another position had been thrust upon him in 1641, when Massachusetts sent him to the Court of St. James, where he showed great ability.   He chose a tomb for himself in New London, but death overtook him on a visit to Boston and he was therefore buried with his father in the family vault in King's Chapel Cemetery.   Henry Winthrop who resides in New London at the present time is a direct descendant of John Winthrop.

The two hundred and fiftieth anniversary of the settlement of New London was celebrated in May, 1896, on which occasion the corner-stone of the monument to

From a photograph by Boston Photo News Co.

ABRAHAM LINCOLN

The St. Gaudens statue, a replica of which was formally presented to the British nation by the Hon. Elihu Root on behalf of the American people, and unveiled in London by the Duke of Connaught on July 29, 1920. This is one of the latest connecting links between the Old World and the New.

From a photograph   *Kindness Ernest E. Rogers, Esq.*

STATUE OF JOHN WINTHROP, THE YOUNGER, IN NEW LONDON, CONNECTICUT,
unveiled in 1905.

He was the first governor of Connecticut by appointment of the original patentees Lord Saye and Sele, Lord Brooke and others in 1635; also the first governor of Connecticut under the charter which he obtained from King Charles II in 1662. His father was John Winthrop, governor of the Massachusetts Bay Colony.

In the background is the oldest cemetery in Connecticut, east of the Connecticut River, and in it is the Winthrop family tomb where he expected to be buried, but as he died while in Boston he was buried in King's Chapel Burying Ground, in his father's tomb.

John Winthrop, the younger, was laid, and also the Soldiers and Sailors memorial was dedicated. Some years later, in 1905, Bela L. Pratt, the sculptor of his statue, received a telegram saying, "John Winthrop has arrived." The monument was unveiled the same year by Master Henry C. Winthrop, Jr., the youngest male descendant of the distinguished Governor bearing the name. The words on the tablet attached to the monument are as follows:

JOHN WINTHROP
1606–1676
FOUNDER OF NEW LONDON
MAY 6, 1646
GOVERNOR OF CONNECTICUT
1657; 1659–1676

THE CHARTER OF CONNECTICUT
WAS PROCURED BY HIM
FROM KING CHARLES II
APRIL 23, 1662

TO COMMEMORATE
HIS GREAT SERVICES
TO THIS COMMONWEALTH
THE STATE OF CONNECTICUT
ERECTS THIS MONUMENT
A.D. 1905

Winthrop Square, where the statue now stands, is the most historic spot in New London, for it was here that the early settlers had a lookout post against the Indians; here also hung the first town's bell, the gift of John Winthrop's son, Gov. Fitz-John Winthrop, in 1698. (The town voted "to ring the bell every night at nine of the clock winter and summer," which custom of ringing the curfew is still in existence and has covered a period of two hundred and twenty-three years, with the change somewhere in the centuries from nine o'clock to eight o'clock on Saturday nights.) Here also was the site of the three successive meeting-houses where Blinman, Bulkeley, Bradstreet and Adams preached; and here in 1745, the troops assembled under Lieut. Gov. Wolcott previous to their sailing on the Louisburg Expedition.

New London was one of the great whaling ports of New England and up to 1860 this was the most important industry of the town.

The bicentennial celebration of the First Church of Christ in New London took place in 1870, this year being chosen for the reason that the church records did not begin until the year 1670, although the church was founded some time before. In "The Early History of the First Church of Christ, New London, Connecticut" by Rev. S. Leroy Blake, D.D., published by him in 1897, when minister of the church, it is authentically shown that the church was organized in Gloucester in 1642 and emigrated with its minister, Rev. Richard Blinman, from Gloucester, Massachusetts, in 1651, to New London, with about fifty of its members. The present Blinman Street received its name from him. During the two hundred and seventy-nine years of its existence there have been but thirteen ministers. The organization of this church is four years older than the founding of the town. The First Church in Hartford, Connecticut, emigrated with its minister, Rev. Thomas Hooker from Cambridge, Massachusetts, in 1636, fifteen years previous to the arrival of Mr. Blinman and his flock in New London.

We quote a few verses written by George Parsons Lathrop on the two hundred and fiftieth anniversary of the founding of New London on May 6, 1896.

> "The river whispered to the sea;
> 'Bring me the men of destiny,
> The men of faith, the men of power,
> From whom shall spring a nation's flower!'
>
> Long, long the waves of ocean bore
> That message to its farther shore;
> At last from ancient realms there came
> The makers of the New World's fame.

VIEW OF THE TOWER OF LONDON AND THE MINT.　　　VUE DE LA TOUR DE LONDRES ET DE LA MONNOIE.

From a print dated 1811
Engraved by Robt. Hazell & Son

Owned by Allan Forbes

A RARE OLD VIEW OF THE TOWER OF LONDON AND THE MINT

Then in the warring Indian land,
Brave Winthrop and his gallant band
Hewed clearings; and from fallen oak
Rose the first hearth-fire's signal smoke."

New London will observe its two hundred and seventy-fifth anniversary on May 6th of this year (1921).

In speaking of the great city for which New London was named all we venture to do is to mention briefly the memorials and places there of interest to Americans, having been helped greatly in compiling the list by Dr. J. F. Muirhead of London. First of all is the recently dedicated statue of Abraham Lincoln in Parliament Square, a replica of the St. Gaudens statue in Chicago, of which we have included an illustration. Next in interest is the fact that Benjamin Franklin spent about a year and a half in London between December, 1724, and the fall of 1726, working as a printer, first with the firm of Palmer, established in what had been the Lady Chapel of St. Bartholomew's Church, and afterwards with Watts, in Wild Court, near Lincoln's Inn Fields. His first lodging was in Bartholomew Close, whence he removed to Duke Street, where he had a room at the modest rental of 1/6 a week. When he returned to London in 1757 in the more dignified position of Agent to the General Assembly of Pennsylvania, he found a home at 36 Craven Street, Strand, which he occupied for several years; there he wrote various humorous papers under the name of "The Craven Street Gazette." The only reminder of George Washington in London is a copy of Peale's full-length portrait of him which was presented to the Government by the Earl of Albemarle in 1919 and which hangs in No. 10 Downing Street, the residence of the Prime Minister, now occupied by Mr. Lloyd George. The associations of John Harvard and Captain John Smith with the city of London were mentioned in Part I.

The visitor to London will find a monument in the Charterhouse to Roger Williams, founder of the State of Rhode Island; also he may wish to see the church of Saint Ethelburga the Virgin in Bishopsgate, associated with Henry Hudson, who named the Hudson River. The American will surely visit Westminster Abbey, where he can see the window placed there in memory of Rev. Phillips Brooks, Bishop of Massachusetts, the bust of Longfellow by Brock, placed there by his English admirers, and the medallion and stained-glass window to commemorate James Russell Lowell. There is also a monument in Westminster, beneath the Tower, to Viscount Howe, erected by the Province of Massachusetts, while still a British colony. General Burgoyne, who capitulated to General Gates at Saratoga, is buried in the North Walk of the Cloisters of the Abbey.

Ralph Waldo Emerson spent a night in Carlyle's House at 25 Cheyne Row, Chelsea, while visiting the city, and there is an interesting tablet and monument in Southwark Cathedral to William Emerson, a supposed ancestor. Washington Irving lodged in Bartholomew Close and was fond of exploring the nooks and crannies of Canonbury Tower.

VIEW OF THE HOUSE OF LORDS AND COMMONS   VUE DE LA CHAMBRE DES PAIRS ET CELLE DES COMMUNES

FROM OLD PALACE YARD   PRISE DE LA COUR DU PALAIS

From a print dated 1811
Engraved by Robt. Havell & Son

Owned by Allan Forbes

A RARE OLD VIEW OF THE HOUSE OF LORDS AND COMMONS, LONDON

From Old Palace Yard.

(Companion picture to the view of the Tower of London)

The Chelsea Public Library contains a bust of Henry James and the Chelsea Parish Church has a memorial tablet in his honour.

In front of the Royal Exchange is a statue of George Peabody by Story, a stone near the west end of the nave of Westminster Abbey marking the spot where the remains of this American philanthropist lay before being removed to Massachusetts. He lived in Eaton Square.

William Penn, the founder of Pennsylvania, seems to have lodged in Holland House in Charles II's reign, having lived also at No. 21 Norfolk St., Strand. He spent nine months in Fleet Prison rather than pay an unjust claim and was also confined in Newgate. He was born on the East Side of Tower Hill and was baptized in All Hallows, Barking. He attended Harsnett's Free School at Chigwell and lived from 1672 to 1677 in Basing House, High Street, Rickmansworth. He was buried at Jordans, together with his two wives and five of his children.

The Pilgrim Fathers' Memorial Church in New Kent Road, the oldest Congregational church in London (1616), is also worthy of a visit. Another place of interest is the Parish Church, Gravesend, where the registers in the vestry contain the record of the burial of Pocahontas, the Indian princess who saved the life of Captain John Smith and who married John Rolfe. Two stained glass windows were placed there in 1914 to her memory by the Society of Virginian Dames, there being also a memorial tablet on the chancel wall.

Edgar Allan Poe, of Baltimore, attended the school kept by the Misses Dubourg at 146 Sloane Street. He also went to school at Stoke Newington from 1817 to 1819. Benjamin West lived for forty-five years at 14 Newman Street; his studio is now St. Andrew's Hall. He was buried in the "Painters' Corner" at St. Paul's. J. M. Whistler died at 74 Cheyne Walk. He lived first at No. 101 from 1863 to 1867 and then at No. 96 for twelve years, during which time the portraits of his mother and Carlyle were painted. He was buried in the burial ground of St. Nicholas Church, Chiswick, beneath a bronze altar tomb. A memorial to him by Rodin is to be placed in the gardens on the Embankment to the West of Albert Bridge.

John Quincy Adams, sixth President of the United States, was married to Louisa Johnson in 1797 in All Hallows, Barking. Another marriage of interest to all the English-speaking peoples is that of Theodore Roosevelt to Edith Kermit Carew, which took place at St. George's, Hanover Square, in 1886. Charles Chauncey, vicar of Ware, who became President of Harvard College in 1654, is commemorated by a tablet in Ware Church, twenty-two miles from London.

The recent death of Francis Hodson recalls to the minds of many Americans and Britons alike the devoted services of this Englishman, who had been acting as chief clerk in the American Embassy during the past thirty-five years. He was an international figure and it was said of him that he was "never in the way and never out of the way." His father, Charles Hodson, who died in 1906, occupied the same position for thirty years, during which time he served under eight American Ambassadors. Francis Hodson's brother, Edward, is to occupy this position now and will doubtless fill the post as his father and brother have done before him, with ability, modesty and tact.

OXFORD, MASSACHUSETTS

WHILE Oxford, England, is universally known as one of the world's greatest seats of learning, it may be a surprise to many to read that there has been an Oxford in Massachusetts since 1683 when the settlement of Nipmuck was named for the famous English city. The first movement toward a settlement in the region now called Oxford was the petition of Hugh Campbell, a merchant of Boston, February, 1680, for land for a colony of Scotch emigrants. The petition was granted, but no effort seems to have been made to take advantage of it. Shortly after this, two prominent men of Boston, William Stoughton and Joseph Dudley, were empowered to purchase this land in the Nipmuck country and reported that with the Hassanamesit and Natick Indians they had agreed for all their land

"lying fower miles northward of the present Springfield road, & southward to that, haue agreed betweene Blacke James & them, of which wee aduised in our late returne, wee haue purchased at thirty pounds money & a coate.

The southern halfe of said countrey wee haue purchased of Blacke James & company, for twenty pounds."

It was undoubtedly at this time that the town received its present name. It was through an associate of these two men, Robert Thompson, merchant of London, England, that the Huguenots were induced to settle in this territory. He got into communication with Gabriel Bernon, who, though he never settled in Oxford, nevertheless was most active in making arrangements for the settlement of the Huguenots here. As a result, from La Rochelle, France, came a letter, dated October 1, 1684, from a representative of the French Protestants there, who, like the Pilgrim Fathers before them, looked to America as a place of refuge from religious persecution at the time of the revocation of the Edict of Nantes. The note in part was as follows:—

"New England, the country where you live, is in great esteem; I and a great many others, Protestants, intend to go there. Tell us, if you please, what advantages we can have, and particularly the peasants who are used to the plough. If somebody of your country would send a ship here to bring over French Protestants, he would make great gain."

To this plantation, then, which had been named for the English city where is the famous University at which many of the Pilgrim Fathers had received their collegiate education, fled bands of the persecuted Huguenots—chiefly from La Rochelle and its vicinity. They endured great hardships to reach America and many died on the voyage, but the sturdy little band that remained arrived in Boston during the winter of 1686 and were hospitably received and cared for at Fort Hill, where they were fed and clothed, the scattered churches of the Massachusetts Bay Colony taking up contributions to meet the needs of the exiles. When spring came they took possession of Oxford, retaining its English name, as they liked it so well.

Many famous names in the history of America appear among this first list of settlers, including Pierre Beaudoin, one of whose descendants, James Bowdoin, became Governor of Massachusetts, and Benjamin Faneuil, an ancestor of Peter Faneuil, benefactor of Boston and donor of Faneuil Hall. André Sigournais was another prominent member of the original Huguenot community and his descendants, the Sigourneys, are well known in Boston and other parts of New England. Andrew Wolcott Sigourney, seventh in descent, still owns the old family homestead in Oxford. In 1884, Miss Myrtis S. Sigourney (now Mrs. William Bacon Scofield) unveiled a splendid monument on Fort Hill erected by the Huguenot Memorial Society to

Photographed by E. B. Luce

HUGUENOT MONUMENT, OXFORD, MASSA-
CHUSETTS,

erected in 1884 by the Huguenot Memorial Society and unveiled by a descendant of André Sigournais, one of the most prominent of the founders of the town. Although the early settlers were French, they retained the name given to this territory by the English owners.

perpetuate the memory of the Huguenots who made the first settlement at Oxford. At the period made famous by Longfellow in his "Evangeline" several other French families also settled here. This town was the home of Clara Barton,

OXFORD, ENGLAND, SHOWING THE CATHEDRAL AND RADCLIFF LIBRARY

The little town of Oxford, Massachusetts, is named for this university city and when the French Huguenots, headed by André Sigournais (spelled also Sigournay and Sigourney), settled here they liked the English name so well they did not change it.

the famous Civil War nurse and organizer of our Red Cross, and here also Richard Olney, Secretary of State under President Cleveland, was born. Olney, by the way, was the last President of the Huguenot Memorial Society, no successor having been chosen since his death.

Judge Sewall, that renowned "Pepys of New England," undoubtedly named the town and he did so because he remembered his rides over the familiar ground in England. He also changed the name of the neighboring town of New Roxbury to Woodstock, his reason for doing so being that there is a town of that name near Oxford, England.

It is interesting to know that the name of Oxford was originally given by Prince Charles of England, later King Charles I, to the territory now known as Marshfield, Massachusetts, when he marked Captain John Smith's map of the New England coast made in 1614.

There is also an Oxford in Maine and one in Connecticut.

The city of Oxford, on that part of the Thames locally called the Isis, ranks among the most ancient corporations in England and its privileges are similar to those of the city of London. At the coronations of sovereigns the Mayor acted as Butler, next to the Lord Mayor of London, and received three mazers, or cups made of maple wood, as his fee until the last feast given by George IV in 1821. Since then no banquet has been given, and while the Mayor of Oxford retains his right he has no opportunity to use it, and, therefore, has no mazers to bring home.

In 912 the Anglo-Saxon Chronicle records:—

"This year died Eathered Ealdorman of the Mercians, and King Edward took possession of London and Oxford, and of all lands which owed obedience thereto."

Its legendary history, however, goes back nearly two centuries earlier and starts with the tale of the holy Frideswide who founded a nunnery there. She is the patron saint of Oxford and one of the three crowned figures in the arms of Oxford diocese is supposed to represent this saintly personage. Churches and castles later sprang up, and the country became famous for its sport, and many of the Norman kings resorted to the forests which abounded in deer. Historians differ as to the origin of Oxford University, though it is generally acknowledged that the movement gained impetus from the intellectual activity that was so apparent in Paris at the close of the eleventh century, at the time that the head of the cathedral school there was William Champeaux. From migrations across the channel this college town of Oxford, which at that time was neither a cathedral nor a capital town, became reinforced by the flood of students that had been turned out of France, so that by the beginning of the thirteenth century Oxford ranked with the most important universities of Europe.

There are many historic landmarks in this English city, the chief of which, however, the famous Osney Abbey, has been totally destroyed. "Great Tom," a

bell weighing eighteen thousand pounds, a relic of this Abbey, is preserved in the
"Oxford Tom Tower." Every night at five minutes past nine "Tom" tolls a
curfew of one hundred and one strokes as a signal of the closing of the college gates.
This tower was built in 1682 by the famous Sir Christopher Wren. Tom's time,
through an old custom, is always five minutes later than Greenwich time, thereby
giving tardy ones a leeway of five minutes in attending chapel, lectures and roll-calls.

The most interesting building among the many in this classical center is perhaps
the famous Bodleian Library, the most ancient part of which was built between
1450 and 1480 to house the books which had been given to the University by
Humphry, Duke of Gloucester. It contains over a million bound volumes and
about forty thousand volumes of manuscripts. By a copyright act it enjoys the
right to a copy of every book published in Great Britain.

Among the men who were natives of Oxford and who won distinction along
various lines were Edmund Ironside, Richard Cœur-de-Lion, and King John.
Cecil Rhodes, one of the most prominent of the famous graduates of the University, is known to the present generation through his endowment of the Rhodes
Scholarships which enable American undergraduates to obtain the advantages of
an Oxford education at the expense of the endowment fund.

READING, MASSACHUSETTS

READING, Massachusetts, set off from Lynn in 1644 as "Redding," was
named for Reading, England, by some of the early settlers of the town who
probably came from the English borough on the upper Thames, or from
that vicinity, having first lived in Lynn on their arrival in this country. John
Poole, one of the leaders, was perhaps responsible for the naming of the Massachusetts town. Among the early settlers were Nicholas Brown, William Cowdrey, Thomas Parker, Thomas Marshall, John Pearson, John Damon, Jonas
Eaton, Richard Walker, John Wiley and Thomas Kendall. Among later, but
still early, comers whose names have been prominent in the town's history were
the Bancroft, Temple, Upton, Nichols and Wakefield families. Some years ago
Hon. Owen Ridley, former Mayor of the English Reading, became much interested in the history of the Massachusetts town, made a visit here and was entertained by the late Chester W. Eaton, Esq., of Wakefield. Later Mr. Eaton and
his daughter, Miss Emma Florence Eaton, who is connected with the Wakefield
Historical Society (Wakefield having once been a part of Reading), visited the
English Reading and Mr. Eaton published an interesting account of his visit in
the "Memorial Volume of Ancient Reading" issued on the occasion of the two
hundred and fiftieth anniversary of the Massachusetts town in 1894. At the time
of this celebration Mr. Philip H. Turner, of Reading, England, carried on a corre-

From an old print owned by Allan Forbes   *Formerly in the collection of J. H. Seers, Essex, England*

READING ABBEY, READING, ENGLAND

spondence with the Wakefield Historical Society, and when the Eaton family made this visit to the old town in England he gave them a most cordial reception. Mr. Eaton in his interesting account spoke particularly of the attractive ruins of Reading Abbey, which was at one time one of the most lordly of the ecclesiastical establishments in England, and which is so well described by Miss Eaton in the following lines of poetry written on the occasion of the two hundred and fiftieth anniversary referred to above:—

> "Now all has passed away
> Save these few stones, near which the Thames doth stately glide.
> Gone are thy black-robed monks with cowlèd heads, gone is thy day
> Of grandeur. Yet still the truths thou stoodest for must abide,
> To make us stronger, nobler; and so I feel, at last,
> That a precious blessing lingers in these ruins of the past."

Mr. Eaton also wrote of the historic churches of the old town, including St. Giles's, a picture of which we have reproduced on the next page. Mr. Eaton explains that Reading, England, dates back to the year 868, although some historians declare that the town formed a part of the Kingdom of Wessex, under the Saxons, towards the end of the fifth century. The name Reading is spelled in a hundred different ways in the ancient English records and, like that of many English places, is probably derived from a Saxon clan name signifying the home of the sons of

Photographed from an old print   *Kindness Ian Forbes-Robertson, Esq.*
ST. GILES'S CHURCH, READING, ENGLAND

"Raed," the head of the clan. Men called Raed, precursors of the modern Reeds and Reids, took their name from their complexion —the Reds, like the Whites, the Browns, etc. To us, of course, the name has lost any significance of this sort and remains simply a link connecting us with that seventeenth-century England out of which the fathers came. There was fought in 1163 a duel that has come down to us in history between Henry d'Essex and Robert de Montford, which took place in the presence of King Henry II. To that town once came John Bunyan, who preached the gospel, and there also is shown to the American visitor the hall where William Penn used to worship. While there Mr. Eaton made a careful examination of the copy of the register of St. Mary's Church during the sixteenth and seventeenth centuries and found a number of names that were equally well known in our Reading, such as Poole, Cowdrey, Parker, Bachellor, Brown, Swain, Townsend, Hawkes, Taylor, Foster, Walker, Marshall, Eaton, Davis, Goodwin and Pearson, many of whom comprised the early settlers of Reading in New England. The famous Huntley and Palmer biscuit factory is situated in Reading, England.

The freedom of the borough was conferred in 1920 on Lord Reading, who had represented this locality in Parliament for over nine years, and who recently has been the British Ambassador to the United States. The American Ambassador, Mr. Davis, was present at the ceremony, during which he said, "No official representative of Great Britain has more truly interpreted the English people to the American people, or more thoroughly won the admiration and affection of the American people than Lord Reading." Our Ambassador, referring to the recent visit of the Prince of Wales to America, said he verily believed that in the recent history of the two countries no visit of greater promise, and certainly none of greater value, had occurred than that of the Prince to the United States, where he had been greeted with overwhelming enthusiasm.

The settlement of our Reading was made in 1639 under a grant of land from the General Court to the town of Lynn, being called Linn Village. The name was changed to Redding in 1644 and the modern form "Reading" appeared in 1647. Territory north of the Ipswich River, extending to the southern border of Andover, was added by a special grant in 1651. South Reading, the original first parish of old Reading, where the first settlement was made, was set off as an independent town in 1812. North Reading, beyond the Ipswich, the original second parish, was incorporated as a town in 1853. The present Reading retains the ancient name and records. The early Reading, therefore, has become in our day three separate towns. The name of South Reading was changed to Wakefield in 1868, in honour of Cyrus Wakefield, a leading citizen identified with the industrial development of the town, and was not derived from Wakefield, England.

There is also a Reading in Vermont.

ROWLEY, MASSACHUSETTS

"What mean these mad men, soon sayes one,
Witlesse to run away
From English beere to water, where
No boon companions stay."

CONSIDERABLE correspondence has been carried on between Rev. L. D. Hildyard, Rector of Rowley Church, Rowley, England, and the town of Rowley, Massachusetts, and we believe his letters, which we quote below, will give an excellent idea of the small but attractive English parish and will also show the love and interest Englishmen have for their offspring on this side of the water:—

"ENGLAND, ROWLEY, LITTLE WEIGHTON, HULL
April 17, 1912

Dear Sir:—

In answer to your letter I am sending some photographs of Rowley Church and Rectory, and Little Weighton Village. There is nothing at Rowley except the Church, Rectory, and farm and park. Little Weighton adjoins and you will find the pictures of it enclosed. Here and at Rowley no doubt resided the people who accompanied Ezekiel Rogers to America. I have also enclosed a photo of myself which is of no interest except that it happens that the Hildyards have held the 'Living of Rowley' since 1704 and Ezekiel Rogers only left in 1638. I believe the church is little altered since that date. It is supposed that Rogers took the Registers to America but I occasionally find a name later on of one or more of those who accompanied him. I have some small photos recently sent by a friend travelling in America of several buildings in Rowley (Mass.) but what I really want is a big picture of the town like a small one I have of 'Rowley from Prospect Hill.' You would know which you considered best and I should be quite satisfied with one good one in return for those I send as you have kindly suggested the question of exchange. I want, if you are pleased to send it to me, to exhibit it in the village and perhaps to put it into one of the papers here.

From a picture sent to Rowley, Massachusetts, by Rev. L. D. Hildyard of Rowley, England   *Kindness Amos Everett Jewett, Esq.*

ROWLEY CHURCH, ROWLEY, ENGLAND,

in which Rev. Ezekiel Rogers preached for seventeen years before emigrating to Rowley, Massachusetts.

With all good wishes from me and the people of Rowley (England) to Rowley (America).

Believe me,

Yours sincerely,

L. D. HILDYARD."

"Nov. 9, 1914.

Dear Mr. Crowdis:—

I read your kind message from the pulpit on Sunday to the Rowley (England) congregation and I have reason to know how deeply touched they were by it. It is indeed gratifying to us to think that although we are separated by so many miles of ocean, and though we are all unknown to one another, yet you still have a corner in your hearts for the dear old place from which Rowley in America took its name.

We have not progressed as you have. The Church in which Ezekiel Rogers ministered is still standing and the village and hamlets remain very much the same, I should imagine, as in the days of long ago. But we often think of those faithful ones, who in the time of Charles First were so beset that they determined to leave their all to maintain their religious convictions.

I have often regretted that there is no memorial of any kind here to Ezekiel Rogers. Before this terrible war began, we had an idea of erecting a window in the church, by which his name and work might be 'had in remembrance.' But alas! the war has put it out of the question. All we can spare now goes to the various Relief Funds, and we have reluctantly had to abandon the idea.

It occurred to me when we were discussing the matter some time ago, how nice it would be if Rowley in America were to take an interest in the matter and possibly to help us in some way. I know you will pardon me for making the suggestion for I dare say, like us, you are a 'poor community.' But it has been in my mind for some time to approach you on the subject. Sometimes I have thought my dream would come true, and I have pictured a great dedication service at Rowley conducted by the Archbishop of York in the presence of representatives from Rowley in America—what a wonderful reunion it would be after two hundred and seventy-five years. As I say, it is only a dream, for the cost of such a memorial would be £150.

Now you must forgive me for digressing in this manner from the consideration of your letter. You ask me for a word of sympathy and greeting from Rowley. Will you please tell your good people that we think of them here, and pray that God may bless them and him who ministers to them?

Believe me,

Yours very sincerely,

L. D. HILDYARD, *Rector*."

A monument has been erected in Rowley Cemetery to the memory of Rev. Ezekiel Rogers, who was the founder and first minister of our Rowley. He with his company of about twenty families came in the ship "John" of London, sailing from Hull and landing at Boston, New England, December 2, 1638. The inscription on this monument is so interesting that we are repeating it here:—

From a photograph   *Kindness Amos Everett Jewett, Esq*

MONUMENT IN THE OLD CEMETERY IN ROWLEY, MASSACHUSETTS,

in memory of Rev. Ezekiel Rogers, a founder and first minister of the town, who had been minister in Rowley, England, for many years. Our town was so named in his honour. He was a cousin of Rev. John Rogers, who came to Dedham, Massachusetts. Rowley, England, has for some time been considering the placing of a memorial to him there. This monument bears a most interesting inscription, which is given in the text.

Rev. Ezekiel Rogers,
first minister of Rowley,
Born at Wethersfield, Essex Co.
England, A.D. 1590, a minister
in Rowley Yorkshire 17 years.
Came to this place with his
Church and flock in April
1639, died June 23, 1660.

This ancient pilgrim nobly bore
The ark of God, to this lone shore;
And here, before the throne of Heaven
The hand was raised, the pledge was given,
One monarch to obey, one creed to own,
That monarch, God; that creed, His word alone.

Here also rest
the remains of his wives.

With him one came with girded heart,
Through good and ill to claim her part;
In life, in death, with him to seal
Her kindred love, her kindred zeal.

We are told that his sparkling wit, judgment and learning delighted his father so much that at the age of thirteen he was sent to Cambridge. Rogers had lived in Rowley, England, where he served as minister for seventeen years, his piety, wisdom and eloquence causing people to flock to hear him from all the adjacent regions. Once, we are told, he preached in the stately Minster of York on a public occasion "which he served and suited notably." Rogers and his company wintered in Salem, Ipswich and Boston whence they began to look about for a permanent home, in the meanwhile attending services in Mr. Wilson's First Church in Boston. New Haven had made the colonists tempting offers, but they finally selected a place on the shore between Newbury and Ipswich where they, with about forty other families who had joined them, settled in 1639. The General Court ordered that the following vote be recorded in the State records and the words used appear on the present seal of the town:—

"The 4th day of the 7th month, 1639. Mr. Ezechi Rogers' plantation shalbee called Rowley."

The pleasant brook which flows through the center of the town is said to have influenced them in choosing this site and they were probably also influenced by the accessibility to the "lectures" on either side of them in Ipswich and Newbury. Ezekiel's father was Rev. Richard Rogers and the following quaint lines concerning him have survived:—

"How shall we passe to Canaan now
The wilderness is wide
Soe full of Tygers Beares and wolves
And many a beast besyde
. . . .

He spared no labour of mynde
Noe bodilie griefe nor payne
That tended to his people's good
And to his master's gayne
When strength of leggs and feet did fayle
On horseback he did ride."

Rev. Ezekiel Rogers was a cousin of Rev. John Rogers of Dedham, England, and Dedham, Massachusetts, a devoted and popular Puritan preacher, whose "lectures" were famous; while his brother Daniel was also a famous Puritan preacher. His family, therefore, was distinguished for its clerical services to the Puritan cause.

In 1643, Mr. Rogers had the honour of preaching the election sermon,—"and the ability he showed on this occasion," said Cotton Mather, "made him famous through the whole country." He married for his second wife the daughter of Rev. John Wilson and for his third wife the widow Barker, who, as has been expressed, "was in years agreeable to him." On the very night of his marriage, his house was burned to the ground with all his goods, probably all the church records and the library which he brought from England containing valuable books given to him by his father. The stout-hearted pastor, however, rebuilt his home and restocked his library. Again misfortune befell him, for he was thrown from his horse and his right arm was broken, causing it to be paralyzed for the rest of his life. Still undaunted, he learned to write with his left hand and continued active until his death which occurred in 1660, Old Style, (1661 New Style). He continually preached against all evil fashions and guises of his age, both in apparel and "that general disguisement of long ruffian-like hair," as he expressed it. On his death he remembered his friends throughout the Colony and even in England and Holland. President Quincy commemorates him as one of the earliest benefactors of Harvard College. Part of his real estate

From a photograph   *Kindness Amos Everett Jewett, Esq.*

COMMUNION CUPS GIVEN BY REV. EZEKIEL ROGERS AND OTHERS IN ROWLEY CHURCH, ROWLEY, MASSACHUSETTS

Those given by Rev. Mr. Rogers were brought by him from England and given to the church in his will.

From a photograph   *Kindness Amos Everett Jewett, Esq.*

TABLET IN ROWLEY, MASSACHUSETTS,

erected by the Jewett Family of America in 1912, in memory of Maximilian and Joseph Jewett, of Bradford, England, who came over in the ship "John" with Rev. Ezekiel Rogers, founder and first minister of the Massachusetts Rowley.

was bequeathed to support the ministries in our Rowley and also in Byfield and Georgetown nearby. The last item of his will reads: "also to the church my silver bowls, which they used for the communion, to be so used still." These same bowls are still used at the first communion service each year, although they have been re-hammered and their shapes, therefore, somewhat changed. Rogers was succeeded by Rev. Samuel Phillips, who came from the English town of Boxford. Almost directly across the drive from the Rogers monument in the cemetery is a memorial tablet, shown in one of the illustrations, erected by the Jewett family of America to the first two ancestors of this name who were buried in this cemetery. There are also stones placed here to the memory of two other early settlers in this New England town, John Trumble first of Roxbury, New England, and William Stickney, who came from Frampton, England, to Boston in 1638, thence to Rowley.

One of the interesting pieces of history connected with Rowley is the fact that the little town was able to supply cloth sufficient for the needs of the Colony, when the supply that had been brought over by the colonists from England had failed them. Johnson in his "Wonderworking Providence" speaks of this incident in these words:—

"These people being very industrious . . . were the first people that set upon making of cloth in this western world, for which end they built a fulling-mill and caused their little ones to be very diligent in spinning cotton wool, many of them having been clothiers in England."

Governor Winthrop also records that in this manufacture "Rowley to their great commendation exceeded all other towns." The name of the pioneer in the manufacture of cloth was John Pearson who shipped his cotton from Barbados, his mill continuing to be the property of his family for the next six generations. A cedar post that was brought from England and put into that first mill was still standing and in good condition at the beginning of this century; it was then cut up into rulers, which were deposited in museums and various other places.

From a photograph sent to Rowley, Massachusetts, by Rev. L. D. Hildyard, of Rowley, England   Kindness Amos Everett Jewett, Esq.

ROWLEY, YORKSHIRE, ENGLAND

Rowley, England, in the East Riding of Yorkshire, is about seven miles from Beverley and is a small parish, for we learn that it consists chiefly of a church and a school. A visitor on alighting at Little Weighton and inquiring for the town, received the reply to go "right awah to your right till you come to a gate." Another traveler to the other side describes a visit to the old parish, where he met Rev. H. C. T. Hildyard, who hastened downstairs to put into the visitor's hands the ancient records and keys of St. Peter's Church, which dates back to the thirteenth century and contains a font that is a century older. A visitor gives in the *New England Magazine* this description of the church:—

"A tiny side chapel contains a tablet to Sir Ralph Elleker and his three sons, Ralph, William and Robert, all four of whom were knighted on Flodden Field in 1513 for their gallantry in that battle. But my mind was full of another hero. I thought how this little church was once thronged to hear the true, brave words of Ezekiel Rogers, how dear its ancient memories must have been to one of his cultivated taste, and how he sacrificed all, including a very comfortable salary, rather than do violence to his conscience. The left part of the rectory, as shown in the accompanying illustration, was that of Ezekiel Rogers. The good rector himself is shown in another picture, beneath a venerable larch that probably had shaded Mr. Rogers. The Rowley living is now a family one, and Mr. Hildyard is to be succeeded by his nephew, Rev. Robert Hildyard. He will be the fourth of the name in the rectorship."

An interesting relic among the Rectory heirlooms is a handsome blanket bearing the date 1733, which has been passed down to each successive Rector for one hundred and seventy-six years.

SALISBURY, MASSACHUSETTS

OF the New England towns, Salisbury ranks among the earliest, a settlement having been made at Merrimac on the Merrimac River as early as 1638, one of the earliest settlers being Roger Eastman, the ancestor of all of that name in America, who sailed to this country from Southampton, England, on the ship "Confidence." The General Court two years later changed the name of this little settlement to Salisbury as several of the first colonists came from the English town of the latter name, among the number being the first minister, Rev. William Worcester. It is also believed that one of the deputies present at the session at which the town was named, was Christopher Batt, who came from the English Salisbury. It has been said of the early settlers of the town that they "were men fitted by education to adorn any station" and by their foresight and care the town early became a pioneer along several lines—notably shipbuilding, and later, the slavery agitation. Here was born Daniel Webster's mother, Abigail Eastman, the daughter of Roger Eastman, who was a great-grandson of the early settler.

There are also Salisburys in Connecticut, New Hampshire and Vermont.

Salisbury, England, at the junction of the Avon and the Wily, is a cathedral city and the capital of Wiltshire. More than seven centuries ago the town and cathedral were transferred to their present location from the windy pinnacle of Old Sarum two miles distant, the direction of the removal, as the tradition goes, being determined by the flight of an arrow. The military and the clergy quarrelled, whereupon the bishops concluded that it was time to move to another locality, the present Salisbury (or New Sarum) being chosen for the site of the new cathedral, which is considered to be one of the finest examples of early English architecture, dating from 1220. The following lines give in a novel way some statistics concerning the construction of the building:—

> "As many days as in one year there be,
> So many windows in this church you see;
> So many marble pillars here appear
> As there are hours throughout the fleeting year;
> As many gates as moons one here may view,
> Strange tale to tell, yet not more strange than true."

The town soon grew in importance and in 1227 Henry III granted a charter to incorporate it, making it a free city.

Queen Elizabeth, while on her way to Bristol in 1574, stopped at Salisbury, and here, too, James I frequently came for retreat. When being taken in captivity and to eventual death in London, Sir Walter Raleigh, on reaching Salisbury, feigned madness and leprosy that he might gain an opportunity to write his immortal "Apology for the Voyage to Guiana." There King James found him and

SALISBURY, ENGLAND,
showing the Cathedral.

ordered his immediate removal to London. Charles I also came to Salisbury many times.

It was at the King's Arms, still standing, that the supporters of Charles II were accustomed to gather when the monarch was in hiding at Heale House. A part of the Old George Inn was built about 1320. It was known in the early days as "Ye Grate Inne of Ye George," and it is said that Shakespeare may have played in the courtyard. Oliver Cromwell slept in the Inn in October, 1645, and the indefatigable Samuel Pepys refers to it in his diary in these words: "Came to the George Inn where lay in a silk-bed and a very good diet."

Nor should the literary associations of the old city be forgotten. There appeared the first edition of Goldsmith's "Vicar of Wakefield" and, in the house still standing near St. Anne's Gate, Fielding lived for some time and there wrote a portion of "Tom Jones." The original Thwackum of the novel was one Hele, who was then master of a school in Salisbury, where Addison received his education "after starting life as such a frail infant that he had to be baptised on the day he was born." Anthony Trollope also laid the scenes of some of his novels there.

During the war Salisbury Plain was the great training ground of the overseas forces of the British Empire and tens of thousands of Canadians, New Zealanders and Australians were constantly thronging the streets of Salisbury to which thousands of American soldiers, no doubt, also found their way.

SHERBORN, MASSACHUSETTS

"There's a little grey-built town
'Neath a windy western down,
Where the streets of stone-roofed houses stand for centuries the same;
In a lap of earth it lies
Over-arched by Dorset skies,
And a gush of crystal water gives it glory and a name.

Mighty monarchs, warriors bold,
Of whose feats the tale is told,
Ruled and wrought there in past ages, though by men remembered not,
Who with valiant deed, or wise,
Lifted Sherborne to the skies,
And their wisdom and their worth remain, the spirit of the spot.

Great and famous were our sires:
Let them be as beacon-fires!
Nurse we well the glowing embers, lest their splendour be forgot,
When the pomp has ebbed afar,
And, like some forsaken star,
O'er the heights beloved of Ealdhelm broods the Spirit of the spot!"

(Part of the verses written by James Rhoades for the Pageant held in Sherborne, England, in 1905.)

EARLY in 1905 Francis Bardwell, Esq., Town Clerk of Sherborn, Massachusetts, wrote a letter to the Vicar of Sherborne, England, the substance of which we quote:—

"TOWN OF SHERBORN, INC. 1674
OFFICE OF THE TOWN CLERK,
SHERBORN, MASS.

Settled 1652.

TO THE RECTOR OF THE ESTABLISHED CHURCH, SHERBORNE, ENG.

Dear Sir: Being Town Clerk of this town and knowing that it was called after the town of Sherborne in England, I write to ask you for information, feeling sure that you can either furnish it yourself, or place this communication in the hands of someone who can.

This town was settled by Hopestill Layland, Thomas Holbrook, and Nicholas Wood or Woods. Do any of their names appear on the Parish Register or among the Church Records?

Tradition has it that it was probably named in honor of Henry Adams, who was supposed to be a native of Sherborne, Eng. Other Incorporators were Morse, Bullen (or Bolyn), Bullard, Hill, Breck, Fairbanks and Perry. Do any of these names appear on your records? Tradition again says that the word Sherborn is derived from the Saxon and means 'pure water,' which is singularly true in regard to this town; is this correct?

I should very much like to know about our Mother Town, its foundation and history, in order to write down the facts and place them among our town records.

Is there a history of your town that can be purchased? I would also like to purchase photographs of the Church and of all places of interest for our Public Library here.

I write you because I think you will perhaps be interested somewhat in this little town of the Colony of Massachusetts Bay and because, when I was abroad in 1895, I was searching concerning my own family (the DeBerdewelles, of Bardwell, Suffolk) and I always found the Rectors and Curates willing and pleased to assist. . . .

With great respect I have the honor to remain

Your Humble Servant,

FRANCIS BARDWELL,
Town-Clerk, Sherborn, Mass. U.S.A."

The answer from the English town spoke of a forthcoming pageant commemorating the twelve hundredth anniversary of the founding of the town. This unexpected result of the letter from our Sherborn encouraged Mr. Bardwell again to write to the mother town, as follows:—

"SHERBORN, MASS. March 7th, 1905.

To THE HON. SECRETARIES,
    SHERBORNE PAGEANT, SHERBORNE, ENGLAND.

Gentlemen:—

The kind letter with enclosures sent me by Mr. Field came duly to hand; I cannot tell you how pleased I was to receive the same. I have delayed in answering until after our Annual Town Meeting on March 6th, because I desired to read the letter to the townspeople there assembled, and request some action. Everybody was interested, and a Committee was immediately chosen to draw up greetings to the Mother town on the occasion of the 1200th anniversary. These greetings will be forwarded to you shortly. I send you by this mail a copy of the Boston Transcript, in which I have called the attention of the readers to the celebration. This paper has a very broad circulation, and reaches everyone interested in genealogical research in the United States.

I cannot tell you how interested I am personally in this matter, and how much it means to this little town, which is, let me assure you, a worthy daughter of so illustrious a mother.

The text of the Folk-play which Mr. Field so kindly sent me I shall have bound and placed in our Town Library.

I wish it were so that some of our townspeople could be present at your celebration, and perhaps it can be arranged; anyway our hearts are with you, and we reach out to clasp your hands across the sea.

Believe me, with the best of good wishes,

Most sincerely,

FRANCIS BARDWELL,
Town Clerk of Sherborn."

This note was followed in a few months by still another letter expressing the greeting of Sherborn, Massachusetts, on the twelve hundredth anniversary of the town of Sherborne, England:—

"SHERBORN, MASS. May 26, 1905.

To THE HON. SECRETARIES,
    THE SHERBORNE PAGEANT, THE PARADE, SHERBORNE, DORSET.

Gentlemen:—

It is my pleasure to inform you that, for and in behalf of this Town of Sherborn, Massachusetts, I sent you today by the American Express our town's formal greeting on the occasion of the 1200th Anniversary of the Foundation of the Mother Town.

I regret exceedingly that our Town has not chosen an accredited representative to bear these greetings and to be with you at this time, for this anniversary means so much to our Town, the foundation of whose existence found root in English soil.

When we look back upon the beginning of this Town and think of the character of its founders, and through them and their influence in the building of a second great English speaking nation, we have profound respect for the Mother Country which reared such sterling men. There is something firm, resolute, fearless, and trustworthy in the New England character, and this is our heritage from those who came from Old England to establish new homes in a strange land.

So then at this time, one of the most remarkable epochs in the history of your ancient

Town, when strangers throng your thoroughfares and marvel at your Historic Pageant, be assured that although an ocean separates us, still your kinsfolk in this little town, your American daughter, feel pride in your great Anniversary, and wish you all joy in your festivities, and the heartiest sentiments of prosperity for your future.

With much esteem, I have the honor to be

Yours with respect,

FRANCIS BARDWELL,
Town Clerk of Sherborn."

The formal greeting reads as follows:—

"TO THE TOWN OF SHERBORNE, DORSET, ENGLAND,
FROM HER AMERICAN NAMESAKE THE TOWN OF SHERBORN, IN MASSACHUSETTS.

GREETING—Our forefathers, men of indomitable spirit and God-fearing ancestry, made their habitation in the wilderness, and, with the homefeeling strong within them, gave to their new abode the ancient name of Sherborn. We, their descendants, have received with filial pride tidings of the forthcoming celebration of the twelve hundredth anniversary of the founding of the Mother Town. Your glorious record of traditions and memories of a thousand years we deem our common heritage.

We greet you on this memorable occasion with a message of esteem and good will, trusting that the ties of a common blood and a common tongue may, through the advancing ages, more closely bind town to town and nation to nation. May the spirit that existed in the eighth century in Old England, and that in the seventeenth century found echo in the wilds of New England, be an inspiration to all our lineage. And may the coming years bring to all peace, prosperity, and happiness, by the grace of God, who for twelve hundred years has cherished the people of St. Ealdhelm's honoured town.

Done pursuant to a vote passed at the annual town meeting held March the sixth, in the year of Our Lord, One Thousand Nine Hundred and Five.

Inhabitants of the Town of Sherborn, Massachusetts,

By its Committee,

FRANCIS BARDWELL,
ROBERT H. LELAND,
CHARLES O. LITTLEFIELD."

This greeting from Sherborn was read by a herald on horseback at the end of the pageant, being received with great applause, and it was also read a second time in Sherborne Abbey. It turned out, however, that our town was represented in three different ways. First of all, a Miss Holbrook, who was a direct descendant of Thomas Holbrook, one of the original settlers of our Sherborn, went all the way from her home here in order to be present at the celebration in Sherborne, England. Secondly,—on one day of the pageant, Sherborn, Massachusetts, was officially represented by Lorin Andrews, Esq., U.S. Consul at Bristol, England. Thirdly,— it was discovered that the daughter of L. N. Parker, Esq., was a direct descendant of Richard Parker who originally owned the land comprised in our Sherborn that was sold to the immigrants who came from Sherborne, England. This interesting information was brought to light by Miss Holbrook and was not known, curiously enough, at the time Miss Parker was chosen for one of the most important parts in the festival. It may be interesting to mention that Louis Napoleon Parker, Esq.,

From *"Sherborne," published by McCann, Sherborne*   *Kindness Francis Bardwell, Esq. and Henry G. Vaughan, Esq.*

LONG STREET AND CONDUIT, SHERBORNE, ENGLAND,
showing Sherborne Abbey in the background.

At the pageant held in the English town in 1905, at which the Massachusetts Sherborn was represented, a message from the Massachusetts town was read in the Abbey. The New England town is spelled without the final "e."

was the music master of the Sherborne School and is well known on account of being the author of the plays "Disraeli," "Rosemary" and "Pomander Walk." He was chiefly responsible for the great success of this celebration. The last scene of the pageant represented the English Sherborne with the British emblem and the American Sherborn with the Massachusetts coat of arms standing together on a pedestal, and below them were four girls carrying a model of Sherborne Abbey, while four boys dressed as Indians had with them a model of the "Mayflower." This picture is shown on the next page. The two towns then embraced while the band played "The Star-Spangled Banner" and "God Save the King." Many tableaux were presented which showed the history of the old town, among the most interesting being St. Ealdhelm receiving the pastoral staff from King Ina; Bishop Ealhstan defeating the Danes; Death of King Ethelbald; Bishop Ealhstan blessing the boy Alfred; Bishop Wulfsy and monks; William the Conqueror removing the See to Sarum; Bishop Roger of Caen laying the foundation stone of Sherborne Castle; Foundation of the Hospital of St. John; Sherborne School receiving its charter and Sir Walter Raleigh's arrival in Sherborne. Sir Walter Raleigh is closely associated with Sherborne, for it was in the castle given to him by Queen Elizabeth in 1599 that he spent some of the happiest years of his life. Vicar W. F. Lyon in writing

From the "Story of the Sherborne Pageant Produced in the Old Castle Ruins at Sherborne in June, 1905"
By Cecil P. Godden, Barrister-at-Law

Kindness Francis Bardwell, Esq.
and Henry G. Vaughan, Esq.

SHERBORNE, ENGLAND, AND SHERBORN, MASSACHUSETTS

Final tableau of a pageant held in Sherborne, England, in 1905, to celebrate the twelve hundredth anniversary of that town.   The lady at the right, holding the American flag in one hand and the arms of Massachusetts in the other, is a descendant of Richard Parker, one of the original settlers of Sherborn, Massachusetts.   One of the Indian boys is holding a model of the "Mayflower."   The pageant was held on the grounds of Sherborne Castle.

From a photograph by F. Frith & Co., Surrey, England   *Kindness Ian Forbes-Robertson, Esq.*

SHERBORNE CASTLE, SHERBORNE, ENGLAND

The older part of this building was built by Sir Walter Raleigh. In these grounds the pageant of 1905 was held, at which time the Massachusetts town was represented, as shown in another illustration.

from the Sherborne Vicarage in 1903 to our Sherborn told the story of the building by Sir Walter Raleigh of the present residence of the Lords of the Manor in Sherborne. There is a seat in these grounds upon which Sir Walter was smoking some tobacco which he had just introduced into the country. The smoke exuding from his mouth caused his servant to think that his master was on fire, whereupon he threw a jug of beer over him to put it out.

The word "Sherborne" is supposed to be derived from "Scir," meaning clear, and "Burne," meaning a brook or spring, the monks having called the place Fons Limpidus, signifying "the clear spring." In 705 A.D. it was the seat of a bishopric founded by Ina, King of the West Saxons, with his kinsman Ealdhelm, Abbot of Malmesbury, occupying the position of first Bishop of Sherborne. This English town, lying in the most picturesque part of Dorsetshire and once the capital city of Wessex, is celebrated to-day for its magnificent abbey, its flourishing school and its two picturesque castles.

The pageant took place near the ruins of the old Castle which was founded by Roger of Caen, Bishop of Sarum and Abbot of Sherborne.

Our Sherborn was settled in 1652 and incorporated in 1674 when it was first called Shearborn, the first settlement having been at "Bogestow." The present historian of Sherborn believes the name of his town was given in deference to John Hull, the "Mint Master," who owned an original grant of land. He was not born in Sherborne, England, but his family was closely associated with Raleigh, who knew Sherborne so well.

SPRINGFIELD, MASSACHUSETTS

WILLIAM PYNCHON of the little parish of Springfield, England, would be pleased and doubtless much surprised if he could see the great city of Springfield, Massachusetts, which was founded by him. It would seem as if the people of our Springfield should place a special memorial to him in addition to the memorial in the Peabody Cemetery which has been dedicated to the Pynchon family. Some years ago, we are told by W. F. Adams, Esq., President of the Connecticut Valley Historical Society, the children of one of the schools of Springfield subscribed eight dollars to start a fund to erect a proper memorial to this early pioneer. There are some additional funds amounting to one hundred and sixty dollars which have been collected by the Historical Society,

From a photograph   *Kindness W. F. Adams, Esq.*

PYNCHON FAMILY MEMORIAL IN THE PEABODY CEMETERY, SPRINGFIELD, MASSACHUSETTS

William Pynchon was rector of All Saints Church in Springfield, England, and in his honour our city of Springfield, Massachusetts, was so named.

From a photograph   *Kindness W. F. Adams, Esq.*

ALL SAINTS CHURCH, SPRINGFIELD, ESSEX COUNTY, ENGLAND,

of which William Pynchon, founder of the city of Springfield, Massachusetts, was warden, and after which
All Saints Church, Springfield, Massachusetts, was designed and named.

also a private subscription of one thousand dollars for this purpose and doubtless
some day the rest of the fund will be raised by the people of Springfield.

William Pynchon was educated at Oxford, was one of the patentees named in
the charter of the Colony of Massachusetts Bay, dated 1628, and was connected
with the government of the company before it was transferred to America. He
lived in Springfield, England, and while there was warden of All Saints Church for
which All Saints Church in Springfield, Massachusetts, was named and from which
it was also designed. He came over with his wife and four children in the "Jewel,"
one of Winthrop's fleet, in 1630 and during his first year in Massachusetts he founded
Roxbury and became the treasurer of the colony. He believed that it was possible to get large returns by trading with the Indians on the banks of the Connecticut
and he recommended, therefore, that his fellow-townspeople establish a new settlement there. Accordingly, the inhabitants of Roxbury in 1635 were granted
leave to "remove themselves to any place they should think 'meet.'"

Springfield possesses the original declaration dated May 14, 1636, under which
the settlement was begun, a few settlers, however, having occupied the lands near
here a year or two before. The names of the earliest settlers are William Pynchon,
Miles Morgan, Henry Smith, Elizur Holyoke, Henry Burt, Lieutenant Thomas
Cooper, John Pynchon, Deacon Samuel Chapin and Richard Sikes. Other important people in the town in later years were the Brewer, Dwight and Bliss families.

This change to Connecticut proved profitable, for Pynchon was soon able to

From a photograph   *Kindness W. F. Adams, Esq.*

ALL SAINTS CHURCH, SPRINGFIELD, MASSACHUSETTS,
named for the church of the same name in Springfield, England.

ship to England more than one thousand dollars' worth of beaver skins. River fishing also became very profitable to these settlers, and at one time shad were so common that a man on being hired was compelled to agree to eat one shad a certain number of times a week.

In 1640 the name of the town was changed from the plantation of "Agawam" to Springfield, in honour, of course, of Pynchon, being therefore, the first town to be settled in Massachusetts west of Boston, Cambridge and Watertown. It is interesting to mention, perhaps, that for one hundred years after the settlement the Connecticut River was still spoken of as the "Great River."

The latter part of William Pynchon's life was unfortunate, for a book written by him that appeared in London, England, was so severely criticised that he was forced to leave this country permanently and to return to England in the year 1652. Much correspondence ensued between England and our Springfield with the final result that the book was burned in Boston by order of the General Court.

Pynchon bought land in Wraysbury, just below Windsor Castle, where he lived until he died in 1662. We give a picture of the Pynchon tablet placed in the church in Writtle, England, and also another showing the interior of the church in Wraysbury, England, where William Pynchon was buried. Pynchon's son, John, took his father's place in Springfield, Massachusetts, and it has often been said that they have been to that city what the Adams family has been to Massa-

From "Springfield" by Mason A. Green   *Kindness W. F. Adams, Esq.*

THE PYNCHON TABLET IN WRITTLE, ENGLAND,

to the memory of ancestors of William Pynchon.

INTERIOR OF THE CHURCH IN WRAYSBURY, ENGLAND,

where William Pynchon, founder of Springfield, Massachusetts, is buried.

chusetts and to the country. It is also an interesting fact that the Pynchon family is still prominent to-day in Springfield, Massachusetts, and as there are fourteen towns in this country named for Roxbury and thirteen towns named for Springfield, William Pynchon deserves a foremost position in the history of New England.

The first minister of the Springfield colony was Rev. George Moxon who was installed as pastor in 1638. The first parish meeting-place was not erected, however, until 1645, and it is said to be the first building devoted to religious worship in this State west of Boston and its vicinity; it was, of course, the beginning of the First Church of Springfield, the present church building not being erected until 1819 when Court Square was laid out as a park. Near this church, on State Street, is the well-known St. Gaudens statue of "The Puritan" erected by Chester W. Chapin, Esq., in memory of Deacon Samuel Chapin, one of the founders of the city. Deacon Chapin was one of the first selectmen, was deacon of the first church and, with Pynchon and Elizur Holyoke, was one of the first magistrates of the town. In Court Square is also a statue of Miles Morgan of Bristol, England,

From Barber's Historical Collections

OLD VIEW OF COURT SQUARE, SPRINGFIELD, MASSACHUSETTS

one of the pioneer band who with Pynchon and Chapin settled in the town in 1636. It is interesting to mention that Miles Morgan married in Beverly, Massachusetts; and it is said that the bride and groom were obliged to return to Springfield on foot carrying with them muskets and household articles.

Traffic on the Connecticut River has been discussed continually and at one of the Springfield celebrations this poem, written by Charles H. Barrows, Esq., entitled "To the New Connecticut," was read; it gives a very exaggerated idea, however, of the possibilities of navigation on this fine river:—

> "Let every sleeper waken
>   And all the waking shout,
> Let measures prompt be taken
>   To dredge the harbour out.
>
> Then silent keep, O doubter,
>   We all shall live to see
> A thoroughfare by water
>   From Springfield to the sea.
>
> Soon the white wings of Commerce
>   Will at our port be found,
> And as one sign of promise
>   We will let Long Island 'Sound.'
>
> We'll keep sperm whales, we dreamers,
>   In flocks, at Windsor Locks,
> When European steamers
>   Tie up at Springfield docks."

Springfield, England, is the eastern suburb of Chelmsford. Here is situated the County Gaol, a gloomy building enlarged in recent years for the accommodation of the "guests" consigned to it, but once past this depressing place Springfield is pleasing and cheerful. Its long street, where the quaint sign of the "Three Cups" stands out, gives place to suburban villas with their attractive grounds. The parish church of All Saints is shown on page 171. Goldsmith lived in the town for some time while writing "The Deserted Village."

Other New England towns by the name of Springfield are in Maine, New Hampshire and Vermont.

STRATFORD, CONNECTICUT

OLIVER WENDELL HOLMES wrote the following poem which was read at the dedication of the Shakespeare Memorial Fountain at Stratford-on-Avon in the year 1887:—

"Land of our Fathers, ocean makes us two,
  But heart to heart is true!
Proud is your towering daughter in the West,
Yet in her burning life-blood reign confest
Her mother's pulses beating in her breast.
This holy fount, whose rills from heaven descend,
  Its gracious drops shall lend—
Both foreheads bathed in that baptismal dew,
And love make one the old home and the new!"

On this occasion Henry Irving made the principal speech and there was also read a letter from James Russell Lowell, which expressed his belief that the dust that is sacred to the Englishman is not the less sacred to the American. This memorial, the gift of George W. Childs of Philadelphia, during the jubilee year of Queen Victoria, was placed in the old Rother Market, not far from Shakespeare's birthplace in Henley Street. One of the inscriptions on this fountain records these words of Washington Irving: "Ten thousand blessings on the bard who has gilded the dull realities of life with innocent illusions."

Other places of interest to the visitor in this ancient Warwickshire town, besides the birthplace and the fountain, are Anne Hathaway's cottage; New Place, where once stood the house in which the dramatist lived and died; the Shakespeare Memorial Theatre, Library and Picture Gallery, where performances of his plays are given each year on his birthday—the dramatic season extending over three or four weeks; and his tomb in Holy Trinity Church, visited each year by thousands of tourists. It may be of interest to mention that in the south end of the Clopton Chapel of this church is a window, which was bought with contributions made by visitors from the United States, and is hence known as the American window. Of the Americans who have been fascinated by the old town, we may mention Washington Irving and Nathaniel Hawthorne, who spent much time lingering "on Avon's banks, whose streams appear to wind with eddies fond round Shakespeare's tomb," to quote from a poem written by John G. Cooper. This beautiful river in its relation to Shakespeare is also well described by Longfellow:—

"Flow on, sweet river! like his verse
Who lies beneath this sculptured hearse;
Nor wait beside the churchyard wall
For him who cannot hear thy call."

Washington Irving has made famous the Red Horse Hotel where he so often stayed and where he wrote his "Sketch Book." There is also the Shakespeare Hotel, the building dating back to the fourteenth century. Its old sign upon which appears Shakespeare's portrait and this legend, "Take him for all in all, we shall not look upon his like again," is now shown inside the hotel. Even the bedrooms are named after some of his plays, while the bar was once, and probably still is, decorated by these appropriate words, "Measure for measure." Another point of interest, of course, is Harvard House, the early home of the mother of John Harvard, described in Part I under Cambridge.

It is told on good authority that the great American showman, P. T. Barnum of Bridgeport, Stratford's neighboring city, once endeavored to purchase Shakespeare's birthplace to exhibit at his circuses in this country, while at another time some German professors asked permission to examine Shakespeare's brain to determine whether its size was in proportion to his genius. This last request was made

Photographed by Douglas McNeill,   *Kindness Ian Forbes-Robertson, Esq.*
Stratford-on-Avon

SHAKESPEARE FOUNTAIN, STRATFORD-ON-AVON, ENGLAND,

presented by George W. Childs, of Philadelphia. It was dedicated in 1887, the jubilee year of Queen Victoria, the principal speech being made by Henry Irving. A letter from James Russell Lowell was read at the dedication, as well as a poem written especially for the occasion by Oliver Wendell Holmes.

in spite of the fact that the poet himself is said to have requested that this verse should be cut on his tombstone:—

> "Good frend for Jesus sake forbeare,
> To digg the dust encloased heare:
> Bleste be ye man y^t spares thes stones,
> And curst be he y^t moves my bones."

The Connecticut town is mindful of the fact that it is named for William Shakespeare's home across the seas and, in his memory and as a further recognition of the common literature and heritage of the two countries, the donor of the Stratford

Photographed by George B. Brayton   *From an old drawing by J. Brandard, owned by J. Murray Forbes, Esq.*

SHAKESPEARE'S BIRTHPLACE, STRATFORD-ON-AVON, ENGLAND

Library, Birdseye Blakeman, a native son of the New England Stratford, placed a Shakespeare rose window, with the poet's bust in the center, in the Library when it was built in 1896. This building, which is situated near the old burial place that was set off in 1670, contains a tablet with this inscription:—

IN MEMORY OF
Six generations of ancestors
residents of Stratford
posterity of
REV. ADAM BLAKEMAN
1598–1665
DEA. JOHN BIRDSEYE
1616–1690
This ground was dedicated
and this house built
by
BIRDSEYE BLAKEMAN
1824–1894

From a photograph   *Kindness Miss Frances B. Russell*

STRATFORD LIBRARY, STRATFORD, CONNECTICUT

The Shakespeare window shown in another illustration is the circular window appearing above.

This earliest Blakeman ancestor was a graduate of Oxford University and was such a learned man that he believed the English language was not a suitable vehicle to express a scholar's work, preferring Latin like many others of his day. Another of the earliest settlers in this Connecticut town was William Beardsley, who lived in the English Stratford during the days when Shakespeare was alive; who probably when a boy witnessed the bard's funeral and who is said to have brought across the waters the name of Stratford for our town. A few years ago his connection with Stratford-on-Avon was established by one of his descendants, Mrs. Margaret Beardsley De Lacour, a native of the Connecticut Stratford, who found his record in the parish register there. The town of Avon in New York State was named for the English river by descendants of Beardsley. Other well-known names of the earliest settlers are Curtiss, Fairchild, Hurd, Peat, Sherwood, Wells and Wilcoxson. Two other Englishmen who took a great interest in the New England town were Thomas Welles and his brother John, who are ancestors of this family now living in our Stratford. It may be of interest to record that the first wife of

SHAKESPEARE WINDOW IN THE STRATFORD
LIBRARY, STRATFORD, CONNECTICUT,

placed there by Birdseye Blakeman, donor of the library,
who was a descendant of Rev. Adam Blakeman, one of
the earliest settlers in this New England town.

Thomas **Welles** (who became a governor of Connecticut) was Elizabeth Foote, daughter of John Dening of England, who is supposed to have been related to Shakespeare. A further proof of this relationship is the fact that Dame Elizabeth, wife of Sir John Berrod and grand-daughter of the celebrated poet, requested in her will that £50 be given to her cousin Thomas Welles.

In the record of the descendants of the widow Elizabeth Curtiss who settled in Stratford, Connecticut, 1639–40, which was compiled by Frederic Haines Curtiss, Chairman and Federal Reserve Agent of the Federal Reserve Bank of Boston, is found the following: "John Curtis of London, England, had his coat of arms described below, confirmed May 9, 1632, just forty-two days before William Curtis of Roxbury sailed for New England." In a note of the inhabitants of Roxbury 1638–40 appears the name of John Corteis, but in 1639 John Curtis was a resident of Wethersfield, Connecticut. In 1640 John Curtis left Wethersfield for Cuphag (Stratford) and his name disappears, but we find the widow Elizabeth Curtiss and her two sons on the earliest records of Stratford. The records of the College of Heraldry in London, England, show that the coat of arms was confirmed to John Curtis of London, Gent., son of William Curtis of Hatton in the county of Warwick, Gent., son of Eustace Curtiss of Malestock—spelled also Makestock and Makestoke—in the said county, Gent., son of William, who was son and heir of John Curtis of Malestock aforesaid, Gent.

The Curtis family was from all accounts one of the most prominent among the first settlers of Stratford and it has been claimed that they suggested naming the town after Stratford-on-Avon, England. If this be true, it adds another proof towards the acceptance of the pedigree with the coat of arms, for Makestoke and Hatton were but small hamlets and Stratford-on-Avon was the nearest town of any size. That the name of Curtiss was well known in Shakespeare's town is shown by the fact that the poet used it for one of the characters in "The Taming of the

Shrew." Thomas Alsop and Richard Booth are also supposed to have been natives of Stratford-on-Avon, and as the Earl of Warwick had letters patent to that part of Connecticut, it is more than probable that many of the early settlers throughout the colony were from Warwickshire. The Beardsley, Booth and Curtis families are still largely represented in the Connecticut town, there being at least twenty-five families of the latter name. Judge Howard J. Curtis of the Supreme Court of Connecticut, who is also the President of the Stratford Library Association, is one of the many descendants.

The Art League in the nearby city of Bridgeport, once part of Stratford, Connecticut, has recognized the city's former connection with old Stratford by building in Beardsley Park a reproduction of the Anne Hathaway Cottage.

In 1896, Rev. N. Ellsworth Cornwall, then Rector of Christ Church in Stratford, Connecticut, visited the English Stratford and preached in Holy Trinity Church where, in the chancel, lie the ashes of the famous poet. On leaving, he was presented by the Vicar, Rev. G. Arbuthnot, with a flag of the Church of England and a tile from the chancel of Trinity Church which was then being repaired; the tile has attached to it the following presentation: "This ancient tile was found under the stalls of Stratford-on-Avon Church when the chancel was restored a few years ago. It is presented to the Rector of Stratford, Connecticut, N. Ellsworth Cornwall, by the Vicar of Stratford-on-Avon, G. Arbuthnot, who hopes that it may be preserved as a slight mark of the unity and concord which prevail between the Episcopal Church of America and the Church of England. XII Sunday after Trinity MDCCCXCVI."

Christ Church celebrated its bicentennial in 1907 and at that time the Rev. G. Arbuthnot sent the following letter of greeting to the Rev. N. Ellsworth Cornwall:—

"The Vicarage,
Stratford-on-Avon,
May 18, 1907.

Rev. N. E. Cornwall,
    Christ Church Rectory,
        Stratford, Conn., U.S.A.

My dear Rector,
    I am much obliged to you for sending me the paper with the most interesting account of the proceedings at Stratford in connection with its anniversary, and I write to extend to you and to your congregation the fraternal greetings of Stratford in the Old Country. I hope we may some day have the pleasure of seeing you here again, and when that takes place that you will spend a Sunday with us and occupy my pulpit. It is indeed pleasant to think that the membership of the one Catholic Church can bridge over so many miles of ocean.
    With kind regards and renewed thanks for your remembrance, I remain,

Yours very truly,

G. Arbuthnot."

Some years later, in April 1911, at the annual Shakespeare festival in Stratford-on-Avon, Mr. H. Snowden Ward, a well-known lecturer on Shakespeare, carried a greeting to the Shakespeare Club of the English town from a number of Shakespeare Clubs in America, including the one in Cambridge, Massachusetts, the Twentieth Century Club and the Art Club in Boston, Massachusetts, and the Stratford Library in Connecticut. At this meeting Mr. Ward declared that he represented Stratford, Connecticut, the first of this name in America. This New England town at the same time sent a wreath to be placed on Shakespeare's tomb and also two greetings in verse written by residents of our town. One of the greetings was written by Arthur Powell, a resident of the Connecticut Stratford, who was born in Warwickshire and who is a descendant of the Quincy family, one of whom, Thomas Quincy, married Judith Shakespeare. He, therefore, can claim relationship with Shakespeare. The other greeting was written by Louise de Forest Shelton and is quoted below:—

"A GREETING TO STRATFORD-ON-AVON
FROM STRATFORD, CONNECTICUT, U.S.A.

From this Stratford in New England
Send we greeting o'er the sea
To old Stratford-on-the-Avon
For this week's festivity.
As you honour the great Poet
We would send our homage, too,
From this small New England village—
Stratford Shakespeare never knew.
But we treasure on our bookshelves
Shakespeare's spirit—heart and thought—
And we feel a closer kinship
For the name the Settlers brought
From that England where our forbears
Lived and loved, before they came
To this strange and unknown country,
Bringing a familiar name.
As you sing the Poet's praises,
We in spirit join the throng—
From this Stratford of the New World
Comes an echo of your song.
Kinship, friendship, even greater
Is the tie that binds us fast—
Proud are we to be the namesake
Born from out so great a Past."

There is also a Stratford in New Hampshire.

SUDBURY, MASSACHUSETTS

WHEN Sudbury celebrated its two hundred and fiftieth anniversary, the presiding officer introduced Dr. Brooke Herford, an Englishman, then minister of the Arlington Street Church, Boston. "I know," said the presiding officer, "one fact that interests us to-day, and that is that the name of our town of Sudbury was taken from the town of Sudbury in England. Our settlers were Englishmen; we are descendants from these representative men, and we are fortunate to-day in having with us an Englishman, a representative Englishman. . . . Dr. Brooke Herford." Dr. Herford in his response emphasized this fact: "I am here to answer for England, as I have been chosen for that purpose. In the speeches that have been made it seems to me that England has most of the glory for what has been done, for it was carefully emphasized that they were Englishmen who came to settle this part of the country."

To the rich lands bordering the Musketahquid, now the Sudbury River, English settlers came in 1638, having previously made plans in Watertown for forming this settlement. The land was purchased from the Indians, and the town incorporated in 1639, being called Sudbury for the mother town in England. Of a splendid type of the historic Puritan were these pioneers in the region of Musketahquid— men of such sterling qualities as Walter Haynes, Peter Noyce, John Blandford, John Bent and John Rutter, all of whom were passengers in the ship "Confidence" that sailed from Southampton, England.

To-day the historic town of Sudbury is sought by visitors from many lands, and the old Wayside Inn, one of the most delightful places of interest in the town, is made memorable by Henry Wadsworth Longfellow in these words:—

"One autumn night, in Sudbury town,
Across the meadows bare and brown,
The windows of the Wayside Inn
Gleamed red with firelight through the leaves
Of woodbine, hanging from the eaves
Their crimson curtains rent and thin.
As ancient is this hostelry
As any in the land may be,
Built in the old Colonial day,
When men lived in a grander way,
With ampler hospitality;
A kind of old Hobgoblin Hall,
Now somewhat fallen to decay,
With weather-stains upon the wall,
And stairways worn, and crazy doors,
And creaking and uneven floors,
And chimneys huge, and tiled and tall."

There is also a Sudbury in Vermont.

Sudbury, England, is in Suffolk County, and is principally noted for its three

Photographed by Charles F. Emeny   *Kindness Ian Forbes-Robertson, Esq.*

GAINSBOROUGH'S BIRTHPLACE IN SUDBURY, ENGLAND

historic churches. St. Gregory's Church attracts the most attention for it is reputed that here reposes the head of that unfortunate Simon of Sudbury, the Archbishop of Canterbury, who was beheaded in 1381 by Wat Tyler's mob. He had previously rebuilt much of this church in which the head is so often viewed by the curious and lovers of the grewsome. His body is laid beneath the altar-stone in Canterbury Cathedral. St. Gregory's Church stands on the site of an earlier Saxon church of wood. A curious tombstone dated 1706, in St. Anne's Chapel commemorating a certain Thomas Carter, states that on the day on which he breathed his last "a Sudbury camel passed through the eye of a needle."

Old Sudbury's greatest man was the son of a clothier and has come down in history as Thomas Gainsborough, the painter. He was born there in 1727 in the house shown above and there is also a statue of him in the town. At the back of this building was an orchard from which fruit was constantly being stolen and no one was able to catch the thief. Gainsborough early in life proved his deftness with a pencil, by sketching the man as he scaled the fence to climb a pear tree. The young artist had risen early to work in a summer house that adjoined the orchard and thus had a very good view of the thief. His sketch was so realistic that every one recognized it as a Sudbury man and ever after the picture was known as "Tom Peartree's Portrait." When the painter became famous he frequently returned to his native town, and many of his paintings are called "a view near Sudbury." In the Grammar School are his initials deep cut beneath a caricature of his master, and his birthplace still stands in the town.

The name "Sudbury" is of Saxon origin and comes from South Burgh. Records show that its charter was granted during the reign of Queen Mary. The town contains some beautiful examples of timbered houses with overhanging upper stories.

TAUNTON, MASSACHUSETTS

"We cannot name them in our song,
    But cherish in our heart,
And in old Taunton's fair renown
    Would bear a filial part."

(Part of a poem written by Mrs. Eleanor S. Deane on the two hundred and fiftieth anniversary of the settlement of Taunton.)

IN 1890 Judge Edmund H. Bennett, first Mayor of Taunton, Massachusetts, visited Taunton, England, this being one of the first, if not the first, of the visits of officials of one Taunton to the other. We give on the next page a reproduction of a photograph taken at Dunster Castle showing Judge Bennett on the steps of the Castle with officials of the English town by whom he was very hospitably entertained. This picture now hangs in the office of the City Clerk, Taunton, Massachusetts.

On September 13, 1900, Mayor William Alfred Wrenn of Taunton, England, visited our Taunton to convey the respects of his borough, and to do honour to the early settlers of our town, who on March 3, 1639, settled here, changing the name from Cohannet to Taunton, as they expressed it, "in honour and love to our dear and native country." His visit may have been made in response to the cable sent some months before by the Aldermen of our Taunton, which read as follows:—

"Ordered that in consideration of the fact that the Taunton and Somerset Society of London, England, holds its annual meeting on May 2nd, and that the Society represents the ancestry of many of the citizens of Taunton and vicinity, the greetings and best wishes of the Mayor and Board of Aldermen of Taunton, Mass. be cabled to that Society."

Mayor Wrenn was enthusiastically received and presented the following resolutions as an expression of good will from his native town:—

"The Council of the Borough of Taunton, England, take the opportunity of the contemplated visit of their Mayor to Taunton, Mass. U.S.A. of continuing the friendly intercommunication which has for some years past taken place between the two towns, by sending friendly greetings and expressing a hope that continued and increased prosperity and happiness is being bestowed upon the citizens of Taunton, Mass. More particularly is the occasion taken advantage of, to accept most gratefully the kind and spontaneous expression of sympathy by the people of Taunton, Mass. with England in the dreadful war in So. Africa. The substantial contribution sent by the people of Taunton, Mass. in aid of the funds collected in England for the widows and children of soldiers who have lost their lives through the war, has awakened feelings of gratitude and affection not only in the town of Taunton, England, but amongst the English people."

From a photograph in the office of the City Clerk, Taunton, Massachusetts   *Kindness Edwin A. Tetlow, Esq.*

JUDGE EDMUND H. BENNETT, FIRST MAYOR OF TAUNTON, MASSACHUSETTS, ON A
VISIT TO DUNSTER CASTLE, NEAR TAUNTON, SOMERSETSHIRE, ENGLAND,

as the guest of the Corporation officials of that town in 1890. Judge Bennett is the third figure from the
left in the second row from the top.

Our Mayor presented to the distinguished visitor a beautiful silver loving cup as
a token and memento of his happy visit to the city and a few days later our Common Council addressed the following lines to the mother town:—

"WHEREAS on September 13, 1900, His Worship William Alfred Wrenn of Taunton,
England, visited us bringing with him a message of friendship, fraternity, and good-will
from the citizens and governing body of that city, which he presented with eloquent and
instructive words, now be it *Resolved*, that Taunton in New England through vote of its
Council express its hearty appreciation of the sentiment contained in the message, and the
pleasure that it has afforded the municipality to entertain the distinguished messenger.
It would further convey to its English cousins the sincere hope and desire that the future
may witness a continuation and greater development of that far reaching spirit of fellowship which exists between the two cities, binding each year closer the ties of international
duty; and be it further *Resolved*, that a copy of these resolutions be suitably engrossed
and forwarded to the Mayor and governing body of Taunton, England."

All of this interesting correspondence is filed in the City Hall of our Taunton.

Our Taunton was not settled directly from Taunton in the mother country, but the early comers were from the southwest counties of England near ancient Taunton and this led them to select this name for their home in the western world. The earliest record we have of new Taunton is that Edward Winslow and Stephen Hopkins walked through Taunton to Narragansett Bay to hold an important meeting with the Indian King Massasoit. The first real record of Taunton, however, was in 1637, when Richard Williams and a few Puritans from Dorchester built some houses there. We are told that the idea of erecting a memorial in memory of Williams has been agitated several times by the family. There is a bridge over the Taunton River which is called the "Williams Bridge," but this was not erected as a memorial. Not long after Williams and his little band settled there they were followed by the families of Dean, Baylies, Tisdale, Morton, Cobb, Crocker, Lovering, Hall, Pool, Crossman, Williams and others. There are memorials erected near

From a photograph   *Kindness Miss Edith M. Hodgman and Edwin A. Tetlow, Esq.*

MONUMENT IN MT. PLEASANT CEMETERY, TAUNTON, MASSACHUSETTS,

over the grave of Elisabeth Pool, who purchased a large tract of land from the Indians near here, and who did much to build up the town in the early days. Her family came from Taunton, England.

the home and on the grave of Elisabeth Pool, who bought a large tract of land from the Indians and became an active promoter of local interests. Miss Pool's family had long lived in Taunton, Somerset County, England. During the two hundred and fiftieth anniversary of the town there was a tableau showing her making this purchase from the Indians, and this scene is depicted on the seal of the city.

There have been many other interesting interchanges of presents and correspondence between the two places, the most important of which occurred during the two hundred and fiftieth anniversary which took place in 1889. The Mayor

Photographed by Montague Cooper from an old print   *Kindness Ian Forbes-Robertson, Esq.*

OLD VIEW OF TAUNTON, ENGLAND
St. James Church is on the right and St. Mary Magdalene's on the left.

of old Taunton presented to the Old Colony Historical Society in new Taunton a stone cherub from St. Mary Magdalene's Church, which is now in the rooms of the Historical Society; also about the same time Edward Lebault of Taunton, England, gave to the Society a piece of the altar railing and pulpit ornament which was formerly a part of this same church. Invitations were sent to the Mayor, Aldermen and Councillors of the English town to be present at this celebration, and the following reply from the Mayor of Taunton was received:—

"I beg to thank you and your Committee for your kind feelings towards us, and to assure you that although we shall not be present at your celebration our hearts will be with you, and we trust you will have a pleasant and enjoyable time. Our Corporation has decided to send you an address of congratulation which is being prepared."

Many letters were exchanged between residents of the two places on both sides of the water, one of which describes in an interesting way a visit that James Russell Lowell made to the old town, on which occasion he delivered a lecture on Henry Fielding of Somersetshire, "The Father of the English Novel."

After the celebration, the English Mayor again wrote and sent an address from his town which was framed in a piece of oak taken from St. Mary's Tower which was torn down thirty years before. This interesting souvenir is now hanging in the Aldermanic Chamber in our Taunton. A view of the old town was also shown attached to this address, also a cut of the old castle which is now used as a museum. The formal message received at the same time read as follows:—

"Although unable to be present ... we can assure you that the ties of kindred and tongue which bind your mighty Nation to the mother country are still further strengthened by the remembrance that there exists on the other side of the Atlantic a city worthy of handing down to posterity the name of Taunton which is endeared to us by the recollection of its historical past, the contemplation of its prosperous present and the promise of a still brighter future."

Our Mayor and Council again replied and sent a souvenir of the celebration, together with an attractive picture showing the "Mayflower" in Plymouth Harbour, a view of Taunton River, a sketch of Taunton Green and a picture of the City Hall. The message shown in the accompanying photograph was framed from a timber that came from the English ship "Sparrowhawk" which was wrecked off Cape Cod in 1626, the hull of which vessel is now one of the relics exhibited in Pilgrim Hall in our Plymouth. The message reads as follows:—

Photographed by Montague Cooper   *Kindness Ian Forbes-Robertson, Esq.*

MESSAGE SENT BY TAUNTON, MASSACHU-SETTS, TO TAUNTON, ENGLAND, IN 1889, on the occasion of the two hundred and fiftieth anniversary of our city. The frame is cut from a timber that came from the English vessel "Sparrowhawk," which was wrecked off Cape Cod in 1626. The hull of this ship is now in Pilgrim Hall, Plymouth, Massachusetts.

"THE MAYOR, ALDERMEN, AND COMMON COUNCIL OF
    TAUNTON, IN NEW ENGLAND

    TO THE
MAYOR, ALDERMEN, AND BURGESSES OF TAUNTON IN OLD ENGLAND.

Greeting ... We have been deeply touched by the reception of your kind Address of Congratulation upon the celebration of the 250th Anniversary of the foundation of our City, which happily arrived on the very day of its occurrence. We assure you that we fully reciprocate your kindly sentiments, so pleasantly expressed, and we fondly cherish the memory of your ancient, brave, and loyal Borough, with its historic castle, its beautiful Church of St. Mary, and its charming river in that lovely vale of Taunton Dean.

We wonder not that our fathers chose our name 'in honour and love to their dear and native country,' and we congratulate ourselves that they brought with them from their own land those lofty and sterling principles of thought and action which have contributed so much to our prosperity, and secured for us the manifold blessings we now enjoy.

May we never bring discredit on our ancient name, but rather lead our English mother to ever feel a just pride in her American daughter, and may the bonds of love and amity between us, and between our respective countries grow stronger till time shall be no more.

Given in our Council Chamber this eighth
    day of August A.D. 1889."

An interesting account of the celebration appeared in one of the English newspapers in Taunton, entitled "Taunton's American Daughter."

Wilfred Marshall of Taunton, England, is very familiar with our town, having visited it three or four times.

That the citizens of Taunton, England, still keep up their interest in the New England city is evidenced by a visit made here in February, 1921, by Thomas I. Perry, a local magistrate of the mother town, who called upon Mayor Coughlin and the other officials at City Hall. In discussing the visit to Taunton, Massachusetts, made by former Mayor Wrenn of his town in 1900, he stated that the late Mayor's widow was the first woman member of the town council of Taunton, England.

"Ich was bore at Taunton Deane where should I be bore else?" is the boast of the inhabitants of old Taunton and the nearby towns, which are situated in what is called "Taunton Dean" or the "Vale of Taunton." The name Taunton is derived from the river Thone, sometimes called Tone, which flows through the town. The name is also sometimes said to have been derived from the Gaelic "Taun" meaning "of the river" and "town," contracted into Taunton. The castle of Taunton built by the Bishop of Winchester (see next page) is the important object of interest in the town. Near this site there was once a castle which was built in 700 by Ina, King of Wessex, who dwelt there. The present castle held out very gallantly against the royal forces in 1625 and the following lines indicate the joy of the town on being saved:—

> "The eleventh of May was a joyful day,
>   When Taunton got relief;
> Which turned our sorrows into joy,
>   And eased us of our grief."

The full history of this castle is one long record of romance and to the New Englander who has read of the witchcraft and superstition of his country, it may be interesting to mention one of the objects that is religiously kept in this old building. It was believed that if a pig died, a witch had "overlooked it," to use an English expression. After the pig's death its heart was filled with pins, stuck into it as in a pin-cushion, and it was then put in the chimney. As long as the heart remained there, it was supposed that no witch could have power over any other pig belonging

Photographed by Montague Cooper from an old print   *Kindness Ian Forbes-Robertson, Esq.*

TAUNTON CASTLE, TAUNTON, ENGLAND

The castle dates back to the eighth century, although it has been much renovated.

to that house. A very old example was found in an ancient house and removed to this castle, where it is still exhibited as a relic of the old days.

It may be interesting to mention that Thomas Chaucer, the son of Geoffrey Chaucer, "the father of English poetry," was at one time constable of this castle, which gives us an idea of its antiquity.

There is a village near our Taunton called Britanniaville, so named because of the fact that britannia ware was first manufactured in the United States in an old building now belonging to the Reed and Barton Corporation. The village arose around this little shop. The ware was so named because it originated in Britain near Sheffield. A number of Englishmen came over from England to work in this trade and their countrymen have continued to come up to the present time.

TOPSFIELD, MASSACHUSETTS

NOT long ago when a visitor from Topsfield, Massachusetts, visited the mother town, the driver of the carriage, in reply to the question as to how the English Toppesfield got its name, said: "Well, they must-a-caught it as it came along. Come by a whirlwind perhaps." Another old character declared it was probable that it was so named on account of being the topmost village in the shire. The place undoubtedly derived its name in Saxon times from a chieftain called Toppa, who owned this territory. At various times the town has been called Toppesfend, Toppesford and Thopefield.

A visitor to the mother town from New England on looking over the church register at St. Margaret's in this Essex village found the following names, all well known to our Topsfield and vicinity: Allen, Barker, Barnes, Clarke, Davison, Hale, Hardy, Palmer, Reed, Rice, Smith, Wildes and Wilson. In this church register appears the name of "Samuel Symonds, Gent." and his wife Dorothy, as well as the records of baptism of their ten children born between the years 1621 and 1633. Samuel Symonds afterwards lived in Ipswich in New England and was a prominent man and "Assistant" or member of the Governor's Council. It was Symonds who was responsible for the change of name from New Meadows to Topsfield in remembrance of the parish in old England where he had worshipped.

From a photograph   *Kindness George Francis Dow, Esq.*

TOPPESFIELD, ENGLAND,

from which place Topsfield, Massachusetts, received its name.

From a photograph　　　　　　　　　　　　　　　　　　　*Kindness George Francis Dow, Esq.*

ST. MARGARET'S CHURCH, TOPPESFIELD, ENGLAND

Samuel Symonds, the Assistant, who settled in Ipswich in the Massachusetts Bay Colony and was instrumental in the naming of Topsfield, was a communicant in this church and here his children were baptized. There are also a number of other names in the register of the English church that are well known in this New England town.

Zaccheus Gould, another early settler, wanted the settlement called Hempstead because he came from Hemel Hempstead in England, but the Court ruled otherwise. Other early settlers besides Gould were William Perkins of London, William Towne, William Howard, Francis Peabody, John Wilde and Thomas Baker.

Topsfield, Massachusetts, received its name in 1650, although it was settled as early as 1639; it was an offshoot of Agawam, the early name of Ipswich and those chiefly responsible for its settlement were two of the party of John Winthrop, Jr., who left Ipswich to come over to this new town.

A well-known minister in our Topsfield was Rev. Joseph Capen of witchcraft times, who married a daughter of John Appleton of Ipswich and whose fine old seventeenth century manse with overhanging second-story has been restored and now is owned and occupied by the local Historical Society. This attractive New England town has become the favorite summer resort of many prominent people.

The only interchange which has taken place between the daughter and mother towns occurred in August, 1900, at the two hundred and fiftieth anniversary of the incorporation of Topsfield. At this time a cable of congratulations from Toppes-field, England, was read at the meeting and a suitable reply flashed back to the English town, while the school-children sang "To thee, O Country."

Mr. George Francis Dow in his address at this two hundred and fiftieth anniversary relates an amusing story concerning "Goodman" Neland, who had built his house across the boundary line between Topsfield and Ipswich. Fcr years the constables called to collect taxes and always found him in the other part of the house and therefore, of course, in the other town. Finally the Topsfield constable on one of his visits climbed into the pig-pen and secured a good fat pig, the sale of which enabled him to recover the necessary taxes.

Topsfield, Maine, a small township in the eastern part of the State, was christened in honour of Topsfield, Massachusetts, by Nehemiah Kneeland who moved to Maine from the Massachusetts town.

WALTHAM, MASSACHUSETTS

ON January 16, 1888, there was held in the Music Hall in Waltham the celebration of the one hundred and fiftieth anniversary of the founding of the town, on which occasion the residents paid their homage to the spirit of the past by flying in the building many American and British flags draped together, and by surmounting one group of banners with a shield bearing the arms and motto of the Prince of Wales. There have been no official visits between the two Walthams, though many people from our city have journeyed to Waltham Abbey, from which our city derived its name. Although at the present time there is little in the appearance of the prosperous Massachusetts city that would recall the historic old English town, it is probable that at the time of the incorporation of our Waltham in 1738, there was some similarity between the "forest home" on the Charles River and that on the river Lea. The name Waltham is supposed to be derived from the Saxon "Wealdham," meaning a "home in the forest," or "wild," and to this day forests cover probably more than half of the territory of the New England city. Certainly visions of "Harold's town" with the Lea winding in and out among the fertile meadows must have been in the minds of William Brown, Samuel Livermore, Daniel Benjamin and other dwellers in the western precinct of Watertown, Massachusetts, when, their petition to have their precinct "erected into a separate and distinct township" having been granted, they conferred upon the newly made town the name of Waltham. As one historian has suggested, it must have been peculiarly gratifying to these early settlers "thus to preserve ever present amid new associations and surroundings the recollections of their old homes across the sea." The first actual settler within the town limits is supposed to have been John Page who in 1643 had a house near the present Watertown line; Samuel Bigelow had a house on the western part of the Great Country Road before 1686, while Allen Flagg and Jonathan Sanderson built at Piety Corner about 1689. Waltham has furnished two Massachusetts Governors, Christopher Gore, who was at one time United States Senator and also special Minister to England, and Nathaniel P. Banks.

The English village is located on the left bank of the river Lea, about twelve miles northeast of London, in the county of Essex, to which locality also belongs Nasing, the birthplace of the Rev. John Eliot, famous for his religious ministrations to the Indians and the early settlers of New England. No small part of John Eliot's early work was among the Indians in the vicinity of Watertown and Waltham, and the fact that Waltham Abbey was near Nasing may have suggested to the early settlers this name for the American town. The exact place where Eliot preached was on the shore of a large sheet of water which was first called the "Great Pond in the Woods," and the Indian tribe to which he preached continued on its shores until the year 1676.

To those familiar with its history, both authentic and legendary, the name of old Waltham will ever be tinged with romance. Thither came Tovi the Proud, standard-bearer to Canute the Dane, King of England, early in the eleventh century, and built for himself in the forest a hunting seat, near which he established a village of "three score and six dwellers." Here also he founded, about 1020 A.D., the Church of the Holy Cross and thus it came about that the town was also called at one time Waltham Holy Cross. Later Waltham came into the possession of Earl Harold, who, out of gratitude for his wonderful cure by the "holy cross," erected in 1059 a monastery upon the site of Tovi's church. After Harold was killed in 1066 in the famous battle of Hastings he was buried in this monastery which, as stated below, came to be known later as Waltham Abbey. In 1177, Harold's college was dissolved and an Augustinian Priory was founded by Henry II, which in 1184 became Waltham Abbey. The history of this edifice is, as old Thomas Fuller says, "the history of the Church of England." To this Abbey came, for various reasons, many of the English royalty, from the time of Harold, its founder, to the days of Charles II.

One of the most picturesque corners of the old town is "Romeland," an open square of quaint, high-gabled and stuccoed red brick houses, while in another part, spanning the Corn Mill stream, is a remnant of very early architecture known as Harold's Bridge. In Waltham also is the house of Master Cressy, in which Cranmer, Fox and Gardner in 1533 discussed the question of the separation of Henry VIII from Catherine of Aragon. Here in the forests the Stuarts did a great deal of hunting and near Waltham still can be seen the house where it is said that James I, during one of his hunts, using his sword for a carving-knife, patted a joint of beef and called it "Sir Loin." Beautiful Epping Forest, the playground of thousands of Londoners on bank holidays, is near Waltham.

WALTHAM ABBEY, WALTHAM. ENGLAND

There is one historic feature in the old English town of Waltham which visitors will always be interested in, and that is old Temple Bar which for several centuries stood at the west end of Fleet Street and was one of the entrances into the real old city of London. In the year 1878 Temple Bar was entirely removed and was subsequently rebuilt at the entrance to Theobald's Park, Waltham. The first mention of the Bar is in 1361, and a curious custom was from time immemorial observed at this point. Before the Sovereign could enter the city proper his carriage was halted while the Lord Mayor presented his sword of office to the monarch, who after receiving the sword returned it to the Mayor, and until this ceremony had been gone through the King was not allowed to enter the city. A huge stone griffin, or dragon, now occupies the site of the ancient Temple Bar.

In 1813, the works of the Boston Manufacturing Company were established in our Waltham, and not only for the manufacturing of cotton goods did the city become noted, but also for the watches made at the famous Waltham Watch factory, supposed to be the largest works of its kind in existence. The Gore and Lyman estates, the most attractive probably of the time, carry out the meaning of the word Waltham, "a home in a forest," on account of their beautiful trees. The Lyman place was originally granted to William Paine, being later purchased by John Livermore, who came to this country in 1634 and who was one of the most important men of the town, besides being the progenitor of most of the Livermores in this country. The descendants of John Livermore owned this place until 1780, when it was sold to Jonas Dix. In 1793 it came into the possession of Theodore Lyman, whose descendants still occupy the old residence. Isaac Stearns, a grandson of one of the early pioneers, and William Wellington also owned much land in the early days of the town. We read of many Fourth of July celebrations held on Stearns's wood-lot and in Wellington's Grove, which were both usually full of partridges and quail.

There is also a Waltham in Maine and one in Vermont.

WARWICK, MASSACHUSETTS, AND WARWICK, RHODE ISLAND

SAMUEL GORTON, who was born in Gorton, England, and who probably named Portsmouth, Rhode Island, was the founder of the Rhode Island Warwick in 1642, those associated with him being Randall Holden and John Greene, both of Salisbury, England, and Francis Weston. They were soon driven out of their settlement by the Massachusetts Bay Colony troops, but after obtaining royal sanction for their settlement returned to it. The final success of Gorton and his few followers against the overwhelming number of their enemies, the Massachusetts Bay colonists, greatly impressed the Indians, as described by Gorton in these words:—

Photographed by F. Frith & Co., Surrey, England   *Kindness Ian Forbes-Robertson, Esq.*

WARWICK CASTLE, WARWICKSHIRE, ENGLAND

"The Indians called the English in their tongue Wattaconoges (meaning those who wear clothes or coat men). They now called us Gortonoges, and being that they had heard of a great war to be in Old England, they presently framed unto them a cause of our deliverance, imagining that there were two kinds of people in Old England, the one called by the name of Englishmen and the other Gortonoges; and concluded that the Gortonoges were a mightier people than the English . . . and therefore . . . thought it not safe to take away our lives because however few there were of us in New England in comparison with those who came out against us, yet that great people in Old England would come over and put them to death if they should take away our lives." This town was named for Robert, Earl of Warwick, Lord High Admiral, rather than for the leading town of Warwickshire, known as the "Heart of England." We have, nevertheless, included Warwick on account of the prominence of the English town and its attractiveness to Americans and Englishmen. The Earl of Warwick was Governor-in-Chief of Foreign Plantations and chairman of the Commission that granted the charter to the Rhode Island town and affirmed Gorton's right to Shawomet. It was out of gratitude to him that the old name of Shawomet was changed to Warwick in the year 1647. Thousands of Americans each year visit the old residential seat of the Earls of Warwick, Warwick Castle, now leased to Henry W. Marsh, Esq., of New York, of

From a photograph

Kindness Herbert H. White, Esq., Dr. Edward H. Nichols and Thomas S. Longridge, Esq.

THE HARVARD SURGICAL UNIT, AT WARWICK CASTLE, WARWICKSHIRE, ENGLAND,

guests of Mr. and Mrs. Henry W. Marsh, on its way to France where it gained a splendid reputation during its uninterrupted service in taking care of one-tenth of the British casualties on the Western front. Mr. and Mrs. Marsh, of New York, have leased Warwick Castle for a number of years. Mr. Marsh, Harvard '85, was the Assistant Manager of the Unit, of which Mr. Herbert H. White was the Manager. The heads of this Unit at different times were: Dr. Edward H. Nichols, Dr. W. E. Faulkner, Dr. David Cheever, Dr. Daniel F. Jones, Dr. Carl W. Robinson, Dr. Benjamin K. Emerson, and Dr. Hugh Cabot, the latter having "carried on" to the end of the war.

the Harvard Class of '85, who was Assistant Manager of the Harvard Surgical Unit which did such splendid work during the war that it was commended in a letter written by King George V. The Unit began service on July 17, 1915, at the 22nd General Hospital in France, where it "carried on" till the end of the war, caring for a tenth of the British casualties on the Western Front. On its return to Boston, the weather-stained Stars and Stripes and the Union Jack which had flown over the hospital during the years of strife were presented at a mass meeting at the Harvard Club of Boston to President Lowell, who turned them over to the Harvard Medical School. The members of this Unit were entertained at the Castle on their way through England and while there had an opportunity to see the wonderful paintings by Van Dyck, Velasquez, Reynolds, Rubens, Holbein and others, also the peacocks for which the Castle has long been famous, and the attractive grounds. One of the curios of the Castle is a huge bowl known as Guy's Punchbowl, so named after the celebrated mythical personage "Guy of Warwick." This curiosity was made for Sir John Talbot, and an old couplet makes reference to him and his odd bowl in these words:—

> "There's nothing left of Talbot's fame
> But Talbot's Pot and Talbot's Lane."

The English borough is situated near the center of the shire, on a hill encircled by a long curve of the Avon and within sight of the Castle grounds where the well-known Warwickshire hounds have often hunted their fox. Nearby is Leamington, a score of years ago one of the great fox-hunting centers of England. Henry James was very fond of Warwickshire, in fact it was a place to which the intellectuals of both hemispheres journeyed, including Sir Walter Scott, Nathaniel Hawthorne, who wrote of Warwick in "Our Old Home," Thackeray, Dickens and George Eliot.

Near the Castle is St. Mary's Church, and in the middle of the choir appear recumbent figures representing the first Thomas Beauchamp, Earl of Warwick, and his second wife, who both died in 1369. This Thomas Beauchamp was one of the ancestors of Randall Holden's wife. The great feature of this church is Beauchamp Chapel and in it lies the body of Richard Beauchamp, Earl of Warwick, who died in 1439, and Robert Dudley, Earl of Leicester, the favorite of Queen Elizabeth. Dudley founded the Leicester Hospital in Warwick. The tower of St. Mary's Church contains a peal of ten bells which plays a tune every three hours, but a different tune every day of the week, which serves to remind the townspeople not only of the hour but of the day. A mile north of Warwick on the banks of the Avon is the famous Guy's Cliff, in far-off ages the retreat of the pilgrim Sir Guy. The present mansion of Guy's Cliff, which dates from the beginning of the eighteenth century, is partially hewn out of solid rock.

The English Warwick held a great pageant during the week of July 4, 1906, on the Castle grounds on the occasion of the one thousandth anniversary of Queen

Photographed by F. Frith & Co., Surrey, England   Kindness Ian Forbes-Robertson, Esq.

LEICESTER HOSPITAL, WARWICK, ENGLAND

Ethelfreda's conquest of Mercia. On that day, the Stars and Stripes were displayed on the grandstand, and the namesakes of Warwick in this country, which doubtless included the Warwicks of New England, were represented on this occasion. This group was photographed, but unfortunately the plate was lost.

The Massachusetts Warwick, which is near Worcester, has sometimes been called the "Switzerland of America." It was one of the four grants made by the General Court in 1735 for his "Majestie's Province in the Massachusetts Bay." Samuel Newall and others signed the first petition for the town, which was called the "plantation of Roxbury," or "Gardner's Canada," so called because the preference of sites was given to those who were descendants of the officers and soldiers who served in the expedition to Canada in 1690. Warwick was incorporated in 1763 and was named either for Warwick or for Guy, Earl of Warwick.

From " Ancestry & Descendants of Sir Richard Saltonstall," Riverside Press, 1897

Kindness R. M. Saltonstall, Esq.

CHURCH OF ST. JOHN THE BAPTIST, HALIFAX, YORKSHIRE, ENGLAND,

in which many marriages and baptisms of members of the Saltonstall family have taken place. Sir Richard Saltonstall, who came from Halifax, founded Watertown, Massachusetts.

WATERTOWN, MASSACHUSETTS

THE family of Sir Richard Saltonstall, who sailed from Yarmouth, England, in the ship "Arbella," and who founded our Watertown, came from the small villages of Nether and Over Saltonstall, which are a part of Halifax, in the West Riding of Yorkshire. Mr. Richard M. Saltonstall, who has edited an interesting book, written by Hon. Leverett Saltonstall, describing Sir Richard Saltonstall's ancestry and descendants, a short time ago visited the two villages in England which are named for his family and when he arrived there the people expressed their fear that one of the family had come back to claim the land. These two hamlets (of which we give pictures, on this page and the next) are very small and almost deserted, yet they form a most interesting link between England and America. Back of these old towns is Saltonstall Moor, which is well known to sportsmen.

The English family of Saltonstall can be traced back from Thomas de Saltonstall to Frederick II, Earl of Guilford, the first record we have beginning with the former. In 1597, a Sir Richard Saltonstall was Lord Mayor of London. We have included a cut of the Church of St. John the Baptist in Halifax, where from the year

From "Ancestry & Descendants of Sir Richard Saltonstall," Riverside Press, 1897   *Kindness R. M. Saltonstall, Esq.*

NETHER SALTONSTALL, NEAR HALIFAX, ENGLAND

Here lived the Saltonstall family so well known in this country, and early settlers in Watertown, Haverhill and Ipswich, Massachusetts.

From "Ancestry & Descendants of Sir Richard Saltonstall," Riverside Press, 1897　　　　*Kindness R. M. Saltonstall, Esq.*

THE OLD CHAPEL, OVER SALTONSTALL, NEAR HALIFAX, ENGLAND

1539 have been recorded forty-four marriages and one hundred and twenty baptisms in the Saltonstall family.

The records in this country show that "Sir Richard Saltonstall, Rev. George Phillips, and a goodly number of planters went up the Charles River four miles to a place well watered" and settled their plantation just below the place where Mt. Auburn is now situated and very near the home of the late James Russell Lowell. This territory, the fourth settlement in the Colony, was first called "Sir Richard Saltonstall's Plantation," but was later named Watertown by the Court, either on account of its natural features or, more probably, from a place by the name of Waterton in England. Saltonstall was the first subscriber to the church covenant of Watertown and he was also an original patentee of Connecticut with Lord Saye and Sele, Lord Brooke and others. Saltonstall remained in Watertown only a short time, but was always interested in the Colony, his two sons remaining there after he had left. Saltonstall Square in Watertown was named after him in remembrance of all he did for the settlement in its first days. President Quincy said of him that after Harvard and Winthrop he was the next greatest benefactor of Harvard College. The Saltonstall family had much to do with the Ipswich settlement and for five generations lived in and helped Haverhill.

There is also a Watertown in Connecticut.

WEYMOUTH, MASSACHUSETTS

"Cohasset for beauty,
Hingham for pride,
If not for its herring,
Weymouth had died."

THE chief feature of interest between the two Weymouths is the visit of Judge Louis A. Cook to old Weymouth in 1914, to attend the unveiling of the memorial that was placed there to John Endicott of Dorchester, England, and Richard Clark, near the wharf from which they sailed, the former to Salem, America, to become Governor of the Massachusetts Bay Colony, and the latter, a "most knowing pilot, ship master and adventurer," as he has been described, to Newfoundland. Judge Cook, who was the delegate from South Weymouth, Massachusetts, was present at the luncheon before the ceremony. In the illustration on the following page can be seen on the table three pairs of shoes which had been brought by him from New England. During the course of his remarks he said that the Massachusetts Weymouth was famous for its shoes and he had been deputed to bring over to this ceremony these three pairs which were made in his town; one pair he said jokingly was for the Mayoress and if they did not fit her, he declared that the Mayor would have to go around the town and find, as in the tale of Cinderella, a lady whom they would fit. The unveiling ceremony was performed by Mrs. Joseph Chamberlain, who was the eighth lineal descendant of Governor Endicott, and her stepson, Rt. Hon. Austen Chamberlain, M.P. The guests were entertained at luncheon by the Mayor and Corporation, at the Gloucester Hotel, which has many historical memories associated with it; it was once the residence of King George III; the peace of Amiens was discussed here; and within its walls the King said farewell to Captain Hardy, one of Nelson's officers, just before the battle of Trafalgar. After luncheon the Mayor and Corporation received Mrs. Chamberlain and all the other guests on the site of the jetty from which Endicott and Clark set out on their voyages to this country. Hon. Austen Chamberlain spoke for Mrs. Chamberlain about the men who went to New England to found a new commonwealth and of the great nation that had sprung up in the land they had settled. He added that he hoped the account was not closed and that between the United States and the mother land there might be an ever increasing interchange of thought and kindly friendship and hospitality. Mrs. Chamberlain asked him to express to the people that she prayed that the country where Endicott lived and to which she had returned to make her home, and the country he had helped to establish, on this hundredth anniversary of peaceful friendship, might now and in the time to come forge fresh links of friendship forevermore. Mr. Chamberlain then took down the British and American flags surrounding the memorial while the band played the national anthems of the two countries. The memorial to John Endicott has been

Photographed by Edward H. Seward

Kindness Ian Forbes-Robertson, Esq.

UNVEILING OF THE JOHN ENDICOTT AND RICHARD CLARK MEMORIAL IN WEYMOUTH, ENGLAND, IN 1914, from which port the former set sail for Salem, Massachusetts, and the latter for Newfoundland. Judge Louis A. Cook of South Weymouth, Massachusetts, was present at the services, the ceremony of unveiling being performed by Mrs. Joseph Chamberlain, eighth lineal descendant of Governor Endicott, assisted by her stepson, Right Hon. Austen Chamberlain, M.P. John Endicott is an ancestor of the Endicotts of Boston, Massachusetts.

placed on the stone column which is shown in the accompanying picture, and the medallion, which is also pictured and which is attached to the monument, bears the following inscription:—

In Memory of
RICHARD CLARK
Captain and Pilot of
Weymouth, who in 1583
sailed thence to join
Sir Humphrey Gilbert's
Voyage of discovery to
Newfoundland, and of
JOHN ENDICOTT
who on June 20, 1628,
set forth from Weymouth in
the ship "Abigail" on the
expedition which led to
the establishment of the
plantation at Salem,
Massachusetts.
Erected by Public
Subscription 1914.

Photographed by Edward H. Seward   *Kindness Ian Forbes-Robertson, Esq.*

BRONZE MEDALLION PLACED ON THE
MEMORIAL IN WEYMOUTH, ENGLAND,

in honour of Richard Clark and John Endicott.

Weymouth in this country was the first permanent settlement in Boston Harbour and is the second oldest town in Massachusetts, antedating Boston by at least six years and, next to Plymouth, is the oldest colony in the State. It is also often referred to as the "Alma Mater of Boston" for the reason that William Blackstone, the first settler in Boston, came from Weymouth. The earliest pioneers in our Weymouth did not come from the town of the same name in England, but many did come here the year after the first settlement of the town in 1623 by Robert Gorges, son of Sir Ferdinando Gorges. At this time our Weymouth was known as Wessagusset. Some years later Rev. Mr. Hall, who was born in Somersetshire, sailed from Weymouth for this country, and it is mentioned in old Weymouth that under date of March 20, 1635, "about one hundred people are recorded as bound here," meaning America. Abigail (Smith) Adams was one of the original settlers of our Weymouth and among other early comers we can mention the names of Bursley, Jeffries and probably Ludden as having come over with Gorges. Some years later the following well-known persons came over and set up their homes in our Weymouth: Henry Adams, John Allen, Robert Abell, Stephen French, John Glover, Edmond Hart, James Parker, Thomas Richards, Thomas Rawlins, Clement Briggs, Richard Sylvester and Clement Weaver. The Weymouth Historical Society in the Massachusetts town possesses some fine pictures of the English Weymouth.

WEYMOUTH BAY, WEYMOUTH, ENGLAND

The town for which our Weymouth is named has often been called the English Naples. It is situated in the county of Dorset on the south side of the river Wey, from which it gets its name, which was originally derived from "Waeye," meaning "water" and "mud," being the Saxon word for "mouth of the river." The town has a fine harbour and has always been a commercial port; it is now also a great watering-place. Into this attractive port the Roman Navy often found its way and years later two ships of the Spanish Armada were brought here as prizes. The earliest history of the town dates back to 938 A.D. in the time of King Athelstan, the next mention of it in history being in the Saxon charter of King Ethelred. One interesting incident occurred at the time King Philip of Spain was driven into the harbour by a hurricane. John Russell, of Berwick House, knew Spanish so well that he was chosen to act as interpreter for the royal party. King Henry was informed of the unexpected arrival of the Spanish King and sent him an invitation to visit him in London. Russell accompanied the visitor and made such a favorable impression on King Philip that the latter recommended him especially to the English King. It happened later that Russell became a favorite with King Henry's son, who created him Duke of Bedford, a name also closely associated with our New Bedford.

WINCHESTER, MASSACHUSETTS

A TEMPORARY memorial to the American soldiers who fell in the Great War has been placed in the south aisle of the Cathedral in Winchester, England, and the inscription reads as follows:—

This window and these panels have been reserved by the Dean and Chapter for the dedication of a perpetual memorial to be erected by the British Nation to those GALLANT AMERICANS who have given their lives for the cause of freedom in the Great War 1914–191 .

A more permanent memorial in the form of a window is now being built in the south aisle of the Cathedral. The ancient city of Winchester is a fitting place for such a memorial because of the fact that one hundred thousand troops of the American Expeditionary Forces came to the city from the nearby port of Southampton where they disembarked. It was at Winchester, too, that one of the largest American rest camps was established, and an added inducement that undoubtedly appealed to the British authorities in the selection of this site for a memorial was the fact that five hundred and fifty-three of our brave soldiers, who died of influenza, lie buried in the military cemetery on Morn Hill in Winchester. A further appropriateness lies in the fact that Winchester was at one time the ancient capital of England and was the home of so many kings that it has often been called "Royal Winchester." Henry I here celebrated his marriage to Matilda of Scotland and their son, William, was born in this ancient city; Henry III was

From a photograph   Kindness Major Evelyn Wrench and Henry
                                                    G. Lord, Esq.

TEMPORARY MEMORIAL PLACED IN WIN-
CHESTER CATHEDRAL, WINCHESTER,
ENGLAND,

to the memory of the Americans who lost their lives in the
Great War.

also born here; Henry IV was married here; Henry V received here the Ambassador of Charles of France; Henry VI often visited here; Henry VII journeyed here with his queen in order that his child should be born in England's old capital, and Henry VIII spent a week here in 1522 and entertained the Emperor Charles V of Austria. King Edward III made Winchester one of his ten staple towns for wool and leather, with the idea of reviving its prestige. Here also Queen Mary entertained Philip, Prince of Spain, previous to their marriage; King James I was the last king to reside in the castle. It was during the reign of Henry III that the city as a governing center began to decline in importance, the chief reason being that the treasury was transferred to London. Outside the west gate of the city was situated the King's hawk-house, in which falconers kept the birds in the days when falconry was so much indulged in. Winchester was the home of Alfred the Great, and here he ruled wisely and well for eighteen years; it was here that he wrote his Saxon Chronicles. It was also in Winchester that the original Domesday Book was compiled and here it was kept as long as the city was the capital of the kingdom. It may be also claimed that Winchester was the cradle of the British Empire, for it was here that King Alfred laid the foundations of the British Navy. It is also interesting to mention that Sir Walter Raleigh was tried and imprisoned in Winchester before his execution in London.

The Cathedral, of course, is the center of interest to visitors, and it will be remembered that Emerson thought it the most beautiful in England with the exception of York Minster. An attraction in the city is the house where Jane Austen lived and died, her body being buried in the Cathedral. New Englanders will be interested to know that the renowned Izaak Walton was also buried there. Bishop Lawrence of our Boston preached officially in Winchester Cathedral in the year 1920.

Like all mediæval cities, Winchester was surrounded by a wall which was origi-

From a photograph   *Kindness Mrs. Mary Fifield King*

WINCHESTER CATHEDRAL, WINCHESTER, ENGLAND,

in which has recently been placed by the British Nation a memorial to the Americans who gave their lives in the Great War. Winchester was the capital of England under Alfred the Great (849 A.D.). The cathedral, built in the eleventh century, is the chief attraction in this ancient city.

nally Roman, but practically nothing of this remains intact. One of the gates was changed to its present aspect by the Normans. It may also be mentioned that the original municipal flag of the English city was presented to its American namesake in Virginia during the latter part of 1919.

Our New England Winchester has taken an interest in the city of the same name in England and the Public Library of our town has several times sent reports and memoranda regarding its war activities, a number of letters in reply having been received describing the large American War Camp near the English city.

Edward Converse, a staunch old Puritan, who came over in Winthrop's colony, was the first settler of the territory now called Winchester, Massachusetts, having built and occupied the first house here in 1640. This humble dwelling stood on the site which many generations later was occupied by the Thompson estate, next to the Post-office. A "corne mill," the first business establishment in Winchester, was also built by this pioneer. This section of the country, considered by the dwellers along the seacoast as a "remote land," was at that time a wild, unsettled part of Charlestown, called Waterfield, included in the original territory granted to Charlestown in 1633 by the General Court. After certain grants by the General Court in 1640 the place was renamed "Charlestowne Village." On October 6, 1642, an act was passed by the General Court incorporating Woburn into a separate town, the act reading, "Charlestowne Village is called Wooburne," so that much of the present territory of Winchester was a part of Woburn until 1850, when

Photographed by H. W. Salmon & Son, Winchester, England
Kindness Ian Forbes-Robertson, Esq.

HOUSE IN WINCHESTER, ENGLAND, WHERE JANE AUSTEN LIVED AND DIED

the town was incorporated under its present name. The territory included in this new township was taken from Woburn, Medford and West Cambridge (now Arlington).

The early settlers in this section had a difficult time gaining a foothold in the wilderness, some of them being obliged to burrow into the hillside to obtain their first shelter. Included within the limits of the town was the farm of John Harvard, the founder of Harvard College.

There is also a Winchester in Connecticut and one in New Hampshire.

WINDSOR

MAINE, NEW HAMPSHIRE, VERMONT, MASSACHUSETTS AND CONNECTICUT

WINDSOR is one of the popular names for towns in America and each of the New England States, with the exception of Rhode Island, has a place so called. The Connecticut town was named for the English Windsor while the Massachusetts town was named for this early settlement in Connecticut, having been called Gageborough in honour of General Gage of Revolutionary fame until the year 1778. The Maine town was first called Malta and later Gerry, and curiously enough was named for the English town by a Frenchman

WINDSOR CASTLE

From a print published in 1799 by Richard Cooper

Owned by Allan Forbes

called Anthony Coombs, the reason for this name, therefore, being difficult to discover. The New Hampshire town is very small, having also received its name from the Windsor in Connecticut, while the Vermont town derived its name in a similar way.

The English town, from which all these places got their names either directly or indirectly, is a municipal borough incorporated by Edward IV, situated on the south bank of the Thames. The ancient name was Windelsora, meaning "the winding shore" (or "winding waters near the Castle"). Windsor itself is chiefly important on account of its Royal Castle which covers a tremendous area. It was begun by William, enlarged by his son Henry, rebuilt to a large extent by Edward III and further enlarged by many of the English monarchs since then. Within the Royal Mausoleum are the tombs of Queen Victoria and Prince Albert. The place is usually called New Windsor to distinguish it from Old Windsor, which is about two miles away. In July, 1896, the Ancient and Honorable Artillery Company of Boston, as guests of the late Queen Victoria, were received very graciously at Windsor Castle, where they were reviewed by the Queen and a large coterie of her distinguished subjects. Nearby is the well-known Eton, with its school, situated on the river Thames.

WOBURN, MASSACHUSETTS

AT the time of the two hundred and fiftieth anniversary celebration of the city of Woburn, in 1892, a number of interchanges of messages took place with the English Woburn and several officials of the latter were invited to be present. During the exercises Rev. Edward G. Porter, of Lexington, who had been a visitor to the old Woburn, told of his trip there, particularly mentioning Woburn Abbey, in which, however, despite the name, there is no longer any trace of a religious establishment. It stands in a park of 3,500 acres, enclosed by a high brick wall, twelve miles in circuit, and the old fish-ponds of the monks are now beautiful sheets of water enlivened by ducks and swans, while herds of deer may be seen quietly grazing over the sloping lawns. The portrait-galleries of this Abbey are famous and include paintings by Titian, Van Dyck, Rubens, Rembrandt, Teniers, Murillo and others. Mr. Porter was so interested in this fine collection that, at his request, the Duke of Bedford, who owned Woburn Abbey, presented catalogues of his collection to the public libraries of Woburn, Lexington and Bedford, in America. Judge Edward F. Johnson, of the Massachusetts Woburn, visited the mother town and its Abbey in 1879. He was treated with great hospitality by Hon. George Russell, M.P., and upon his return home he wrote an account of his visit which was afterwards published in England and resulted in a very cordial letter from a member of the Russell family.

Old Woburn, or Woubourne as it was once called, dates from Saxon times, and

From "Views of Woburn," Fisher & Sons, Woburn, England   *Kindness Judge Edward F. Johnson*

WOBURN ABBEY, WOBURN, ENGLAND

The seat of the Russell family, which has taken a great interest in Woburn, Massachusetts.

although little is known of its early history, it was chosen for the site of an abbey in the twelfth century, when fourteen monks took up their residence there and gave much attention to the mill facilities that were offered by the brooks. In the reign of Henry VIII, on the dissolution of the monasteries, the Abbey reverted to the crown. When this monarch came to the throne he gave the estate to John Russell, who was created Earl of Bedford. The latter's successors, up to the year 1892, had included four Earls and ten Dukes. The famous Woburn Abbey is now the seat of the Duke of Bedford.

Previous to the introduction of railways, Woburn, Bedfordshire, was a great center for stages and was a larger and busier town than it is at the present time. To-day its nearest railway station is known as Woburn Sands, which is some three miles distant from the town itself and about forty miles from London.

There are three places in England from which it was thought for some time that the Massachusetts Woburn might have derived its name: Woburn in Bedfordshire, Woo-burn in Bucks County and O-burn in Dorset, all three spellings having been used by the earliest settlers of the Massachusetts town. It is rather remarkable, as Mr. Porter says, "that not one of the first sixty towns in the colony received an Indian name, and only one or two were honored with Scripture names,

From "Views of Woburn," Fisher & Sons, Woburn, England   *Kindness Judge Edward F. Johnson*

TOWN HALL AND GEORGE STREET, WOBURN, ENGLAND

although the Puritan element was then so strong." It is also an interesting fact that no other town in America bears the name of Woburn, so far as we can learn.

There is no contemporary record which explains the naming of our Woburn, but it is now known definitely that it derived its name from Woburn, Bedfordshire, and was so named by Captain Edward Johnson, the "father" of the town, in honour of his friend, Major-Gen. Robert Sedgwick, who was born in the Bedfordshire town. Sedgwick came to this country in 1635, was one of the earliest settlers in Charlestown and commander for several years of the Ancient and Honorable Artillery Company, of which both he and Johnson were charter members. Sedgwick was also at one time commander of the Castle. He was a neighbor of Johnson's in Charlestown, and in his famous book entitled "Wonder-working Providence of Sion's Saviour in New England" Johnson refers to Sedgwick in eulogistic terms, calling him "stout and active in all feats of war, nurst up in Londons Artillery garden, and furthered with fifteen years experience in N. E. exact theory, besides the help of a very good head-piece." In his first mention of Sedgwick in the Woburn Town Records, Johnson calls him "Noble Captain Sedgwick;" and Sedgwick's part in the work of exploring the land for the settlement of the town, and the influential position he held in deciding upon its present site, are also set forth by Johnson in the first volume of the Woburn Records. Sedgwick, however, never lived in Woburn and apparently never intended to. Johnson was its first town clerk, the chairman of its first Board of Selectmen and the first deputy from Woburn to the General Court, and his leadership and influence were such in all matters relating to the organization and government of the new town that he would naturally have had the say as to its name. In recognition of the nativity of his distinguished friend, he chose the name of Woburn; and, at the General Court holden in Boston September 27 (October 7, N.S.), 1642, it was ordered

"That Charlestowne Village is called Wooborne."

It may be interesting to mention that Charles Goodyear, the inventor of the process of vulcanizing India rubber, lived in our Woburn as early as 1835 in a house now standing, in that part of Woburn called Montvale; he was at that time poor and unknown, and it was while warming himself one cold night in the village store that his great idea occurred to him. In Woburn also was born Benjamin Thompson, afterwards made Count Rumford, who became a famous philosopher and scientist, known throughout Europe. John Fiske, the historian, in his History of the United States, says that Rumford was the greatest scientist America has produced, and it is as a scientist that he is honoured in his native town. In 1784, he was knighted by the King of England, and in 1791 was created a Count of the Holy Roman Empire by the Elector of Bavaria. He chose the title of Rumford in honour of Rumford, now Concord, New Hampshire, with which town his wife's family was prominently identified in the days of the early settlement. Count Rumford was founder, with a large endowment, of the Rumford Medal of the American Academy of Arts and Sciences, and of the Rumford Professorship in Harvard College. In an article published in the *Youth's Companion*, August 26, 1920, the late President Dr. Maclaurin of the Massachusetts Institute of Technology gives an interesting account of some of Rumford's inventions and experiments—"experiments that set the scientific world thinking and working in the right direction."

A statue of Rumford was erected on the lawn of the Woburn Public Library in 1900, the inscription on the pedestal, prepared by President Charles W. Eliot of Harvard College, reading in part:—

THE EARLIEST
SCIENTIFIC PHILANTHROPIST
HE PROVED THAT HEAT IS MOTION
AND HAD A GLIMPSE
OF THE GREAT DOCTRINE
KNOWN LATER AS
THE CONSERVATION OF ENERGY

The house in which Rumford was born is still standing in North Woburn and is owned and maintained as a museum of local antiquities by the Rumford Historical Association, organized and incorporated in 1877 for that purpose.

In North Woburn there is a statue of Loammi Baldwin, a contemporary and lifelong friend of Rumford. The inscription states briefly his career, mentioning also the fact that he was one of the proprietors and a principal constructor of the Middlesex Canal, the first sheriff of Middlesex County, and then recording that he was

DISSEMINATOR OF THE APPLE
IN HONOR OF HIM CALLED
THE BALDWIN
WHICH PROCEEDED FROM A TREE
ORIGINALLY GROWING WILD
ABOUT TWO MILES NORTH
OF THIS MONUMENT

The Rumford Historical Association erected a monument some years ago near Chestnut Street (formerly Butters Row) in that part of old Woburn now Wilmington, Massachusetts, to mark the site of this original Baldwin apple tree.

It may be interesting also to mention that ancestors of Presidents Pierce, Harrison and Cleveland are buried in the old cemetery on Park Street in Woburn, while North Woburn has the distinction not only of being the birthplace of Count Rumford and of Col. Loammi Baldwin, but is also proud of the fact that it is the home of Grover Cleveland's first American ancestors.

In its Library building, Woburn possesses one of Richardson's masterpieces of architecture and on the walls of the reading-room is a collection of views of Woburn Abbey.

The citizens of Woburn still take a great interest in the mother town, and several of them have visited there in recent years.

YORK, MAINE

YORK, Maine, may well be proud of the source from which she received her name, for that ancient cathedral city in Yorkshire on the banks of the Ouse, with its quaint and narrow streets, is most attractive and appeals to people of almost every taste. One of the lanes is called the Shambles and it is so narrow that neighbors on opposite sides can shake hands from the upper floors; there is another street in the city called Whipmawhopmagate, so named because it was the boundary for the public whipping of delinquents at the cart tail, a practice used even on women at one time. According to legendary history, York was founded about 1000 B.C. by a Northumbrian king who christened it "Ebauricus." One thousand years later, authentic history records this city as being in the hands of the conquering Romans, who called it "Eboracum." Its present name of York is thought to be a possible contraction of the name "Jorvick," which was given to it during Danish occupancy. With the second campaign of Agricola in 79 A.D., the history of York is clearly defined and soon afterwards we learn that the

View of the CITY of YORK from the River Ouse.

YORK, ENGLAND

From an old print owned by Allan Forbes

Formerly in the collection of J. H. Seers, Essex, England

YORK CATHEDRAL, YORK, ENGLAND

From an old print owned by Allan Forbes

Formerly owned by Brooks Reed of Boston

Emperor Hadrian here completed the famous chain of forts known as the "Pict Wall," which almost surrounds the city and provides a delightful walk. Examples of their ancient buildings also exist. Constantine the Great was proclaimed Emperor in 306 by the Roman Legion then stationed there. There, also, was held the great slave market where many a maid and lad were sold in the Roman days to be conveyed to Rome.

In mediæval days, the place became the scene of struggles between Britons, Saxons and Danes. There is a tradition that the famous King Arthur, after defeating ninety thousand Saxons on Baden hills, took up his residence in York and with the chivalrous knights and fair ladies of his Court celebrated the first Christmas festival ever held in England. In these days York was surrounded by deep forests and no one dared leave the city without an armed guard on account of the bandits and robbers who infested the outlying regions. In 1486, Henry VII visited York and the citizens, to quote the records on this occasion, "drank the city dry." To Americans, York will have another special interest, for in the Fulford Cemetery lie many of our brave boys, including some from our York, who died in the English city during the Great War.

From a photograph   *Kindness Ian Forbes-Robertson, Esq.*

THE SHAMBLES, YORK, ENGLAND

This street is so narrow that neighbors on opposite sides can shake hands from the upper floors.

York Minster is one of the most majestic cathedrals in the world and is enriched by innumerable historic associations. After having passed through the changes and additions of eight and a half centuries and the many sanguinary and thrilling scenes enacted at its feet, it was reconsecrated in 1472. The magnificent windows of mediæval glass, the stone carvings and tracery, and the famous bell called "Big Tom," which tolls forth the hours to the passing generations, are features of this Cathedral.

Photographed by Joseph Duncan and M. A. C. Lewis, York, England *Kindness Ian Forbes-Robertson, Esq.*

CITY WALLS, YORK, ENGLAND,

part of the ancient defences of the city, upon which one can walk for miles.

From "The Beginnings of Colonial Maine," by Henry S. Burrage, D.D., Historian of Maine

ST. BUDEAUX CHURCH, NEAR PLYMOUTH, ENGLAND, IN WHICH IS THE MEMORIAL TO
SIR FERDINANDO GORGES

Sir Ferdinando Gorges took a great interest in the early colonization of New England and particularly of the territory now included in Maine. He was interested in the voyages of Captain Waymouth and the Popham colonists to Bath; he was given the title of "Governor of New England," received a royal charter and changed the name of the territory near the present York, Maine, from Agamenticus to Gorgeana. The name York was given later, in 1652.

In York, the State of Maine possesses the first chartered city of America, and Sir Ferdinando Gorges, its founder, has been called "the Father of American Colonization." Of his thus honouring the little hamlet of Agamenticus at the base of the mountain bearing this same Indian name, Bancroft says, "She became a chartered borough, and Sir Ferdinando, like another Romulus, resolved to perpetuate his name, and under the name of 'Gorgeana' the land around York became as good a city as seals and parchment, a Mayor and Aldermen, a Chancery Court, Courtleet, Sargeants and white rods can make of a town of 300 inhabitants." Sir Ferdinando opened his grand and imposing Charter, creating Gorgeana a city of twenty-one square miles, by saying, "Whereas his Majesty, King of England, hath created me Absolute Lord of ye Province of Mayne,"—then he proceeds to confer on his beloved city, which he idealized with promise of future glory, a chartered form of government, nobly planned, which covered many feet of parchment. An anonymous poet refers to the founding of this First City in America in the following lines:—

> "For hither came a knightly train
>   From o'er the sea with gorgeous court;
>   The mayors gowned in robes of state,
> Held brilliant tourney on the plain.
> And massive ships within the port
>   Discharged their load of richest freight.
> Then when at night the sun went down
>   Behind the western hill and tree,
> The bowls were filled,—this toast they crown,
>   'Long live the City by the Sea!'"

This city by the sea, the favored namesake of Gorges and later of old York, fell heir to the tragic fortunes of both its founder and the elder city, although Thomas Gorges, coming here as Deputy Governor for his uncle Sir Ferdinando, strove most faithfully to carry out the constructive plans of his relative. The two Gorges made most of their plans from Bristol, England, although the memorial to Thomas Gorges is in Heavitree Church, near Exeter, and the one to Sir Ferdinando Gorges is in St. Budeaux Church, near Plymouth. With the fall of King Charles, involving the elder Gorges, a staunch royalist, in financial ruin and imprisonment, the struggling city of Gorgeana was left without head or support from the adverse Cromwellian rule. Its inhabitants found their lands and possessions tossed back and forth for the next forty years, while they defended themselves, unaided, from their garrison houses against the treacherous Indians. One of these garrison houses, built in 1645, is still standing in perfect condition just above the old swinging bridge on the bank of York River.

In 1652, Massachusetts having succeeded for the time being in her claim upon Maine territory, Gorgeana was reorganized into the town of York, as the shire town of Yorkshire County. In 1623, Christopher Levett, who was born in York,

From "The Beginnings of Colonial Maine," by Henry S. Burrage, D.D., Historian of Maine

CHURCH AT LONG ASHTON, ENGLAND, IN WHICH SIR FERDINANDO GORGES WAS
BURIED

England, in 1576, had bestowed this same name of York on the territory then called by the curious name of "Quack," situated on the western shores of Casco Bay, off Portland. Levett explored the Maine coast, returning in the following year. He was in Salem when John Endicott came there and welcomed him to these shores. He sold his interests in Maine and died on the homeward voyage. His father, Percival Levett, was City Chamberlain of York, England, in 1584 and sheriff in 1597–98. The county jail in York, built in 1653, is still standing and is now put to beneficent use by the York Historical Society, which maintains it as a museum of local antiquities.

York's crowning tragedy, however, befell in January, 1692, when a force of Indians gathered under the darkness of a winter's night on the snowy slope of Mt. Agamenticus, overlooking the sleeping town, and in the grey of the morning pounced upon the unwarned settlement, ruthlessly tomahawking family after family until over half the inhabitants were thus cruelly massacred. The feeble remnant still refused to desert the beloved locality, and struggled on, later becoming a prosperous fishing and farming community.

Rev. Shubael Dummer, who organized the first Congregational church in York in 1662, was a graduate of Harvard College in 1656. As late as the year 1769 we find a curious regulation among the church records that "singing was permitted to the lower floor, if persons occupying the designated pews fit them up at their own expense."

Of recent years, York, Maine, has become one of the most fashionable and attractive summer resorts of our entire New England coast.

CROSSED SWORDS OF COLONEL WILLIAM PRESCOTT AND CAPTAIN JOHN LINZEE

mounted on a tablet in the library of the Massachusetts Historical Society.   Colonel Prescott was a leader of the American troops at Bunker Hill while Captain Linzee commanded the British sloop-of-war "Falcon" which acted against the Americans during this famous battle.   By a romantic coincidence these swords came into the possession of the Massachusetts Historical Society through the will of William Hickling Prescott, the celebrated historian, grandson of Colonel Prescott, who married Susan Amory, a grand-daughter of Captain Linzee.   The international fame of these weapons has been recorded by Thackeray in "The Virginians."   The occasion of the presentation of the swords to the Historical Society brought forth from Rev. Nathaniel Langdon Frothingham, D.D., a poem entitled "The Crossed Swords" which for many years appeared in American school books.   To the people of Massachusetts a further interest attaches to the history of these swords as a granddaughter of William Hickling Prescott became the wife of Roger Wolcott, late Governor of this Commonwealth.

In concluding this account of the ties which exist between New England and Old England, Ireland and Scotland, it is, perhaps, fitting to recall, in view of recent world events, the vision of Alfred Tennyson who, in 1852, expressed what he hoped America's part would be if England were ever called upon to fight a "tyrant's" power.   Little did he then know how his hope was to be fulfilled after a lapse of sixty-five years.   This was the noble feeling to which he then gave utterance:—

"Gigantic daughter of the West,
    We drink to thee across the flood,
We know thee most, we love thee best,
    For art thou not of English blood?
Should War's mad blast again be blown,
    Permit not thou the tyrant's power
To fight thy mother here alone,
    But let thy broadsides roar with ours.
        Hands all around!
    God the tyrant's cause confound;
To our great kinsmen in the West
    And the great cause of freedom, round and round."

THE END